Jeremy Hutchinson's Case Histories

Jeremy Hutchinson's Case Histories

THOMAS GRANT

JOHN MURRAY

First published in Great Britain in 2015 by John Murray (Publishers)
An Hachette UK Company

2

© Thomas Grant 2015

A CIP catalogue record for this title is available from the British Library

ISBN 978-1-444-79973-6
Ebook ISBN 978-1-444-79974-3

Typeset in Bembo MT Pro by Palimpsest Book Production Limited,
Falkirk, Stirlingshire

Printed and bound by Clays Ltd, St Ives plc

John Murray policy is to use papers that are natural, renewable and recyclable products
and made from wood grown in sustainable forests. The logging and manufacturing
processes are expected to conform to the environmental
regulations of the country of origin.

John Murray (Publishers)
Carmelite House
50 Victoria Embankment
London EC4Y 0DZ

www.johnmurray.co.uk

To Hester

Contents

PART IV: The Secret Society

PART V: Mary Whitehouse v Jeremy Hutchinson

Preface

I T WAS FOUR years ago that a friend first mentioned to me the name Jeremy Hutchinson. I had recently moved with my family from London to the Sussex Downs. My friend and I visited the nearby Charleston Farmhouse, country home of the Bloomsbury Group. Did I know, she asked, that a second-generation 'Bloomsberry' was alive and well and living just over the hill from me? And did I know that he was, like me, a barrister, and had appeared in some interesting cases during his time at the Bar? Intrigued, I wrote a letter to Lord Hutchinson (he had been made a life peer in 1978). The first lesson I learned is that one must never call him Lord Hutchinson; and he has been Jeremy ever since. He will be Jeremy throughout this book.

Jeremy replied to my letter graciously. We met a few times. He has an abiding love of cricket and he came to a few matches in which I was playing for a local side. And we talked. It became clear that my friend's reference to 'some interesting cases' had been a considerable understatement, but the truth emerged only through a brazen persistence on my part. Jeremy is one of those people whose modesty is disproportionate to their achievements. I had always been an avid reader of the old Penguin Famous Trials series and revelled in reading about the careers and cases of the great advocates of the past: the Edward Marshall Halls, the Patrick Hastings, the Norman Birketts. Through wheedling and tenacity I discovered that he was a man who had emulated those great figures of the past to become the leading criminal advocate of his own generation. What was more, he had appeared in some of the greatest criminal cases of the period from the 1950s through to the 1980s; cases that defined the age and which stood as landmarks of the revolution in behaviour and thinking that gave birth to modern Britain.

I would seize any opportunity to walk over the hill to the tiny hamlet of Lullington, where Jeremy lived, and would casually raise with him another case which, through my own covert researches, I had discovered he had appeared in. It made me feel rather giddy. Here was incarnated the cultural and legal history of the mid-twentieth century: the man who had defended Penguin Books in the *Lady Chatterley* and United Artists in the *Last Tango in Paris* trials; who had battled Mary Whitehouse in the *Romans in Britain* case; who had appeared for the Soviet spies George Blake and John Vassall; who had acted for Christine Keeler, the Great Train Robber Charlie Wilson, the art faker Tom Keating and the cannabis smuggler Howard Marks.

Our conversations ranged beyond his career at the Bar. It became apparent that, quite apart from his life in the courtroom, this was a man who had grown up an intimate of the literary and artistic giants of the early twentieth century (I was regaled with his vivid memories of T.S. Eliot, Virginia Woolf, Lytton Strachey and many others); who had been at Oxford with one of the most brilliant generations of undergraduates of that century; who during the Second World War had been an officer on HMS *Kelly* with Louis Mountbatten; who had fought the 1945 election in the Labour interest; who had married the foremost actress of the time; who had been a prominent member of the House of Lords; who became the chairman of the Tate Gallery; and who had maintained close friendships with some of the most fascinating figures of the century.

And then there was his character. Here was a man in his late nineties who spoke and thought as if he were in his forties. Although age had made him slightly unsteady on his feet, it had had no other discernible effect on him. He still carried within him a passionate engagement in life, an engagement that was not political in any sort of party sense, but which drew from a deep taproot of liberalism. His convictions remained those that had shaped his life both as a lawyer and beyond: the sanctity of the jury as a bulwark of English liberty; the futility of prison as a means of punishment in most cases; the need for rehabilitation of offenders both in prison and after; the vital importance of a vigorous and independent criminal Bar to the functioning of justice; and, more broadly, the hatred of censorship and cant; the importance of conversation as the vigorous exchange of ideas; the cultivation of friendship as a supreme value in itself; delight in the natural world and the visual arts.

After a time I hesitantly asked him whether he had ever thought of writing his memoirs. No, came the answer. He was far too busy living in the present to rake over the past. Had anyone else written his life? It appeared not. Surely, I suggested, it would be of considerable interest were someone to set down his experiences and memories? He was not keen. He is a private man and a biography seemed immodest and, anyway, an intrusion. Anyhow, who would be interested? A lot of people, I retorted, but I did not press the point. (It was only later that I came across letters from various publishers over the years urging him to write a memoir or a monograph on the art of advocacy: all in vain.)

After a while, I started on a different tack. I told him I thought it would be fun to write up a few of his most interesting cases, perhaps for private publication, to mark his hundredth birthday, which was then a couple of years off. Jeremy hesitated, but eventually agreed. Perhaps the pull of the past had been a little stronger than he thought. I started on a short but charming case in which he had triumphed, the trial of Kempton Bunton. It had attracted considerable press coverage at the time, and for good reason. Bunton had apparently committed the first and only successful theft in the history of the National Gallery: the purloining, via a lavatory window, of Goya's famous portrait of the Duke of Wellington. Jeremy had defended him at the Old Bailey in 1965 and had successfully persuaded the jury that Bunton – a retired Newcastle bus driver outraged that £140,000 could be forked out for an old painting when OAPs had to pay for their television licences and who wished to make a public protest about this state of affairs – had not been guilty of theft, because he had never intended to deprive the gallery permanently of the painting.

Jeremy was amused by the product of my researches, and I wrote a couple more pieces on other cases – including *Lady Chatterley*. By now he had mentioned, and thrown open to me, his 'archive' – in fact a large tin box in which had been stashed away a vast number of legal papers, correspondence and newspaper cuttings over forty years of practice. This archive has proved to be the proverbial gold mine.

The writing up of these cases galvanized Jeremy's interest in the past and, in particular, his own past. Most people do not think of their life as a thing of intrinsic general interest. But through my (no doubt sometimes tiresome) enthusiasm, Jeremy became engaged in the process. His initial mantra – 'It was so long ago I have no memory of what happened' – I am thankful to say proved to be entirely wrong. In fact his recollection of events that had occurred many decades previously proved to be razor-sharp; sufficiently minute to recall the look of a witness when a critical question was asked, or the laugh of a jury that signalled the demise of the prosecution case.

But all this was still just intended as a small project, a distraction from my own chancery practice and the writing of black-letter law books. It was at this stage that the friend who had first introduced me to Jeremy, the historian Juliet Nicolson, looking at my pieces, said that she thought they could be of wider interest. She introduced me to the literary agent Caroline Dawnay and Jeremy and I were astounded when Caroline, whose client list makes for dizzying reading, said that she shared Juliet's view. And so we were introduced to Roland Philipps of the publishers John Murray. For Jeremy, the prospect of this book being published by John Murray was enjoyably apt. He had been a close friend of the great Jock Murray, who had presided over the publishing house for several decades, and had often visited Jock at Albemarle Street. In a letter to Jeremy dating from the late 1970s Jock had written that 'when next we meet I shall ask you when you will write me a book.' There is also in Jeremy's archive a lovely exchange of correspondence between the two. Jock writes asking Jeremy to assist in hunting down the meaning of an obscure legal maxim quoted by Byron in one of his letters to Hobhouse (the great twelve-volume *Complete Letters* was then in the process of being published). Having consulted a legal academic at the LSE Jeremy was able to clear up the point. Now, more than thirty years later, John Murray was returning the favour and, after a fashion, receiving the book Jock had requested.

The book that follows is not a conventional biography; nor is it conventional history. Rather, what I have attempted is a kind of social history of the 1960s, 1970s and 1980s told through the lens of its leading criminal cases, bound together by the common thread that in each case the defence was conducted by the same man. Out of the many hundreds of trials in which Jeremy appeared I have chosen fourteen for inclusion in this book, arranged thematically rather than chronologically. While I have written the chapters, Jeremy has, over many hours, poured out his recollections to me, and commented on my multiple drafts. My choice of cases was dictated by two criteria. First, the case must be fascinating in its own right; second, it must act as a prism for the political, moral or cultural issues of the day. I have been helped by the fact that, perhaps uniquely, the period of Jeremy's maturity at the Bar coincided with a time when the criminal law was the anvil on which many of the great public issues were being hammered out. Certainly never before, or since, has the law been so close to centre stage in this country's life.

The inevitable result of the application of these two criteria is that most of the cases that make up the body of this book are well known in their own right. They might suggest that Jeremy's life at the Bar was devoted to the defence of the famous, the infamous or the glamorous. He is anxious to dispel that suggestion. He is emphatic that the vast majority of the cases he undertook were for the unknown and the underprivileged, cases of little interest other than to their protagonists, the kind of cases that make up the daily meat and drink of the criminal Bar.

The result is a book that has multiple aims. I have tried to recreate the atmosphere of the courtroom and to explain the way that trials work, and the way that barristers try to win them. (But I have striven to ensure that legal technicalities play only a very minor role in the dramas recounted below.) I have also tried to place those cases very firmly within their political, social and cultural context. But the lens is also personal: I have tried to describe a fascinating and brilliant man, both in and out of court. Although the core of this book is a series of legal cases the significance of which was felt far beyond the four walls of the courtroom, it is on Jeremy's role in them that I focus. So the reader can understand and know the man better I have written a biographical sketch of Jeremy, which appears at the beginning of this book. It tells the story of a remarkable life that is far more than the sum of his courtroom triumphs, a story that was told in part in the edition of *Desert Island Discs* on which Jeremy appeared in 2013.

There is one final purpose to this book. The criminal Bar faces unprecedented attacks on its integrity and existence. It is no exaggeration to say that its future is imperilled by current (and past) government policy. As a result the criminal Bar is fast losing its senior practitioners, while good junior barristers are tending to practise in non-criminal areas of law. The principle that a person charged with a crime is entitled to representation by an independent person of their choice, whose skills as an advocate and lawyer are of the highest order, is in jeopardy. This is a subject that, even in his hundredth year, and several decades into his retirement, exercises Jeremy. His Postscript stands not only as a reflection on his life at the Bar, but also as what he expresses to be a requiem to an idea of justice that he espoused and embodied. And here lies the book's final aim, which is, in a small way, to celebrate the criminal Bar and the barristers in it who work to maintain the integrity of justice and preserve a vital aspect of our democracy.

Thomas Grant
March 2015

Jeremy Hutchinson

A Biographical Sketch

T HIS BOOK IS not a biography in the traditional sense. Rather, as mentioned in the Preface, its focus is a series of key trials that took place in the 1960s, 1970s and 1980s in which Jeremy Hutchinson was a leading protagonist – a set of remarkable court-room dramas that played a significant part in forming the legal, political and social culture of contemporary Britain. To help the reader to understand the character who dominates the chapters that follow, a brief sketch of his life is provided below. It is of course an impossible task adequately to précis a life of a hundred years, especially one lived so richly and intensely, in just a few pages. Nonetheless I hope the account below gives a flavour of what may be described as a 'life of the century'.

Jeremy was born in March 1915. His early childhood was spent on the banks of the Thames at River House in Upper Mall, Hammersmith, a small early eighteenth-century house that sits beside Kelmscott House, where William Morris had lived – and had died twenty years earlier. A spread in a 1919 edition of *Vogue* shows River House as the exemplary Bloomsbury town house, arrayed with furniture and rugs from the Omega Workshops and paintings by Duncan Grant. It would be Jeremy's home for the first decade of his life; his parents, St John and Mary Hutchinson, eventually gave it up (in the manner of the period it was rented) in favour of a larger residence in Albert Road,[1] Regent's Park.

Jeremy's first memory – he can have been only two – is of sitting in the cellar sheltering from a Zeppelin raid overhead. He recalls no particular feeling of fear. His second memory is of a boy riding precariously bareback down the drive of his parents' (also rented) house in the country at Robertsbridge in East Sussex: 'The war is over! The war is over!' As he was in the act of delivering news of the Armistice, the boy fell off his mount into the mud, which retained the impression of his limbs: his 'trademark' as Jeremy's father described it. This was the first 'grown-up' word Jeremy learned. Although he did not know it then, that night his parents, along with his mother's cousin Lytton Strachey, who was staying with them, went up to London to attend Monty Shearman's legendary Armistice party at the Adelphi (the party that features in the film *Carrington* and which was noted for Strachey's 'stick insect' dancing).[2]

Jeremy has particularly vivid childhood memories of his parents. Another early recollection captures the character of his mother. To get to Hammersmith Underground station at the time from Upper Mall one had to pass through a slum, long since cleared. Mary, wearing clothes made at the Omega workshops, and hand-painted by Roger Fry or Duncan Grant, would lead Jeremy and his sister to school, hand in hand. 'Here comes the Queen of Sheba,' the slum children would cry, as Mary walked imperturbably on.

Jeremy's direct ancestors include Dr Benjamin Hutchinson, who was Byron's doctor in Nottinghamshire and who prescribed a diet and exercise regime to the teenage poet, with a view to controlling his notoriously fluctuating weight. Jeremy can trace his ancestry even further back, to Colonel Hutchinson, one of Charles I's regicides, whose wife Lucy wrote *The Memoirs of Colonel Hutchinson*, one of the great eyewitness testaments of the Civil War period. The Hutchinson family motto is 'Neither rash nor fearful' – and moderation is one of the factors to which Jeremy attributes his longevity.

Jeremy's father, generally known as Jack or 'Hutchie' (as he was called by his close friend, Diana Cooper[3]) was a barrister (he would become a KC in 1935) and a discriminating buyer of modern art. Some of the fruits of his collecting can be seen on Jeremy's walls even now, seventy years after his father's death. Jeremy's mother was a Strachey and an intimate of many members of the Bloomsbury Group. A confidante of Lytton Strachey, and Virginia Woolf's inspiration for Mrs Dalloway, Mary also had a long relationship with Clive Bell, which was apparently tolerated by her husband, whose equable temper and generosity of spirit is testified to in many of the memoirs of the period. Perhaps in some form of veiled revenge, Vanessa Bell painted a portrait of Mary, now at the Tate Gallery, which brings out none of her beauty. It is a painting Jeremy has never liked: 'To me it's not like my mother at all. It accentuates various things in her face and exaggerates them. I think it is a rather unkind portrait.'

The Mary Hutchinson archive is now kept at the Harry Ransom Humanities Research Center in the University of Texas. Mary's reputation as having an extraordinary gift for friendship is borne out by the holdings in the archive: 1,400 letters from and to Clive Bell; 141 letters to Lytton Strachey; and a vast corpus of correspondence with an array of the great names of the day.[4]

Mary was a close friend of T.S. Eliot and she appears as a frequent correspondent in the edition of his collected letters which is still in the process of being published. He and Vivienne would often retreat to a house in Bosham on Chichester Harbour, close to the weekend cottage that the Hutchinsons started renting in 1915, Eleanor House, which was set back a hundred yards from the sea at West Wittering in Sussex. Mary and Tom would visit each other by means of an ancient ferryman who ran an irregular service at Itchenor in his rowing boat. (Jeremy still recalls having to shout out 'Ferry!' over to the cantankerous Mr Haines, to encourage him to row across to pick up his fare.)

To Jeremy, Eliot seemed a very closed man, buttoned up in his tightly fitting jacket and waistcoat, very much, at least on the outside, the bank clerk. Jeremy and his older sister, Barbara, coined a private nickname for Eliot: 'the eagle', in homage to his pronounced nose (a theme of Jeremy's childhood is the private hilarity with which he and his sister viewed the famous people they encountered. Aldous Huxley received his own moniker: the 'quangle-wangle'). The first volume of Eliot's collected letters[5] has two charming photographs of Jeremy as a boy of four or five posing with his mother and Eliot. Jeremy has a cache of photographs of life during the long summers at Eleanor; to look at them now, almost a century on, is to trace some of the cultural icons of the period: Duncan Grant, Roger Fry, Mark Gertler (who painted a portrait of Jack one summer at Eleanor and was the recipient of substantial financial support from the Hutchinsons), George Moore, Sacheverell Sitwell.

The central experiences of Jeremy's early life, which he sees as being essential to the formation of his personality, occurred at Eleanor House. Long summers would be spent with his sister Barbara under the sole and undemanding guardianship of a governess, Mrs Brereton, their largely absent parents occasional visitors from London.

> It was at Eleanor that I learned my love of the outdoors, the sea and estuaries, and of the simple life. For weeks on end Barbara and I would devise our own entertainments far from the reaches of the outside world. I remember catching butterflies, pressing wild flowers and spending days on the nearby farm in the company of a wonderful labourer called Alf. I learned to milk the cows and sit proudly on the carthorses as Alf went to work in the fields. The house was lit by candles and lamps, we bathed in a copper bath, we drank water drawn from a well and made daily use of the earth-closet. The local fisherman would spend the night fishing and in the morning would pass our house and throw dabs – soles too small to sell – into our porch. I think that all the values that shaped my life were somehow born during those summers.

Jeremy's father Jack Hutchinson was himself a remarkable man. He became one of the leading criminal barristers of his time and his career at the Bar foreshadows Jeremy's. He featured in many of the great cases of the period, including conducting the defence of Compton Mackenzie on Official Secrets Act charges (the case is vividly described in Octave 7 of Mackenzie's autobiography[6]) and acting for George McMahon, the would-be assassin of Edward VIII. He also appeared for Oswald Mosley in his famous libel case against the *Star*, which had published an article alleging that Mosley was advocating armed revolution. In a kind of precursor to one of Jeremy's triumphs at the Bar, Jack Hutchinson acted for the Warren Gallery, in a case brought against it on obscenity charges arising from an exhibition of D.H. Lawrence's paintings in London in 1929: the police apparently operated a policy that the depiction of any trace of pubic hair merited a painting's seizure. A compromise was brokered by Jack, with Lawrence's encouragement, whereby the paintings were saved from the flames on condition that they were never shown in England again. In a letter to Jack written shortly afterwards, Lawrence referred to him as the 'real St George in the fight against censorship', a description that would prove to be equally apt for Jeremy.[7]

The profession of criminal barrister was very much less demanding in Jack Hutchinson's day than it was in Jeremy's time, or is now. There were then four courts at the Old Bailey (there are today over thirty). Jeremy remembers his father's clerk telling him that often the six members of chambers would play cards in the afternoon in the Temple, having returned early from court. Jeremy rarely saw his father working at home and it was only on Sundays that legal briefs appeared on his bed before he got up for lunch. He had a lifelong interest in politics (he unsuccessfully fought the 1910 and 1929 elections as a Liberal candidate) and led a very active social life. A diary from 1919 shows him out almost every night, at the Garrick or Beefsteak clubs, at the theatre, or at a music hall. He was also a man of letters: when Eliot had the nervous breakdown that took him to Margate for recuperation (and from which was born *The Waste Land*) Eliot called upon Jack to take over the writing of his 'London Letter' for the American literary magazine, the *Dial*.[8] Another early memory of Jeremy's is of being taken by his father to the Holborn Empire, to see the 'Prime Minister of Mirth', George Robey; or Lily Morris, whose song 'Don't Have Any More, Mrs Moore' remains one of Jeremy's favourites. A week before his death Jack was appointed a trustee of the Tate Gallery – another instance of his career anticipating that of his son.

Jeremy first entered a courtroom at the age of fourteen, when, in Court 1 at the Old Bailey, he heard Norman Birkett, as Jack Hutchinson's leader, plead in mitigation for the notorious fraudster Clarence Hatry. (Birkett was perhaps the most famous barrister of the pre-war period. He would later become a law lord, and struck up a friendship with Jeremy at the end of his life.) Hatry is largely forgotten now, but the collapse of his group of companies in September 1929, with debts of £19 million (an astronomical sum then), was said to be one of the contributing factors in the Wall Street Crash. Jeremy still has a clear image of the vigour of Birkett's advocacy in the face of a judge, Mr Justice Avory ('his face like a skull, thin-lipped and utterly lacking in emotion'), who went on to sentence Hatry to fourteen years' hard labour, the maximum sentence available. Jeremy describes the broken Hatry stumbling as the sentence was pronounced, held up by the two guards standing beside him to prevent him sinking, and turning to walk down the stairs back to his cell, only for the judge to bark out the word 'Stay!'; Hatry swung round, to hear further concurrent sentences being heaped upon him on the various other counts to which he had pleaded guilty. (The *Manchester Guardian* report of the trial confirms the accuracy of this recollection.)

The memory of Birkett's marvellous oratory remains embedded in Jeremy's consciousness and from this moment one can trace the lineaments of his own later career. Court 1 would become his own primary stage and his fame and reputation would be carved from his representation of some of the most famous, as well as notorious, figures of the post-war period. Certainly the central image of the advocate making his case fearlessly and passionately before a hostile tribunal is one that Jeremy himself embodied in his career at the Bar.

Jeremy's parentage meant that much of his childhood was spent in the company of many of the literary and artistic giants of the period, as well as assorted members of the Bloomsbury Group. He is mentioned in Virginia Woolf's diaries as a visitor to Monk's House in Rodmell; and he recalls being taught, aged about fifteen, how to knot his first bow tie by Lytton Strachey (Jeremy's library contains a number of first editions of Strachey's works, inscribed by the author with charming messages to his younger cousin). He remembers how he and his sister would delight in imitating Strachey's quavering voice. Osbert Sitwell also described one occasion when Barbara performed her imitation before the man himself, to which 'with a look of utmost distaste', he responded, 'I expect it's amusing, but it isn't at all *like*!'[9]

Jeremy was sent to Stowe School where he was an indifferent scholar but discovered a lifelong enthusiasm for cricket. Before going to university he spent several months in France and Germany. The horror he felt at the sight of members of the Hitlerjugend bearing toy weapons and marching down the street outside the house where he was staying was an early stepping stone in his political awakening. He went up to Oxford in October 1933, reading Modern Greats (what is now known as PPE) at Magdalen College. The Oxford of the time was fizzing with intellectual energy and Jeremy found himself thrown into the company of a dazzling generation. 'I suddenly discovered what learning was all about.' He shared rooms in his last two years at 7 Beaumont Street, just down from the Ashmolean, with Stuart Hampshire, later to become a well-known philosopher, the future art historian Benedict Nicolson, son of Harold Nicolson and Vita Sackville-West, and David Wallace, son of a Conservative Cabinet minister (he would later be killed in the war). The editor of Harold Nicolson's diaries would later describe this group, together with Jasper Ridley, Lionel Brett and John Pope-Hennessy, who lived a little further down Beaumont Street, as 'the most intellectually active group of their generation of undergraduates'.[10] The Beaumont Street set is the subject of a tender appreciation in Philip Toynbee's *Friends Apart*: 'It could be said, perhaps, that this group was a late off-shoot, a second generation, of that Cambridge world of forty years earlier which subsequently assumed the general title of "Bloomsbury".'[11] The primary values of Jeremy's group of friends were emotional integrity and the cultivation of intense personal relations, but to these Bloomsbury ideals were superadded engagement in the outside world and socialism.[12]

Oxford at the time was a place where undergraduates and academics did not hold themselves at arm's length from one another. The older and younger generations socialized and exchanged ideas. A particular friend was Isaiah Berlin, eight years Jeremy's senior and then a fellow of All Souls, who in a letter in 1936 referred to Ben Nicolson and Jeremy Hutchinson as like the chess king and chess queen in Oxford highbrow circles.[13] On Jeremy's sitting room wall there is a beautiful Duncan Grant pastel of two dancers. When I asked him about it Jeremy explained that it had been a gift from Kenneth Clark, then a curator of the Ashmolean, on his twenty-first birthday – a marvellous example of the nature of Jeremy's friendships in the 1930s, friendships that lasted for decades afterwards.

There was still room for undergraduate japes. It was while living at Beaumont Street that Jeremy was caught by a passing policeman practising his marksmanship – such as it was – with an air pistol. It was unfortunate that the policeman, while walking his beat, had felt a stray pellet glancing off his trousers. The *Oxford Chronicle* reported Jeremy's plea of guilty to a charge of 'firing an air-pistol within 50 feet of the highway'. Harold Nicolson recorded a wholly exaggerated version of the event in a letter to Vita of 5 May 1936 thus:

> Jeremy, David and Stuart Hampshire have all been arrested for shooting a policeman with their air-revolver. Ben is a trifle ashamed as he funked taking part in the game and was therefore exempted. The policeman telephoned that he had been shot and armoured cars gathered around Beaumont Street at 1am and the house was surrounded by the whole Oxford police force. They then 'effected an entry' and the three foolish boys were dragged out of bed in their pyjamas and arrested. They are to be summoned this week. I do not quite like the idea of Ben being such an old cautious cissie as to refrain from shooting policemen with air-pistols.[14]

Jeremy makes the point that he thus started his career at the Bar with a 'criminal record'.

Before going up to Oxford Jeremy had entertained thoughts of working for the League of Nations, which seemed to him to be the only hope of avoiding another war. However he realized that his roots were too deep in England to contemplate a life abroad. As is often the way of the children of barristers, he alighted upon the law as an alternative. Having come down from Oxford, Jeremy lived with Stuart Hampshire in rooms at the top of a tall old house in Mecklenburgh Square. While Hampshire was conducting a torrid liaison with A.J. Ayer's wife, Jeremy had formed a relationship with Laura Bonham Carter, his first serious love,[15] while studying law at Gibson & Weldon, the tutorial college. Life in London was full of gaiety and Jeremy discovered a passion for the ballet, influenced by the fact that his friend Guy Branch, later to be a Battle of Britain ace,[16] was himself conducting a liaison with the dancer and actress Pearl Argyle. His upbringing had been a liberal one but it was during this period, both at Oxford and later in London, that Jeremy's political allegiances were cemented. 'I remember seeing the Jarrow marchers walking down Piccadilly in October 1936. I was so moved by their plight and determination that I immediately joined the Labour Party.' He would remain a member for more than forty years.

In preparation for a career at the Bar Jeremy served on two occasions as a 'marshal' to a High Court judge, Mr Justice Charles, while he was trying criminal cases on the north-eastern and western circuits. The job of marshal involved, for two guineas a day, acting as a form of social secretary and general factotum while dressed in a tail coat. Jeremy recalls sitting at Charles's side after dinner in his lodgings, forced to stay awake and listen as the judge nursed a glass of whisky and ruminated on the day's events. He would also accompany Charles to football matches and Boots' lending library. 'He would ask the young assistant for a book on the top shelf so he could admire her legs as she walked up the library steps to fetch it.' An eccentric, Ernest Charles had developed in childhood a private language with his brother, known as Carolingian, which remained their lingua franca and which Jeremy was expected to learn. As a witness whose collar was heavily carpeted with dandruff came into the box Charles, resplendent in his robes and wig, leaned over to Jeremy on the bench and whispered portentously, 'Marshal, sturf on u tollar.'

It was while acting as a marshal that Jeremy struck up a friendship with Vyvyan Holland, Oscar Wilde's surviving son, who was marshal to a fellow judge, Mr Justice Roland Oliver. Oliver, disliking students, always took a friend on circuit with him as marshal. Jeremy recounts receiving notes sent by Holland from the next-door court describing excitedly the more bizarre criminal offences that were passing through his court (including a particular case of bestiality that prompted Holland to write a lengthy ode to the farmer who was charged). Eccentricities apart, it was an invaluable education. 'I was able to see criminal advocacy in action from the perspective of the judge's bench and to learn from Charles what worked and what did not.'

After his legal studies Jeremy decided to have a concertinaed 'gap year'. He embarked at Glasgow on a Norwegian fruit ship (which admitted four passengers) to Los Angeles, by way of the Panama Canal, to stay with Aldous and Maria Huxley, friends of his parents and then living in Los Angeles. A whirlwind of socializing ensued: Aldous informed him the day after he arrived that he had organized for Jeremy to have lunch with 'Charlie and Paulette' (Chaplin). Aldous was also anxious to show him the Forest Lawn Cemetery (resting place of the great figures of Hollywood, later immortalized by Evelyn Waugh in his satirical novel *The Loved One*) and he remembers the eternal Wurlitzer music issuing from the trees as the novelist marvelled at the kitschness of the funerary statues: 'What beautiful bottoms, don't you think?' They also visited the Disney studios and dined with Edwin Hubble, the famous astronomer, and peered through his telescope. Jeremy looks back: 'For a young man it was all pure delight. Maria was so down to earth, so poetical, so full of humour and teasing, and of course for the adolescent so sexy.[17] Aldous was so gentle, so enquiring and fascinating; and fascinated too with every fact, every thought, hesitatingly brought out with the amazed inflection of his voice. For a young man he aroused a deep response. I loved them both. My whole memory was one of gaiety and stimulation.'

Jeremy then started on a protracted bus journey across America, visiting the Grand Canyon, eventually ending up in New Orleans, and then on to Mobile, Alabama, where he embarked on a tramp steamer back to London; this time as the only passenger. The journey took six weeks, which were spent reading the Russian classics and learning to type (a skill he would never make use of).

Arriving back in England in spring 1939 Jeremy saw that the international situation was grave. He had met Winston Churchill in the mid-1930s at Chartwell and Cranborne Manor[18] (a vivid memory is of Churchill in his boiler suit building a wall at Chartwell). Jeremy recalls hearing the future Prime Minister railing against the prevailing policy of appeasement and the scourge of Nazism. Churchill's warnings made a profound impression. Another key experience from this time, which also shaped Jeremy's thinking (and which remains lodged in his memory), was a dinner party thrown by his parents that was attended by Duff Cooper, then the First Lord of the Admiralty.

I remember my father asking Duff to give an account of his usual day. Duff explained that he would typically get into the office at about ten in the morning. At about noon he would go off to the Beefsteak or the Carlton Club for lunch. He would then go to another club to play a game or two of backgammon. He would get back to the office at about four, or perhaps five if the games were going well. He would then leave at about six. Although I was probably being unfair to him – and Duff was of course a fierce anti-appeaser – I remember this sense of outrage welling up in me that, as the international situation became dire, there were the English upper classes still living this leisured existence, detached from any sort of reality.

On his return from the United States Jeremy took a momentous decision. He determined to suspend his legal ambitions and, in anticipation of what he felt was the inevitable war, join the navy in order to make his own personal contribution to the defeat of Nazism. Jeremy had already acquired his sea legs sailing dinghies in Chichester Harbour (after leaving university he had asked a farmer if he could construct a small hut near the sea on the farmer's land, a request that was granted and provided the opportunity for Jeremy to pursue his obsession for sailing). He now applied to join the Royal Naval Volunteer Reserve on HMS *President*, the recruiting ship moored on the Thames opposite the Temple. He was initially turned down because of poor eyesight, but his father intervened with a call to a friend who was a senior officer in the Admiralty.

The next seven years were spent in the Royal Navy. It is a testament to Jeremy's modesty and lack of hauteur that this son of Bloomsbury and Oxford graduate proudly started his naval career as a rating. He was delighted with his uniform: the bell-bottom trousers, the tight-fitting top, the collar (which passers-by would touch for luck) and the black neckerchief, worn in honour of the death of Nelson.

In the first six months of the war Jeremy was stationed at Gosport and served as a signal rating (ironically, requiring particularly good eyesight) on troopships leaving Southampton for Cherbourg, ferrying British soldiers to France in preparation for the anticipated German invasion. The winter was a biting one and the ships would scurry across the Channel in darkness, haunted by the fear of predatory U-boats.

By spring 1940 it had been decided that Jeremy was officer material, and he was sent to Hove for training to become a sub-lieutenant. In April 1940 a woman with whom he had been acquainted since his boyhood, and whom he had met in Oxford when she played Juliet in a memorable OUDS production, suddenly became central to his life. Peggy Ashcroft was by then on her way to becoming one of the most famous Shakespearean actresses of the age. Seven years Jeremy's senior, she was already twice married and divorced. She had first married Rupert Hart-Davis, a friend of Jeremy's parents and later to become a well-known publisher and editor of Oscar Wilde's letters. That marriage had foundered early and Peggy went on to marry the extraordinary Theodore Komisarjevsky, a Russian émigré theatre director and committed follower of Stanislavsky, whose productions of Chekhov and Shakespeare were landmarks of the London theatre scene of the 1920s. 'Komi', as he was known, had been a prominent figure in the pre-revolution Moscow theatrical avant-garde and had been appointed director of the Bolshoi Theatre after the revolution. He had fled to England when Lenin had instigated the artistic repression of the early 1920s. Twenty-five years Komi's junior, Peggy had come under his Svengali-like spell and flung herself into a hasty marriage after he had directed her in his three-hour stage adaptation of Arthur Schnitzler's novella *Fräulein Else*. Komi proved impossible to live with, and within months Peggy had left him.

Now, here she was appearing at the Theatre Royal in Brighton. Jeremy came to see the play and knocked on her dressing-room door. He recalls: 'I was reading the paper and saw that Peggy, whom I hadn't seen for several years, was playing at the Royal. I made my call at the stage door to see her. There was nothing premeditated about it: it was pure chance. We made a date to see each other and went for a long walk over the Sussex Downs. Partly I suppose because of the shadow of war, we had something of a whirlwind romance.'

Peggy evidently fell for Jeremy in his smart rating's uniform – 'the one time I ever looked really attractive'. A photograph taken at the time shows him cutting a gallant figure. After the briefest of war romances they married on 14 September 1940, at the height of the Battle of Britain. As the wedding breakfast started at his parents' house at 3 Albert Road Jeremy remembers receiving a delivery – it turned out to be a rare Bonnard screen, a gift from the director of a London gallery much visited by Jeremy, and who had been success-fully defended on a loitering charge by his father. The whine of the air-raid sirens cut short the celebrations and the bridal couple made a hasty escape from London, driving hurriedly through empty streets peopled only by air-raid wardens, to a honeymoon at Burton Bradstock in Dorset.

Jeremy then joined HMS *Kelvin*, a destroyer of the 5th destroyer flotilla, under the command of Captain Lord Louis Mountbatten. After some months on Atlantic convoys, he was transferred to HMS *Kelly*, the flotilla leader, as the only RNVR officer on Mountbatten's staff, an appointment Jeremy looks back on with pride. Jeremy was on board when *Kelly* was sunk by German Stuka dive-bombers off Crete on 23 May 1941, during the evacuation of the island.

> I will always remember that morning. When dawn came it was absolutely beautiful, the most beautiful, still dawn, the most wonderful light. And I remember the smell of the herbs coming from the island. Everything was still and then, sure enough, the first group of specks of black appeared in the air, which were of course the high-level bombers. And then came the dive-bombers, coming down with this terrible, screaming noise, and then when they got what seemed terribly low they would swoop up and, as they swooped up, drop their bombs. It was only when the third lot came that we were hit. I was one of the lucky ones. Half the crew were lost. I was on deck when the bombs struck and was swept into the sea.

He recollects plunging 'down and down and down into the water, feeling as if my ears would burst, before popping back up, covered in oil'. He remained in the sea, clinging to wreckage with Mountbatten and the other survivors for many hours until they were rescued by another British destroyer, HMS *Kipling*. A vivid memory is of cheering the stricken ship as she slid beneath the waves. 'We then sang stirring songs such as "Roll out the Barrel" to keep up morale.' Noël Coward's great 1942 film *In Which We Serve*, telling the story of 'HMS *Torrin*' and her crew, is based on the career of the *Kelly*. Coward, a friend of Mountbatten, himself played the captain. The story is framed by scenes of the ship's sinking just as Jeremy describes it, and he confirms that Coward's farewell speech to the surviving members of the crew, gathered together for the last time in Alexandria, is accurate: 'We didn't leave the *Torrin* [*Kelly*], the *Torrin* [*Kelly*] left us!'

Mountbatten's great ambition, to captain a major warship, was fulfilled when, at the age of forty-one, he was appointed captain of the aircraft carrier HMS *Illustrious*, which was then being repaired following bomb damage at Norfolk, Virginia. He asked that his surviving officers from the *Kelly* be sent over to join him. Jeremy now found himself in America for several months, spending a treasured week in Manhattan with his old friend, the artist Edward McKnight Kauffer, who had designed a series of celebrated posters for London Transport while living in England. 'Ted took me to Harlem or Greenwich Village every night and introduced me to the music of Teddy Wilson, the jazz pianist. Jazz became a lifelong love of mine.' Jeremy returned to England in the *Illustrious* at the end of 1941.

> We did not have any destroyer support so the *Illustrious* and the *Formidable* zigzagged across the Atlantic in formation and at maximum speed. The *Illustrious* was astern of the *Formidable* keeping station on one small blue light. A young officer took over the watch from me and got too close in the dark so that *Illustrious* bumped the *Formidable*'s stern. One of my most vivid war memories is seeing the next morning a huge gash in our bows, which were covered with thousands of bananas which had been bought in Jamaica and stored on the after-deck of the *Formidable*. It was for me a stroke of good luck, as the ship had to be repaired in Liverpool, the crew got Christmas leave, and I found myself spending Christmas with Peggy and our new daughter Eliza. My sister Barbara had married Victor Rothschild in 1933[19] and Victor lent us an eighteenth-century folly on his estate at Tring Park, where Peggy spent the war years with our daughter.

Early the next year the *Illustrious* set off for the Indian Ocean, stopping en route to retake Madagascar from the Vichy French. The ship then joined the Far Eastern fleet, based at Trincomalee in what was then known as Ceylon. After eighteen months awaiting the feared Japanese encroachment into the Indian Ocean, Jeremy applied successfully to join the first specialist Long Signals course to include RNVRs at the Naval Signal School, which had been evacuated to East Meon in Hampshire, inland from Portsmouth. It was from Portsmouth that most of the ships participating in D–Day set sail, while the course was still in progress. 'So I avoided D–Day.' Having qualified, he was posted to the staff of the Commander-in-Chief Mediterranean at Caserta, outside Naples. After four years at sea Jeremy found himself on dry land and to his joy in Italy: 'Back in civilization! I remember the delight of going to a production of *La Traviata*, staged soon after the reopening of the San Carlo Opera House in Naples.'

It was then that Jeremy was given his first legal brief: to prosecute an English sailor on a capital charge. In Rome in 1944 a group of Allied deserters, styling themselves the Sailor Gang, had set up as outlaws, stealing and plundering and selling their wares on the black market. In November 1944 the body of a soldier, shot three times, was found in a ditch outside Rome. He was identified as a Canadian private, 'Lucky' McGilvary, a member of the gang. He had fallen out with his confederates over the division of the spoils and, in the heat of the argument, had been shot in a room on the via Pistoia by a fellow gang-member. The leader of the Sailor Gang, an Englishman called Bill Croft, then dumped the body in a ditch outside Rome. Over a few weeks those involved in the killing were arrested and charged with murder. Each service was instructed to try its own member(s). In peacetime, any capital charge in the Royal Navy was always sent back to England to be tried at the Old Bailey. Here, uniquely, the case had to be tried where the crime was committed.

The only lawyer available to prosecute was Jeremy. 'I was given a jeep and a driver and ordered to gather evidence and build the case. We drove up to Rome and I interviewed all the witnesses. I had to take statements, read up the law and present the case. It was one of those extraordinary things that happens in wartime. You just get on with it.' Despite his never having yet appeared in a courtroom, Jeremy led the case for the prosecution in an ornate room set up as a temporary court in the San Carlo, where he had seen *La Traviata* weeks earlier, in front of a court martial of five senior officers dressed in full naval regalia. The papers Jeremy retains from the case show how seriously the killing of one man, himself a criminal, amid so much wider destruction, was taken by the military authorities. Seventeen witnesses were called for the prosecution and elaborate preparations were made to have them brought to Naples.

Jeremy sums up the crux of the case: 'What was incontrovertible was that Croft had shot Lucky in the head while he was in the ditch. There were two critical issues in the case. The first was whether Lucky was already dead. Croft claimed that he had only fired the shot to prevent identification of what was then a corpse; but the minuteness of the bullet wound contradicted that account. Secondly, even if Croft had shot Lucky's corpse, and although he did not fire the original shot, was he nonetheless guilty of murder under the doctrine of joint enterprise.' There followed a prolonged trial. 'I will never forget Croft's dark-eyed Italian girlfriend giving evidence against him. She walked proudly into this gloriously baroque room with naval officers all around bearing their ceremonial swords and in their full pomp. On her arm was a six-month-old baby – the child of Croft. As she gave evidence she suddenly opened up her dress and out came this beautiful breast to feed the baby. In typical naval fashion, nobody batted an eyelid.' Croft was found guilty and sentenced to death. He was the last British sailor to be executed. Jeremy claims to be the only member of the English Bar to have had as his first brief a prosecution for murder.[20]

As the war in Europe was coming to an end, Jeremy seized the opportunity to get some badly needed home leave by contesting the 1945 general election. A signal had been sent from the Admiralty that any candidates in the forces would be granted a month's campaigning leave. Jeremy telephoned an old friend, Philip Noel Baker, who helped to get him selected as the Labour Party candidate for the Abbey Division in Westminster, a rock-solid Tory seat. Jeremy threw himself into the campaign with vigour, attending public meetings and canvassing what was then a constituency that embraced the City of London, the West End, Soho and the working-class districts of Pimlico. A young man of nineteen in an RAF uniform drove Jeremy's loudspeaker van – his name the Honourable Anthony Wedgwood-Benn.[21]

On 30 June 1945 the *News Chronicle* reported that Jeremy, with Peggy accompanying him, had attempted to canvass in Downing Street. As they approached, a police officer had stopped them: 'You – the public cannot come in here.' Jeremy retorted, 'But I am permitted to canvass any of my constituents!' It was reported that PC 494A relented and Jeremy asked the commissionaire at the famous door of Number 10: 'Is the householder in?' The commissionaire testily replied that Mr Churchill was not in, but Jeremy insisted on meeting the domestic staff, who were eventually lined up in the hall. 'I received a number of friendly winks.' However Westminster remained solidly Conservative and Jeremy was thankful not to be elected: after six years of military service he was anxious to start his legal career and embark on family life.

First there was the business of finding a house in which to set up his family (his son Nicholas was born in 1946). Monty Shearman, who had been legal adviser to the Foreign Office and a bachelor (and who had thrown the Armistice party at the Adelphi), had recently died, bequeathing to Jeremy a small snow scene by Monet. 'What extraordinary generosity and how fortunate I was.' Jeremy recounts that he allowed himself ten minutes to look at the painting before wrapping it up and promptly taking it down to Cork Street to sell. 'Any longer and I might have fallen in love with it.' With the proceeds of the sale Jeremy bought a house on Frognal Lane, Manor Lodge, the old manorial bailiff's house of Hampstead Village.

He was finally demobilized in 1946 and arrived at his father's chambers (Jack Hutchinson had died in 1942) at 1 Garden Court in the Temple the same year, to undertake his twelve-month pupillage. He was thirty-one, years older than the average pupil starting out at the Bar. His pupil master was James Burge, later counsel for Stephen Ward in his infamous trial, a Pickwickian, rumbustious figure who would be, with his pupil, one of John Mortimer's inspirations for Horace Rumpole. Jeremy reminisces: 'My grounding was the dock brief – chosen by a prisoner in custody, standing in the dock behind a row of barristers, one pound seven-and-six in the palm of his hand, and a choice based on the promise disclosed by the back of a bewigged head. If chosen I would hurriedly go down to the cells to take instructions from my newly found client and then fight the case.' And still in Jeremy's archive is a letter from the Clerk to the Old Bailey, dating back to February 1946, adding Jeremy's name to the list of counsel willing to defend under the Poor Persons Defence Act.

Jeremy's first important briefs were for the navy stoker Henry Herbert Rose, accused of espionage for the Germans during the war,[22] and on behalf of one of the parties whose conduct was being examined by the Lynskey Tribunal, set up to investigate allegations of corruption against government ministers and civil servants. In 1952 he acted as junior in the prosecution of the child murderer John Straffen. Straffen, suspected of strangling two children, had been found unfit to plead and committed to Broadmoor. The next year he escaped, and on his first day on the run strangled another child. Jeremy's leader was the then Solicitor General, Reginald Manningham-Buller, who was later to figure largely on the opposite side of the court in Jeremy's career. Straffen was somewhat surprisingly found 'fit to plead', found guilty and sentenced to death, although his sentence was commuted on account of his insanity. He would go on to become the longest serving prisoner in British legal history, eventually dying in prison in 2007.[23]

Although he would become known as a great defender, Jeremy did his fair share of prosecution work throughout the 1950s. Jeremy insists that it is crucial for any criminal barrister to both prosecute and defend if he is really to learn his art. He recalls vividly the prosecution of Lord Montagu, arrested in 1953 during the so-called 'Lavender Scare', and charged with a sexual assault on a scout in a bathing hut at Beaulieu. The trial was heard in December 1953 (attended by massive public interest) and resulted in a hung jury. While Montagu was awaiting a retrial, it was proposed that he be prosecuted for further homosexual offences, this time along with the journalist Peter Wildeblood, Michael Pitt-Rivers and two airmen. Jeremy was sent the papers in relation to the second charge by the Director of Public Prosecutions. Jeremy robustly advised the DPP that while the retrial on the first charge was pending it would be quite wrong for Montagu or the other co-defendants to be tried for a second set of offences, which could only fatally prejudice his

defence in the retrial. This was advice that the prosecuting authorities were not interested in receiving and the second case was swiftly
removed from him. Jeremy thereby lost out on a very good brief
(Montagu and his co-defendants would later be convicted in April
1954 on the second set of offences and sentenced to lengthy periods
of imprisonment) but his behaviour demonstrated one of the qualities of the independent Bar: putting the interests of justice first,
rather than seeking to obtain a conviction at all costs.[24] (Jeremy's
view was echoed by a later article in the *New Statesman* which
deplored 'the extraordinary decision of the Director of Public
Prosecutions to launch a second prosecution against Lord Montagu
while similar charges, on which an earlier jury had disagreed, were
still pending'.[25]) In the event the DPP agreed that, Montagu having
been convicted of the second set of charges, it would be wrong to
proceed with the earlier case. Jeremy later received a letter from Sir
Theobald Mathew, the DPP, recording his gratitude to Jeremy for
his work. 'I really appreciated your assistance and advice, perhaps
the more because you did not agree with some of the decisions, as
it is very valuable to have the other side cogently presented.'

Through the 1950s Jeremy built up a successful criminal practice
in London. He was admitted to the Western Circuit and cut his
teeth in the courts of Hampshire, Somerset, Wiltshire and Dorset
as well as the magistrates courts of London. He also became standing
counsel to the Post Office, an appointment that Jeremy puts down
to the general policy that prevailed after the war of rewarding those
who had been engaged in prolonged war service.

The variety of work that he undertook is evident from a press
cutting from 1955 headed 'The Forgetful Professor' which records
an incident during a holiday being taken by the great conservative
philosopher Michael Oakeshott. There follows a wonderful vignette
of the 1950s. Camping near Chesil Bank on the Dorset coast,
Oakeshott, then in his fifties, is recorded as having brewed a pot of
tea on an oil stove before going down to the sea to bathe. Eschewing
any bathing costume, he was reported to the police by a shocked
couple on a seaside walk. Hauled up before the Dorchester Quarter
Sessions, Professor Oakeshott pleaded guilty to 'unlawfully, wilfully
and publicly exposing his naked person on the beach'. Jeremy's

speech in mitigation included the following delightful lines: 'You can wear a bikini on Brighton beach for all to see you. You can stand naked on the London stage without any offence in law. But if you are a forgetful professor sitting in your tent unclothed, you do, in fact, commit an offence against common law if anyone should happen to see you.' Oakeshott was given a conditional discharge. On the face of it, a job well done. But Jeremy remembers the case as providing an early lesson in advocacy. He had leafed through the brief on the train down to Dorchester, cogitating how to pitch his mitigation. The case seemed a wholly ridiculous one and Jeremy decided to introduce an element of levity into the proceedings. As hinted at by the newspaper report, his speech made allusions to the Windmill Theatre in Soho, infamous for its nude *tableaux vivants*, to an increasingly stony-faced tribunal, which consisted of a chairman, who was a local chancery barrister, and two lay magistrates. The bench retired for more than an hour to consider their sentence. Although the ultimate sentence was a light one, Jeremy would later be told by the chairman that the reason for the delay was that the magistrates had taken a very dim view of Jeremy's apparently blasé attitude to the offence and had had to be worked on by the chairman before they were willing to consent to leniency. Jeremy remembers: 'I discovered that it could be very dangerous to assume that everyone thought like myself.'

The same year, Jeremy appeared for the Belgian government in its (ultimately successful) attempts to extradite 'Dr' Emil Savundra for a fraud committed in Antwerp. Savundra would later resurface as the unnamed 'Indian Doctor' (in fact he was Sri Lankan) who visited Stephen Ward's flat for assignations with Mandy Rice-Davies and was the man behind the notorious Fire, Auto and Marine insurance fraud of the 1960s. On this occasion he claimed to be too ill to attend the court, so the lawyers all trooped to his bedside in the London Clinic where, as the newspapers put it, 'with eyes closed he lay in bed at the foot of the long board table, watched by a doctor and a nurse.' Jeremy recalls him surreptitiously opening one eye and giving him a conspiratorial wink before quickly shutting it again.

There were also more glamorous briefs. Jeremy successfully

defended Lady Bridget Parsons on a drink-driving charge in which her passengers were the Duke and Duchess of Devonshire. After a police officer standing guard outside the German Embassy had arrested her and locked her in the embassy building, she was seen to sway as she got into the Black Maria that had been called. Jeremy persuaded the court that Lady Bridget's uncertainty on her feet was caused by her high heels and tight evening dress. The photographs in the newspapers show her being led out of court by John Betjeman ('A wonderful show! This way, Bridget, old girl!') and embracing Jeremy as she offers him effusive thanks. Another client was the actor Trevor Howard, also prosecuted for drink-driving (a very useful stream of income for barristers in those days). Jeremy managed to secure his acquittal by showing that, while awaiting the police doctor (these were the days before the breathalyser), Howard, a cricket lover, had had a long conversation with the police officer about the differences between a googly and a leg break. 'Is it really likely, members of the jury, that a man could have such a conversation and yet be incapable of having a proper control of a car?' asked Jeremy. The jury agreed.

He also acted for Stirling Moss on charges of dangerous driving, but with less success. Moss had his licence suspended for twelve months and gave birth to the cliché asked by so many police officers since: 'Who do you think you are, Stirling Moss?' A few years later Jeremy found himself defending Arthur Koestler on a charge of driving under the influence. He had apparently been stopped for driving with exaggerated caution at too slow a speed down the Brompton Road. The author of *Darkness at Noon* was fined twenty guineas and received the mandatory sentence of having his licence suspended for twelve months. He wrote an indignant letter to *The Times* complaining of the injustice, as he saw it, of a law that imposed a mandatory sentence, regardless of culpability. Jeremy followed this letter up with his own broadside in the same columns against compulsory sentences: 'Is it not remarkable that whereas English Courts are trusted to decide whether to deprive a man of his liberty, they are not allowed to decide whether to deprive him of his driving licence?'[26]

Although Jeremy's archive is filled with newspaper cuttings

reflecting the growing practice of a fashionable barrister, the most poignant documents I came across when researching his life are the reams of handwritten letters sent to him by the countless unknown and unheralded individuals whom he represented during his years at the Bar, all carefully preserved by him. These were ordinary people, out of the public eye, who at a moment of often supreme difficulty in their lives placed their confidence in him as their counsel. The letters demonstrate the bond of trust between client and counsel and reveal so much about how a criminal barrister is more than just a person doing a job for a fee. They are filled with heartfelt thanks to Jeremy not just for what he did for them in court, but for his interest and concern for them both before and after the case had finished. It is very moving to read them. Two examples will suffice. 'I am writing to you in a vain attempt to convey my gratitude for all you have done on my behalf in the last few months. I must confess that it wasn't until I actually listened to your oratory that I fully realised just how fortunate I was for you to be representing my interests. I now know that I could not possibly have been in safer hands, a fact which I appreciate in no small measure.' And: 'Though a desperately serious matter for me, I must confess I have seldom spent a more fascinating, stimulating, interesting and exciting three days than the days of my trial. Having lived with the case for 4 months very actively, I, better than anyone else, am able to say that my defence was BRILLIANT down to the last detail and not a trick was missed. I have taken part in a great event.'

In his turn Jeremy speaks of the privilege that he felt as a barrister of being asked into a person's life, often during a period of great crisis for them, and of the weight of responsibility he experienced when presenting their case before a jury or judge.

> Some of the most important cases I did were not the ones which made big headlines. Often they took place in magistrates courts or in obscure courts across the country. There was one in the early 1960s where I defended a senior civil servant, the under-secretary at the Ministry of Public Works, charged with importuning, based on evidence that he had entered a public lavatory late in the evening and smiled and nodded in a suggestive way at the two plainclothes policemen who were there for the specific purpose of trying to

catch out homosexuals. We lost the case before the magistrate. A
fine of £25 was imposed — but the reality was that the man was
ruined. He was sacked from his position and of course the stigma
at that time was terrible. Thankfully, we won the appeal. It is one
of those examples of what is, on the face of it, a relatively minor
criminal charge having the power to destroy a person's life. And it
is your responsibility as counsel to defend him. I always found that
a heavy responsibility.

Jeremy's breakthrough case came in 1960 when Penguin Books was
prosecuted under the recently enacted Obscene Publications Act
1959 for publishing *Lady Chatterley's Lover*. The trial was of course
a sensation; it has been described by Geoffrey Robertson QC as the
most socially impactful trial of the twentieth century. Although
Jeremy was led by Gerald Gardiner QC,[27] who was briefed at a very
late stage, Jeremy had prepared the case, selected the battery of expert
witnesses, and conducted many of the examinations of the witnesses
called by the defence. Afterwards Jeremy received a short poem from
his old friend Vyvyan Holland, who had attended the trial.
Commenting in the wake of the acquittal that he thought 'It was
the Bishop that did it' (a reference to the Bishop of Woolwich, John
Robinson, who, famously, gave evidence for Penguin Books), he
continued:

> It was very swish
> To have tee-d up a bish
> But it would have been fun
> To have chartered a nun.

The Penguin Books trial had many immediate effects on Jeremy's
life. First, it sealed his reputation and led to his taking silk the next
year. Second, it enabled him to buy a small rectory in the tiny
hamlet of Lullington in East Sussex, a place of magical beauty which
was captured by Dirk Bogarde (who had spent his childhood summers
there in the 1920s and 1930s) in his memoir *A Postillion Struck by
Lightning*. Jeremy remembers that the decision to purchase Lullington
required him to sell an island (or rather the remains of it) in the
Walton backwaters in Essex, known as Skippers Island, which he
had bought in the early 1950s. 'I bought Skippers as a place to go

at the weekend with the children, to be in total isolation and to sail. Arthur Ransome wrote a book called *Secret Waters* which was set on this island. Just above the high-water mark was an old beached houseboat where we would sleep. It was there, surrounded by seabirds and a small heronry, that I taught my children how to sail on the day boat which I kept there and which I named after Ransome's book.' Lullington is close to Charleston, home of Duncan Grant and Vanessa Bell, and Rodmell, home of the Woolfs. When asked recently about a tree in his garden, Jeremy replied that it had been given to him by Leonard Woolf. Lastly, Jeremy's conduct of the *Chatterley* case led to him being offered the chairmanship of Penguin Books by Allen Lane, an offer he declined, not without hesitation. 'I seriously considered the offer; the thought of a working life outside the public eye was very attractive. One of the drawbacks of life at the Bar is that one is constantly on show.'

Applying for silk is not now, and was not in 1961, a step to be taken lightly. As a newspaper at the time put it: 'Taking silk is a milestone in a lawyer's life. It carries great risks. Not every prosperous junior makes the grade. Some forfeit a lot of income.' In 1961 the thirty-four successful applicants were described by the *Observer* as 'juniors with busy practices which have left little time or opportunity to make an impact on the public'. Jeremy's own success was not exactly met with undiluted applause. The *Observer* continued: 'Jeremy Hutchinson, for all his flourishing criminal practice – and his Labour candidature in 1945 – has not been able to compete with his wife, Dame Peggy Ashcroft.'

The next twenty years were to disprove that comment. They were a period of extraordinary legal activity. Jeremy became the most sought-after criminal defence barrister at the English Bar. In the memoirs of the period he is identified as among the greatest advocates of his generation. (For instance, Lord Goodman, in his autobiography, *Tell Them I'm on My Way*, described Jeremy as the 'most brilliant criminal counsel of our day'.[28]) Rarely has a barrister so completely dominated his field.

The barrister's work is an ephemeral business. Great causes are often soon forgotten. Professional reputations are unceremoniously ushered out of view as new generations step into the limelight. But, in researching his life and work, what has stood out is the peerless reputation that Jeremy acquired during the 1960s and 1970s as the leading criminal barrister at the Bar, lauded not just for his skills as an advocate but also for his passionate devotion to the interests of his clients and the integrity of his profession. This is something that I have had to winkle out: Jeremy would never suggest that himself. Yet reading the newspapers of the time, and the effusive letters from judges and other members of the Bar after some particular triumph, one can piece together a vivid picture of achievement. As one barrister wrote: 'He has the unique ability of being able to create an atmosphere in court.'

In 1961 Jeremy was retained to act for George Blake, the spy who would be sentenced to the longest determinate sentence ever handed down by an English court. Presciently, in the appeal to the Court of Appeal, he would warn that a man visited with such a sentence would be faced with only two options: 'lose his sanity or gain his freedom'. This case led to the 'Committee of 100' Official Secrets Act trial in 1962 (notable for many reasons, not least that Vanessa Redgrave and Bertrand Russell gave evidence for the defence) and the defence brief in the other notorious spy scandal of the period, John Vassall, a case that Harold Macmillan feared would bring down his government. Jeremy would become the leading barrister in espionage and Official Secrets Act cases. He personally regards his greatest success as securing the acquittal of the atomic scientist Giuseppe Martelli in 1963 on charges of spying for the Russians. A profile in the *Daily Express* afterwards provides an ample testament to his prestige:

> Every man is innocent until he is proved guilty. That is the heart of English justice. And it was the key to the defence of Dr Martelli, acquitted last night. A defence conducted by Jeremy Hutchinson QC. Hutchinson, in court, is totally absorbed in the facts he elicits from a witness – seeking the fact which reveals a doubt. The jury sees a handsome man of 48, his powerful features beneath the high domed forehead set in forbidding lines: a face to fit a judge. Now and again the tension he has built up is relieved by a sudden smile. But all the time he is building the wall of doubt to clear the man in the dock.

The writer then describes some of Jeremy's well-known cases. He continues:

Tough cases. Some lost. Many won. By the serious voice asking juries: 'Is there no doubt?' Hutchinson, the son of a great barrister father, has been married for 23 years to Dame Peggy Ashcroft, the actress. They live in Frognal-lane, Hampstead, with their son and daughter. There ought, by rights, to be a celebration tonight. Not just for another Hutchinson triumph. For a triumph of that proud claim: Every man is innocent until he is proved guilty.[29]

Another newspaper referred to an urbane court manner with a touch of a certain 'Oxford languor'. Yet this was also a man who was not afraid to confront judges when he thought they were being overbearing or showing bias against his client. In one case a newspaper reports a 'dramatic' moment in court when a magistrate remonstrated with Jeremy over his prolonged cross-examination of a prosecution witness. 'I am getting absolutely strangled – by wool!' Courageously, Jeremy demanded that he recuse himself from the trial (that is stand down) for his intervention. The magistrate meekly acceded. Yet life at the Bar is not all about contention and disputation. There are two letters in Jeremy's files that reveal a very different side: the camaraderie. The first is a letter sent by Peter Rawlinson, then the Solicitor General, who had unsuccessfully prosecuted the Martelli case, congratulating Jeremy on his victory. The letter shows real magnanimity in defeat and admiration for forensic skill. The second is a letter from Mervyn Griffith-Jones, Jeremy's principal opponent in some of his greatest cases – *Chatterley*, George Blake, *Fanny Hill* and the Committee of 100. As I explain in the chapters that follow, Griffith-Jones was a kind of inverse of Jeremy in terms of outlook and values. When Griffith-Jones was made up to a judge in 1964, Jeremy wrote him a letter of congratulation. Griffith-Jones's reply is revelatory. An entirely different man is disclosed from the grim and relentless moralist who seemed to be incarnated in court. 'Bless you for your letter – I cried.'

Many of the great cases of the 1960s that followed are narrated in the chapters below. It is a shame that reasons of space prevented others receiving proper attention: these include Jeremy's defence of Charlie Wilson, the Great Train Robber, the theft of the World Cup in 1966, and the prosecution of the Irishman who threw CS gas canisters into the House of Commons in protest against the use of that gas in Northern Ireland.[30]

There was also time for devotion to causes close to Jeremy's heart. A fervent cricket lover, he had become friendly with Len Hutton (one of his heroes) and spent many Sundays watching Sussex play at Hove in the company of his great friend Alan Ross, then the cricket correspondent for the *Observer*. In 1968 Jeremy found his political convictions overlapping with his affection for the game. That year the original team picked by the MCC to tour South Africa had left out the outstanding all-rounder Basil D'Oliveira, a celebrated Test cricketer who was of mixed Indian and Portuguese ancestry. (In the event, owing to the injury of another player, D'Oliveira was picked and the tour was cancelled by the apartheid regime in South Africa, which refused to welcome a team containing a player who was classified under their race laws as 'coloured'.) This led to the historic Special General Meeting of the members of the MCC at Church House in Westminster, called by Rev. David Sheppard, former captain of England, to protest against D'Oliveira's initial non-selection, widely believed to have been influenced by the South Africans, and to call for a cricketing boycott of South Africa. Jeremy was asked by Sheppard to act as his informal legal adviser, and to speak on behalf of the motion put before the hall that there should be no further tours to or from South Africa until non-racial cricket had been established in that country. Jeremy recalls a fervid atmosphere. 'There were about 1,000 members of the MCC physically present. There was also a lot of bad feeling from the old guard who hated the idea of their sport being mixed up in larger political and moral questions. I had never spoken to such a large and hostile audience.' The *Observer* pronounced his arguments 'unanswerable' and the motion received significant support at Church House, but was ultimately defeated by the postal vote of all the members. Nonetheless the battle would later be won.

Other liberal causes also attracted Jeremy's attention. Ever since he had first visited a dank Victorian prison in the 1930s, Jeremy had been a zealous advocate of prison reform. He also campaigned for the abolition of the 'dock' in the courtroom and challenged the imposition of excessive prison sentences. The letters pages of *The Times* and the *Guardian* carried frequent lapidary contributions from him.

★

Jeremy's marriage to Peggy Ashcroft came to an end in the mid-1960s. He later described the difficulties of being married to a theatrical genius: 'Great artists are primarily married to their art, and so it should be', and he speaks frankly of the loneliness he felt in the marriage as Peggy pursued her stage career. (It is another insight into the times that his divorce created some consternation at the Middle Temple and cast into doubt his appointment as a Bencher of the Inn. He would eventually be made a Bencher in 1967, after he was safely remarried.) He and Peggy would remain friendly for the rest of her life and Jeremy organized Peggy's memorial service at Westminster Abbey in 1991.

In 1966 Jeremy remarried. June Osborn was the daughter of 'Boy' Capel, Coco Chanel's lover and patron, who had died in a car crash in southern France in 1919, before June was born. She had been married to the pianist Franz Osborn, who had died early, and had subsequently been wooed by two unlikely suitors: Cecil Beaton and Edward Heath. She and Jeremy remained very happily married until June's death in 2006.

Jeremy never had any ambition to take up a full-time judicial role. He explains: 'First of all, I couldn't have borne having to be respectable, and secondly, I wanted to retain my freedom, because the joy of being at the Bar is you are self-employed. You do not have to come into an office at a fixed time, and leave at five thirty. Once you become a judge you become part of the establishment, you have to go where you are sent and sit for regular hours.' Nonetheless, for ten years from 1961 he sat as the Recorder of Bath. This role required him to spend three or four weeks a year sitting at the Bath Quarter Sessions dispensing justice, whether by handing down sentences on those who had pleaded guilty to offences that were too serious to be tried by the magistrates or conducting jury trials. He found immense satisfaction in this position and enjoyed being the city's second citizen. Perhaps unsurprisingly, he became known for his enlightened sentencing policy. He was eventually retired from this position when, as a result of the Courts Act 1971, the Quarter Sessions courts were abolished and the title of Recorder of Bath was swept away. Jeremy gave a mournful speech on his last sitting day. He looks back: 'There had been a Recorder of Bath for almost 700 years. As a result of the changes the concept of local justice conducted in the interests of and with the participation of local inhabitants was removed in the name of efficiency. In my view this was a fundamental error.'

By the late 1960s Jeremy was acutely conscious that there was a disjunction between the crucial role of the criminal Bar as a bulwark of liberty and its low professional status. 'I remember people would approach me in the Inn and say, disapprovingly, that they were surprised to see me in such-and-such a case, as if it was somehow undignified to be associated with some particular alleged criminal.' There was a tendency at the time to treat the criminal barrister as a sort of hack, plying a dubious trade for the benefit of undeserving people. 'I felt that if the criminal Bar was to organize into a formal body then it might be able to raise its reputation and, more importantly, increase public awareness and understanding of its vital role.' Accordingly, in 1969 he and other colleagues at the criminal Bar, including Basil Wigoder, John Hasan and Michael Hill, formed the Criminal Bar Association. Jeremy was its chairman for six years, with Basil Wigoder (later to become a Liberal peer) his vice-chairman. Jeremy's chairmanship involved advocacy on a wider stage than that of the courtroom of his profession and of the fundamentals of criminal law. There were frequent clashes with governments of the day, bent on undermining the rights of defendants. The CBA remains a thriving and vigorous body.

The 1970s were the years when Jeremy's position as the leading figure at the criminal Bar was undisputed. Some of the great cases of that decade – *Sunday Telegraph*, *The Mouth and Oral Sex*, the *ABC* case, Tom Keating and *Last Tango in Paris* – are described in the chapters that follow. But there were many others which, had space and time allowed, would have merited similar treatment – including the trial of T. Dan Smith, the leader of Newcastle Council (in his first trial Jeremy sensationally secured his acquittal, for which services, he recalls, wistfully, he was never paid[31]); the 'supergrass' bank robbery case trial, in which Bertie Smalls turned Queen's evidence; and the court martial of Commander Swabey.

This last case deserves elaboration. It was to be one of the longest legal sagas of the twentieth century and drew into its clutches – as either supporters or opponents – many of the prominent figures of the day to become a kind of small-scale Dreyfus scandal. Born in 1926, Christopher Swabey came from a distinguished naval background and followed his father, a vice-admiral, into the Royal Navy. In 1950 calamity befell him. He was charged with indecently assaulting a rating – an offence that, if proved, would lead to instant dismissal from the service and social pariahdom. At a court martial convened in Malta he was acquitted of the indecency charge and, although he was convicted of a lesser charge of disturbing ratings while they were sleeping, that conviction was later annulled. Swabey went on to serve with distinction in the Korean War and to gain promotion to lieutenant-commander. But no doubt the whispering persisted and memories of the case remained live.

In 1956 he was appointed to command HMS *Redoubt* in Malta. On one of the first evenings on his new ship, Swabey invited the other officers to dine with him on shore. Only one, a twenty-two-year-old sub-lieutenant, took him up on the offer. The two men proceeded to embark on a protracted crawl round the bars and clubs of Valletta. As they returned late that evening back on their ship, having drunk their fair share, the younger man accused Swabey of having indecently assaulted him. The alleged act giving rise to this charge seems, from today's perspective, ludicrously trivial: it was said that, in the taxi back, Swabey ran his hand along the sub-lieutenant's knee in a way that suggested homosexual intent. Swabey vigorously denied the charge, and a court martial was convened on the very island where the earlier trial had been held. Swabey was convicted and dismissed from the service in disgrace.

There followed appeals, reviews and petitions, all of which hit a brick wall. But beyond the formal legal processes, there was a growing sense that justice had not been done. In particular, it became apparent that it remained common knowledge in Malta that Swabey had previously been tried for a similar offence; the risk was that the officers sitting on the court martial (who, in the absence of a jury, were the tribunal of fact) were influenced by that knowledge. The matter was then taken up by various peers, Lords Shackleton and

Russell and the Marquess of Salisbury included, and, over the years, there were three debates in the House of Lords concerning Swabey's plight, Jeremy's old foe Viscount Dilhorne, the former Attorney General Reginald Manningham-Buller, being notable in his resistance to any suggestion that there had been any miscarriage of justice. But Swabey remained absolutely determined to clear his name and, after byzantine machinations, the case finally came back before the Court of Appeal sixteen years after his initial conviction. Jeremy represented him. 'A critical piece of evidence against Swabey was the fact that, after he had been accused, he did not publicly denounce his accuser, but showed what appeared to be a terrible disturbance of mind. This demeanour could be taken as consistent with guilt; in fact, it flowed from his horror that what had happened in 1950 was about to happen again. After a three-day court battle we persuaded the court that the conviction was unsafe and the appeal was allowed. Swabey was vindicated. It was a wonderful moment – all his supporters in court were in uproar.'[32]

Jeremy had been close friends with many Labour politicians, most notably Roy Jenkins, since the 1940s. He had been appointed by Jenkins, when he was Home Secretary, to sit on the Committee on Immigration Appeals in 1966 and Jenkins had tried, unsuccessfully, to have Jeremy appointed as a legal adviser to him while he was Home Secretary.[33] Nonetheless his elevation to the House of Lords, as Lord Hutchinson of Lullington in 1978, came as a surprise to him. It was apparently a move by the Labour government to increase the party's legal presence in the House of Lords. Jeremy remembers his wife June asking, 'Why you?' It was, in one sense, a good question. After all, Jeremy had not participated in politics in the party sense for many years. But taking the Labour whip in the Lords did not dim his anti-establishment proclivities. In the *ABC* trial, a politically motivated and thoroughly misconceived Official Secrets Act prosecution heard in September 1978,[34] he poured scorn on the conduct of the Labour government law officers who had instituted the proceedings.

While remaining a fully engaged barrister, Jeremy also became a very active member of the House of Lords. He contributed most vigorously to debates on criminal and penal policy as well as issues relating to legal services – and yet, as he points out, his maiden speech was about the importance of poetry to the culture of England. His speeches retain on the pages of Hansard the passion with which they were delivered. The following comes from his last speech in the Lords, delivered at the age of eighty-six in 2001, opposing the controversial Hunting Bill (an example of his liberalism in action):

> My Lords, for me this Bill is overwhelmingly a matter of civil liber-ties, human rights, tolerance, democracy and freedom itself. Every countryman knows that the Commons' vote seeks to destroy not only a country pursuit – a disciplined and historic form of fox and deer control – but also a part of the very culture of the countryside.
>
> In the other place reference was repeatedly made to 'the declared will of the majority', to be respected by country people and, remark-ably enough, by this elected House. Of course, the rural population is a minority and the hunting community is a substantial part of that minority, which comprises decent, civilised, caring people who live, protect and understand, as the majority do not, animals in the wild and who preserve and manage their habitat.
>
> There are men, women and, yes, children – the hunting fraternity and the followers – who are bewildered, shocked and now deeply angry that an ignorant, uninformed and urban and suburban majority should now demonise their community and seek to make their historic way of life criminal; their families open to arrest on suspicion; their premises open to search without warrant and their dogs liable to destruction.
>
> What is democracy about if it is not respect and tolerance for the beliefs and way of life of minorities in one's midst and, indeed, respect for the views of this second Chamber under our constitution? Since the 17th century hunting has been an integral part of country life.[35]

Many of Jeremy's Lords speeches were focused on defending the integrity of the legal system. One of his most deeply held convic-tions is of the fundamental importance of the jury to the criminal process. He speaks of the role – and collective wisdom – of the jury with almost mystical reverence and it is fitting that it was he who first came upon and exposed the practice of jury-vetting during the *ABC* trial[36] – an occasion that inspired one of his greatest courtroom speeches.[37] It is therefore no surprise that Jeremy used his position in the Lords to make his mark on jury-law. In the wake of Jeremy Thorpe's acquittal in 1979, the *New Statesman* had interviewed one of the jurors and published an article explaining the jury's reasoning. Contempt proceedings had been brought against the magazine, which had been dismissed by the court. 'I was horrified by what had happened. To my mind if anyone, whether a journalist, an academic or a member of the defendant's family, was allowed to interview jurors about their deliberations and the reasons for their verdict, the very integrity of the jury was placed in jeopardy.' During the debate on the Contempt of Court Bill in 1981, Jeremy moved an amendment that would make it a criminal offence for any person to enquire into or disclose the deliberations of a jury.[38]

> The jury is indeed becoming the last bastion and guarantee of our freedom in this country, and here the ordinary citizen stands firm of purpose between the subject and the Executive. It is a guarantee in every case that human justice, as opposed – I say it expressly – to lawyers' justice, is in fact arrived at. A verdict is reached by 12 ordinary untrained people, giving consideration to a whole complex of relevant matters, and feeling their way to a joint decision on the question: in the end in this case is there a reasonable doubt? . . . Blackstone said that the liberties of England cannot but subsist so long as this palladium remains sacred and inviolate. If we want the jury system to continue then, in my submission, it is vital that it should remain inviolate.[39]

His intervention provoked a furious article in the *New Statesman*[40] which accused him of an attack on the freedom of the press. 'The curious point about Lord Hutchinson and his allies is not one of them can have the slightest idea what they are talking about, for none of them is allowed to serve on juries.' Jeremy wrote to the *New Statesman* in rebarbative terms:

> I appreciate your admitted difficulty in your piece on the Contempt Bill in casting me as a reactionary leader of a lawyers' pressure group 'spouting . . . foam flecked rubbish' and crushing the radical left represented by the N.S. and Lord Hailsham.[41] To surmount the difficulty you had, of course, to invent the rubbish. In speaking to the amendment, made necessary by your approach to a juryman after

the Thorpe trial, you say my 'elegant argument' was that 'jurors are wee timorous beasties . . . quite incapable of deciding whether they want to answer questions.' In fact I said the opposite.

This letter reveals another aspect of Jeremy's character. He was not afraid of controversy and frequently found it in the House of Lords. When he spoke out against a suggestion that the right to jury trial in cases of fraud should be restricted, his speech was characterized as 'rhetoric and special pleading' by Lord Wilberforce. Hansard records him interrupting a speech given by Lord Gifford during the debate of the Legal Profession Green Paper with the word 'Rubbish!' After his friend Bernard Levin had attacked the Bar as a closed shop in need of exposure to the cold winds of the market, Jeremy described him as one of the 'intellectual Murdoch mafia', who had been given 'a field day as they pop up from the squalor of their own profession, which they dare not criticise, singing from their masters' hymn sheet of the great God of the morality of the market place'. A heated correspondence ensued.

By the 1970s Jeremy felt that the Labour Party had lost its radical element and become reactionary and anti-European. It was no longer a natural harbour for him. He crossed the floor in 1982, following his friends Roy Jenkins and Shirley Williams, to join the SDP (and later sat as a Liberal Democrat). He formally retired from the House of Lords in 2011 (the first life peer to do so under the new dispensation). He is now the oldest life peer.

For many barristers legal practice is an all-consuming obsession that can occlude other interests. Jeremy never fell into that trap. 'I always ensured that I never worked too hard and had time to preserve a "hinterland".' One of his greatest enthusiasms had always been the visual arts. Jeremy had grown up in the company of artists and counted many as friends in his adult life.

He joined the Arts Council in 1974 and became deputy chairman in 1977, at a time when this institution had a very high profile and was at the centre of the debates about public support of the arts. In the same year, while he was still in legal practice, he was invited to become a trustee of the Tate Gallery and three years later became the chairman of the trustees, a position he held until 1984. His comment on appointment: 'For me a greater privilege than being appointed Lord Chancellor.' What an irony that the man who had defended Kempton Bunton on charges of the theft of a Goya from the National Gallery[42] a few years earlier was now heading one of the great London public galleries. He looks back on a fascinating period dominated by the Turner controversy:

> At the time the great debate which was raging concerned the Turner Bequest. Turner had left a large body of work to the nation with the request that it be housed in a dedicated gallery. In the late 1970s there was a move to create a Turner Gallery in some rooms at Somerset House. We at the Tate opposed this move as totally unsuitable, and were vilified by many. I then found myself seated next to Mrs Vivien Duffield at a dinner given by my nephew Jacob Rothschild. We got talking and it became clear that Mrs Duffield was anxious to find some form of memorial to her father, Sir Charles Clore, who had recently died. I put to her the idea of a new gallery, in his name, to house the Turner Bequest. It was this conversation which eventually led to the extension to the Tate which became known as the Clore Gallery.

The Turner Society, which had vigorously supported the Somerset House plan, was persuaded to back the new gallery, and the National Gallery and the V&A disgorged a large part of their holdings. Designed by James Stirling,[43] his first commission for a public building in England, the Clore Gallery would eventually be opened in 1987 by the Queen. It was built with over £6 million from the Clore Foundation's generosity. Yet it was a project fraught with controversy and the finished building attracted criticism from many quarters – though it also won an RIBA award.

Under Jeremy's chairmanship there were other important developments. Barbara Hepworth's studio came under the aegis of the Tate Gallery in 1980. It was in 1981 that the idea of 'The Tate of the North' (eventually 'Tate Liverpool') was born, the result of a direct approach by Jeremy and his director, Alan Bowness, to Michael Heseltine, the Secretary of State for the Environment, after an unsuccessful attempt to gain support from the Minister for the Arts, Norman St John-Stevas. 'Heseltine was very enthusiastic and backed to the hilt our idea of the conversion of a beautiful disused warehouse in the old docklands on the Mersey. It became a key part of his plan to revive the city after the Toxteth riots.' Jeremy is especially proud of two great exhibitions, the 1983 Cubist exhibition curated by Douglas Cooper[44] and the Turner exhibition which was exported with huge success to the Grand Palais in Paris, as well as of other, and innovative, ideas: a sculpture show for the blind, the display of pavement artists round the gallery and an exhibition about paint as a medium. There was also a retrospective of the works of Reg Butler which was especially poignant for Jeremy, who had in the 1950s prosecuted a Czech artist for having desecrated Butler's work *Unknown Political Prisoner* while it was on display at the gallery. An exhibition of the eighteenth-century land-scapist Richard Wilson, curated from a Marxist viewpoint, also had resonance for Jeremy. The Wilson exhibition brought with it condemnation from the right-wing press. At the same time Jeremy was defending Brenton's play *The Romans in Britain*, also ridiculed for its political content, from the attacks of Mary Whitehouse.

In her history of the Tate, Frances Spalding writes that Jeremy, along with Alan Bowness, effected substantial changes, transforming what she describes as a rather tight, inward-looking institution into something more international and European.[45] 'I wanted to be a hands-on chairman and made sure I attended every event and worked closely with Alan to ensure that artists, and the public, were much more involved in the life of the gallery. In an age of government austerity I also encouraged commercial sponsorship, which proved controversial, but necessary.' Just before his retirement from the Tate[46] Jeremy was given a seventieth birthday party by the gallery which he remembers with delight. 'I had a birthday cake iced with a reproduction of Matisse's cut-out *The Snail*. I was very moved to find that Francis Bacon, John Piper, Anthony Caro and a host of other artists had attended to celebrate with me.' Jeremy recalls that Lucian Freud was unable to attend, explaining that he 'always worked up to midnight' but suggesting that they meet at Annabel's at 1 a.m. 'I declined that offer.'

The year 1984 was something of a watershed in Jeremy's life. Not only did it see his formal retirement as chairman of the Tate Gallery but it was also the year when he finally gave up practice at the Bar. His last case was an appeal in a legally aided case, which pleased him. A letter he received on his retirement from one of his loyal solicitors, for whom he had worked over many years, sums up his career: 'Since 1965 when you first accepted a brief from me, I have taken comfort from the thought that *in extremis* there is one fighter with the consistency and all round fighting ability to take on all comers, whether it be a short three-rounder exhibition match, or a fifteen-round slogging contest. A good punch, fast footwork, stamina, fighting spirit against all the odds, and a killer instinct at the finish, together with real professionalism. In my experience, a combination so rare as to leave a gap which I can see no prospect of being filled.' Jeremy's clerk of many years, Ronald, wrote mournfully: 'He had reached a unique position at the Bar, which I am certain will not be repeated in my time. I know I could have kept him at the top for many years to come. He became the idol of the criminal bar.'[47]

Thereafter he resisted attempts to lure him back to practice. There are in his files letters from solicitors asking whether he would appear for Clive Ponting in his Official Secrets Act trial in 1985 and the Guildford Four in their appeal in 1989. Enticing as these opportunities were, Jeremy resisted the pull. 'I had made a definite decision and I thought it would be dangerous to allow myself to slip back into the law. If one is to be a lawyer one has to be entirely up to date with the law. I thought it would be wrong to drop in and out of it in retirement.'

But although he might have formally retired, his life has remained a full one. He continued to be an active member of the House of Lords until 2001 and has thrown his weight behind an array of organizations. Jeremy was the chairman of the Elephant Trust, set up by Roland Penrose and Lee Miller with the proceeds of the sale to the Tate of Max Ernst's famous painting *Celebes*, with the intention of supporting original artists unable to get support elsewhere; he served on the Council of the National Association for the Care and Resettlement of Offenders (Nacro) for twelve years under the enlightened directorship of Vivien Stern; he was deeply involved in the New Bridge Foundation, working with ex-offenders; he became Professor of Law of the Royal Academy in 1988.

At one hundred Jeremy divides his time between St John's Wood and Lullington. Until only very recently he was enjoying daily walks to the nearby village of Alfriston (indeed he claims that walking has been his sole exercise throughout his life). He remains entirely a man of the present, wholly up to date with the political and legal issues of the day, bringing acuity and vision to any subject, engaging in vigorous correspondence with a vast number of people. This aspect of his life deserves to be noted. His archive is replete with letters from a galaxy of correspondents, including Isaiah Berlin, Noel Annan, Stephen Spender, Roy Jenkins and Ludovic Kennedy. He lived in an epistolary age, where the letter was still a vehicle for sustained expressions of feeling and thought. That age has largely passed and reading through his correspondence makes one regret that. He has never sent an email. But of course it is Jeremy's voice which was, and remains, his chief asset. Listening to him speak now one can understand the mesmeric quality that he exercised in the court room. It is also a voice which serves as a link to an earlier age and allows one to conjure up a speaking manner, lyrical and intonated, but with the capacity for sustained intensity, which has been largely overtaken by the flatter tones of the twenty-first century.

While he has outlived almost all his contemporaries, his friendships have constantly renewed themselves and his social life is (almost) as active as it ever was. Perhaps the most important truth about the man that has emerged from my research is his capacity for friendship and his ability to inspire the affection and respect of others. His is truly an example of the life well lived.

PART I

The Twilight of Conservatism

I

'Lose his sanity or gain his freedom'

R v Blake (1961)

IN MARCH 1961 Jeremy Hutchinson 'took silk', that is he became a Queen's Counsel. Although by then almost forty-six, seven years had been carved from his twenties and early thirties by the war and so lost to his professional life. After his demobilization he was thirty-two and knew he had time to make up. Having started out on his legal career in 1946 Jeremy became a QC after only fourteen years in practice – an astonishingly short period of time. For most barristers, taking silk is the crowning moment in their career and it is one they will have doggedly strived towards over years of hard work as a junior barrister. A new silk will hope to graduate to more glamorous and better paid work. But the quid pro quo is that the cases become more difficult and challenging. And there is the ever present fear that work will dry up: the Bar was then, and remains, filled with advocates bearing the coveted letters after their name but with no briefs to fill their days.

Jeremy's first substantial case as a silk could not have involved a more demanding introduction to this new life. It also provided the reassurance that he would thrive in silk. In May 1961, two months after he had attended the QC ceremony in Westminster Hall, with all its ancient pomp and flummery, Jeremy was instructed to represent the man who would become perhaps the most notorious spy of the post-war period.

One of the great mysteries of life at the Bar was, and to an extent remains, how a barrister comes to be instructed in any particular case. When asked why he was briefed on behalf of George Blake, Jeremy professes ignorance. 'It is not the kind of thing one raised with one's solicitor then. The briefs just arrived in chambers.' This reticence was compounded by the rule that prevailed at the Bar until well into the 1980s, which prevented barristers from engaging in any form of touting for work. Taking clients out for drinks or dinner, throwing professional parties, having business cards or brochures, in short all the apparatus of marketing that is now near obligatory in the professional world – all this was unthinkable in 1961. Indeed it was more than unthinkable: it was a breach of the barrister's Code of Conduct. All students reading for the Bar when Jeremy started out were provided with a copy of a little book by a judge named Sir Malcolm Hilbery entitled *Duty and Art in Advocacy*.[1] Between its ominously black covers Hilbery thundered that the 'first commandment which the barrister finds he must obey is: "Thou shalt not advertise or solicit for work." Anything like asking for work or touting for it, directly or indirectly, is in the highest degree improper. It is beneath the dignity of the Bar. So strong is the rule that if he writes articles for publication he can sign his name, but not proclaim himself "Barrister-at-law".' This commandment remained equally sacrosanct into the 1960s: in 1964 Quintin Hogg MP QC, the future Lord Chancellor and a Tory leadership contender the year before, was subject to disciplinary proceedings brought by the Bar Council because, after six years as a Cabinet minister, he had told newspaper reporters that he was returning to private practice at the Bar. This was apparently a form of unlawful touting. Although the charge was eventually dismissed it cast a shadow over Hogg's life for some time.[2] On the other hand Jeremy recalls that this professional fastidiousness had its advantages: 'It was so liberating not having to jump through all the hoops required to market oneself. One did one's work and sought to do it well, and it was on that one was judged. I can say with confidence that I never entertained a solicitor during the entire period of my practice at the Bar.'

In May 1961 Britain was already seized by spy fever. After a trial at the Old Bailey in March of that year five defendants had been convicted for their part in the so-called Portland spy ring and sentenced to between fifteen and twenty-five years in prison. The case had been an acute embarrassment to the government and prompted opposition demands for the resignation of Lord Carrington, the First Lord of the Admiralty.[3] It was revealed that two clerks working at the Admiralty Underwater Weapons Establishment in Portland, Dorset, had been photographing swathes of classified material and passing it to the Russians.[4] The story involved a cast of colourful characters, which had only heightened the public's interest. A shambolic alcoholic and his middle-aged spinster mistress both worked for the Admiralty at Portland and sold the secrets to a man posing as a Canadian (who was apparently in the business of selling bubble-gum dispensers and jukeboxes), but who was in fact a Russian member of the KGB. The secrets would then be transmitted to Moscow by two American communists living under false names in an unassuming villa in Ruislip and posing as antiquarian book-sellers. The security lapses exposed were so startling that an enquiry was immediately instituted, to investigate how security procedures could be tightened.

The Portland case was just the latest in a series of security blunders that had strained relations with the Americans. As the *Daily Mail* put it the day after the trial ended: '[It] is regarded as the worst penetration of our security system since Klaus Fuchs gave the atom-bomb secrets to Russia . . . There will undoubtedly be serious repercussions on Anglo-American relations. It is only recently that the Americans have got over their mistrust of British security caused by the Fuchs case, the Pontecorvo case, and Burgess and Maclean.'[5]

But worse was to come. On 6 April 1961 George Blake, an employee of the Secret Intelligence Service (SIS), confessed under interrogation to having worked as a Soviet spy for the past nine years. It rapidly became apparent that the scale of his treachery dwarfed that of the Portland ring. Despite the government's initial inclination to grant Blake immunity and cover up the whole episode, American anger at yet another security lapse demanded action. Blake was charged with five counts under the Official Secrets Act and his trial was fixed to commence on 3 May 1961 at the Central Criminal Court, otherwise known as the Old Bailey.

This was the first of a series of cases from the early 1960s that played themselves out on the various stages of the courts, Parliament and the press, in which Jeremy was intimately involved and which hastened Harold Macmillan's resignation, and the eventual end of a Conservative government that had held uninterrupted office since

1951. The recent judgement of Dominic Sandbrook is amply justified: 'Blake's arrest was the first major step in a series of security scandals in the early sixties that severely tarnished the reputation not only of the intelligence services but also of Macmillan's Conservative government. Such was the extent of Blake's betrayal that Macmillan is supposed to have remarked "The Government could fall over this" when Sir Dick White, the head of the Secret Intelligence Service (SIS), told him the news.'[6]

George Blake was born George Behar, in Holland in 1922, into a family of Sephardic Jewish origin.[7] In 1936 his father died and he was sent to live with his aunt in Cairo. Educated first at a French school and then an English one, he developed an intense Calvinist faith and considered going into the Church. He returned to Holland in 1939, experienced the bombing and near destruction of Rotterdam, acted as a courier for the Dutch resistance and eventually decided to escape to England where his mother and sister had already gone. After a long and hazardous journey across Europe he reached Gibraltar and boarded a ship for England. Later he managed to join the Royal Navy Volunteer Reserve (which Jeremy had himself joined a few years earlier), and after a short period training for duty on two-man submarines, he was seconded by the SIS (otherwise known as MI6) as an officer in their Dutch section. Blake was overjoyed. He later recalled: 'I could hardly believe it was true . . . that I would actually become an officer in the British Secret Service, this legendary centre of hidden power commonly believed to have a decisive influence on the great events of this world, was something that far exceeded my wildest expectations.'[8] For the rest of the war Blake worked to build up the Dutch intelligence network.

Following the end of the war Blake was posted to Hamburg, where he was given the task of recruiting German naval officers as agents to obtain information about the Soviet military and also political developments in the Soviet zone. Blake was startlingly successful in his efforts to recruit agents and by 1947 he had built up two intelligence networks in East Germany, staffed largely by ex-naval and Wehrmacht officers. In April of that year Blake was offered, and accepted, a permanent position in the secret service.

After six months in Cambridge learning Russian, he was posted to Seoul as Vice-Consul to the British delegation in South Korea. This was an official title only. His true brief was to recruit agents in the north-eastern provinces of China, and eastern provinces of the Soviet Union. His posting reflected a growing concern in the West regarding the vulnerability of the Far East to communist encroachment.

In 1945 Korea had been divided at the 38th parallel. The North remained a Soviet client state even after Russian troops pulled out. On 15 August 1948 Syngman Rhee was elected the first President of South Korea, with American backing. On 9 September North Korea proclaimed the Democratic People's Republic of Korea, under the leadership of Kim Il-Sung.

Relations between the two ideologically opposed states worsened and, on 24 June 1950, North Korean troops invaded the South and advanced to the capital. As, at this stage, the British were officially non-belligerents in the conflict, the legation in Seoul remained in post. Then followed the American-sponsored United Nations Security Council Resolution 83, calling for armed intervention in South Korea, which the British government felt obliged to support. Suddenly the British in Seoul were no longer neutral observers but enemy aliens. On 2 July 1950 Blake and fellow members of the British legation were taken into custody. Just after midnight they were ordered into the back of a lorry and driven out of the city. After an hour, they stopped in a wooded valley, and the detainees were ordered to get out and stand in a line. It was apparent to Blake and the others that they had been brought here for summary execution. Commissioner Herbert Lord, of the Salvation Army, who was of the party, recalled: 'We nodded at each other, and we thought we might as well go happily. I said a short prayer.' But it was not to be. After about an hour, the prisoners were loaded back into the truck, and the journey resumed.

Blake was held prisoner in North Korea for three years. His internment included periods of extreme deprivation, illness and trauma. In the late autumn of 1950 Blake, fellow members of the British and French delegations, several European nuns and missionaries, and 700 captured American GIs were force-marched 120 miles to the north-eastern town of Chunggangjin, with little food and in freezing conditions. This has become notorious as the 'Death March'. The prisoners, several of whom were in their seventies and eighties, were subjected to unspeakable cruelty. Stragglers were shot.

The next two and a half years were spent in an internment camp. The only reading matter provided was copious quantities of communist literature. One of Blake's fellow captives later described its effect:

> Meanwhile we lay on our backs, driven by boredom to the umpteenth reading of the . . . so-called communist classics – works by Marx, Engels, Lenin and Stalin . . . we occasionally had modern Russian novels, magazines and newspapers, which concentrated on proving that all was wrong with the West, and that only the East was capable of giving the human being a chance. Every bad aspect of our civilization was pounced upon, mounted on a pedestal of words, spotlighted, magnified, analysed . . . And there was a mass – an overwhelming mass – of words following one another towards the same goal. It was not indoctrination by an interlocutor who irritates you and whose arguments you're goaded to refute. It was endless repetition – a monotonous and single-minded repetition which began to make an impression.[9]

It was during these years of confinement that Blake was converted to communism, a mental journey later described in detail by Jeremy in his speech in mitigation. In autumn 1951 Blake took the preliminary steps towards his career as a Russian spy. Blake describes how, one evening, he approached the commander in charge of the camp: 'I put my finger to my lips as I handed him a folded note. He looked at me somewhat surprised, but took it without saying anything. I closed the door and went back to bed.' The note, which was written in Russian, was addressed to the Soviet Embassy in Pyongyang. According to Blake, the note stated that he had 'something important to communicate which they might find of interest'.[10]

Blake was freed from captivity in March 1953. On returning to England, and after a fairly perfunctory debriefing, he resumed his position in the SIS, where he was treated as a hero. On 1 September 1953 Blake joined Section Y, which was responsible for the decoding and translation of Soviet intelligence obtained through phone taps.

That October Blake met Soviet agent Sergei Aleksandrovich Kondrashev near Belsize Park Underground station. Blake handed over details of SIS bugging operations of Soviet and Eastern bloc embassies in Western Europe, and a list of phones being tapped in Vienna. Blake later referred to this meeting as one of defining importance in his passage of betrayal. He felt an 'exhilarated feeling of achievement which comes whenever one has overcome fears and apprehensions'.[11] His aim was simple: to undermine and disrupt the British intelligence service. Thereafter, Blake met Kondrashev every few weeks. The Russian gave him a Minox camera, which he used to photograph relevant material.

In December 1953 Blake was present at a meeting between CIA and SIS representatives in which 'Operation Stopwatch' was discussed. This was an audacious scheme to dig a tunnel, from the American into the Soviet Zone in Berlin, to enable interception of phone communications between Moscow and the Soviet military command in Berlin. On 18 January 1954 Blake handed a copy of the minutes of the meeting to Kondrashev. The scheme, into which the Americans invested vast resources and effort, was known to the Soviets before it even started.

On 23 October 1954 Blake married an SIS secretary called Gillian Allan. Gillian's father, Colonel Arthur Allan, a Russian expert, also worked for the SIS. In his autobiography, Blake describes the dilemma that faced him in relation to his marriage to Gillian. 'I fully realised that, in my position, to marry anyone would be the height of irresponsibility and, of course, I should never have allowed things to develop to this point in the first place. How to get out of it now?'[12] Faced with the prospect of breaking off the relationship without ostensible reason, and hurting Gillian, he determined to marry her. Blake tried to convince himself that he was 'really in no different position from a soldier during the war who got married before he was sent to the front'.

Then in April 1955 Blake flew to Berlin to take up a posting at the SIS station there. He was attached to the section responsible for collecting intelligence on the Soviet Union. Blake's particular brief was the recruitment of Soviet intelligence officers to work as British agents. Meanwhile, Blake was introduced to his Russian handler in Berlin, Nikolai Sergeevich Miakotnykh, codenamed 'Dick'. During these years Blake passed information on a massive scale to the Russians concerning the British intelligence operation in Germany, including the names of hundreds of agents SIS employed behind the Iron Curtain.

Blake and Gillian lived in a pleasant part of West Berlin. There was a large British community, and the staff of the SIS station enjoyed a busy social life. There were a great deal of cocktail parties, Blake recalls, and Gillian rode and played tennis. In 1957 Gillian gave birth to a son, Anthony. This compounded the strains of Blake's double life: 'I was building with one hand a happy family life . . . and with the other hand I was pulling the foundations from underneath it so that it might crumble at any moment',[13] and he began to look for a way out. The opportunity eventually came with an invitation to learn Arabic at the Middle East Centre for Arabic Studies in the Lebanon. The Blakes arrived in Beirut in September 1960, and were given accommodation in the mountain village of Shemlan, close to the MECAS School. Gillian had given birth to a second son while the couple were in England, and she became pregnant with a third while they were in the Lebanon.

It was at this time that the SIS began to harbour suspicions regarding Blake's activities. This was in part due to the revelations of the Soviet defector, and one-time double agent, Lieutenant Colonel Michal Goleniewski ('Sniper') who, as early as April 1959, had revealed the existence of 'two very important spies in Britain: one in British Intelligence, the other somewhere in the navy'. 'LAMBDA 2', as the navy spy was known, was subsequently identified as Harry Houghton, the alcoholic clerk in the Underwater Weapons Establishment who was a member of the Portland spy ring. 'LAMBDA 1', the intelligence mole, was harder to pin down.

The arrest of another double agent, Horst Eitner, in Berlin in October 1960 provided further intelligence. By early 1961 SIS officers in London had come to the conclusion that Blake was 'LAMBDA 1'. On 25 March 1961 Nicholas Elliott, the head of the SIS station in Beirut (and Kim Philby's best friend[14]), met Blake at a production of *Charley's Aunt* staged by the local British drama group. The encounter appeared accidental, but was in fact contrived. Elliott told Blake that he had that morning received a letter from head office in London to the effect that Blake should return to London 'for a few days' consultation in connection with a new appointment'.[15]

The news threw Blake into a ferment of indecision. He knew there was something wrong about the recall: 'Why this highly inconvenient, sudden interruption?' By the time he had arrived home that evening, Blake had determined to drive with Gillian and the children over the border to Damascus, and there 'explain the situation to her exactly as it was, however painful this might be, and leave her to decide whether to accompany me to the Soviet Union or take the car and the children back to Beirut and return to England'.[16] Plagued by doubts, and a nagging worry that he was overreacting, Blake got in touch with his Soviet contact in Beirut, who, following consultation with Moscow, reassured him that as far as they were aware there was nothing to fear. This calmed Blake, and he decided to fly to London.

From 4 to 6 April 1961 Blake was interrogated at SIS's offices in Carlton Gardens. A surreal game of cat and mouse ensued as Blake resolutely maintained his innocence. He remained a free man, although he was being closely watched, and spent the evenings with his mother at her flat in Radlett, as if all were as normal. In his autobiography, Blake refers to these evenings as 'without doubt, the most difficult hours of my life. Knowing that I was in serious danger . . . I had to pretend to my mother that all was well and continue to discuss with her the plans for her forthcoming trip [to Beirut] and all the purchases we had to complete before the end of the week. I remember in particular how one item high on my wife's shopping list was mosquito nets. My mother had found out that these could only be bought at Gamages.'[17]

Blake maintained his innocence until the afternoon of the third day. Although he did not know it, without a confession SIS felt they could do nothing. Dick White told a colleague that if Blake didn't confess 'we'll invite him to fly to Moscow.' Then, with half an hour of questioning left to go, Harry Shergold, the chief interrogator, suggested to Blake that he had started spying for the Soviets after having been tortured and blackmailed in Korea. Blake felt a sudden upsurge of indignation. He wanted, he recalls, his interrogators 'and everyone else to know that I had acted out of conviction, out of a belief in Communism, and not under duress or for financial gain'. He burst out: 'No, nobody tortured me! No, nobody blackmailed me! I myself approached the Soviets and offered my services to them of my own accord!'[18] SIS now had their man.

The discovery of Blake's treachery caused consternation in government. It was clear that it had the potential to inflict grave damage on the reputation of the Macmillan administration. Here was an SIS officer who had, over almost a decade, systematically disclosed all information he learned to the Soviets without detection. It was suggested by Harold Macmillan that Blake should be offered immunity to avoid the publicity of a trial. But Dick White insisted on a prosecution. In Whitehall steps were being taken to minimize the impact of such a prosecution on public opinion. Harold Macmillan noted in his diary that 'Naturally we can say nothing. The public do not know and cannot be told that he belonged to MI6 – an organisation which does not theoretically exist.'[19] On 15 April 1961 a meeting of Foreign Office and government personnel chaired by Edward Heath determined on a strategy that involved giving the press as little information as possible. On 1 May a 'D-Notice'[20] was sent to newspaper editors which stated that: 'Blake is an employee of MI6, and therefore comes under "D" Notice dated 27.4.1956, requesting you not to disclose the identities and activities of employees of MI5 and MI6.' It continued: 'There is special reason for requesting your co-operation in this case in that the lives of MI6 employees are still in danger.' This was an era when newspaper editors were more willing to do the government's bidding in matters of secrecy and a form of partial news blackout prevailed for some weeks.

Having resisted pressure from the Prime Minister to hush up the case, on 10 April 1961 Dick White gave authority for Blake to be charged under section 1 of the Official Secrets Act 1911. In the end Blake would be charged with five counts, each count relating to a distinct period in Blake's life as a spy, ranging from 1951 to 1959. In the evening of the same day, Gillian, still in Beirut, was informed of her husband's perfidy. She later recalled: 'Clearly it was hard to believe, but I didn't think for a moment that they'd made a mistake.

I didn't think, "They must have got hold of the wrong man, or this can't be true" – even though, of course, I had no idea he was working for the Russians.'[21]

Soon after that Jeremy's clerk at his chambers in Queen Elizabeth Building in the Temple received a telephone call from Bill Cox, a partner in the firm of Claude, Hornby and Cox of Great Marlborough Street, and the solicitor acting for Blake.[22] Jeremy had, over the years, been instructed by Cox on various criminal matters, but this was something altogether bigger. Jeremy had only ever acted in one spying case before, and that was many years earlier when he had defended Stoker Henry Rose, who had, in 1946, been convicted of passing on information to the Germans.[23]

The trial was fixed to start on 3 May 1961, just over three weeks after the initial charges. It was a hectic time. Here was perhaps the biggest spy scandal of the century, and there were just a few weeks to gather and present Blake's case. By this stage Blake had signed a confession and so there was no question of defending the charges. But there remained the vital issue of the sentencing. It would be Jeremy's task to present to the court Blake's account of his conduct, which would influence the sentence to be passed on him. Blake was on remand in Brixton prison and Jeremy paid him a number of visits. 'I had to understand Blake's motivation and the extent of his spying activities.' He and Blake had both served in the RNVR during the war and found that they had an instinctive liking for each other. Jeremy remembers: 'Blake was a man who exuded this great and intense charm. I was immediately taken with him.'

In the course of their discussions at Brixton, Blake sought to explain his reasons for working for the Soviets. As Jeremy recalls, he emphasized two things. One was the behaviour of the American GIs in captivity: 'He felt they were so spineless, and so corrupt, and so third-rate in every way, and he took terribly against them. They were wimps, you know, in his view. Blake said that he began to question the values of the American way of life of which these young boys were the product.' The other was Marx. 'He read *Das Kapital* from cover to cover and he said it was a remarkable book and completely convincing. He said, "I had a lot of time to think, and it seemed to me a basis for a better world."' Blake struck Jeremy as completely genuine in this regard:

> I didn't feel he was trying to justify himself in any way. On listening to his story I accepted that his decision to work for the Russians was based on an almost religious conversion. He said that throughout his life he felt he had lacked aim and had been distracted by the pursuit of pleasure and personal ambition and that, in that internment camp, he decided to devote the rest of his life to what he considered a worthwhile cause, and to sacrifice to that cause not only possibly his life and liberty but even more his honour and the affection and esteem of his friends and relations – to live no more for himself but only for this purpose.

Jeremy had grown up during the thirties when the debate about communism and capitalism raged intensely among the young. Faced with the onset of a Second World War and the menace of Fascism it seemed to many at the time that it was only the communists in Europe who were prepared to stand up to the dictators. Jeremy had himself never flirted with the extreme left but Blake's account of his conversion from Christianity to communism was a journey familiar to him. Through the mists of the latter-day triumph of the consumer society, it is difficult to recall now that even in the 1950s and 1960s there were still many who saw capitalism as a decaying economic system, which would with historical inevitability be replaced by communism. The Soviet Union remained for millions across the world the avatar of a new Utopian world. Blake later explained: 'The formula, "from each according to his ability, to each according to his need" defines, to my mind, the only right and just relationship between men, born free and equal into this world. To help build such a society, was this not to help build the Kingdom of God on earth? Was this not the ideal that Christianity for two thousand years had been striving for?'

In Jeremy's view, Blake spied because of his commitment to communism, which was absolute. As he recalls, 'It was this that gave me my great interest for doing the case; it wasn't a squalid money arrangement with the Russians, and it wasn't a sex thing. I accepted it was a true conversion and he had that kind of mind that would be 100 per cent committed, and that his spying was based on this absolute and almost religious conversion.' Yet it remains intriguing that Blake's conversion – a voluntary one as he insists – should have taken place while he was a captive of a brutal communist regime, a witness to countless atrocities perpetrated in its name. But Jeremy remembers many who at this time, and before, were so attracted by the idea of communism that they were wilfully purblind to the deeds done in apparent furtherance of it.

Early in the morning on the day of the trial, Jeremy held his final conference with Blake in the gloomy interview room in the cells at the Old Bailey. 'I remember walking down the stairs to the cells. There was all the shouting of other prisoners awaiting their trials that one always heard. It was a beautiful spring day, the kind of day when one is inclined to be light-hearted, but as I spoke with George Blake about what was to happen in the courtroom above everything seemed very tense. Finally I asked him whether he wished me to tell the court that he regretted what he had done.' Blake recalls how he replied: 'I could not agree to this. In the first place it was untrue, for I felt that what I had done was right. In the second place, it seemed to me undignified that somebody, who in the course of nearly ten years, had photographed almost daily every important and interesting document which had passed through his hands in order to transmit [it] to the Soviet authorities, should suddenly feel sorry for having done this, simply because he had been found out and arrested.'[24] Such an unequivocal, if morally honest answer, made the task of seeking mercy from the court even more difficult.

The trial took place in Court 1 of the Old Bailey, where, a few months earlier, Jeremy had defended D.H. Lawrence's novel *Lady Chatterley's Lover*[25] and where, rather less happily, notorious criminals such as Dr Crippen, Lord Haw-Haw and Christie had been tried in the previous decades. Jonathan Aitken would, a decade later, find himself in the same dock where George Blake was now quietly sitting, and describe it as like a rather run-down municipal swimming baths. As if to emphasize the centrality of the defendant to the whole proceedings, the dock, accessible only from a hidden staircase leading up from the cells below, directly faces the bench and is disproportionately large compared to the court itself. Writers have noted how, as one enters Court 1 from the imperious marble hall of the Old Bailey, it is disconcerting to find it rather smaller and more cramped than its reputation might suggest. And yet the high-windowed, wood-panelled courtroom has a grandeur and formidable aspect which is impressive. The judge sits high up, under a huge carved pediment that is designed to instil in jurors, lawyers, defendants and members of the public alike a sense of the majesty of the law.

On this occasion the judge chosen to fulfil that role was the Lord Chief Justice, Lord Parker of Waddington, the most senior member of the English judiciary. Jeremy knew Parker as a pillar of the establishment. Quiet, well-mannered and polite, to Jeremy he came over more as a distinguished civil servant than as an enlightened member of an independent judiciary. Unlike his predecessor, Lord Goddard, Parker rarely sat as a trial judge (he would usually be found sitting in the more rarefied atmosphere of the Court of Appeal) and his decision to take this case was symptomatic of its perceived national importance. And this was a case where the establishment was represented in droves. There, sitting in the well of the court below the prosecution benches and in the public gallery, Jeremy saw ranks of Whitehall panjandrums. Though he did not know it then they included Sir Dick White, head of the SIS, and Sir Roger Hollis, head of MI5, both there to witness Blake's sentencing. Jeremy also saw Sir Theo Mathew, the Director of Public Prosecutions, who had instructed him for the prosecution in some of the most notorious cases of the 1950s, and who now sat tight-lipped alongside White and Hollis.

Finally Jeremy looked over at the formidable figure of counsel for the prosecution, the Attorney General himself, Sir Reginald Manningham-Buller QC, standing in leading counsel's row a few yards down from him. As Blake sat in the vast dock, he remembers thinking how much he preferred the 'thin intellectual' features of his own advocate, to the 'wobbling crimson cheeks and . . . apoplectic, bulging eyes'[26] of Manningham-Buller. The Attorney General would do battle with Jeremy on a number of occasions in the next couple of years. Theirs was a relationship of semi-cordial mutual dislike. Jeremy was everything Manningham-Buller despised: an associate of the effete Bloomsbury Group and a leftist who was willing to strive on behalf of his clients, no matter how objectionable they might be.

Manningham-Buller had a few years earlier prosecuted in the notorious case of Dr John Bodkin Adams, the Eastbourne doctor who, it was alleged, had murdered scores of his patients in the expectation of substantial legacies. His conduct during that trial had mesmerized the judge, Mr Justice Devlin, who would much later, and from the safety of retirement, take the unprecedented step of writing a book about the trial. There Devlin pronounced a brutal, and often quoted, judgement on Manningham-Buller:

> What was almost unique about him and makes his career so fascinating is that what the ordinary careerist achieves by making himself agreeable, falsely or otherwise, Reggie achieved by making himself disagreeable. Sections of the press, which he permanently antagonized, liked to parody his name by calling him Sir Bullying Manner. This was wrong. He was a bully without a bullying manner. His bludgeoning was quiet. He could be downright rude but he did not shout or bluster. Yet his disagreeableness was so pervasive, his persistence so interminable, the obstructions he manned so far flung, his objectives apparently so insignificant, that sooner or later you would be tempted to ask yourself whether the game was worth the candle: if you asked yourself that, you were finished.[27]

In his dealings with Jeremy, Manningham-Buller would certainly live up to the 'Bullying Manner' moniker. Even now Jeremy remains shocked by what happened. In the days prior to the trial Jeremy had requested a private meeting with the Attorney General, who grudgingly received him in his offices at the Royal Courts of Justice. Jeremy said he must know what the prosecution was going to allege as to the extent of the damage that Blake's conduct had caused to this country, so that he could properly focus his mitigation speech. Manningham-Buller replied curtly that no details of any kind could be given in open court or even to the judge sitting in camera, so sensitive was this information. When Jeremy asked how in that case justice could be done, he was brusquely told, 'That is a matter for you and the judge. I have nothing more to say.' With that he was shown the door. Manningham-Buller was the Attorney General. The judge was the Lord Chief Justice. Jeremy was a new silk. This was still, just, the age of deference and Jeremy feels to this day that if he had been more experienced he would have given vent more strongly to his suppressed feelings of outrage and indignation at such an answer. Jeremy explains: 'There has always been a culture at the Bar of equality and civility. I remember once, before the war, being sent over to court to deliver a message to Sir Stafford Cripps, then a pre-eminent silk at the Bar. I addressed him as "Sir Stafford". I will always remember his reply: "The name is Cripps." His point was that he and I, as members of the Bar, were in a position of equality despite our age difference. That taught me a lot. Now, years later, Manningham-Buller was treating me in this extraordinarily contemptuous way.'

Jeremy's meeting with Manningham-Buller had yielded one concession. It had been agreed between them that they would jointly submit to the judge that the whole case should take place in camera. This was not a position that Jeremy was happy with, but Manningham-Buller had made it clear to him that he would object to Jeremy referring to any of Blake's activities in open court, because to do so would be 'prejudicial to the interests of the state'. Indeed Manningham-Buller insisted that Jeremy could not even mention that Britain operated an intelligence organization at all! Jeremy recalls: 'Of course, in principle, I would have liked an open trial, but the conditions they laid down would have meant that I didn't have the freedom to tell George's side of the story. I conferred with him, and reluctantly – because of the disadvantage that the outside world would not hear any of the mitigation – we decided it would be better if it was held in camera so I had complete freedom in my address to the judge.' It was also agreed by Manningham-Buller that if Jeremy could not present his mitigation on behalf of Blake publicly then it would be wrong, and unfair to Blake, for any part of the case, including the prosecution opening, to be held in public.

So matters were left. But, on the day of the trial itself, and just before they went into court, Manningham-Buller collared Jeremy and peremptorily announced that he would be presenting the prosecution case in open court. The effect of this volte-face was to unbalance the trial and mean that the press reporting would be entirely one-sided. It also meant that Jeremy had no time in which to tailor his submissions so that at least some part of Blake's mitigation could be heard by the world at large. Jeremy is convinced that this decision on the part of the prosecution, and the last-minute manner in which he was informed of it, was part of a strategy designed by Manningham-Buller to bully his opponent into submission.

Manningham-Buller addressed Parker for eight minutes only. He referred obliquely to Blake's employment as being 'in the government's service both in this country and overseas'. He told the court that Blake had worked as a Soviet agent for nine and a half years. He was, he said, unable to 'publicly reveal the nature of the information he has communicated', but referred Parker to a section of Blake's signed confession in which Blake admitted that 'there was not an official document of any importance to which I had access which was not passed to my Soviet contact.' As Blake had access to 'information of very great importance' it was the Crown's case that he had 'done most serious damage to the interests of this country'. Finally Manningham-Buller made a reference to the Portland spy ring trial, where he had appeared as the prosecutor and Parker had again been the judge and which had concluded the month before: 'That was a grave case . . . But that this is an even graver case is in my submission clearly shown by the confession made by the accused.'

At this point Jeremy rose. He first made a veiled complaint at Manningham-Buller's conduct:

> My Lord, I indicated to the [Attorney General] some of those matters which I shall urge in mitigation and which are of the most vital importance to this man. I am told that much of which I wish to say should not be said in public. Therefore my choice must be as to whether the full facts can be laid before Your Lordship or whether I should leave out much of what should be said, but at least some mitigation of this man should be known to the outside world. That is the choice I have had to make during the last ten minutes. I had no idea until then that these proceedings were going to be in public.

Jeremy had decided, in the short time available to him, that he simply had insufficient opportunity to unpick from his speech material which could be publicly stated. Therefore everything would have to be said in closed court and Blake's side of the story could not be told to the world at large. So the court went into camera, the journalists shuffled out resentfully, and Jeremy began his plea in mitigation. The contents of what he said have only been made public in the last few years.

How does one seek to mitigate the offences of a man like George Blake? The task was a daunting one. Blake looks back at what happened that morning and remembers Jeremy's speech on his behalf as 'able and eloquent'. Jeremy had explained his client's motives for treachery 'so lucidly, and with such understanding', that he felt that the judge must be moved by it. The speech is interesting not only as the clearest statement we have of Blake's justification of his conduct, but also as an example of advocacy in action in the most testing circumstances.

Jeremy opened with an appeal to Parker's humanity. While conceding that 'any man who pleads guilty to an offence of this kind must be looked at by any court, indeed, by any Englishman with distaste, and therefore I cannot claim any sympathy from Your Lordship', he asked nonetheless for 'some patience and under-standing'. Knowing Parker to be an establishment judge and sensing some kind of unspoken understanding between him and the Attorney General, Jeremy was concerned that any sentence handed down might well be politically motivated. So, Jeremy also reminded the judge that 'this is not a political trial and it is not a propaganda trial.' Nor was it, he continued, 'a move in a cold war'. He went on: 'I know Your Lordship would take the view that we here in modern days have never had trials in order to give comfort to our allies or bring fear to our enemies.'[28]

Jeremy constructed Blake's mitigation on four principal grounds. The first of these was an attempt to explain Blake's conversion to communism. Jeremy began: 'If he had been brainwashed, if he had been tortured, if he had been subjected to Russian pressure, Your Lordship would, I am sure, count it strong mitigation.' He then painted a portrait of Blake's early life that emphasized its instability and periods of trauma: 'he was either in Egypt or running messages for the underground, involving himself in war, deprivation, murder and suchlike.' Jeremy contrasted Blake's adolescence with that of an English boy, who, with the privilege of 'attachment to this country by birth, by growing up, by tradition, by education . . . had all these things in quiet and peace'.

Compounding the dislocation of Blake's early life, Jeremy continued, came Korea. He asked the judge to consider the young man's condition in 1951 'after going through what he had on these marches, five times in his young life faced with death . . . pneumonia, dysentery, and seeing people dying like flies'. It was, he said, a condition that could be equated with that of a man who had undergone 'brainwashing and torture'. In other words, the experiences of Blake's adolescence, compounded by the horrors of Korea, put him in a position of vulnerability akin to a man who has been brainwashed or tortured. Jeremy pursued this argument further by asserting that Blake had in fact been subjected to a form of brainwashing, in the form of the copious quantities of communist literature that was provided to the prisoners in the Mon Yong Nee camp and supported his argument by quoting at length from the book written by his fellow captive Philip Deane about their experiences (see earlier, p.46).

The second plank of Jeremy's case was that, in evaluating the moral culpability of Blake's betrayal, it was unfair to judge him by the standards of an ordinary Englishman. He reminded the judge that, 'as regards allegiance to this country, this man's name was only Blake by deed-poll. He was called Behar by birth.' His father was a 'Spanish Turk', his mother was Dutch and he had spent his childhood in the Netherlands and Egypt. When he joined the SIS as a permanent officer he had been resident in the country 'for a year, or a year and a half altogether out of his life so far'. Blake was without 'attachment to this country by birth, by growing up, by tradition, by education', and for this reason his allegiance to it was less developed than it would have been in a young man who had enjoyed these privileges. In conclusion, as Blake's allegiance to this country was, inevitably, weaker than that of an Englishman born and bred, this should be taken into account as a mitigating factor when determining the moral culpability of his betrayal.

Next, Jeremy argued that it was a mitigating factor that Blake's crimes were motivated by idealism, rather than money or other personal gain. Blake had turned to communism, Jeremy explained, because he believed that it was the 'theory of life which had more hope for the future than all the things he had seen in the past'. His experiences in Korea and earlier had left him in a state of dislocation from Western values, which he saw embodied in the feebleness of the American GIs, and the corruption of the Syngman Rhee regime in Korea. Blake embraced communism because he sincerely believed that, in a manifestation true to the spirit of Marx's founding principles, it would make the world a better place.

Jeremy described how Blake, on the first evening of his Korean captivity, had asked himself, as he stood waiting as he thought to be executed: 'Why am I going to die? What am I dying for?'; and had come to the conclusion that 'so far in his life he had done nothing which was of any value.' Communism, Jeremy argued, had given Blake a sense of purpose in his life, which he had hitherto lacked, and the means to make 'a positive contribution'. It was, further, a means of surviving the ordeal of the present: 'something to give him strength, and fibre, and hope, to keep him alive.'

So, Jeremy contended, in the misery and deprivation of a North Korean prison camp, and with the noblest of intentions, Blake adopted communism as a means to keep himself alive, and with the ulterior purpose of improving the lives of others. He received not 'one penny piece for what he did' and obtained no other advantages.

In response to this argument, Parker testily interjected: 'This court will not sentence a man for becoming converted to a genuine belief in a system which he thought was better.' But he asked Jeremy to explain why, assuming that the belief was genuine, Blake chose to stay on in government service and betray his country, rather than resign. In response, Jeremy described the dilemma facing Blake consequent on his conversion to communism. He had three choices: to go to Russia; to stay in this country and further the cause of communism here; or to retain his position as an officer in the secret services. Blake chose the third of these options because, as Jeremy explained, it was the means by which he could make 'the maximum contribution' to the communist cause. Parker did not look impressed, but there was no other honest answer that could be given to his question.

Jeremy argued that on his return to England, and the resumption of a normal life, Blake began to regret his choice. 'Of course from that moment onwards he begins to understand, become more normal, to see life as it is led here, and he begins to realize how mistaken he was in many ways.' Going to Beirut, where he was not a recipient of classified information, and could provide nothing of value to the Russians, was Blake's way of trying to escape the bind that he found himself in. In time, Jeremy explained, Blake hoped to use his Arabic to get a job in an oil company and 'finally rid himself of the course which he had taken'.

The fourth ground of mitigation referred to the nature of Blake's treachery and its consequences. Jeremy argued that Blake had only ever intended 'the disruption of the Intelligence Service', that is, to frustrate the efforts of the West to spy on the Soviet Union and its allies. He had never, in Jeremy's words, 'given information which in his view could be used against this country in the sense of doing military damage, or anything like that'. Critically, Blake took care to ensure that the consequences arising from the information he gave to the Russians were kept within limits. In particular, whenever he revealed the name of an SIS agent, he sought and obtained an undertaking that 'they would be neutralized in their usefulness but not physically harmed.' In support of this contention, Jeremy argued there was evidence of only two arrests having been made as a result of information supplied by Blake. Finally Jeremy drew the distinction between Blake's case and that of Fuchs, the atomic scientist tried in the same court by Parker's predecessor Lord Goddard, a very experienced and formidable criminal judge. He also faced four separate charges covering a continuing offence over seven years. Fuchs had betrayed the secrets of the atom bomb. Jeremy had noted Manningham-Buller's words in opening the case: 'Fortunately, Blake's employment did not give him access to secret weapons or nuclear or atomic energy.' So, Jeremy quoted Goddard's words on passing sentence: 'How can I be sure that . . . the working of your mind may not lead to betraying further secrets of the greatest possible value to this country? The maximum sentence which Parliament has ordained is fourteen years and that is the sentence I pass upon you.'

After his speech in mitigation the hearing was adjourned for a short period before being reopened to the public for sentence. Blake recalls that he was optimistic that the plea had made an impression on the judge. It was Bill Cox's view that Jeremy had 'conducted the matter beautifully to the point where I anticipated a comparatively light sentence'. Such is the power of advocacy. But neither Blake nor his solicitor had reckoned with the Lord Chief Justice.

Parker then slowly walked back into court to deliver his sentence. The silence that prevailed was more total than Jeremy had ever experienced; or at least so it seemed that morning. Blake's and Cox's optimism would be quickly snuffed out. The judge drily accepted that Blake had been motivated by a 'genuine belief in the communist system'. But the 'gravamen' of the case against him was that he had not resigned from his position in the secret service, but instead 'retained his employment in positions of trust in order to betray your country'. It was the judge's view that the information communicated by Blake to the Russians was 'clearly of the utmost importance to that power', and 'has rendered much of this country's efforts completely useless'. The judge referred in particular to Blake's admission that 'There was not an official document of any importance to which I had access which was not passed to my Soviet contact.' In Parker's view, Blake's treachery was 'akin to treason' and was 'one of the worst that can be envisaged other than in time of war'.

For such 'traitorous conduct extending over so many years', there must, he said, be 'a very heavy sentence'. For 'a single offence of this kind', the judge continued, the highest penalty laid down by statute was fourteen years' imprisonment. Blake, however, was charged with five separate offences, each of which referred to discrete periods of spying activity. For this reason, the judge felt entitled to impose a sentence of fourteen years in relation to each count. The sentences in respect of counts one to three would be served consecutively; those specific to counts four and five would run concurrently. 'The total sentence,' the judge concluded, 'is one of forty-two years in prison.'

There were gasps from the public gallery. The journalists who once again crowded the public gallery scribbled vigorously, taking down the judge's unyielding judgement. Sitting in the public gallery, Dick White and Roger Hollis nodded in quiet satisfaction.[29] By the early 1960s those given a life sentence could expect to serve about ten years before being released. The term of imprisonment given to Blake was the longest in English legal history and meant that he would spend far more time in prison than the average murderer. Jeremy himself was stunned: this was not a moment of legal history with which he had wished to be associated. What was novel was the imposition of consecutive sentences in respect of what was in reality a continuous course of conduct. As Jeremy had mentioned, ten years earlier the spy Klaus Fuchs had been sentenced to fourteen years for many years of nuclear espionage for the Soviet Union. This had been considered the maximum sentence the court could impose.

As for Blake, when Jeremy and Bill Cox went down to see him in the cells they found a man who seemed remarkably unaffected by the personal catastrophe that had just befallen him. Jeremy recalls: 'The newspapers at the time reported that Blake had had a nervous collapse immediately after the sentence. Nothing could be further from the truth. Blake was remarkably serene. He realized the sentence was purely political. He saw himself as akin to a prisoner of war. I suspect he thought he would be swapped at some point in the future.' Jeremy returned to his chambers in low spirits. In defeat most barristers experience a lingering sense of personal responsibility. Was there something he could have done or said differently? His dejection was partly alleviated the next day when he received a letter from Bill Cox. 'I am writing this letter to you whilst my mind is still more unbalanced than usual as a result of the sentence which we received this morning, but I would like to say in all sincerity that I thought you dealt with the matter in the best possible way and I cannot think that you could possibly have done or said more than you did. I am quite bitterly disappointed with the result, which leads one to conclude that it did not really matter what we said or did.'

As Jeremy read his solicitor's words of comfort the Prime Minister was making a statement in the House of Commons about the 'grave case of George Blake'. Amid raucous scenes Harold Macmillan, in contradiction to Lord Parker, assured the House that Blake had not done 'irreparable damage' to national security and defended the security services against the charge that they had failed to detect Blake earlier. Hugh Gaitskell, then leader of the opposition, pounced upon a Prime Minister already wounded by the Portland spy ring case. 'Is the Prime Minister aware . . . that there is wide-spread disquiet that this kind of thing could have been allowed to happen and that a man could for nine and a half years have supplied information to the Soviet Union and thus, in the words of the Lord Chief Justice, rendered much of this country's efforts useless?'[30] That night Macmillan wrote in his diary: 'The case of George Blake – a traitor – has shocked the public. The LCJ has passed a savage sentence – 42 years! . . . I had a rather rough passage in the HoC . . .'[31]

Faced with this unprecedented sentence there was nothing else to do but appeal. However Jeremy remained exercised by the way that Manningham-Buller had, as he saw it, hoodwinked him. He insisted on another meeting with the Attorney General. This time, before the Court of Appeal, he wanted to explain openly Blake's justification for his conduct. Three days before the appeal was due to be heard they had another tense discussion in the Attorney General's room at the Royal Courts of Justice. Jeremy challenged Manningham-Buller as to the prosecution's position on whether the court should sit in camera. The Attorney General was implacable. No facts about the work Blake had done could be stated publicly and he was not prepared to give any reasons for that position. He then unleashed a stinging personal attack on Jeremy which is still etched on his mind:

> He said he could not understand why I should want to mention anything in public, as it was for the court not the press to listen to the mitigation; nor could he understand my point that the press had misrepresented the prosecution case and had suggested all sorts of things which Blake was not guilty of. He then said he understood that I wanted to make a 'good publicity splash', i.e. that I wanted to obtain cheap publicity for myself as an advocate. I couldn't believe it. It was also extraordinary that he refused to speak to me directly, but addressed himself throughout to my junior Bill Howard.

So shocked was Jeremy by Manningham-Buller's behaviour that he immediately wrote out a lengthy memorandum, headed 'For the Record', which he has kept to this day. There, in numbered paragraphs, Jeremy noted what the Attorney General had said to him. A number of comments stand out now, more than fifty years later. First, he wrote that Manningham-Buller had stated that 'We were welcome to outline Blake's conversion to communism, but this could not conceivably be mitigation. Nor could the fact that he was trained to do to others precisely what he did himself. THAT'S NOT MITIGATION.' Jeremy recalls that Manningham-Buller was shouting as he said this, presuming to tell defence counsel what he should or should not say in mitigation of his client's conduct. Second, Jeremy noted that the Attorney General had 'said that the court would be in possession of nothing other than the depositions and the transcript – but didn't look as if he meant it'. Was Manningham-Buller hiding the existence of secret, off-the-record communications with the court? Third, Jeremy recorded the delight expressed by Manningham-Buller that Mr Justice Salmon, a notably liberal judge, had been removed from the panel to hear the appeal, and replaced by a much more 'sound' judge. Finally, Jeremy concluded that 'he was bullying, offensive, torturous, and displayed a heart of stone.'

So came the day of the appeal. It was to be presided over by Mr Justice Hilbery, seventy-seven years old, the author of *Duty and Art in Advocacy*, and, as Jeremy recalls, 'an awful acidulated man'. Jeremy knew he was going to be in for a rough ride. He valiantly referred to the forty-two-year sentence as 'so inhumane that it was alien to all the principles on which a civilized country would treat its subjects. No man could survive a sentence of more than twenty years. There was nowhere in the prison system where such a sentence could be administered.' Effectively Blake was being sentenced to prison for the rest of his natural life. Faced with such a sentence a man had only two options: 'lose his sanity or gain his freedom'. Jeremy did not shy away from asserting that the sentence that had been passed had not been simply based on the offence itself: 'A political sentence would be completely alien to the basis of the administration of English law. It would be wrong to pass sentence with any desire of comforting allies or discomforting enemies of this country.' He then addressed the issue over which he had sparred with Manningham-Buller: he wished, so far as possible, to make his mitigation speech in public so that the world could know the true facts about Blake's conduct.

Hilbery's response was withering: 'We are not concerned with press conjecture. We are solely concerned to administer the law. We are not here to scotch some rumour. We are here to consider whether this sentence was wrong in principle or manifestly excessive. It does not matter to Blake or anybody else whether certain things are made public.' Jeremy battled on, emphasizing once again the impropriety of evading the maximum sentence of fourteen years, but it was obviously hopeless. In refusing permission to appeal, Mr Justice Hilbery poured scorn on everything Jeremy had said. Conduct such as Blake's 'should not only be condemned, should not only be held in utter abhorrence by all ordinary men and women, but should receive, when brought to justice, the severest possible punishment'. According to Hilbery, the sentence had 'a threefold purpose'. It was 'intended to be punitive, it was designed and calculated to deter others, and it was meant to be a safeguard to this country'.[32]

The front cover of the *Daily Express* on the day following the appeal, 20 June 1961, pictured the silhouettes of forty men under the headline '40 Agents Betrayed'. The paper's defence correspondent, the legendary Chapman Pincher, was the author of the article, which claimed that as a result of Blake's treachery forty agents working for Britain had been executed. Pincher has now confirmed[33] that his source was the then deputy leader of the Labour Party, George Brown, who had been apprised of the full details of the Blake case, via an agreement between the Prime Minister and Hugh Gaitskell. Pincher and Brown regularly lunched together at the Ecu de France, a restaurant in Jermyn Street so well-known as the venue for 'off the record' briefings to journalists that its banquettes were bugged by MI5. It has been claimed that the D-Notice Secretary, Rear Admiral Sir George Thomson, allowed the publication of the Pincher article, notwithstanding the severity of the restrictions placed on press coverage of the case generally, because the government wanted to explain the harshness of the Blake sentence.

The Pincher article is the source of a theory that associates the length of Blake's sentence with the number of deaths of the agents he betrayed. According to the theory, each year of the forty-two-year term equated to the death of an individual agent consequent on information provided by Blake to his Soviet handlers. If such a theory is right then it means that the Lord Chief Justice was apprised of more information than he was officially provided during the court proceedings.

There are some grounds for suspicion. The Attorney General had himself proposed that Blake be charged with five counts, each relating to a particular period of Blake's espionage activities for the Russians. This would allow the court to impose consecutive sentences and so evade the fourteen-year maximum imposed by section 1 of the Official Secrets Act. Manningham-Buller is reported to have told the Prime Minister that he would hit Blake 'with the biggest hammer possible'.[34] Yet, one of the oddities of the trial is how little Manningham-Buller actually told the court about Blake's crimes. In particular nothing was said to the court, other than in the broadest terms, about the consequences of Blake's revelations to the Soviets. So there was very little material before the court on which its sentence could actually have been based. Although the idea that Parker would have totted up years in jail by reference to a crude tallying up of deaths seems far-fetched, it has been suggested that there were private communications between Manningham-Buller and Parker in advance of the trial at which Parker was given much more information about Blake's case than was officially presented.[35] Indeed it has even been suggested that Macmillan, Parker and Manningham-Buller privately agreed the sentence before trial.[36]

If that is right, or even half right, then, regardless of the gravity of Blake's crimes, the sentence passed on him was a grave miscarriage of justice. It is a cardinal principle of law that neither side should engage in private communications with a judge. If Parker was given information through unofficial channels about the consequences of Blake's conduct, then, whether that information was right or wrong,[37] Jeremy was given no opportunity to attempt to meet it. It is in this context that Manningham-Buller's half-hearted protestation to Jeremy that the Court of Appeal would be in possession of nothing but the depositions and the transcript of the trial before Parker ('but didn't look as if he meant it') should be seen.

The dismissal of the application for permission to appeal was, for Jeremy, the formal end of his involvement in George Blake's case. But he remained haunted by a sense of personal outrage at the sentence that had been passed on Blake. He remains convinced that the sentence was politically motivated and that the passing of three consecutive (rather than concurrent) sentences of fourteen years was an abuse of the legal process.

Jeremy had reason to fear a 'political' trial. The Blake case was a source of significant embarrassment to the Macmillan government, especially in the context of its relations with the US. The CIA was furious when it discovered that Blake had compromised the Berlin tunnel, which had hitherto been considered a daring and brilliant achievement. A hefty sentence was a means of appeasing US disquiet, and also of softening domestic criticism of a seemingly dysfunctional, and 'leaky', SIS. Jeremy considers it likely that Parker was leaned on to sentence as he did. 'Parker was a creature of the establishment,' he says, 'and as such, likely to do its bidding. He passed an administrative, not a judicial sentence.' For Jeremy, Blake's sentence inspired fifty years of campaigning for sentencing and prison reform.

Up to 1961 Blake's life had been a remarkable one. It was assumed by everyone involved in his case that the sentence passed on him that year meant that, immured in some high-walled Victorian prison, he would fade from the public memory. That was not to be: the walls were not high enough.

Blake began his sentence in Wormwood Scrubs prison in west London, awaiting transfer to a maximum security prison. As a prisoner, Blake showed many admirable qualities, including a remarkable mental fortitude in the face of the seeming inevitability of spending the rest of his useful life behind bars. He practised yoga and exuded, to all who encountered him, an air of serenity and calm. Blake also continued his studies, gaining an A-level in Arabic, O-levels in the British Constitution and Russian, and later a degree in Arabic. The extraordinary length of Blake's sentence ensured him an elevated position in the prison hierarchy, and, notwithstanding the notoriety of his crimes, the dignity with which he faced it made him popular with fellow inmates.

Jeremy continued to help Blake. Jeremy's archive contains many letters from Blake and his wife Gillian, thanking him for his help in securing the easing of security restrictions on Blake's mother's and Gillian's visits to prison. In one, Blake tells Jeremy of his 'deep appreciation for your continuing interest in my affairs'. (Jeremy's involvement in the affairs of his clients long after he had stopped acting for them is a significant feature of his professional life: his archive is littered with correspondence from old clients on prison notepaper.) Gillian complained that she could only see her husband in the presence of a prison guard. In one poignant letter she wrote that it was difficult enough 'to keep our marriage going on a few hours together a year, without the added strain of these times together being listened into'. Jeremy raised the issue directly with Frank Soskice, the Home Secretary, who replied to him personally. The answer was no. 'I have looked again into this question, but I am afraid I should not feel justified in authorizing any change in the arrangements which have been made for the visits.'

Jeremy also persisted in his attempt to get Blake's sentence overturned. The appeal having failed, he shifted his attention to Parliament. It was to Lord Birkett that he turned first. Norman Birkett was, in his view, the greatest advocate of his time at the Bar and had become a personal hero for him. As a law student Jeremy had managed to listen with fascination to a number of his performances in court. He found that Birkett was shocked by the passing of the forty-two-year prison term, and the manipulation of the maximum sentence laid down in the statute. He agreed at once that he would seek to initiate a debate on long sentences in the House of Lords based on the Blake case. He was working on the debate when he died in 1962.[38] Next Jeremy corresponded with Jo Grimond, the leader of the Liberal Party, who also promised to raise the matter in the Commons, although in the end nothing came of this.

In his autobiography, Blake recalls that he felt it incumbent upon him to try to escape from prison. 'The sentence was such that it was almost a question of honour to challenge it. Moreover, I looked upon myself as a political prisoner and as such, like a POW, had a duty to escape.' In Blake's view, the severity of the sentence was instrumental to his escape, not simply because it spurred him on, but because it encouraged others to help him. According to his autobiography, 'it is to this long sentence that I owe my freedom. It secured me the sympathy not only of many of my fellow inmates, but also of the prison staff. It made me determined to attempt to break out of prison, as I truly could say that I had nothing to lose

but my chains.' Blake continues: 'Had I been given fourteen years
. . . it would have excited much less interest and sympathy in others,
and very likely, I would have served my sentence to the end.'[39]

Among the sympathetic inmates whom Blake met in prison were
Pat Pottle and Michael Randle, two young radicals whose passionate
belief in the cause of unilateral disarmament had led them to organize
an attempted sit-down on an RAF airfield in an attempt to prevent
nuclear bombers from taking off. After a trial at the Old Bailey in
1962, where they had been represented by Jeremy[40] (they had in fact
been inspired to retain him because of his involvement in the Blake
case), they found themselves as fellow prisoners with Blake at
Wormwood Scrubs. While they did not share Blake's political
ideology, they were outraged by the sentence that had been meted
out to him and soon found themselves engaged in lively discussions
with him under cover of a 'Music Appreciation Class'.

To the intense embarrassment of the British government, on the
evening of 22 October 1966 George Blake, perhaps the most high-
profile prisoner in Britain, escaped from Wormwood Scrubs. A
massive manhunt revealed no trace of him and it was generally assumed
that the escape had been masterminded by the KGB. In fact Blake's
escape was the work of three men, all former inmates with Blake
and motivated solely by their sympathy for Blake's predicament.

The real mastermind was a rackety Irishman called Sean Bourke,
who had got to know Blake while serving a seven-year sentence for
sending an explosive device through the post to a police officer
against whom he bore a grudge. The other two participants were
Jeremy's old clients Michael Randle and Pat Pottle. Jeremy, himself
ignorant of the real story behind the escape, read the news with a
certain grim satisfaction. He had famously told the Court of Appeal
a few years earlier, when seeking to reduce Blake's sentence, that
such a prison term would result in either madness or escape. His
prediction had come true.

The escape itself involved Blake slipping through the broken panes
of a window on the second floor in D Wing. He scaled the perimeter
wall with the assistance of a rope ladder, the rungs of which were
made of knitting needles, thrown over by Bourke from the other
side of the wall. Bourke then drove Blake to a safe house. From the

evening of his escape until 17 December Blake lived incognito in a series of flats found by Pottle and Randle. Blake was then spirited out of the country in a specially converted 'Commer' camper van. Michael Randle had spent three weeks creating a hidden compartment in which Blake could be concealed. Randle agreed to drive the Commer for the purposes of the escape, and his wife Anne and their two young children came too, to give the impression of a family holiday. The party left London on the evening of Saturday 17 December. From Dover they caught a ferry to Ostend, and drove to Brussels, then Aachen and the West German border. After crossing over to East Germany, Blake emerged from his place of concealment at the East German checkpoint near Berlin. Here he parted company with the Randles, who drove home, completing their 'holiday'. Blake, meanwhile, was swiftly removed to Moscow where he was fêted as a national hero and made a colonel in the KGB.

Almost fifty years later Blake remains a resident of Moscow. He has never left the confines of what was the Soviet Union and he is, of course, unwilling to return to England. It is doubtful that this curtailment of his freedom of movement has caused him much concern. His connection with Great Britain was always a tenuous one and he spent relatively little of his life actually living here. This form of cosmopolitanism may be the ultimate key to the decisions he made. Blake considered himself unbound by the ties of nationality and class. In fact he despised both. He wrote: 'I feel above nationality. I don't approve of national feelings. Loyalty to humanity, loyalty to a human cause, loyalty to religion is higher than loyalty to country.' Blake finally published his memoirs in 1990. It will be enough to quote the title – *No Other Choice* – to realize that this was not a book for the expression of remorse. But the book did lead to another spat with the British government, which successfully sued him for all the profits he made from the book on the basis that he remained bound by his contract of employment with SIS.[41]

Blake now lives with his Russian wife in retirement and for many years he has refused most requests for interviews. His ninetieth birthday was marked by a telegram from President Putin, pitched in terms of calculated provocation to the British establishment:

'You rightfully belong to the constellation of strong and courageous people. You and your colleagues [presumably a reference to Philby, Maclean and the other members of the 'Cambridge Five'] made an enormous contribution to the preservation of peace, to security, and to strategic parity. This is not visible to the eyes of outsiders, but very important work deserves the very highest acknowledgment and respect.'

There was to be one final trial. In 1987 Montgomery Hyde published a biography of Blake in which, for the first time, he referred to the roles of Pat Pottle and Michael Randle in the escape, barely disguising their names. Having been so unceremoniously 'outed', the two of them decided to go on the record as to what they had done and why. They sought advice on the question from Jeremy, who advised that, if they went ahead and published, he thought a prosecution would be almost inevitable: what governments and the civil service dislike most is to be made to look foolish. Nonetheless Pottle and Randle's book *The Blake Escape* was published in 1989. As Jeremy had predicted, this was too much for the British government and *R v Pottle and Randle* was duly tried in Court 1 of the Old Bailey in 1991. Jeremy was approached to give evidence on their behalf but, however sympathetic he felt towards his old clients, he was concerned that his evidence would not assist their cause. The two men defended themselves, admitting the facts alleged against them but explaining that they had acted 'under duress': so outraged were they by what they considered was a vindictive and unjust sentence that they had to take the course they did. It was a brilliant performance. Notwithstanding the judge directing them that the defence did not amount in law to duress and that they should convict, the jury acquitted them. Michael Randle wrote to Jeremy afterwards: 'As you say, the cycle of events from the Blake and Wethersfield trials,[42] to George's escape and finally our acquittal is extraordinary and − finally − satisfying.'

∼

George Blake has always been adamant that his work for the Russians did not lead to the death of any agents working for the British security services. In a statement made by him for the purposes of the preparation of the defence case in April 1961, Blake testifies that he disclosed the names of agents reluctantly, and on his own terms. 'I stipulated,' he recalls, 'and repeated this every time I passed a name that these agents should not be arrested and that the only use the Russians should make of this information was to protect themselves from the activities of these agents by denying them access to information which they thought valuable.' Apparently the 'Russians agreed to this' but with the caveat that 'if the East Germans obtained independently evidence of the activities of these agents, they could not prevent them from taking action.'

Blake maintained, and continues to maintain, that the Russians respected his wishes. In his autobiography, Blake accepts that he revealed the identity of 'a large number of agents to the Soviet Intelligence service, not forty as alleged, but nearer 400'. He continues: 'I challenge anybody, however, to name one who has been executed. Many of them are today taking an active part in the democratic movements of their respective countries in Eastern Europe.'[43] In an interview in Moscow in 1990 Blake reiterated his assertion that none of the agents he betrayed was killed by the KGB.

On the basis of information that has subsequently become available, Blake's insistence on this point is evidence either of naivety, or an unwillingness to accept the consequences of his actions. The KGB at this time was led by Stalinists such as Ivan Serov. It strains belief to contend that a man such as Serov would have held back from his usual ruthless ways in deference to the sensitivities of a British mole.

By inserting the caveat in their 'undertaking' to Blake that, in the case that 'the East Germans obtained independently evidence of the activities of these agents, they could not prevent them from taking action', the Soviets retained complete freedom of manoeuvre. They could maintain that the arrest of a particular agent was the work of the Stasi, while neglecting to mention that the information leading to the arrest was, at least in part, provided by the KGB. Blake seems to have fallen for this ruse. In his April 1961 statement he recalls that 'In every case when an agent whose name I had passed on was arrested, I raised the matter with the Russian Controllers officer and in every case he assured me that the action had been taken by the East Germans on their own evidence and without information having been passed to them by the Russians.'

Stasi archives provide ample evidence of the consequences of Blake's betrayal of British agents. In the mid-1950s the East Germans were struggling to restrict penetration of their operations by Western spies. Erich Mielke, who later became head of the Stasi, was given responsibility for stemming the tide. Information given by Blake to the KGB, and passed to the Stasi, was of incalculable assistance to him. In April 1955 Mielke was able to tell the party's Central Committee that 521 agents had been arrested, of whom 105 were agents of the 'British secret service'. A further 251 spies were detained in the last three months of the year. In 1956, 679 spies were arrested, and 582 in 1957.[44]

A paper published by Stasi's counter-intelligence branch some years after the events in question reported that 'Blake's work substantially laid the foundations for the liquidation of networks of British secret service agents in the GDR. So it was possible from 1956 to 1961 to identify around 100 spies working in the GDR.' Among them were (the names are blacked out) 'dangerous agents such as [ ] stenographer at the GDR Council of Ministers; [ ] Colonel of the NVA; [ ] Member of the State Planning Commission; [ ] Senior Advisor at the Ministry for heavy machinery; [ ] Department head in the Ministry for Trade; [ ] Employee in the building committee in Potsdam'.[45]

The prosecution file for the Blake trial, which has only recently been made public, includes a report by SIS 'Officer B'. It is heavily redacted. 'Officer B' states that he has investigated the cases of individual agents working for the Berlin station of the SIS between 1955 and 1959, who were 'either arrested by the Russians, or disappeared without trace, or became known to the Russian Intelligence Service as our agents'.[46] There are then several blacked-out pages.

The former head of Soviet counter-intelligence, Oleg Kalugin, discussed the issue with Blake when he met him in Moscow many years later. According to Kalugin, Blake 'didn't want to know that many people he betrayed were executed. I think we even discussed this subject at one point, and he wouldn't believe it – he would say, "Well, I was told this would not happen."' Kalugin concludes: 'It did happen; he was not told.'[47]

2

'Untough'

R v Vassall (1962)

'We have arrested a spy who is a bugger and a minister is involved.'[1]

A YEAR AND a half after Blake had been incarcerated news of another spy case emerged to send fissures through the fragile hold on public trust that Macmillan's government was slowly seeking to regain. This time the spy was no rugged ideologue but a lowly clerk working at the Admiralty. Yet his arrest and trial provoked a far greater public furore and, in the end, inflicted far greater damage upon Macmillan than Blake's treachery had done. The fatal ingredient that was introduced into the mix this time was sex, and gay sex at that. Added to this were the embellishments of Soviet blackmail and the suggestion, ostensibly sincerely made by both the press and the parliamentary opposition, of indiscretions by a government minister. Out of this toxic brew sprang a scandal that served as the prelude to the disaster – in the shape of what has come to be known as 'the Profumo affair' – that was to occur the next year.

The political implications of the case were immediately apparent to Harold Macmillan. He was writing a speech on the EEC for the forthcoming Conservative Party conference when he was informed of the arrest of John Vassall, a clerk at the Military Branch II serving the naval staff in the Admiralty. In his diary entry for 28 September 1962 Macmillan recorded: 'There has been another "espionage" case – and a very bad one – in the Admiralty.'[2] Sir Roger Hollis, head of MI5, expressed his surprise, in the course of a meeting with Macmillan on the subject, at the Prime Minister's apparent lack of enthusiasm for the spy's exposure: 'You don't seem very pleased,

Prime Minister,' he remarked. The Prime Minister replied: 'No, I'm not at all pleased. When my gamekeeper shoots a fox, he doesn't go and hang it up outside the Master of Foxhounds' drawing room; he buries it out of sight.' There would now, he said, be a 'great public trial. Then the security services will not be praised for how efficient they are but blamed for how hopeless they are. There will then be an enquiry . . . [which] will say – like the Magistrate in "Albert and the Lion" – that no one was really to blame. There will be a terrible row in the press, there will be a debate in the House of Commons and the Government will probably fall. Why the devil did you "catch" him?'[3]

But catch Vassall they had, and that meant a trial.

John Vassall was born on 20 September 1924 at St Bartholomew's Hospital in the City of London, where his father William was chaplain. The Vassalls were, in a minor way, an established and well-educated clerical family. Vassall's mother converted to Roman Catholicism six years after her marriage, which put great strain on her relationship with her husband and his family. Vassall was brought up in what he later described as 'a good home, but an unhappy one'.[4] His sympathies lay with his mother, and he remained close to her throughout his life. A fey child, uninterested in games, he was a lacklustre scholar. He attended a minor public school where he earned a reputation as the best-dressed boy in the school, and acquired the nickname 'Serf', a reflection of his servility towards his elders and eagerness to please. Hopes of an Oxford education were dashed when he was forced to leave school at sixteen as a result of financial constraints. In his autobiography he describes, in the mannered but earnest Edwardian style that permeated his character, how early on he realized that he was attracted to his own sex: 'I began to form secret and intimate friendships with older boys, whom I thought of as mature beings, strong, masterly and physically attractive. I lived in a secret world, one which I felt nobody could ever possibly know or understand. My whole being was stimulated by my sense of their awareness and virility. I did not think of my friends as boys; they were virile young men, whom I looked up to as Greek gods.'[5]

Vassall joined the civil service at the age of seventeen and worked in the Admiralty Records Office. After the outbreak of war he trained as a photographer and saw active service. In 1946 Vassall returned to the Admiralty as a clerical officer, and worked successively in the Air Equipment Department, Naval Law, and the War Registry. Vassall's capabilities as a civil servant appear to have been limited, and he was passed over for promotion on the two occasions that he applied. His official annual income never overtopped £750. Though apparently 'defective in the power of judgment and of limited intellectual capacity', nearly everyone found Vassall 'pleasant to work with', and he was considered 'a discreet, reserved, and obliging man, well spoken and in appearance neat and well dressed'.[6]

In 1954 Vassall applied and was accepted for a post in the office of the British Naval Attaché in Moscow. Vassall's first few months in Moscow were difficult; he disliked the excessive formality of the British Embassy where he was based, and later criticized what he considered the lack of care and consideration shown by senior members of the diplomatic staff. A snob himself, Vassall was undoubtedly in turn himself a minor victim of the prevailing snobbery of the period. And if he was slighted he no doubt felt it the more keenly because of his sense of his own inadequately recognized qualities and the unfairness of his education having been brought to such an early end. He prided himself on what he considered his artistic sensibility and delicacy of thought, and was wounded when these traits were an insufficient passport to the dinner tables of the higher echelons of the British Embassy. Instead Vassall found friends in other embassies, and established himself as a regular and apparently sought-after guest on the Moscow diplomatic circuit. In his autobiography, Vassall describes his social life at this time with obvious pride: 'invited to the Mexican Embassy for cocktails and then on to play bridge with the Afghan Counsellor at his flat. The Argentinian Ambassador gave a tennis party', then 'to the Swedish Embassy where there was a party for the Swedish Opera Company.'[7]

Vassall became friends with a Pole named Sigmund Mikhailski, who worked as a translator and fixer in the administration department of the British Embassy. Mikhailski introduced Vassall to a Russian man (referred to in Vassall's autobiography only as 'the skier') with whom he had a physical relationship. According to Vassall (and we have no way of corroborating his own testimony), he attended a number of dinner parties at the invitation of the skier. In his autobiography Vassall recounts how on the evening of one such party, the skier notified Vassall that he was unable to attend himself, but that he had a friend who wanted to invite Vassall out to dinner. Vassall accepted and was taken to a private room in the Berlin Hotel where he ate dinner with several Russians whom he describes as 'formally dressed, friendly and courteous'. After dinner, and substantial quantities of brandy, Vassall felt befuddled and unwell and was helped on to a large divan. He was asked to take his clothes off, and remembers lying on the bed with three other men, and 'having my underpants in my hand and holding them in the air at the request of others'. He saw the skier's friend taking photographs. Suddenly, Vassall recalls, 'everything became very painful.' The inference to be drawn is obvious, though Vassall is too delicate to explicate. Later he was helped to dress 'and we all behaved as if nothing had happened. It was like a painful dream.'[8]

Any sensible man would have read a sinister significance into this bizarre evening and would have been more careful in his future dealings with Russians. But Vassall was not a sensible man. According to his autobiography, several months later, on the evening of 19 March 1955, Vassall accepted a further invitation from the skier, which involved Vassall meeting 'a friend of his, a military officer, who was on leave in Moscow'. The scene that follows has a Pinteresque quality. Vassall had been told that the three of them would go to the theatre. Instead he was taken, without explanation, to a large block of flats. In a room in the top-floor apartment he and the officer engaged in sexual activity, which was interrupted by 'a polite but firm knock on the door' and a voice telling him to 'come into the next room when I was ready'. The officer hastily dressed and left, never to be seen again. Vassall was interrogated by members of the Russian secret service, who produced photographs of Vassall participating in oral and anal sex with a variety of different men. The agents told Vassall that he had committed a serious offence under Russian law and that if he did not cooperate, they would expose him variously to the press, the Soviet government and the British Embassy.[9]

Vassall was later adamant that he felt unable to confide his misfortune to an appropriate member of the British diplomatic community and, terrified by the threat of public exposure, he succumbed to Soviet demands. For the next fifteen months Vassall met his Russian handlers every three weeks or so and gave them information about the British Embassy. At first this related to routine matters of personnel and administration. Later Vassall brought documents to his meetings with the Soviets, which were examined, or photographed, and returned. In December 1955 Vassall accepted his first payment from the Russians.

On his return to England in July 1956 Vassall took up a posting in the Naval Intelligence Division. Thereafter, in June 1957, he was transferred to the private office of the Civil Lord of the Admiralty, a genial Scot named Thomas ('Tam') Galbraith MP, where he worked as a clerical officer assisting Galbraith's private secretary, delivering documents to Galbraith's home in Scotland, making travel arrangements and suchlike. Then, from the autumn of 1959 until September 1962 Vassall worked in Military Branch II serving the naval staff in the Admiralty. Before leaving Moscow Vassall was introduced to a Soviet agent called Gregory, who he was told would be his contact in London. Vassall was required to meet Gregory every three weeks at an appointed place, for example outside the Finchley Road Underground station. If he had documents, they would be taken away and photographed, and then returned. At Christmas 1957 Vassall was given money to buy a Minox mini camera, and thereafter provided Gregory with undeveloped films. But the Soviet bounty extended to more than just the acquisition of the paraphernalia of spycraft; the Russians were careful to feed Vassall regular sums of money – roughly doubling his annual income – which allowed him to indulge his love of foreign travel and Queen Anne furniture. This combination of threat and encouragement was a well-tested Russian technique. For a character such as Vassall's the natural desire to appease those in a position of power, whether that was a master at his school or his Russian handler, to play the 'Serf', completed the nexus of dominion. Thus was the Russians' hold on Vassall complete.

Intelligence provided by high-ranking KGB officers, Anatoli Golitsin and Yuri Nossenko following their defection to the West, led to

Vassall's arrest on 12 September 1962.[10] By this time Vassall was living in fashionable Dolphin Square. His rooms were searched and ten undeveloped films containing photographs of seventeen secret Admiralty documents dated between 4 July and 3 September 1962, and the Minox camera, were recovered from the secret compartment of a bureau bookcase in his flat. The contents of Vassall's wardrobe were almost equally interesting: thirty-six Savile Row suits, three cashmere overcoats and thirty pairs of hand-made shoes. This was not the wardrobe of a junior clerk on £750 a year.

It was still common in the 1960s for those charged with serious offences to sell their story to newspapers, which were less punctilious then at the prospect of the potentially guilty profiting from their crime. In homage to this tradition, and while in prison awaiting trial, Vassall sold his story to the *Sunday Pictorial* for the considerable sum of £5,000, which he used in part to pay his legal costs. But the newspaper had not contracted for thin gruel. It can have done Vassall few favours when there appeared in the pages of the *Pictorial* the following charming sentiment: 'On my dressing-table stood a miniature toy white poodle and other furry animals and on my bed my favourite friend – a cuddly toy cheetah. I had a photograph specially taken in colour of me and my cheetah. I wish I had it with me now.' It was with the money that such observations bought that Vassall's solicitor retained Jeremy, by now fast becoming the most fashionable criminal silk at the Bar, as his leading counsel.[11] His retainer as Vassall's counsel even made it into the papers: the *Evening Standard* headline told its readers 'Vassall chooses Blake case's QC for his defence' with a suitably serious photograph of Jeremy wearing his full-bottomed wig. Vassall remembers Jeremy visiting him in Brixton prison prior to the trial: 'Mr Hutchinson I admired from the moment I saw him.'[12] These were the days when barristers only ever had one first name to their clients: Mister.

Vassall recollected this time: 'my life seemed to be now a series of apologies for what I had done.'[13] And to Jeremy this sentiment sums up Vassall's whole attitude to his spying. He recalls:

> He saw his behaviour as a matter for apology rather than shame. He found it difficult to understand that he had been charged at all – he could hardly accept that he had even committed a crime. It was

as if what he had done was just an awful *faux pas*. I discerned no real contrition in him at all. The predominant feeling was self-pity – as if he was a victim rather than a perpetrator. He came across as a weak and rather vain young man who considered himself superior in many ways to those with whom he worked. His job may have been of no great distinction but he thought of himself as a cultured man able to enjoy the most intellectual pursuits of a well-educated gentleman.

Jeremy's own view of Vassall was equivocal: it was difficult to warm to him, but pity came easily.

Vassall's trial was heard at the Old Bailey on 22 October 1962. There, sitting on the bench, was the same judge who, eighteen months earlier, had sentenced George Blake to forty-two years in prison – the Lord Chief Justice, Lord Parker of Waddington. Ever the snob, Vassall described the atmosphere of the courtroom as 'so quiet that one might have been in the Athenaeum Club'.[14] Immediately upon his arrest Vassall had confessed everything. So there was no choice for Vassall but to plead guilty to the four counts under the Official Secrets Act with which he was charged. The first referred to 'a day in 1955', at a time when Vassall was in Moscow; the second to a period between 'August 1, 1956, and May 31, 1957' when he was employed in the Naval Intelligence Division; the third to 'August 17, 1962' at the time of his posting to Military Branch II; and the last to a period between 'August 17 and September 12, 1962' just prior to his arrest. The indictment followed the precedent set in the Blake case. Each charge carried with it a maximum term of fourteen years and it seemed that the court was being given once again the opportunity to impose a draconian punishment made up of consecutive sentences.

The Attorney General, Sir John Hobson MP QC, appeared for the prosecution. It was a relief for Jeremy to have, after Manningham-Buller (who had become Lord Chancellor a few months previously), a reasonable and courteous opponent. There would be no repeat of the bullying of the Blake case. Hobson told the court that, while Vassall had been 'entrapped by his lust', he was also motivated by greed. It was claimed that the Russians paid Vassall between £500 and £700 a year. Vassall, the Attorney General stated: 'has been well rewarded by those who have used him as their tool and has sold some part of the safety and security of the people of this country for cash'.[15]

In her contemporary account of the Vassall case[16] the doyenne of British spy-writing, Rebecca West, castigated the prosecution for its willingness to accept Vassall's explanation of his behaviour. 'By tradition the prosecution always receives with kindly gullibility statements made by persons accused of treachery, even when these are patently absurd.' West's portrayal of Vassall was of a smooth and experienced operator, at ease with his sexuality, a man who would have been constantly alert to the risk of blackmail in Moscow. She found it preposterous that he would have succumbed to a Russian honey-trap and argued that Vassall hoodwinked the establishment into believing that he was a weak and irresolute victim of a ruthless power. The inevitable logic of this line of argument is to impute an ideological or financial motive to Vassall's spying, yet West was unable to propose any coherent alternative account of what in fact had lured Vassall into his course of spying. Jeremy will have none of it. 'A man less interested in communism it would be hard to find. No doubt the money oiled the discomfiture of his predicament, and he clearly had a penchant for foreign travel, tailored clothes and antique furniture, all of which he funded with the proceeds of his crime. But it provided no initial motive.' Vassall's defence of himself, self-serving as it was, has some vestige of sincerity: 'Who on earth would do it for money? One would have to have nerves of steel, to be super-human . . . All money does is give you a false feeling of security and a certain amount of personal freedom. The whole thing is an illusion, a stay of execution, nothing more.'[17]

Like conversation, or theatre, the essence of advocacy is the impression it makes, at the moment it is given voice, to the immediate audience to whom it is made. The words themselves, and the meanings they are intended to convey, are only half of the effect. Put fine words into the mouth of a poor advocate and those words can die on the tongue, whereas a great advocate can conjure magic out of the proverbial laundry list. Virginia Woolf described in her memoir *Old Bloomsbury* the difficulty of capturing the conversation of the early Bloomsbury Group: 'Talk, even talk of this interest and importance is as elusive as smoke. It flies up the chimney and is gone.' The same is true for oratory. Great speeches read on the page decades or centuries later can seem so many dreary words. No English advocate's courtroom speeches are ever recorded. The most one can hope for is a transcription of what was said. And yet, in the transcript that survives of Jeremy's speech on behalf of Vassall, some sense of the power of the spoken word has been smuggled out of a cold and gloomy courtroom of fifty years ago and has escaped from the bubble of the ephemeral. And we can also see in this speech, described by the *Guardian* at the time as 'quiet, serious and moving', the power of persuasion at work upon a judge naturally inclined to do the bidding of the executive.[18]

First, Jeremy emphasized the difficulty of his task: the greatness of the judicial process and the smallness of the man in its grip. But with that power came a special responsibility.

> My Lord, it is never easy to swim against the tide and my learned friend Mr McEwen [Jeremy's junior] and I are very conscious of the fact that we cannot hope to tap the springs of sympathy from Your Lordship when a man has pleaded guilty to four charges of committing acts which are prejudicial to the safety of the state. My Lord, the sentencing of this man, John Vassall, is not an executive act by the state: it is, of course, a judicial process, and this is a trial. At this stage this trial has only reached halfway. We are not here to see this man removed from society as if it were the squashing of a fly. Our task, as I see it, is to assist Your Lordship to come to a just decision here as to the penalty which should be imposed, to assist the court to maintain a sense of proportion and to set the facts as you have heard them against the grim and squalid background of this particular facet of what are called 'international relations', to try to help you to assess the actual harm done and the degree of guilt in this individual.

Parker will have understood precisely the message Jeremy was seeking to convey: his sentence on Blake had been interpreted by many as precisely such 'an executive act by the state'.

Jeremy continued the theme of emphasizing Vassall's smallness and insignificance before the might of the law. He did so in terms that were designed to demonstrate the difference between the pathetic

Vassall, the very embodiment of the amateur, and the hardened professional spy, Blake.

> Your Lordship has come down to this court to try this case and my learned friend has come here to represent the Crown, and this case, of course, has attracted and will attract the maximum publicity. But the chief actor in the case, of course, has the shortest part; he has one word, albeit repeated four times. My Lord, it is too serious a matter to worry about personal feelings. The man who sits in this dock – and I say it in his presence – does not measure up to the role which he has chosen to fill. He is a very ordinary, a very unremarkable man. His background is a very normal and ordinary background; perhaps it is a background which might on the face of it justify a higher rating of job than the one he has pursued for a number of years now with the civil service . . . whatever the security arrangements were, surely no one can believe that a man of this calibre in that job, whatever he has done, has really disclosed over a long period information which can do the greatest damage to this country.

And now to the question of Vassall's sexuality. It was on this that the whole case hinged:

> As I say, he is an ordinary man, and a man no doubt with some weaknesses in his character. He is an untough man. He is a man who when you talk to him is possibly more interested in the contemplative side of life rather than the active life. Perhaps one might describe him as somewhat unadult when one sees him and talks to him about the situation he is in. My Lord, he is a man who has a weakness – and which of us can say that this does not apply to him? – he has a weakness, and his particular weakness is that within him, ever since I suppose he came into this life, he has a latent homosexuality, which of course brings in its train all the inner turmoil and suffering which we who practise in this particular court know only too well. [In 1962 homosexual acts remained illegal and this was still a period when homosexuals were rigorously prosecuted.] Therefore I have nothing to unfold to Your Lordship of interest, no revelations of a master spy for people in search of sensation in this case. Your Lordship does not have before you a brilliant scientist with a unique and intellectual gift or a rugged ideologist determined to uphold his faith . . . My Lord, this is a story of a vulnerable

and possibly irresolute man who became the victim of a ruthless and pitiless apparatus which has in fact squeezed him into submission.

And Jeremy then delineated the events leading to the entrapment.

It was the receipt of money where the difficulty lay for Jeremy. Vassall was not simply a victim of a honey-trap: he had received money which he had not been slow in spending. The problem was met head-on:

> As far as the money is concerned, perhaps it is too simple to go into. Obviously from the Russians' point of view − and this is so well known − it is essentially another technique that money should be given and taken. Obviously for every psychological reason that would be so: it is the final degradation of a man who is in your power. It was vital from their point of view that that should be the relationship − and I dare say it is some relief from the state of affairs into which he had got himself to have money − and let us face it, if he was the man to stand up and say, 'No, I won't take money although I am being blackmailed', no doubt he would never have given any information at all and the efforts of the Russian police would not have been successful, as they have been on his mind and his resistance.

And so to the conclusion, whereby Vassall was pitched as victim rather than perpetrator:

> I finish, of course, by directing my attention to the question of sentence. So long as powerful nations train men to suborn and to seduce, equipped with modern scientific psychological methods, so long as these organizations are built up, so long there will be victims such as John Vassall. Just so long as this canker of espionage continues to rot the goodwill between men, so long there will be trials such as this, and if this trial has disclosed something of the pressures to which ordinary men are now put it will have served a greater purpose than only to affect Your Lordship's sentence and society's condemnation of one of its members.

Jeremy now permitted himself an attack on the sentence imposed on Blake. This was bold but necessary. After all, why should Parker not conclude that Vassall's disclosures had inflicted more harm upon the state than Blake's?

In a recent case Your Lordship imposed a number of consecutive sentences on separate counts covering a course of continuous action, for offences against a similar section of the Official Secrets Act as the one which is now before the court. Your Lordship imposed a sentence which in aggregate covered a period which was really the equivalent of that man's whole natural life. The indictment in this case has been drawn so that a similar course could be followed by Your Lordship and this prospect, unknown until 1961 by any English advocate, is indeed a daunting one. My Lord, I ventured at a later date [a reference to Jeremy's submissions to the Court of Appeal in the *Blake* case] to submit that perhaps an inordinately long sentence was not in this class of case such an effective deterrent as might at first be thought, and one cannot help but notice that the dates of counts three and four, when this man was passing the information he did, lie after the imposition of those sentences in that previous case.

In short, even after Blake was sent down for forty-two years Vassall was squirrelling documents out of the Admiralty to pass to his Russian handler. For Jeremy this was a moment of immense satisfaction.

The conclusion of his submissions showed Jeremy reaching for an almost Olympian mode of address.

A long, long sentence of the kind I have described can only, can it not, be justified if the man before the court is so dangerous that he should not be allowed again into society. My Lord, there cannot, can there, be any other justification for the incarceration of a human being for a length of time which means to all intents and purposes the rest of his life. No one – no one – could conceivably describe this man in that category. He has now confessed to everything that he has done and I hope Your Lordship can therefore accept and believe what he has said, and can accept and believe what is not disputed as to how all this began. My Lord, it is a question always to be posed, I suppose: Is it worse to do this because you believe you are doing right, because you want to assist a potential enemy, because you believe it is right, or is it worse to do it because you have been blackmailed and you are a weak vessel and have succumbed to a system which is designed for that very purpose?

Note the repetitions here, which were not accidental, but almost incantatory. And, having posed the question just quoted, Jeremy was assiduous to avoid answering it head-on. Rather he is back to the task of differentiating Vassall from Blake:

> In my submission the cases are utterly different. As I have said before, so long as this apparatus exists, so there will be victims; but, My Lord, you will not find the victims in the toughest stratum of society, you will find the victims among the weaker vessels and those who have their weaknesses through no fault of their own. Whatever may be the views and practices of other countries, whether friendly countries or potential enemies, here an inordinately long sentence has never been part of our penal system. Your Lordship will remember the words of Sir Alexander Paterson:[19] 'It requires a superman to survive a sentence of more than twenty years with his soul intact.' He was a man who knew perhaps more than anyone else of what happens to persons when they leave this dock. My Lord, this is no superman, and I ask Your Lordship to impose a penalty which allows him at least to do what Sir Alexander Paterson said was impossible to do if a sentence is inordinately long, and I would ask Your Lordship by imposing a just penalty to prove once again that in this country humanity goes hand in hand with justice.

So the speech ended, with a challenge to Parker to redeem himself: to act as an independent judge rather than an adjunct member of the executive.

It is always difficult for an advocate to know what effect his words have on the judge or jury. Judges do not often overtly concede that their decision has been influenced by the power of advocacy. To do so is to suggest an acceptance that the just solution is not an objective fact, to be reached regardless of the skill of the advocate. Here, plainly Parker was not going to follow Jeremy down the path of painting Vassall as a helpless victim of the psychological warfare that permeated the Cold War. But that was not Jeremy's hope. The task was to instil in Parker a sense of expectation that he would do independent judicial justice. And while Parker inevitably referred, when passing sentence, to Vassall's failure to make a clean breast on his return from Moscow and his willing acceptance of Russian bounty, the actual sentence he passed was generally considered a light one: six years' imprisonment on the first count and twelve years on the remaining three, the two sets of tariffs to be run consecutively giving a total sentence of eighteen years.

The next day Jeremy received a letter from his junior, Robin McEwen. Few advocates, however eminent, are free from self-doubt, and reassurance is always welcome. Jeremy concurs: 'There is always the terrible fear that one has struck the wrong note. The difference between a moving speech and bathos can be paper-thin.' So the terms of McEwen's charming letter were gratifying: 'This is just to convey the warmest admiration of your so-called junior for the moving and eloquent plea which you made on behalf of J Vassall – which must have penetrated the granite form of Parker in deciding his sentence, even though he didn't like to admit it in so many words.'

So ended Vassall's role in his case. But his sentencing proved to be just the prelude to the scandal that was about to ensue. It was a scandal that unravelled against the backdrop of the Cuban missile crisis, the first time in history when 'you could meet people who seriously thought the world was about to end'.[20] In fact the crisis erupted on the very day of Vassall's trial: 'The first day of the World Crisis!' as Macmillan termed it in his diary entry for 22 October 1962. 'I do not remember a more worrying time,' he noted of the three previous weeks in his entry of 15 November 1962. 'I had been engaged in facing what seemed the opening phase of a Third World War, involving not merely the intellectual strain of constant talks with the President, but the physical disadvantage of scarcely sleeping one or two hours each night.' Yet 'so strangely is the human brain constituted, this terrible danger seemed to distress me less than the personal and human anxieties' of the Vassall affair.[21] For, during those three weeks, while the world held its breath over the Cuban stand-off, Vassall's conviction unleashed a torrent of local agitation, both in the press and Parliament. The questions became louder and louder: How could a man like Vassall have come to be employed? Was it not obvious that he was a homosexual and so a blackmail risk? Who had been sheltering him at the Admiralty? Perhaps there was a vast homosexual conspiracy permeating the upper echelons of the civil service? And what of the relationship between Vassall and the amiable

Tam Galbraith? When Macmillan referred – accurately – to the hullabaloo as 'a sort of mass hysteria worked up by the Press and the less reputable members of the Opposition like Brown and Crossman and Gordon-Walker'[22] he could not have foreseen that it was but a foretaste of the collective insanity that was to settle over the country just a few months later following the resignation of John Profumo.

It has been said of the modern tabloid press that once it has decided to fell a politician then its pursuit of him will be as relentless as a pack of hounds on the scent of a fox. The exact same bloodlust was at work in late 1962. Barely was Vassall immured in Wormwood Scrubs than rumours were circulating about an improper relationship between him and Tam Galbraith. Delighted at the prospect of a story involving sex and spies and a minister, the press pursued Galbraith with zeal.

Galbraith attempted to clear his name in an article in the *Daily Mail*. But his protestations concerning Vassall that 'My relations with him were no different from those with other civil servants' and that 'I felt rather sorry for him – I felt he had a screw loose' served only to inflame suspicion. If Vassall had indeed a 'screw loose', why was he carrying around secret government documents? On 1 November 1962 Galbraith felt forced to put out a statement through his lawyers that he had not known that Vassall was homosexual. Meanwhile the *Sunday Pictorial* had obtained letters from Galbraith to Vassall and sent copies of them to the government and the opposition. The letters, which were later published in full, reveal nothing salacious, but rather the kindness and courtesy shown by a thoughtful man to his ingratiating junior. So, for example, a letter of 15 April 1962: 'Dear Vassall, We much enjoyed your visit and it was very nice of you to write'; Easter 1960: 'My Dear Vassall, Goodness knows what you will think of me for having taken so long to write'; 18 September 1957: 'Dear Vassall, it isn't often a Civil Lord has the chance to write a note to one of his staff when over the North Pole'. But the press could not read a letter that commenced with the greeting 'My Dear Vassall' without assuming impropriety.

On 28 October 1962 the *Sunday Pictorial* began its serialization of Vassall's story. It was accompanied by a photograph of a gamin Vassall, in a sort of Tony-Curtis-in-*Spartacus* pose, luxuriating in a no doubt very hot bath. On the following Sunday, 4 November 1962, the paper linked Vassall with a wider homosexual 'conspiracy' operating in the higher echelons of government. Meanwhile it was being reported that Vassall had been known to wander the streets of the West End in women's clothing and that his sexuality was an open secret in Whitehall: he even apparently had a pet moniker – 'Aunty'. On the following Monday in the House of Commons, at the end of the debate on the Queen's Speech, the egregious Deputy Leader of the Labour Party, George Brown MP, returned to the subject of Vassall. He told the House that he had seen letters (from Galbraith to Vassall), which indicated 'a degree of ministerial responsibility that goes far beyond the ordinary business of a Minister'.[23] Brown's imputations were wholly baseless given the paucity of the evidence on which they were founded. Nonetheless the press and the opposition had got their man: Galbraith resigned on 8 November 1962, his only fault being to have demonstrated an unduly fastidious sense of *noblesse oblige* to his fawning underling. Accounts differ as to the circumstances of his resignation. Macmillan claims that he accepted Galbraith's 'insistent' offer of resignation with reluctance.[24] But it seems more likely that it was a resignation extracted by the Prime Minister.[25] Forcing Galbraith's resignation, and so sacrificing an honourable man to appease a carnivorous press, would be one of Macmillan's greatest regrets.

And yet Galbraith's resignation, rather than quieting criticism of the government's handling of the Vassall affair, served only to intensify it. The *Sunday Times* of 11 November 1962 accused the government of losing control in the face of 'public clamour'. The result: 'a most unedifying spectacle – of a Junior minister being sacrificed in a premature resignation before he had even the chance to justify his conduct before a committee of enquiry'. The *Observer* of the same date noted that the government had succeeded only in focusing public attention temporarily on 'a minor aspect of a major scandal', while 'the major aspect – the Admiralty's continuing inability to distinguish Russian spies from civil servants' remained at large. The Tory backbenchers blamed senior members of the government for 'botching the affair'. According to *The Times*, Galbraith's resignation caused 'a wave of anger' in Conservative ranks. It was felt that the fiasco had 'overshadowed and detracted' from what was perceived to be a 'significant recovery in form and élan of the Government and Conservative Party'.

On the day of Galbraith's resignation the opposition tabled a censure motion, which read: 'This House regrets the refusal of the Prime Minister, despite widespread and continuing public concern, to set up an independent inquiry into the Vassall case.' On 14 November 1962 Macmillan announced to the Commons that, as a result of what he termed a 'changed situation', he was now of the opinion that the current internal security review that he had instituted was inadequate as an organ of enquiry, and that he was setting up an independent tribunal instead. The circumstances of this changed situation were indeed sensational: that it was apparently being rumoured within the security services that just prior to his arrest Vassall and Galbraith had been planning to 'do a Pontecorvo' — i.e. to defect together to the Soviet Union! But Macmillan's crucial gambit was to ensure that the remit of this tribunal extended beyond simply a review of security procedures to an investigation of the conduct of the press. It was intended to be a masterstroke, to turn the tables on both the press, whose conduct Macmillan found reprehensible, and the opposition.

The tribunal was chaired by Lord Radcliffe, a Law Lord, the man who had drawn the partition between Pakistan and India on independence, and the very essence of probity and eminence. It solemnly sat over a number of months, and much of its time was taken up enquiring into the vast welter of allegations that had spewed out from the newspapers in the weeks after Vassall's conviction. There was a sense at the time that, however objectively the tribunal carried out its tasks, its focus was turning upon the excesses of the tabloids, just as Macmillan had intended. There was ostensible justification for this. If, as it did, a newspaper had posed the question 'Why did the spy catchers fail to notice Vassall, who sometimes wore women's clothing on West End trips?', then the issue of whether Vassall did indeed wear women's clothes had to be investigated. The problem was that such an investigation inevitably required an enquiry into the sources of the various journalists who had made these allegations. And at this three journalists jibbed, though there was dispute as to whether this was on a point of journalistic principle or because there were in fact no sources to reveal. Lord Radcliffe duly sent these journalists over to the Royal Courts of Justice to be committed for contempt of court. There were interesting legal arguments about whether a journalist could be compelled to reveal his sources but here again we find Lord Parker agreeing with the Attorney General that journalists enjoyed no privilege to protect their sources.[26] In the end two of the three journalists were, to the lasting outrage of Fleet Street, sent to prison for six and three months. And it was perceived, at least by Fleet Street, that Macmillan bore the brunt of the responsibility for their incarceration. The martyrdom of Brendan Mulholland and Reg Foster would be avenged.

The report of Lord Radcliffe's tribunal was published on 26 April 1963. With limited exceptions it exculpated those involved in Vassall's training and employment, and found no fault with those who failed to detect him as a spy. Inevitably the press shouted whitewash and, reading the report now, it does appear to be remarkably tender to the powers that be. Galbraith was entirely, and rightly, exonerated. But the press emerged tarnished. Radcliffe summoned a number of journalists to give evidence to the enquiry (all those women's clothes had to be enquired into). According to Bernard Levin, himself a scourge of the English legal establishment and with no obvious animus against his confrères: 'The press witnesses cut, almost without exception, a poor figure, as, one after the other, they turned out to have got most of what they printed by taking previously printed articles and repeating them with embellishments.'[27] So, in his report Radcliffe referred to an article that appeared in the *People* on 4 November 1962 under the headline 'For two years I saw him strutting around Moscow like a dressed-up doll'. The article quoted Mr Stanley Johnson, former Moscow correspondent for Associated Press: 'More than once I saw his face covered in cream. And I shall always remember him strutting about Moscow like a dressed-up doll.' Mr Johnson conceded to the tribunal that his allegation of extravagant dress was based upon seeing Vassall in a woollen hat and an 'excessively long' scarf in preparation for going skating; he did not disagree with Vassall's own account that the cream was probably 'Nivea cream used as a protection in extreme conditions of weather'. And it is the press aspect of the imbroglio that resonates down the decades. The article in the *People* was but one example of a welter of largely invented and unashamedly homophobic reportage which shocks even now. Was the press chastened by the tribunal's findings? Certainly not: rather, to quote Levin again, it was 'resentful at the way in which its less reputable methods, of building a tower of innuendo upon a foundation of rumour and labelling the result a house of fact, had been exposed. There could be little doubt that the man at the Head of the Government which had put them on such public trial would, if he was ever caught in their trap, be shown no mercy.'[28]

Vassall proved an exemplary prisoner. Following in his mother's footsteps, he converted to Catholicism while in prison. Released early in 1972, he changed his name and started work on his autobiography. Written in the seclusion of a monastery, it was published in 1975. The book revealed a man who had still not found adulthood; a man still unable to accept any portion of personal responsibility for his actions. Looking back to the day of his trial Vassall wrote: 'As I stood to plead guilty to four counts under the Official Secrets Act all I wanted to say was that I was not guilty. But how could I in the circumstances? There was not a thing I could do or say. If one is blackmailed into action of this kind, surely one is not acting freely. England had always looked upon blackmail as the most despicable crime. But no one was interested in that defence. It meant nothing in my case.'[29]

In Jeremy's papers there are numerous letters written to him by Vassall in the years after his conviction. It is apparent from the pervasive expressions of gratitude that Jeremy devoted a good deal of time trying to assist Vassall in finding employment after his release. But the mantle of the past weighed heavy on his shoulders and prospective employers proved reluctant. The correspondence shows a man struggling to hold his head high, extracting simple pleasure from books he has read, country walks he has taken, friends who have shown kindness. It also shows a man eschewing self-pity: a contrast with the tone of his book.

Opinion is divided as to the extent of the damage wrought by Vassall's spying activities. Vassall claimed to be a 'pygmy among spies', on the apparent grounds that, as a junior civil servant, he had little access to sensitive material, and also because of a lack of sophistication in technique. It is certainly the case that, for much of his career, for example during his time in Moscow, and while working for Galbraith, he did not have access to classified documents. The work on which he was engaged in Military Branch was also 'of low classification and the Russians found his material of little interest'.[30] It was only on the few occasions that he acted as personal assistant to the head of his section in 1962 that he was able to abstract material of a significant nature, as was shown by the photographic evidence found in his flat. It was Radcliffe's view that had Vassall been a 'more adventurous spy' he could have passed on more secret material than he did. On the other hand, the Russians clearly prized Vassall. General Gribanov, Head of the Second Chief Directorate, the body responsible for internal intelligence operations in the Soviet Union, personally supervised Vassall's recruitment,[31] and he was run in London by Nikolai Borisovich Rodin ('Gregory'), a KBG general and the official 'KGB Resident' in Britain. Chapman Pincher contends that 'the recruitment and running of Vassall was a major triumph for the KGB. He provided information of the highest value to the Soviet defence chiefs in their successful drive to expand and modernize the Red Navy.'[32] Oleg Gordievsky agrees: he contends that, over a period of four years, Vassall handed over 'thousands of highly classified documents on British and NATO naval policy and weapons development'.[33]

John Vassall died in 1996, while travelling on a London bus, a largely forgotten figure.

3

'Society's pound of flesh'

R v Keeler (1963)

A CARTOON BY Cummings appeared in the *Daily Express* on 10
July 1963 headed 'The Adventures of James Macbond'. It
showed the beleaguered figure of Harold Macmillan fleeing from
three assailants. Kim Philby and his fellow spy John Vassall are both
dressed as shady hoodlums, one wielding a knife, the other a pistol,
both aimed at Macmillan. Christine Keeler is the third, incarnated
on the page as a sort of vampiric harpy, her long-nailed hand
outstretched, trying to clutch at the Prime Minister's coat tails.

That year was a kind of horror show for Macmillan, and he was
not to see out 1963 as Prime Minister. His resignation was accepted
by the Queen in October. We have already seen the damage the Blake
and Vassall affairs inflicted on him.[1] Kim Philby, the so-called 'Third
Man', had disappeared from Beirut in January while working as a
journalist for the *Observer* and *Economist*. In May he had reappeared
very publicly in Moscow, dealing another security embarrassment to
the government.

The Profumo affair itself, in which Christine Keeler played the
starring role, came to a head, after festering for months, on 5 June
1963 when the Secretary of State for War, John Profumo, resigned
from the Cabinet, having admitted that he had earlier lied to the
House of Commons about his relationship with Keeler, a twenty-
year-old model. Various participants in the Profumo affair found
themselves in the criminal courts throughout 1963. But the final act
of what was for most of its central players a tragedy took place in
December of that year when Keeler herself was tried at the Old
Bailey on charges of perjury and conspiracy to pervert the course
of justice.

As her counsel, Jeremy provided the swansong to the affair. The story he told the court is the one set out below. It was the first time that an account of Christine Keeler's life had been told without painting her as some version of the caricature of Cummings's cartoon. It is a classic example of how the courtroom can be used to alter and shape the public mood. Until December 1963 Christine Keeler was a figure of either desire or contempt in the public mind. Jeremy's speech, described at the time as one of the greatest ever heard at the Old Bailey, was quoted at length by the press not only in England but the world over. Afterwards she became a figure who at least laid claim to pity and sympathy too.

Christine Keeler was the central figure of the Profumo affair, an axis around whom the destinies of many men were to be disarranged. Her passively feline allure, and her blank face, which seemed to mock the folly of male desire, were captured by photographer Lewis Morley in the famous portrait taken at the height of her notoriety, in which she sits, apparently naked, astride a (fake) Arne Jacobsen chair. It was an allure that was, in different ways, to destroy the lives of a clutch of men, of high and low degree, and alter the course of English political life.

Born in 1942 to an eighteen-year-old mother and a father who soon disappeared, Christine was brought up in dismal circumstances in two converted railway carriages in Wraysbury, Berkshire. In her autobiographies she portrays herself as an ingenuous tomboy, rushing around on bicycles and hauling herself up trees, whose life was irreversibly changed by the onset of puberty, a full chest (in an age that was breast-obsessed) and incessant and unwanted male attentions. She fell pregnant at the age of sixteen to an American GI[2] and, after frantic efforts to self-abort the foetus failed, she gave birth to a premature baby who died at six days. Having gone through a succession of dead-end jobs she then headed for London to re-fashion herself. All vestiges of the provincial ingénue were soon left behind. She found work as a showgirl at Murray's Cabaret Club in Beak Street, Soho. Murray's was an upmarket, if slightly tawdry, hostess club where the banquettes were of red velvet and the girls struck 'poses plastiques' under elaborate headdresses. The clientele seems to have been predominantly made up of middle-aged businessmen.

They were allowed to ogle but not to touch. It was at Murray's that Christine met Stephen Ward, a fashionable, if rather louche, osteopath, whose celebrity client list included Winston Churchill, Nubar Gulbenkian and Ava Gardner, and who had also achieved a certain cachet as a dextrous, if unadventurous, portrait artist.

Ward was a bachelor – a brief early skirmish with matrimony had set him on a path of detachment from any form of exclusive relationship – and thirty years Keeler's senior. He invited her to live – platonically – at his London mews flat. So started a haphazard ménage, the unconventionality of which would have fateful consequences. It was temporarily disrupted by Christine's various forays to live, less platonically, with other men, including Peter Rachman, the notorious acme of slum landlordism.

One of Ward's close friends was Lord Astor, who had let Ward a Thameside cottage, at a peppercorn rent, on his country estate, Cliveden. Ward had a standing invitation to use Cliveden's swimming pool, which he frequently availed himself of in the company of the many attractive young women he invited down to stay with him.

In July 1961 John Profumo and his wife, the actress Valerie Hobson, were invited to a weekend party at Cliveden by Astor. In the course of an after-dinner stroll, Astor's guests – a Fellini-esque assemblage that included the President of Pakistan as well as Osbert Lancaster – encountered Ward and his own demi-monde friends frolicking in the pool. One of Ward's guests that weekend was Christine. The precise sequence of events on that sultry Saturday evening by the pool has been pored over on countless occasions, but what is uncontroversial is that there were pool-side antics during which Christine somehow lost her swimming costume. The naked nymph caught Profumo's eye. On Christine's later account she was then taken on a personal tour round Cliveden by an increasingly libidinous Profumo and eventually took refuge in a suit of armour. Profumo asked for Christine's phone number. Stephen Ward gave it to him.

Also visiting Ward at the cottage that weekend was another friend of his, Yevgeny Ivanov, the assistant naval attaché at the Soviet Embassy and (as it turned out) a Soviet Military Intelligence officer. After swimming races between Profumo and Ivanov on the Sunday afternoon, Christine was driven back to London by Ivanov. Christine subsequently claimed that, after a number of glasses of vodka, they made love at Ward's flat.[3] Some have doubted whether Christine ever had any form of liaison with Ivanov[4] but it was this central motif – the Cabinet minister and the Soviet spy sharing the favours of a young 'model' – that was to dominate public perceptions at the time and create the impetus for the final denouement.

Back in London, Profumo made the inevitable telephone call to Christine. An affair ensued. Most of Profumo and Christine's subsequent encounters took place at Ward's flat, although Christine later conjured up the remarkable image of the two making love in a side street in Profumo's Mini. Christine apparently proved an uninspiring lover – a disappointment corroborated by other partners – and the affair fizzled out after a few months.

Many months later rumours started to circulate in Fleet Street that a Cabinet minister had been sharing a lover with a Russian spy. For the time being the fear of a libel writ cowed editors into silence. Meanwhile Christine was continuing her picaresque erotic progress through London society. With an eclectic taste in men she seems to have discovered a particular penchant for West Indians. During the following year, her brief stint as mistress to a minister of the Crown over, she embarked upon a series of byzantine dealings with various Notting Hill petty criminals. These are delineated in dizzying detail in her autobiographies. Christine flits from one flat to another, either hiding from maddened, axe-wielding beaux, attending Mayfair 'sex parties', or making coffee and running errands for Stephen Ward and various members of his 'spy ring', which, according to her later account, supposedly included Roger Hollis (then head of MI5) and Anthony Blunt.

In the shebeens of Notting Hill two men in particular were vying for Christine's attentions. Aloysius 'Lucky' Gordon was a thirty-year-old sometime jazz singer whose primary occupation appears to have involved hanging out in bars and clubs waiting for the onset of trouble. He had arrived from Jamaica in 1948 and acquired a string of convictions. Contemporary photographs show a ratty, tight-framed man without obvious attractions for the opposite sex. His character was marked by a tendency to violently possessive behaviour towards women. From Christine's later accounts it is difficult to come to a clear conclusion on the nature of their relationship. Gordon appears to have been mesmerized by Christine and obsessively stalked her around London. Had he lived his youth in the twenty-first century he is the kind of man who might have bombarded Christine with text messages, alternating between menacing threats and supplicatory pronouncements of love. But, deprived as he was of the accoutrements of modern stalking, Gordon had to content himself with the time-consuming business of hunting Christine down to her latest flat (it is difficult to keep up with her changes of address at this period) and waiting outside for her to emerge. Christine recounts a chilling episode in which Gordon lures her to his lodgings and then subjects her to a prolonged ordeal of multiple rapes at knife-point.[5] On another occasion he keeps Christine a prisoner in her flat for two days while threatening her with an axe. But, bafflingly, a few weeks later, she then agrees to a prolonged form of 'bed-in' with Lucky at his brother's house in Leytonstone. 'We stayed together in that room for three days and all that time Lucky waited on me as though I were a princess. I was so mixed up inside that I thought that this was the escape that I wanted.'[6]

Needless to say the love-nest broke up and Gordon was soon back terrorizing Christine. She found comfort in the arms of Johnny Edgecombe, another small-time criminal, who vowed to protect her from Gordon. They lived together in a short burst of mutual enthusiasm and, after Gordon had ambushed Christine in another access of jealousy, there was a confrontation between the two men in October 1962 at the Flamingo club (sometimes referred to as the 'All-Nighters') in Wardour Street, Soho. In the mêlée, it appears that Christine's new champion slashed Gordon's face with a knife. The wound required seventeen stitches, which Gordon, fresh from having had them removed at the hospital, later presented to Christine 'with his love'.

Christine's affections were being liberally bestowed and her relationship with Edgecombe soon foundered. On 14 December 1962 he arrived at the door of Ward's flat in Wimpole Mews, where Christine had taken refuge. Mandy Rice-Davies, who was herself staying at the flat, mourning the recent and sudden death of her own quondam lover, the same Peter Rachman who had kept Christine two years earlier, looked out of the window to see an agitated West

Indian waving a pistol and demanding admittance. Christine told Mandy to tell 'the Edge', as he was known, that she had gone to the hairdressers. Edgecombe was not taken in by this story, and, in a jealous rage, fired five bullets at the door and windows, in what Bernard Levin subsequently referred to as 'Sarajevo-like shots'.[7]

His motives remain obscure. It has been said that Edgecombe was overcome by the thought that Christine had taken up once again with Lucky Gordon – or that he had convinced himself that she had given him a venereal disease. If that was so he was wrong on both counts. But it is clear that Christine had, again, cast her intoxicating spell and unwittingly driven a man out of his reason. Ward called the police and Edgecombe was arrested. His trial was fixed for 14 March 1963 and Keeler was to be the prosecution's star witness. The newspapers were agog: a West Indian indiscriminately firing into the dwelling of a society osteopath and artist, in which were holed up a twenty-year-old self-styled 'model' and an eighteen-year-old 'actress' was a story that had all the ingredients of a sensation. And the icing on the cake was that the 'model' was also known to have had a brief affair with a government minister the year before. Once Christine was in the witness box anything she said could be published without fear of a libel action.

Meanwhile Christine was doing her best to stoke the flames of rumour. Flattered by the interest she had aroused, she started telling all and sundry about her various entanglements, not only with Profumo, but also with Ivanov. It was perhaps natural that, in her eagerness to please her audiences, she was prone to exaggerate the depth and range of her attachments. Soon she was claiming that Ward had asked her to tax Profumo on the proposed deployment of nuclear weapons to West Germany, for this to be passed on to Ivanov. In fact this was simply the reheating of a joke told by Ward, who no doubt found the idea of Christine engaging in such post-coital pillow talk with a minister of the Crown ludicrous. But such talk lodged in her auditors' minds and soon the newspapers were buzzing about her, seeking to buy up her story.

As the date for Edgecombe's trial approached, it must have become apparent to Ivanov and his superiors in Moscow that there was a serious risk of his name cropping up during the proceedings in a way that could be profoundly embarrassing. In January 1963 he was recalled to Moscow. In the event he never returned to England – although he maintained a spectral presence throughout the remaining events of that year. As for Christine, she had sold her memoirs to the *Sunday Pictorial*. The article, which was ghosted for her, was never published, but Lord Denning quoted it at length in the report he subsequently wrote about the whole affair.[8] Through the miasma of untruths that Christine was made to utter, three sentences have the ring of authenticity: 'Men are such fools. But I like them. I have always liked them.'

Profumo, Lord Astor and Ward, all fearful of the contents of Christine's story, and the likelihood of being named, were doing their best to suppress publication. There were conversations between Profumo's solicitor and Christine's: a figure of £5,000 was mentioned as the price of her silence. Profumo baulked at such a proposition and tried to persuade the Attorney General to prosecute Christine for blackmail.

But the threat, directed at the *Pictorial*, of multiple libel writs had the desired effect. For the moment Christine's story had been neutered. Yet soon Christine was telling it to the police officers who were dealing with Edgecombe's prosecution. This time the man most prominently in her sights was not Profumo or Ivanov, but Stephen Ward. Ward had been Christine's mentor, confidant and generous landlord. She had been Eliza Doolittle to his Professor Higgins. But he had now alienated Christine in a way that was to have fatal consequences for him. She thought he had cut her loose as she became too hot to handle; she blamed him for the whole Lucky Gordon affair; she held him responsible for the loss of her hefty fee from the *Pictorial*. Now she was happy to regale the police officers who came to remind her of the date of Johnny Edgecombe's trial with tales of Ward's sexual proclivities and his role as a 'procurer of women for gentlemen in high places'. She also recycled once again the silly story of Ward having tried to use her to elicit nuclear secrets from Profumo. Her account was dutifully taken down and passed to the relevant authorities. Nothing was done about Christine's indiscretions. The police were not interested in the alleged sexual misdemeanours of the upper classes and MI5 knew all about Ward's involvement with Ivanov (not least because Ward frequently updated his own MI5 handler about it: when it was discovered that Ward was friendly with Ivanov he had willingly agreed to report back to MI5). Ward may have been a meddler who luxuriated in intrigue, but he was no traitor.[9]

When the day of Edgecombe's trial arrived, the star witness had vanished. It turned out that she had been spirited away to Spain, possibly because it was thought by Christine's de facto manager, Paul Mann, that the value of her story would be diminished if it poured out – free of charge as it were – under cross-examination.[10] The case of the 'missing model' made the headlines, while Johnny Edgecombe was sentenced to seven years for possessing a weapon with intent to endanger life. In Christine's absence he was acquitted of the more serious charge of shooting at her with intent to murder – and of the knife attack on Lucky Gordon at the Flamingo.

It was at this moment that the Labour opposition decided to pursue its advantage under cover of parliamentary privilege. In the evening of 21 March there was a Commons debate on the recent imprisonment of the journalists Mulholland and Foster for their refusal to name their sources to the Vassall tribunal.[11] In the course of that debate Colonel George Wigg MP, implacable enemy of Profumo and scandalmonger extraordinaire, finally brought Christine's affair with the minister into the open:

> There is not an hon. Member in the House, nor a journalist in the Press Gallery, nor do I believe there is a person in the Public Gallery who, in the last few days, has not heard rumour upon rumour involving a member of the Government Front Bench. The Press has got as near as it could – it has shown itself willing to wound but afraid to strike. This all comes about because of the Vassall Tribunal. In actual fact, these great Press lords, these men who control great instruments of public opinion and of power, do not have the guts to discharge the duty that they are now claiming for themselves.
>
> That being the case, I rightly use the Privilege of the House of Commons – that is what it is given to me for – to ask the Home Secretary, who is the senior member of the Government on the Treasury Bench now, to go to the Dispatch Box – he knows that

the rumour to which I refer relates to Miss Christine Keeler and Miss Davies and a shooting by a West Indian – and, on behalf of the Government, categorically deny the truth of these rumours.[12]

Barbara Castle, to her eternal discredit, then stood up and suggested that Christine's disappearance had somehow been orchestrated by 'people in high places'. The innuendo was obvious: Profumo was behind Christine's failure to give evidence at Edgecombe's trial.

The Conservative government felt it now had to act decisively to slay these insinuations. A befuddled Profumo was pulled from his bed and a meeting was urgently convened in the early hours of Friday 22 March. Profumo was bounced by his Cabinet colleagues, including both the Attorney General and the Solicitor General, into drafting an ill-judged, and false (though only Profumo knew that then), denial of any impropriety with Christine. This statement was read by Profumo to the House at eleven o'clock in the morning on that same Friday, with a supportive Macmillan next to him. Journalists in the press gallery described the event as the most highly charged parliamentary moment they could remember. The statement, however eloquently read, reeked of tergiversation.

I last saw Miss Keeler in December 1961, and I have not seen her since. I have no idea where she is now. Any suggestion that I was in any way connected with or responsible for her absence from the trial at the Old Bailey is wholly and completely untrue.

My wife and I first met Miss Keeler at a house party in July 1961, at Cliveden. Among a number of people there was Dr Stephen Ward, whom we already knew slightly, and a Mr Ivanov, who was an attaché at the Russian Embassy.

The only other occasion that my wife or I met Mr Ivanov was for a moment at the official reception for Major Gagarin at the Soviet Embassy.

My wife and I had a standing invitation to visit Dr Ward.

Between July and December 1961, I met Miss Keeler on about half a dozen occasions at Dr Ward's flat, when I called to see him and his friends. Miss Keeler and I were on friendly terms. There was no impropriety whatsoever in my acquaintanceship with Miss Keeler.

That Profumo's legal colleagues actually believed this statement was a source of astonishment to Bernard Levin, writing at the end of the decade: 'One of the more interesting things to emerge from this case, though perhaps not widely enough, is the extraordinary naivety of the legal profession.'[13] Levin saw the whole saga as the vestige of an era that even seven years later seemed irretrievably part of the old world.

In the event, notwithstanding the optimistic verdict of the *Daily Telegraph* that the 'boil has been lanced', Profumo's statement merely inflamed the rumour-mongering. The photographs of 'the missing witness', which now crowded the pages of the newspapers, did not lend full support to the claimed lack of impropriety. Lord Denning's risibly prim later verdict on a particular photo spread of a bikini-clad Christine in the *Daily Express* summed up the views of many at the time: 'On an inner page there were four striking photographs of Christine Keeler from which most people would infer her calling.'

A few days later, having been hunted down in her Spanish fastness by journalists, packs of whom were marauding the Sierra Nevada in her pursuit, Christine purported to support Profumo's story: 'Certainly both he and his wife were friends of mine. But it was a friendship no one can criticize.' The notion of Mr and Mrs Profumo being 'friends' with Christine did not carry immediate plausibility.

Meanwhile the net was slowly closing around Stephen Ward. After George Wigg's intervention in the House of Commons the Labour MP appeared on the BBC's *Panorama* to discuss the supposed (though in fact non-existent) security issues arising out of the affair. Ward was incensed by various errors in Wigg's account of Ivanov's behaviour and arranged to meet Wigg to put him right. On 26 March he had a very public session with Wigg in a tearoom of the House of Commons. Ward was a well-known figure and this meeting must have come to the attention of the government: was Ward, whose flat was of course the principal stage on which Profumo and Christine's liaison had played itself out, spilling the beans to the opposition? It was certainly known that Ward was himself gossiping about the Profumo/Keeler liaison across the dinner tables of London.

The very next day there took place an extraordinary meeting between the Home Secretary, Henry Brooke, the head of MI5, Roger

Hollis, and the Commissioner of the Metropolitan Police. The ostensible purpose of this meeting was to investigate certain poison pen letters that had been sent to Valerie Profumo. But the discussion quickly turned to Stephen Ward. Brooke was interested in establishing whether Ward had committed any offence under the Official Secrets Act. Hollis's view was that he had not. What then appears to have been decided was that the police should embark on an enquiry to establish whether Ward had committed any crime at all. As Geoffrey Robertson has recently demonstrated, it is unconstitutional for a member of government to direct a police investigation.[14]

And so started a concerted and relentless police investigation designed to pin an offence on the hapless Ward. Some 140 witnesses were interviewed (in Christine's case no fewer than twenty-four times); Ward's clients were collared as they arrived at his consulting rooms and asked whether he had ever made lewd suggestions to them; his telephone was bugged; witnesses were threatened to give statements prejudicial to Ward.[15]

It was in the course of this investigation that Lucky Gordon was reintroduced into the picture. Back from her Spanish adventure, and with Edgecombe safely incarcerated, Christine was now living with a friend, Paula Hamilton-Marshall, in Devonshire Street. On the evening of 17 April 1963 Christine had a violent argument with Paula's brother, John. During a scuffle Christine received a black eye and a few bruises. Later that evening Christine's latest boyfriend, Rudolph 'Truello' Fenton, and another friend, Clarence Camacchio, arrived at the flat. They all left after midnight to go dancing. Lurking on the street was the unwelcome figure of Lucky Gordon. He lunged at Christine, half menacing half adoring. She fell to the ground and retreated while Fenton and Camacchio held Gordon back and saw him on his way. Safely back in the flat, Christine decided to phone the police and pin the injuries inflicted on her earlier by John Hamilton-Marshall on Gordon. She had had enough: 'This time he will pay.' Gordon was quickly arrested and charged.

An alternative version of the events of that evening has been put forward by historians of the Profumo affair.[16] It goes like this. At this time Christine was speaking regularly to the two police officers leading the investigation into Ward, Chief Inspector Herbert and

Detective Sergeant Burrows. She was now entirely in the thrall of the pair. When they got to hear about her altercation with John Hamilton-Marshall they suggested that she assist them in framing Lucky Gordon, whom they wanted to deploy in the intended prosecution of Ward. Gordon was informed of Christine's whereabouts and, true to form, later that same evening there he was banging on the door demanding to see the woman he still professed to love. Gordon was let in, made a hullabaloo but no more, and was soon ejected by Fenton and Camacchio. As arranged, Christine then telephoned the police who duly arrived and were told that the injuries inflicted by John Hamilton-Marshall were the handiwork of Gordon. Gordon was arrested and told that, if he could provide evidence against Ward, no charges would be brought against him. Gordon refused to play ball. The price of this non-cooperation was that he was prosecuted for a crime he had not committed, and which the police knew he had not committed.

Jeremy dismisses this theory. Later that year he interviewed Christine at length about the events of that night. Christine made no mention of this elaborate arrangement at a time when she was at risk of incarceration on perjury charges, and it would have been in her interests to cast herself as the puppet of the police. In subsequent accounts she seeks to exculpate herself not by pointing to pressure imposed by Herbert and Burrows, by then both long dead, but by asserting Gordon's own responsibility for some of the injuries she sustained that day.[17]

Stephen Ward's world was crumbling under the assault of the police investigation. His clients and friends were deserting him. Astor asked him to give up the cottage at Cliveden. In his desperation and panic Ward started lashing out, writing to whomever he could think of, trying to get the police dogs called off. If the Home Secretary's intention had been to frighten Ward into shutting up, the plan had misfired horribly. Ward wrote to Harold Wilson, revealing the true facts of Profumo's liaison. Soon the speculation against Profumo, temporarily stifled by his statement to the House of Commons in March, was reaching fever pitch again. Questions were once more raised in Parliament. Wilson took up the matter directly with Macmillan. He demanded to know the full facts. Macmillan sought to appease Wilson's concerns by appointing the Lord Chancellor, Jeremy's old adversary Reginald Manningham-Buller, to conduct an enquiry.

Finally Profumo's nerve broke. On 4 June 1963, some ten weeks after he had personally assured the House of Commons of the propriety of his relations with Christine Keeler, he wrote a letter of resignation to Macmillan in which he admitted his affair with Keeler and that he had misled the House of Commons in his earlier statement. It was Profumo's resignation that now unlocked the sluice gates. All fears of libel actions having evaporated, the press went into a frenzy of false moral indignation. Bernard Levin's theory was that, the Radcliffe tribunal having scotched any idea of establishment corruption in the context of John Vassall's spying, and two journalists having been jailed during its currency for refusing to name their (alleged) sources, Fleet Street had been biding its time, waiting to take its revenge on the 'establishment': 'The pent-up lake of disappointment sought an outlet; deprived of scandal once by the fact that there was no scandal, it seethed and bubbled and waited. When the dam went the second time, with the announcement of Mr Profumo's resignation, the flood-waters poured, unchecked, into the valleys of public life, sweeping everything before them in a great release of joy in the depravity of others.'[18]

Levin recalled the early summer of 1963 as a period of collective insanity, in which, on the evidence of nothing so much as a short affair between a minister and a young woman, Britain fell prey to the delusion that the 'establishment' was in a terminal state of moral decay. This was the period when one could read or hear about the Mayfair sex parties at which, apparently, a Cabinet minister dressed only in a mask and a pinafore waited at table begging to be beaten; when nine High Court judges supposedly attended the same orgy (Macmillan was said to have commented, 'One or two I could understand, but nine?'); when a (presumably different) member of the Cabinet was found under a bush in Richmond Park in a compromising position with a prostitute. It was in this period of madness and vindictiveness that Stephen Ward was charged with knowingly living on the earnings of the prostitution of Christine and Mandy.

Christine herself cashed in. For an unprecedented fee of £23,000, she sold her story to the *News of the World* and became the most famous young woman in England. The fig leaf of a supposed public interest was provided in the shape of her supposed liaison with Ivanov and its alleged implications for national security. These are the words Peter Earle, the chief crime reporter of the *News of the World*, invented for Christine to describe her first (and probably only, if it ever took place at all) encounter with the Russian, on the Sunday evening after the Cliveden weekend: 'Here was my perfect specimen of a man. And he wanted me. He couldn't have stopped now anyway. We crashed through the room. A little table went flying. He pinioned me in a corner by the door. I relaxed. Because he was just kissing me with all the power of a man in a frenzy of passion.'[19] Such was the taste for overheated prose of the newspaper-buying public of the early 1960s.

The insanity spread even to *The Times*, which published its infamous 'It is a Moral Issue' editorial,[20] accusing Macmillan of having debauched the nation. 'Eleven years of Conservative rule have brought the nation psychologically and spiritually to a low ebb.' Of course the sanctimony extended also to the House of Commons. In the notorious debate of Monday, 17 June 1963, the day after Christine's most salacious revelations had been printed, Harold Wilson and his colleagues unleashed a flow of humbug at the government front benches. 'This is a debate without precedent in the annals of this House,' Wilson pontificated. 'It arises from disclosures which have shocked the moral conscience of the nation. There is clear evidence of a sordid underworld network, the extent of which cannot yet be measured.'[21] The next day the newspapers predicted Macmillan's imminent resignation.

The day after Profumo's resignation, on 5 June 1963, Lucky Gordon went on trial charged with the assault on Christine in Devonshire Street. The timing was perfect. Christine arrived each day in a specially hired Rolls-Royce, dressed in 'a simple mauve outfit', and gave evidence against Gordon. *The Times* reports provide an illustration of the chaos of the proceedings. Gordon was originally represented by counsel whose attempts to cross-examine Christine seem to have got nowhere. Gordon then dispensed with his lawyers and represented himself: no doubt the shock of the bogus prosecution made him suspicious of any emanation of the law.

In his confusion Lucky Gordon found a sort of tragic, if misguided, eloquence; he told the judge that 'since I have known Miss Keeler she has caused me extreme provocation, humiliation and indignation and everything that is degrading. Regardless of these things which she has caused me, sir, I have loved her within my heart.' To the delight of the tabloids he demanded that Profumo and Ward, as well as Fenton and Camacchio, be called as witnesses, because they could confirm his story. The police falsely stated that neither witness could be traced. As things got more desperate for Gordon he started accusing Christine of having given him a venereal disease (it will be remembered that Edgecombe had been under the same delusion) and of being a prostitute under the spell of Ward. Christine's response, from the public gallery, was so violent that she was ejected from the court; counsel on her behalf attended the next day to offer her apologies to the judge.

On the back of Christine's evidence Gordon was duly convicted, the jury deliberating for thirteen minutes. He was sentenced to three years in prison. Now both of Christine's principal lovers of the year before were behind bars. This would not however be Gordon's final involvement in the saga.

To round off one of the most eventful weeks in English political and social life, on 8 June Stephen Ward was charged. Ward's trial started on 22 July 1963. Billed even then as the 'trial of the year' it has since been the subject of a vast corpus of critical analysis. Most recently, Geoffrey Robertson has demonstrated the sheer scale of the miscarriage of justice that was perpetrated.[22] But even in 1963 there were some who were appalled by the merciless pursuit of a man who had done nothing obviously wrong except choose to live a life that was out of kilter with received opinion.[23] Needless to say, for the press one of the highlights of the trial was the arrival at the Old Bailey of Christine to give evidence against her old mentor in support of a charge that Stephen Ward had been living off earnings she had made as a prostitute. It must have been an excruciating and humiliating experience for Christine. Crowds of women waited to jeer and taunt her. Rebecca West was an eyewitness to events and captured the scene at the earlier committal proceedings, which was repeated at the trial:

Christine Keeler was every afternoon led out by the police and put in her car, which was covered by a tent of photographers, who climbed on the footboards, the bonnet and the roof. Then they fell away and their place was taken by a mob of women, mostly old or middle-aged, without exception ill-favoured and unkempt, and shabby elderly men. Inside Christine Keeler sat in terrified dignity, her face covered with the pancake make-up which levels the natural toning of the skin, and her determination not to show her fear ironing out her features to the flatness of a mask. The cries and boos of the crowd expressed the purest envy. It was disagreeable to see a number of women candidly confessing that at the end of their lives they bitterly resented not having enjoyed the happiness of being prostitutes; and a number of men in the same situation wishing that they had been able to afford the company of prostitutes.[24]

Ward's counsel, James Burge, had been Jeremy's pupil master and they remained close friends in chambers at Queen Elizabeth Building. An ebullient, kindly man who was well suited to more minor cases[25] he was, in many commentators' view, the wrong man to defend in a case such as Ward's. In fact, according to Jeremy, Burge told Ward that a case of such importance required an experienced silk – but Ward, impressed by Burge's performance at the committal proceedings, insisted that he should conduct the case himself. This was a mistake: Burge was eclipsed by counsel for the Crown, Jeremy's perennial opponent Mervyn Griffith-Jones, a man whose name will figure largely in the chapters below. It has been remarked that Jeremy should obviously have been the man to defend Ward. Had he done so the outcome may well have been very different. Jeremy recalls reading about and hearing of the events of each day in court and feeling increasingly aghast at the way Griffith-Jones was steam-rollering his way to a verdict. This was a case that required to be exposed and denounced as a political prosecution, as an establishment revenge on a man's morality, not brushed aside with a jovial grin. But, as it happened, Jeremy was already engaged in the other *cause célèbre* of the summer of 1963 at the Old Bailey: successfully defending the Italian nuclear physicist Giuseppe Martelli from spying charges.

While Ward's case was coming to court, Lucky Gordon had launched an immediate appeal against his conviction for assaulting

Christine. After his trial John Hamilton-Marshall, Truello Fenton and Clarence Camacchio had all come forward contradicting Christine's account of what had happened that April evening. A lengthy tape recording made by Christine's new 'manager' Robin Drury, with a view to a book being produced about her, had also passed into the hands of the police. It was clear that Christine had perjured herself at Gordon's trial. She was now repeating the same lies during Stephen Ward's trial.

The Court of Appeal actually heard Gordon's appeal while Ward's trial was continuing. The circumstances in which the appeal was allowed attracted adverse comment at the time[26] and over the years have been the subject of a sustained chorus of criticism. The court was presided over by the Lord Chief Justice, Lord Parker, whom, as we have seen, Jeremy regarded as an executive placeman. Parker plainly realized the potential public interest in the case given Christine's profile and its critical relevance to the Ward trial; no sentient being living in England at that time could have been unaware of Ward's trial and the evidence given in it. Yet the court sat early (at 9 a.m.) and disposed of the appeal within eleven minutes. There was no public or full explanation of the basis on which the appeal was allowed, notwithstanding that the court was presented with substantial evidence that showed that Christine had committed perjury a few weeks earlier. Instead the court provided a thin-lipped statement, to be conveyed to the court where Ward was being tried, that if the new evidence had been called 'the jury, to say no more than that, might have had a doubt in the matter. It might well be that the complainant's [i.e. Christine's] evidence was completely truthful. It was not for the court to say.'

But Parker said nothing about what that evidence actually was. Indeed, notwithstanding that he had before him sworn statements from both Hamilton-Marshall and Camacchio as to what had really happened that night, as well as Christine's own confession in the tapes, Lord Parker again went out of his way to confirm that 'the court was not holding that the complainant's evidence was untruthful.' It was this disingenuous flummery that was conveyed to the jury in Ward's trial, then in its penultimate day. It allowed both the judge and Griffith-Jones to tell the jury in honeyed terms that the outcome of the Gordon appeal was entirely irrelevant to the Ward case. Yet even as they said this a report had been passed to the Director of Public Prosecutions recommending that Christine be prosecuted for perjury.

That night, the evening of 31 July 1963, having heard a summing-up from the judge which he rightly interpreted as the prelude to his inevitable conviction, Stephen Ward took an overdose of nembutal. As he lay dying Ward was convicted of living off the immoral earnings of a prostitute. The truth of the matter was that it was Ward who gave Christine and Mandy money and neither was a prostitute in any recognizable sense. Yet the vindictiveness of the newspapers was not satiated by Ward's death. Rather they treated it as the cowardly escape of a degenerate 'whore-master'. And the vitriol poured on Christine by the crowds witnessed by Rebecca West was replicated in print. This was Cassandra's verdict in the *Daily Mirror*: 'From the age of sixteen Keeler was abed with all and sundry. She showed a catholicity of undiscriminating sexual taste that makes all-in wrestling seem like a monastic pursuit. When Stephen Ward was at the end of the lonely, disgraceful road that he has followed, where was his Christine? Right there in the witness box, ratting on him as hard as she could, betraying right and left and grabbing and clutching at every odd thousand pounds she could lay her hands on.'

Gordon himself was obviously a very unhappy man. The day after he was released from prison he issued a writ against Christine for malicious prosecution. And in early September 1963, five weeks after her evidence had helped convict Stephen Ward, Christine was herself charged with perjury and conspiracy to obstruct justice.

At the committal proceedings Gordon now found himself giving evidence for the prosecution, rather than the defence. He explained why he had gone round to the flat in Devonshire Street that April evening: 'She was pregnant and Dr Hughes [a local doctor] got rid of the kid. That is what I went there to prevent. She was sick, you want to know.' Christine denied this. But some other evidence that was given does shine a vivid light on the nature of Christine's life in 1963. On the night of the fight with John Hamilton-Marshall, Christine was expecting Truello Fenton, a married man, to arrive later that evening. Christine was under some kind of unspecified pressure to see Fenton every night in London. After her altercation with John Hamilton-Marshall Christine was terrified of Fenton's jealousy if he learned who was the author of the violence. So she invented for Fenton's benefit a story that she had been hurt in a fight with a girl. From these hints, which emerge from the prosecutor's submissions, and evidence led by the prosecution, one can piece together a picture of Christine's life at this time. If Edgecombe had replaced Gordon then Fenton had, by April 1963, replaced Edgecombe as Christine's controlling lover. She had come a long way from the high-jinks of the Cliveden swimming pool.

Christine's trial was set for 5 December 1963 – the final act in the drama of the Profumo affair. The judge was the Recorder of London, Anthony Hawke, whom Jeremy had succeeded as Recorder of Bath and before whom he had appeared many times. Jeremy considered him the best judge of this period – a man of justice and humanity, a man utterly unlike Mr Justice Marshall, the judge who had condemned Stephen Ward. By now Macmillan had succumbed to the pressure of events and resigned as Prime Minister and the Denning Report into the circumstances of Profumo's conduct – composed in the style of a cheap novelette and perhaps for that reason the most widely read Command Paper ever written – had been published. It was now that Jeremy came on to the scene.

He remembers vividly the day when Christine came to see him in his chambers. 'As she arrived every head in chambers turned. Colleagues of mine peeped their heads round their door as she walked upstairs and through the corridors. Here was the most recognizable face in England at the time and she was at Queen Elizabeth Building.' She was shown to Jeremy's room, lined with books and filled with papers, and sat opposite him. 'This figure of beauty was sitting in my room. What sticks most forcefully in my mind is the disparity between her porcelain, mask-like looks, still undeniably beautiful, and her voice. It was the voice of a person who had lived many years longer than her twenty-one years and who seemed to have grown entirely weary of life. It was a voice which had lost any joy in life.'

What Jeremy discovered in his interviews with Christine was that there was a vast gulf between her public and her private face. She may have been at the centre of a vortex that had seen a Cabinet minister resign, a government rocked, two men jailed and one take his own life, but, in truth, she was a wholly passive party. Events happened to her; she did not instigate them. She was the very opposite of her street-wise former friend Mandy Rice-Davies. Jeremy looks back sardonically on the events of that year. 'The Profumo affair has been painted as one of the first eruptions of the swinging sixties. I saw it as anything but. Christine in the flesh was far removed from Christine astride the famous chair. She was a victim of circumstances and of a kind of unquenchable male desire. The history of the previous two years was one of sleaziness not sexiness.'

It was, however, clear that Christine had not told the truth at Gordon's trial and that there was a battery of witnesses now ready to step into the witness stand to condemn her. Christine had to plead guilty. But Jeremy had a difficult task. How to present the true, private face of Christine; how to cut through the false public face? Whatever was said on her behalf at the trial would be reported across the world and could alter for ever the public perception of her. Jeremy recalls: 'The real difficulty lay in the fact that here was a woman who had brought down a Cabinet minister and come to epitomize a sense of moral decline. I had to somehow rescue her from that reputation and the retribution that some judges might have felt inclined to visit on her.'

In a packed courtroom Jeremy finally gave voice to a version of the true Christine. It was a speech described by many at the time as one of the most brilliant, and one of the longest, ever heard at the Bailey. According to the *Daily Mail*, 'in 150 minutes of legal drama the whole sordid story of her life and loves was retold.' But the portrait to be painted was not of the femme fatale who, as the *Daily Sketch* put it, had left a 'trail of ruin across Whitehall and the West End' but of a girl who had grown up in poverty, who had lost a child at sixteen, and who had, in her short period of near-adult life, become the plaything of assorted men.

Delivering an effective plea in mitigation is one of the key skills of any criminal barrister. It is that speech which will often determine the sentence that is imposed by the judge. There is no duty to emphasize points that stand against one's client. But the barrister cannot tell untruths about his client or their offence. The key is to

On holiday at Eleanor House, West Wittering, 1919. From left: Mary Hutchinson, Barbara (aged eight), T.S. Eliot, Jeremy (aged four), St John Hutchinson, Osbert and Sacheverell Sitwell.

Mary Hutchinson, muse to Bloomsbury. Lytton Strachey declared her to be 'the only sympathetic person in London'.

Father and son on holiday in Holland, c.1937. Desmond MacCarthy remembered St John's 'kindness and laughter, his amiable and alert intelligence and his generous response to life'.

At Lasky Ranch, California, on the set of George Cukor's *Susan and God*, 1939.
From left: Aldous Huxley, the actress Constance Collier, Maria Huxley, Jeremy.
Maria wrote of him as being 'an adorable boy . . . I'd like to keep him here forever.'

The jaunty rating, 1940.

Westminster Abbey Division — Parliamentary Election, 1945
Polling Day : THURSDAY, JULY 5th, 1945

Lieut. JEREMY

HUTCHINSON
R.N.V.R.

THE LABOUR CANDIDATE

If you are a Supporter please show this in your Window

Five years later, now a serious
lieutenant and Labour candidate for
the Abbey Division, Westminster.

Peggy Ashcroft, Jeremy's first wife, at Buckingham Palace with their children Eliza and Nick, after receiving her DBE, 1956.

The determined young barrister.

Jeremy with June, his second wife, 1990s. The Boris Anrep mosaic was given to Jeremy's mother by the artist.

George Blake after his arrest, 1961. Jeremy recalled that 'he exuded this great and intense charm'.

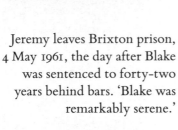

Jeremy leaves Brixton prison, 4 May 1961, the day after Blake was sentenced to forty-two years behind bars. 'Blake was remarkably serene.'

The Attorney General, Sir Reginald Manningham-Buller QC, 1961. Jeremy and he did not see eye to eye.

John Vassall as a young man in the RAF. At his trial for espionage Jeremy described him as 'an untough man . . . possibly more interested in the contemplative side of life rather than the active life.'

Vassall's arrest and conviction led to a media frenzy and claimed the career of a minister. Note the photographs of Christine Keeler and John Profumo carefully juxtaposed, though still unconnected in the public mind.

Hubert Parker, the Lord Chief Justice, who presided over the trials of George Blake and John Vassall. He believed that the courts 'have a positive responsibility to be the handmaiden of administration rather than its governor'.

Harold Macmillan, the beleaguered Prime Minister. Cummings' cartoon in the *Daily Express* of 10 July 1963 shows him being harried by two of Jeremy's clients, John Vassall and Christine Keeler, as well as Kim Philby and the cadaver of Peter Rachman.

"It's all very well Maudling talking about youth, but I happen to be taking part in an X-certificate film..."

Christine Keeler arrives at the Old Bailey, 1963.

Christine's nemesis, Aloysius 'Lucky' Gordon, strikes a relaxed pose outside court on the first day of his trial, 6 June 1963.

'As if on his way to his own martyrdom.' Gerald Gardiner QC is appointed Lord Chancellor, 1964.

The starting pistol of the 1960s is fired. *Lady Chatterley's Lover* goes on sale, November 1960.

The man who 'could make a honeymoon sound obscene'. Senior Treasury Counsel Mervyn Griffith-Jones marches into court. In private he was a warm and affectionate man.

The verdict delivered, members of the jury in *R v Penguin Books Ltd* leave court, having retained their sense of humour.

"*Is anything the matter, Moleskin? You seem so nervous all of a sudden!*"

Osbert Lancaster's Maudie Littlehampton talking to her gamekeeper. Never has a case provided better copy for cartoonists.

Ralph Gold reads *Fanny Hill*, February 1964. The magistrate ruled that it was obscene after considering his verdict for two and a half minutes.

The counter-culture arrives. Margaret Drabble gave evidence in defence of *The Mouth and Oral Sex* at the trial in 1971: 'I found it readable, entertaining and well written, although not a very serious medical work.'

place an interpretation on behaviour and an account of a life that explains the defendant's criminal conduct. Often the reality of a person's life is occluded by the desire to place their criminality in the best possible light. But the picture presented by Jeremy did have a fundamental truth.

The first step was to establish Christine's clear acceptance of guilt. 'The first thing my client said to me when I first met her was: "I have done wrong and I know I must face it."' But what was the level of that guilt? In truth, Jeremy explained, it was minimal. Gordon may have been wrongly convicted but he was on a more fundamental level guilty. In fact the real story of Christine's life over the last two years was not her affair with Profumo – which amounted to no more than a brief flickering episode of wordless and loveless sexual encounters – but the abuse she had suffered from Gordon and Edgecombe, and the fear that they had instilled in her. This was the dismal reality of her case. There had been precious little glamour in Christine's London life, and the hate-filled envy of the crowds who taunted her as she arrived at the Old Bailey was undeserved.

Jeremy then dealt with the massed ranks of the moralists demanding that Christine be made an example of. 'There are people, and wicked people, who want to see this young woman – let me say it quite simply – sent away. I know Your Lordship will take that into consideration when deciding what the proper course is.' Jeremy explains: 'There was this prevailing sense at the time that somehow Profumo's downfall was Christine's fault. Nobody seemed to take any account of the fact that she had barely left childhood. I wanted to confront all the self-righteous humbugs.' Hence his subsequent point: 'Nowadays many children seem to think that sexual experience can be equated with maturity, but, as Your Lordship knows from sitting in this court, that is untrue. This girl may be experienced in matters of sex but she remains exceptionally immature about what happens in the real world outside.'

Next Jeremy had to deal with Stephen Ward. This was an uncomfortable moment.

> Dr Ward was on his own admission a man without morals. What he
> lacked in morals he made up for in charm. He had great artistic flair
> and won his way into a snob world of power and privilege, taking

with him young girls. Miss Keeler was one of them, whom he groomed and fashioned – rather a sort of perverted Professor Higgins. She went with him and learned his outlook, was educated by him in the ways of life. By the time she was seventeen Ward had introduced her to Peter Rachman and she became his mistress. For three years she lived in a completely dream-like world.

In his book on Stephen Ward's trial, published early in 1964, Ludovic Kennedy commented adversely on what Jeremy had said about Ward. 'The voice was Mr Hutchinson's but the words might have been those of Mr Griffith-Jones. Yet, only a few months earlier Mr James Burge, Mr Hutchinson's friend and colleague in chambers, had stood in the same building and said the opposite. "Ward did *not* introduce her to Rachman: they met entirely by accident . . . Ward did *not* introduce her to drugs, which he strongly disapproved of . . ." One cannot blame Mr Hutchinson for he had a client to defend and he was following instructions. But let no one pretend that our system of justice is a search for truth.'[27] Richard Davenport-Hines has recently repeated the criticism of Jeremy's speech for recycling the false image of Stephen Ward that had been peddled by Lord Denning in his report – that of a lascivious Svengali: Christine's 'counsel's rhetoric might have been taken from Denning'.[28] But this is to misunderstand the advocate's task. Jeremy responds: 'I took no pleasure in the spectacle of Ward's trial and remain convinced that Ward's conviction was a travesty of justice. But in presenting Christine's case I owed a duty first and foremost to her and a duty to follow her instructions.'

And what of Christine, the ostensible sexual predator? 'I do not want to say anything about her character and make-up. If I say anything in her favour it will only be looked upon as some form of sentiment. I say only this. With everybody who has met her it is perfectly clear that her straightforward and curiously naive outlook contrasts very, very strongly with the public image which she seems to have created.'

And so to a conclusion.

Your Lordship now comes to write the last scene of the last chapter in this long saga which has been called the Keeler affair. Ward is dead. Profumo is disgraced. And now, I know, Your Lordship will resist the temptation for what I might call society's pound of flesh. I ask you to take in this case a course which will bring this long public and private struggle to a quiet and dignified and unemotional end, and not do anything which will exacerbate and aggravate even further the problem of the future. I leave her in the hands of the court and the last words I wish to say in this case are not my words but the words of Lord Denning. 'Let no one judge her too harshly: she was not yet 21 and since the age of 16 she was enmeshed in a net of wickedness.'[29]

With that Jeremy sat down.

Keeler told friends that she thought she would get two years. Instead she received a comparatively light sentence of nine months' imprisonment. She heard her sentence impassively and showed no emotion as she was led down to the cells. Her former friends at the *News of the World*, who had paraded her story to the nation Sunday after Sunday in June, were in the minority in not being moved by Jeremy's plea. In an extraordinarily cruel form of 'open letter' to her headed 'Goodbye Christine, it's the End of the Affair', Peter Earle wrote: 'No – we never thought you would cry. Because we always knew you saw yourself as the irresistible kiss-of-death *femme fatale*.' Malice aside, this is a complete misunderstanding of Christine.

In her later autobiographies Christine writes of going to prison as a form of relief. It is notable that, unlike his other clients who wrote later accounts of their trials (and many did), in each of her autobiographies – Christine has now written four – Jeremy is not mentioned at all. Whereas Jeremy made a point of keeping in contact with his former clients, once the doors of Holloway clanged shut behind her he never heard from her again. Having served six months of her nine-month sentence she was released into a new world of which she had been a partial progenitor. Her life thereafter has been, by all accounts, a troubled one.

The affair blighted other lives. John Profumo retired from public life and lived the rest of his long life working as a volunteer at Toynbee Hall, in what was regarded as a form of expiation for his conduct (Jeremy met him often there; they never talked about the events of 1963). Lord Astor died of a heart attack in 1966, shunned by his former friends for his part in the affair and broken in spirit.

Finally there was Jeremy's old friend Jimmy Burge, who would be known for the rest of his life as the man who defended Stephen Ward. Jeremy remembers that the case haunted him for years afterwards. Some element of the Pickwickian ebullience had gone.

The one person who now emerges as a kind of counter-cultural hero of the Profumo affair is Stephen Ward. He was sympathetically played by John Hurt in the film *Scandal* in 1989. In Richard Davenport-Hines's definitive account of the affair Ward emerges, for all his sexual idiosyncrasies, as the only truly sympathetic figure. His rehabilitation was confirmed when a musical of his life, written by Andrew Lloyd Webber, was staged in London in 2013.

As for Jeremy, within days of Christine's imprisonment his clerk had received a call from the solicitor acting for the former Viscount Hailsham, now plain Quintin Hogg. As Macmillan's supposed anointed successor, Hogg had been a prominent leadership contender for the Conservative Party at the Blackpool conference in October. In order to strengthen his prospects he had promised to renounce his peerage; he would be adopted as the Conservative candidate in the Marylebone by-election that eventually took place in December 1963. However his standing in the party had suffered earlier that year and in the end his challenge for the leadership faltered.

A last-minute 'Stop Quintin' campaign saw Alec Douglas-Home instead emerge as Macmillan's successor. Hogg had been the chief Pharisee within the Conservative Party denouncing the conduct of Profumo, his former Cabinet colleague. In a notorious BBC interview at the height of the midsummer madness he had accused Profumo of having 'lied and lied; lied to his family, lied to his friends, lied to his solicitor; lied to the House of Commons'. As for Christine, he intoned that the Conservative Party would not be brought down 'by a woman of easy virtue and a proven liar'. This performance, greeted with amusement or irritation by most who watched, led to one of the great parliamentary put-downs when the Labour MP Reginald Paget said, a few days later, during the 17 June debate: 'From Lord Hailsham we have had a virtuoso performance in the art of kicking a fallen friend in the guts. [Hansard records here an 'Interruption'.] It is easy to compound for sins we are inclined to by damning those we have no mind to. When self-indulgence has reduced a man to the shape of Lord Hailsham, sexual continence involves no more than a sense of the ridiculous. [Interruption.] Yet this is the performance which made the Tory Party say, "Here is our missing leader."'[30] Bernard Levin would devote nearly four pages of his seminal book on the 1960s, *The Pendulum Years*, to this single episode ('His behaviour was, to many, so extraordinary that a rumour was rapidly put about to the effect that he had been drunk').[31]

Yet just a few months later Hogg was seeking out the very same barrister as had acted for the 'woman of easy virtue' in respect of his own legal difficulties.

The backdrop has a certain humour. This was the back end of the period of the 'Liberal Bubble'. After their triumph at the Orpington by-election in 1962, for a dizzy few weeks the Liberals topped the polls, pushing the Tories into third place. At the time the Young Liberals were a radical movement that had energized a stratum of modern youth. One of their principal mantras was the reduction in the voting age from twenty-one to eighteen. The Young Liberals seized on the Marylebone by-election as a choice moment to project their message to the electorate. One of their number was a twenty-year-old service engineer called Roy Grundon. As Hogg emerged victorious from Marylebone Town Hall as his constituency's new MP he was barracked by a number of Young Liberals waving their home-made placards demanding votes for eighteen-year-olds and 'oinking' in chorus. Hogg, a famously bellicose campaigner, tore the placards down and hurled them to the ground. There was further jostling and Grundon later told newspaper reporters that Hogg 'turned round and belted me one. I was utterly amazed.' Having failed to secure an apology Grundon issued a private prosecution for assault against Hogg, who countered by issuing, together with his wife, their own prosecution against Grundon, alleging that in fact it was the Young Liberal who had assaulted them.

Although Hogg had narrowly missed out on the leadership that October he remained, as the Science Minister, a front-runner when Douglas-Home stepped down. This was anticipated to be an event likely to occur in the near future, given that a Labour victory in

1964 seemed inevitable. Jeremy saw it as his duty to Hogg to try to avoid a trial at all costs.

> If Quintin Hogg had been convicted that would have been the end of his prospects for the leadership. I advised him to reach some form of accommodation with Grundon. But Quintin's response to me demonstrated the nature of his character. He was a man of absolute principle; he would bang the table and insist that he would not countenance any form of apology or compensation to Grundon. He was quite prepared to see the matter through to a trial, irrespective of the cost to his reputation. But I knew the magistrate at Marylebone – a Mr Raphael – who would have taken the greatest pleasure in putting Quintin in his place if he could. In the end I arrived at court for the trial and thankfully reached an accommodation whereby both prosecutions were dropped. Quintin remained in Whitehall throughout, ready to come down if the trial fought.

So ended Hogg's run-in with the Young Liberals.

Jeremy notes the irony that within the space of a month he had acted as counsel for both Christine Keeler and her principal Conservative condemner. But both had played their parts in an extraordinary moral drama, which hastened the demise of an older, more deferential England. Jeremy looks back on the events of that year:

> Although I am not sure there was any actual evidential basis for it (certainly I never attended any orgies!) what emerged from the various trials which took place and the rumours that were rampant was a sense that the ruling class was degenerate and decaying. A class which had been looked up to was apparently revealed as having no moral compass. And it all happened at the end of the administration of a man who seemed to represent a long distant past. Wilson came into power as a man who was going to clean the Augean stables and usher in a new classless society. And I felt that after 1963 there was a real sense that the old deference which had been an intrinsic part of life had gone.

PART II

Is This a Book That You Would Even Wish Your Wife or Your Servant to Read?

4

'Virtuous and puritanical'

R v Penguin Books Ltd (1960)

OF THE MANY obscenity cases which Jeremy defended, the most celebrated is *R v Penguin Books Ltd*. The prosecution of Penguin for the publication of D.H. Lawrence's novel *Lady Chatterley's Lover* attracted vast publicity at the time, and remains perhaps the most famous English trial of the twentieth century. Indeed, as a set-piece courtroom drama, with its explicit sexual references and 'four-letter' words, a cast list of distinguished writers, clerics and literary scholars, and its thinly disguised class antagonisms, it could hardly be surpassed.

Penguin's acquittal is rightly considered as a milestone in the history of the freedom of literary expression. But the trial's significance goes beyond its immediate compass and it now stands as a watershed moment dividing two worlds: the repressive past and the liberal future. No doubt the truth is a lot more nuanced; but in the public imagination, as best exemplified by Philip Larkin in his poem 'Annus Mirabilis', the ending of the *Chatterley* 'ban' signalled the beginning of the discovery of sex.

The fact that the trial took place at the threshold of the 1960s has helped it acquire its status as the first shot fired in the cultural revolution that transformed Britain in the decade that followed. But it is a fact, not just a convenient reshaping of history, that the 1950s was a period that had seen a concerted effort by the authorities to crack down on literary 'obscenity' and curtail sexual freedom. In 1954 alone, five avowedly 'literary' novels had been prosecuted for obscenity[1] and the decade was marred by the so-called 'Lavender Scare', which saw a spate of vindictive prosecutions against homosexuals.[2] From a distance of more than fifty years, the centrality of the *Lady Chatterley* trial to the shaping of a new public consciousness remains clear.

Lawrence wrote *Lady Chatterley's Lover* in three complete consecutive drafts, between October 1926 and January 1928, while living at the Villa Mirenda, near Florence. Lawrence was forty-two when he completed the novel and suffering from tuberculosis, the disease that killed him two years later. The novel is set contemporaneously, at Wragby Hall, the home of Sir Clifford and Lady (Constance) Chatterley, in the mining country of the East Midlands. Sir Clifford is paralysed, and impotent, as a result of injuries sustained in the recent war. Connie is lonely, and increasingly detached from her husband. She embarks on an affair with Sir Clifford's gamekeeper, Mellors, for whom she eventually leaves her husband.

Scholars broadly agree on the status of *Lady Chatterley's Lover* in the Lawrence canon: it is not the novelist's finest work, but it contains some of his most beautiful writing, and its themes and subject matter inform a general appreciation of his work. Of these, two are of particular significance in relation to the subsequent trial. The first is Lawrence's treatment of Connie and Mellors's sexual relationship, which he describes in explicit and reverential detail. The second is Mellors's use of what were then (and are sometimes now) considered obscene words, to describe his and Connie's sexual organs and activity.

Lawrence considered his novel 'beautiful and tender and frail as the naked self'. It was his own favourite work. Of the sex scenes, Lawrence explained: 'I always labour at the same thing to make the sex relation valid and precious, instead of shameful. And this is the furthest I've gone.' He justified his copious use of words considered obscene as being an attempt to 'purify the ancient language of sex'.

Lawrence failed in his attempts to find an English publisher for *Chatterley*. As the law of obscenity then stood, publication would have led to almost certain, and almost certainly successful, prosecution. Instead, Lawrence published the novel in Italy, as a private venture with the assistance of a Florentine friend and bookseller, Giuseppe Orioli. Copies were available by subscription only. A thousand were printed. Lawrence personally chose the paper and binding, and drew the image of the phoenix that was printed on the front cover and was later adopted by Penguin.

The novel was ruthlessly pirated. Five unauthorized editions had appeared by March 1929. In an attempt to forestall them, Lawrence agreed to the publication of a cheap paperback edition by the Paris publisher Edward Titus, copies of which found their way to England with apparent ease. Over the years, magistrates courts periodically convicted booksellers in England for handling the novel: for instance, in 1955 a prison sentence of two months was imposed on one hapless retailer. It was a feature of the subsequent trial that the thirty-five witnesses who gave evidence for Penguin had all read the novel in its unexpurgated form without difficulty of access. This led Colin MacInnes to suggest that the trial was redundant: anyone who wanted to, and was clever enough to appreciate it, could already obtain *Chatterley* in England.

Lawrence considered, but rejected, authorizing an expurgated version of the novel. Bowdlerization was impossible, he concluded: 'I might as well try to clip my own nose into shape with scissors, the book bleeds.' Nevertheless, in 1932, two years after the novelist's death, an expurgated version of the novel was approved by his widow Frieda and published in Britain and the US. It is certain that Lawrence would have disapproved of this mutilated version of his work, a point made by several witnesses at the trial.

The *Bookseller* of 9 January 1960 carried the following full-page advertisement: 'To mark the thirtieth anniversary of the death of D.H. Lawrence Penguin will publish in June 1960 a further group of seven books including the unexpurgated *Lady Chatterley's Lover.*' Although Penguin had published many of Lawrence's other novels in inexpensive paperback editions, there had been no previous attempt to publish the unexpurgated *Chatterley* in Britain. In giving evidence at the trial, Sir William Emrys Williams, Penguin's editor-in-chief, explained its reasons for choosing to do so then. Not only was 1960 the thirtieth anniversary of Lawrence's death, it was also the twenty-fifth anniversary of the founding of Penguin Books. Lawrence was a Penguin author. In Williams's words: 'we were hoping to attain a summit of achievement, and we thought the most appropriate unpublished novel which should appear in the jubilee year was *Chatterley.*'

Other factors had been important. The first was the publication of an unexpurgated edition in the US the previous year. The decision to ban the novel at first instance was overturned by Federal

Judge Frederick Bryan. In his reasons – which are relevant to the subsequent English proceedings – Judge Bryan referred to the undoubted literary merit of the book: 'a significant work of a distinguished English novelist'. As for the candid sex scenes and 'four-letter words': while these might shock a sensitive-minded reader, they were justified as 'relevant to the plot and to the development of the characters and their lives as Lawrence unfolds them'. Bryan distinguished between a work of literature, such as this, and a work of pornography where 'dirt is for dirt's sake'. In conclusion, a ban on *Chatterley* on grounds of obscenity would 'fashion a rule which could be applied to a substantial portion of the classics of our literature. Such a rule would be inimical to a free society.'

Of the reasons given by Williams for publication, the most significant was the passing into law on 29 August 1959 of the Obscene Publications Act. The impetus for a reform of the law of obscenity had gathered momentum after a spate of obscenity prosecutions directed at literary works in the mid-1950s, instigated by a succession of socially conservative home secretaries. The initiative was taken by the Society of Authors, under Sir Alan Herbert. Norman St John-Stevas (who would later serve as a notably 'wet' minister for the arts in the first Thatcher government) drafted the proposed bill, which was introduced to the House of Commons by Roy Jenkins, and passed after considerable delay and amendment. The purpose of the Act, as defined in its preamble, was more clearly to distinguish, in considering an obscene work, between literature and pornography, so that the law concerning pornography was strengthened, and literature better protected.

The 1959 Act represented a significant remodelling of the law. Of the changes it wrought, three were of particular importance. First, whereas previously the prosecution could rely on individual passages of the work as evidence of obscenity, shorn of its context, now the book must be considered 'as a whole'. Second, prior to the Act, the test for obscenity was whether the work had a tendency to deprave and corrupt those whose minds were 'open' to such immoral influences (a hypothetical fourteen-year-old schoolgirl being a favourite example), regardless of the likelihood of such persons actually reading it; now it must be proved to deprave and corrupt only those persons who were *likely* to read it. The last change of significance was the most profound in its effects on the subsequent trial. In cases where a prime facie case of obscenity was made out, nonetheless a defence was now available that publication was justified 'as being for the public good on the ground that it is in the interests of science, literature, art or learning, or of other objects of general concern'. Further, expert evidence could now be deployed by both the defence and the prosecution to support, or contradict, such a 'public good' defence.

On 10 March 1960 Penguin's solicitor, Michael Rubinstein, commenting on a proof of *Chatterley* that had been sent to him for his opinion, advised that he considered a prosecution under the new Act 'possible, if unlikely'. After all, was it really likely that a novel by D.H. Lawrence could be prosecuted under an Act whose avowed purpose was to 'afford protection to literature'? Rubinstein no doubt also drew comfort from the fact that Weidenfeld & Nicolson had not been prosecuted for their recent publication of Nabokov's *Lolita*. Penguin's printers Hazell, Watson & Viney were less sanguine. On 11 April 1960 they informed Penguin that they were not prepared to print the 200,000 copies ordered by the company. Several printers subsequently approached by the company also declined. Penguin was rescued by Sir Isaac Pitman, who offered the services of his subsidiary firm Western Printing Services. Publication, originally planned for June 1960, was delayed until August.

The decision to prosecute Penguin was taken by the Director of Public Prosecutions, Sir Theobald Mathew, the man who had instructed Jeremy in the notorious prosecution of Lord Montagu six years earlier.[3] It was founded, at least in part, on the advice of the Senior Treasury Counsel, Mervyn Griffith-Jones, who had prosecuted – with almost total success – many of the obscenity cases in the 1950s, and later led the case for the prosecution at Penguin's trial. Griffith-Jones had advised the DPP that 'the unexpurgated version of *Lady Chatterley's Lover* . . . is obscene and prosecution for publishing an obscene libel would be justified. Indeed if no action is taken in respect of this publication it will make proceedings against any other novel very difficult.' The decision to prosecute was enthu-siastically endorsed by the Conservative government's Attorney

General, Sir Reginald Manningham-Buller, who, as we have seen, crossed swords with Jeremy on a number of occasions. Having read the first few chapters on the train going down to Southampton en route to a holiday in France, he scribbled a hasty note back to Mathew in London: 'If the remainder of the book is of the same character I have no doubt you were right to start proceedings – and I hope you get a conviction.'

The prosecution proceeded with Penguin's full cooperation. On 16 August 1960 Detective Inspector Monahan of Scotland Yard attended the company offices at Northumberland House, High Holborn, and was handed twelve copies of the novel. This form of technical 'publication' was devised by Penguin to avoid the risk of criminalizing a third party, for example a bookseller. On the following day, Penguin advised the public in a press statement that 'as they must anticipate legal action against them in the immediate future under the Obscene Publications Act 1959, publication of D.H. Lawrence's *Lady Chatterley's Lover*, which was planned for Thursday 25 August, has had to be postponed until further notice.' On Friday 19 August a summons was issued against the company.

Preparation of the defence had started eleven days earlier. At a meeting held at the company offices, solicitor Michael Rubinstein and members of the board met to discuss tactics, choice of counsel and potential witnesses. It was at this early stage of the proceedings that Jeremy was briefed as junior counsel for Penguin. Quite apart from his qualities as a lawyer he was a fitting choice as defence counsel, for several reasons. In 1929 Jeremy's father, St John, had been briefed by the Warren Gallery, which had put on the first English exhibition of Lawrence's paintings. Several of the pictures had been seized by the police as allegedly obscene (the policy having apparently been adopted that if they showed any trace of pubic hair they were deserving of seizure). St John Hutchinson successfully negotiated the return of the pictures against Lawrence's undertaking never to show them again in England.[4] In a letter thanking St John for his work on the case, Lawrence referred to him as the 'St George of the censorship battle'. Aldous and Maria Huxley, who were close friends of Lawrence and had been present at the novelist's death at Vence in 1930, had also been friends of Jeremy's parents. (Jeremy recalls how in 1939, as a young man of twenty-four, he had visited the Huxleys in Los Angeles. They had talked a great deal of Lawrence. Maria had, she told him, herself typed the second, and more explicit, half of the final draft of *Lady Chatterley*, 'to spare the blushes of the printer', as she put it.) Further, Jeremy was connected to the mining country of the East Midlands where Lawrence grew up, and which is the setting for much of his writing. Jeremy's ancestor, the regicide Colonel Hutchinson, had defended Nottingham Castle against the royalist army; his forebears had continued to live in the country around Nottingham and Newark. And Jeremy's father had been a childhood friend of the Sitwells, whose family seat, Renishaw Hall, near Sheffield, was used by Lawrence as a model for Wragby Hall.

Jeremy knew at once the likely significance of the case. For him it would be a career-defining, and career-changing, case. Once briefed, he turned all other work away. The next three months would be dedicated to preparing the defence. The first question was, what kind of evidence could Penguin deploy? Penguin's case was that the novel was not obscene, but if it was, publication was still justified as being for the public good. As we have seen, the Act permitted expert evidence to justify a publication prime facie obscene as being for the public good 'on the ground that it is in the interests of science, literature, art or learning, or other objects of general concern'. The phrase 'objects of general concern' was not further defined. This was only the second prosecution to be brought under the Act (the first, of *The Ladies' Directory*, a guide to the various services of London prostitutes, was of little practical relevance[5]), so there were no precedents. Jeremy and Rubinstein chose to interpret the phrase elastically. They approached 300 potential witnesses who might testify on behalf of the book's literary or ethical merits. Of these, the majority were approached for their expertise on literature in general, and Lawrence in particular. They included the novelists Aldous Huxley, Graham Greene, E.M. Forster and Iris Murdoch; the poets T.S. Eliot, Stephen Spender and John Betjeman; and the intellectuals and scholars Bertrand Russell, Helen Gardner and Noel Annan. Jeremy knew most of these potential witnesses personally. In support of the 'objects of general concern' limb of the defence, Rubinstein contacted teachers and head-teachers, theologians, senior members of the Church of England and other denominations, politicians, journalists and television presenters, doctors, psychologists and psychotherapists.

Rubinstein developed an appraisal system to determine the suitability of witnesses, based on their letters of response. 'A' was awarded to those considered 'Probably excellent or necessary'; 'B' was 'Probably necessary'. 'D', the lowest grade, was for those 'Not in top category'. Candidates for 'D' grade status included Evelyn Waugh, who, in his reply to Rubinstein, wrote that he considered the novel 'dull, absurd in places and pretentious'; and Robert Graves: 'D.H. Lawrence, even at his purest, is the writer I like least of my contemporaries, and I won't have a book of his on my shelves.' It is no surprise that Waugh and Graves were not troubled further. Others responded more equivocally, and Jeremy was surprised at how many potential witnesses expressed themselves as 'on your side', but were nonetheless strongly against selling the book at 3s 6d.

As Jeremy explains, several factors determined the choice of witnesses. Being an expert, or well known, was not enough. An expert needed to be reliable, and capable of withstanding hostile cross-examination. It was important, Jeremy considered, and so it proved, that the witness was capable of talking in simple terms. The witness should not come across as remote or stuffy. Jeremy thought it as much his job to keep witnesses out of the box as in. Some, like T.S. Eliot, had their own agendas: in his case, to redress the balance of his earlier criticism of Lawrence's art. In the end, Eliot was not called to give evidence. Jeremy felt that the danger of Eliot being confronted with his previous pronouncements on Lawrence was too great; and that, by the time Eliot was due to appear, the previous expert witnesses had done their job. But it is clear from a letter written by Eliot to Jeremy on 24 October, after the trial had started, that he still anticipated being called: 'Forster is now to appear on Friday and you will call me on Monday . . . I should very much like to have another talk with you before I appear.' Jeremy also received a letter from John Betjeman expressing his willingness to be called: 'Of course I am on your side (at whatever price the book was to be sold).' Again, Jeremy eventually decided not to call Betjeman.

Penguin's case was prepared with meticulous care. Rubinstein and

Jeremy met many of the witnesses personally and statements were gone through in detail. Thought was also given to the likely thrust of the prosecution case, and witnesses were advised as to the kinds of question they might be asked. The success of Penguin's anticipation of the prosecution case was obvious during the trial and there were no moments of hesitation or difficulty.

The distinguished criminal advocate Geoffrey Lawrence QC, famous for his recent defence of Dr Bodkin Adams, the Eastbourne GP and alleged serial killer, was briefed to lead Jeremy, but circumstances required him to withdraw shortly before the trial started. His place was belatedly taken by Gerald Gardiner QC. Jeremy was surprised at the decision. Gardiner was an admired civil practitioner, but had little or no experience of criminal trials. He was certainly not accustomed to 'slumming it at the Old Bailey', as Jeremy put it. In looks, and character, Gardiner was exceptional. A Quaker, he had been a pacifist during the war, and went on to be one of the founders of CND and the Howard League. An ascetic figure, Gardiner's only known indulgence, according to Jeremy, was to have his hair cut at the Savoy Hotel. Jeremy describes him as an 'El Greco figure, very tall, with hollow eyes and a pale complexion, and a look of injured innocence'. He entered court 'as if on the way to his own martyrdom'. Jeremy wondered how 'this innocent' would withstand the blandishments and wiles of prosecuting counsel. Would the 'four-letter words' trip off his tongue? In the event, Gardiner's handling of the trial was masterly. According to Jeremy, he 'dominated the court' and gave 'an immaculate performance of jury advocacy'.

The trial began at ten thirty on the morning of Thursday, 20 October 1960 in Court 1 of the Old Bailey. The case was heard by Mr Justice Byrne, a High Court judge of eighteen years' experience, who was shortly to retire. Ominously, Byrne had previously held the position of Senior Treasury Counsel at the Old Bailey, the very position now held by Mervyn Griffith-Jones. A devout Roman Catholic, it was suspected, with good reason, that Byrne would be sympathetic to the prosecution case. A correspondent for the *New Yorker* magazine, who was present in court, described him as a 'compactly-built grey-haired man with a quietly pugnacious expression'. To modern eyes, it is an extraordinary fact that Byrne was joined on the bench by his wife, Lady Byrne, who remained there throughout the trial. Jeremy explains that it was at the time unremarkable for judges to be sometimes accompanied during trials by their wives, or even on occasion a friend, though it is baffling that this judge should want to subject his wife to the salacious material that the trial would inevitably rake over. Perhaps Mr Justice Byrne hoped that no jury would dare acquit in the face of her moral authority. Jeremy remembers Lady Byrne, seated beside her husband with her arms crossed, glaring down at him, a grim and disapproving spectator. A photograph that appeared in the *Evening Standard* at the time shows the judge, his wife beside him, on his way to court to deliver his summing-up on the last day of the trial, both faces seemingly locked in determined grimaces.

The moments before the trial started remain imprinted in Jeremy's mind. He was struck by the extreme irony of the situation. 'Although on that October morning the dock, planted in the very middle of the courtroom, was empty (because only the company had been prosecuted, not its individual directors), the person who was really on trial was D.H. Lawrence. I had an image of Lawrence, slight, pale-skinned and red-bearded, with his sharp darting eyes, sitting alone in that enormous dock, normally reserved for those on trial for the most heinous crimes. And for what? For writing an allegedly pornographic book, with the avowed purpose, in Lawrence's words, of restoring the beauty and sacredness of the physical relation of two people in love.'

The prosecution was led by Mervyn Griffith-Jones, the man who had initially advised on the obscenity of the novel. A product of Eton, Cambridge and the Coldstream Guards, it was widely noted at the time that he seemed the very epitome of the establishment. His dislike of the novel, and personal support for the prosecution, was apparent throughout. *Esquire*'s Sybille Bedford described his voice as 'quivering with thin-lipped scorn'. And the trial was unusual in this way: in the normal case, counsel in a criminal trial are, in a sense, interchangeable, in that they have no strongly held personal views as to the guilt or otherwise of the defendant, other than in their professional capacity of seeking a conviction or acquittal, as the case may be. In England, the traditional role of prosecuting counsel, unlike defence counsel, is simply to present the facts fairly and without emotion. Yet in *Chatterley* the manner in which the prosecution was presented (at least in the person of leading counsel) exuded a stern, deep-seated belief in the obscenity of the novel and the justice of the case for the prosecution, whilst Penguin's legal team were equally strongly motivated by their belief in freedom of literary expression.

As it was a trial of obscenity, Penguin was entitled to have an all-male jury. It waived that right. According to Jeremy, he and Gardiner had agreed that in matters of indecency women tended to be more relaxed and sensible. Two male members of the jury were challenged by the defence. The journalists in the press gallery wondered why those men in particular had been asked to stand down. Jeremy recalls that they 'just looked rather nasty – there was no more science in it than that'. The hope was that they would be replaced by women: and so they were. In its final form, the jury, drawn at random from the public, nameless people about whom nothing was known, was composed of nine men and three women. Observers noted that, of the twelve, five read their oath with some difficulty and hesitation.

It was explained to the jury by Griffith-Jones, in opening the prosecution case, that they were required to answer two separate questions. First: was the novel obscene? If they considered that it was not obscene, then that was the end of the matter, and there should be an acquittal. It was for the prosecution to prove that the novel was obscene, and the jury should consider it so only if they were sure beyond reasonable doubt. If, and only if, the jury considered the novel obscene, they should go on to consider the second question: that is, whether publication was justified for the public good. It was for the defence to prove that, and they were required to do so on the balance of probabilities; in other words, that it was more likely than not that the publication was justified for the public good.

It was noted that the foreman of the jury nodded encouragingly as Griffith-Jones continued his peroration. Perhaps he felt encouraged as he explained that the novel was obscene within the meaning of section 2 of the new Act if it would 'deprave and corrupt persons who are likely, having regard to all relevant circumstances, to read . . . it'. In answering this question, the jury must consider the book as a whole, and not only certain passages within it. The jury was also reminded that their decision must be unanimous. At that time a majority verdict was not permissible.

The prosecution case, as outlined in opening by Griffith-Jones, was that *Lady Chatterley's Lover* was obscene within the meaning of the Act, because it contained passages of detailed sexual activity, and 'four-letter words'. The novel, Griffith-Jones argued, 'sets upon a pedestal promiscuous and adulterous intercourse. It commends . . . sensuality almost as a virtue. It encourages, and indeed even advocates, coarseness and vulgarity of thought and language.' He constantly emphasized the adulterous nature of the affair, the unsaid point being the disapproval of Lady Chatterley, a married woman of high social station, associating with a gamekeeper. Griffith-Jones told the jury, as if the mere fact of repetition might be relevant to the issue of obscenity, that he had counted the 'four-letter words': 'The word "fuck" or "fucking" occurs no less than thirty times . . . "cunt" fourteen times, "balls" thirteen times, "shit" and "arse" six times apiece, "cock" four times, "piss" three times, and so on.'[6] Sybille Bedford, sitting in the press gallery, recorded her shock at the 'deliberate brutality' of Griffith-Jones's speech; not because of the words themselves, but because of the insensitivity of his attack – the approach of the 'bookkeeper'. Several of the phrases used by Griffith-Jones in opening were reused repeatedly during the trial, and acquired an almost emblematic quality. Scenes describing sexual activity were 'purple passages'. Connie's and Mellors's sexual encounters were 'bouts' (bout one, bout two, etc.). The portions of the book not concerned with sex were 'padding'. On the second issue of justification for the public good, Griffith-Jones conceded that Lawrence was a 'well-recognized and indeed great writer'; and that the novel had some literary merit. It was the prosecution's case that such literary merit as the novel possessed did not outweigh its obscenity, so as to justify publication.

Reading Griffith-Jones's opening speech now, it is easy to agree with Jeremy's recollection that he seemed to walk into court entertaining no doubts that the prosecution would succeed. His approach to the case seemed to be built upon the central idea that it was inconceivable that a book so replete with 'four-letter words', so explicit in its description of sexual acts, could be acquitted. Yet his approach to the jury demonstrated a disastrous failure of tact. Here was a jury quite obviously drawn from all walks of life. Nonetheless Griffith-Jones spoke at, rather than to, them as if they were a group of elderly grandees sitting round the dining table at his club. The most infamous instance of this, of course, was when he invited the jury to 'ask yourselves the question when you read it through: would you approve of your young sons, young daughters – because girls can read as well as boys – reading this book? Is it a book that you would even wish your wife or your servants to read?' Jeremy remembers the suppressed smiles that flickered over the faces of the jury members as they listened – and that the foreman's nods became from that moment less encouraging. Griffith-Jones would later report that he realized, even as the words came out of his mouth, what a disastrous rhetorical question it was, though, in the event he learned nothing from that realization. Jeremy also remembers giving the jury a conspiratorial gaze before throwing a sideways glance at Lady Byrne. The message was clear. From that moment the case became one of 'them and us'; a battle between the establishment, as so admirably personified by the ramrod-straight figure of Mervyn Griffith-Jones and the stern Mr Justice and Lady Byrne, and the 'people'.

To be laughed at by a judge or jury is one of the most disconcerting things that can happen to an advocate. But, especially in a case such as this, if the jury once began to think that the prosecution was comic, or absurd, then its prospects of success could be fatally undermined. And yet Griffith-Jones persisted along his chosen furrow. Just a few minutes later we hear him reading to the jury a description of the book as a story of 'phallic tenderness' before saying, as an aside: 'Members of the jury, for those of you who have forgotten your Greek, "phallus" means the image of the man's penis.' This remark raised another smile from the jury: doubtless most had never learned any Greek to forget. Patrician condescension would remain the tone adopted by Griffith-Jones throughout the case.

When Gerald Gardiner QC opened the case for Penguin stridency retreated and gentleness flooded the courtroom. That the novel contained repeated descriptions of sexual intercourse was of course admitted. This was necessary, Gardiner argued, for what Lawrence was trying to say. The importance of a tender and mutually fulfilling sexual relationship between two people in love was a 'natural theme' of the book. Descriptions of successive episodes of lovemaking were necessary both to establish this theme, and also to develop the characterization of Connie and Mellors, and their relationship. The use of 'four-letter words' was Lawrence's attempt to rid them of their 'shameful connotations'. If the description of sex was shocking, this did not mean that it was obscene: 'We are not sitting here as judges of taste.' That this was literature, of the kind specifically protected by the Act, and not pornography, was testified to most convincingly by Penguin's decision to publish it. Penguin's repute as a publisher of outstanding enterprise, decency and taste was the foundation of the defendant's case. Even if, Gardiner argued, the jury found that the novel was obscene, then that obscenity was outweighed by the literary merit of the book, already conceded by the prosecution, and Lawrence's status as one of the greatest novelists of the twentieth century.

The opening statements of prosecution and defence having concluded, the court was required to consider how and where the members of the jury should read the book. The jury room was considered by Mr Justice Byrne as the appropriate place, notwithstanding Gerald Gardiner's submission that the 'hard wooden chairs' provided there were inimical to a comfortable reading of the novel. In the end, the jury were given a special room provided with deep leather armchairs, and read in comfort.

The trial resumed on 27 October 1960. Penguin called thirty-five witnesses. They included nine university academics, thirteen authors, journalists and editors, three publishers and four Anglican churchmen. Of these, twenty-two were examined by Gardiner, and thirteen by Jeremy. Before the trial Gardiner had asked Jeremy which of the witnesses he would like to examine. He replied without hesitation: Richard Hoggart, Roy Jenkins, E.M. Forster and Sir Allen Lane, chairman of Penguin. It was the evidence of these four witnesses, as drawn out by Jeremy's examination-in-chief, that, in their different ways, proved decisive.

The literary experts all spoke to a common theme. This included an assertion of Lawrence's status as a writer, and a defence of his use of graphic sexual description. Graham Hough, Lecturer in English and Fellow of Christ's College, Cambridge, gave evidence that 'the repeated descriptions of sexual scenes' were necessary to show 'the development of Connie Chatterley's awareness of her own nature'. On the subject of obscenity, Hough argued that Lawrence was trying to find a language in which sex could be discussed openly and not irreverently. Helen Gardner, Reader in Renaissance English Literature at Oxford, agreed: 'I think that by the very fact that this word ['fuck'] is used so frequently in the book, with every subsequent use the original shock is diminished, and . . . by the end Lawrence has gone very far within the context of this book to redeem this word from low and vulgar associations.'

The most convincing of the literary experts was Richard Hoggart, Senior Lecturer at Leicester University and author of *The Uses of Literacy*, published three years previously. To C.H. Rolph, who was present in court and later edited the Penguin book of the trial, Hoggart came over as a 'self-composed, determined and unshakeable witness'. Jeremy remembers him as 'small, clear, and the most perfect witness in the case'. Jeremy's examination of Hoggart is a high point of the trial and many consider Hoggart's evidence its turning point. Jeremy wanted Lawrence's 'beautiful prose to ring around the contaminated walls of the Old Bailey', so he read out long passages from the novel, before asking Hoggart to comment on them. 'As I read them out,' Jeremy recalls, 'there was absolute silence in the court. I felt the atmosphere changing as the words went round the courtroom. I found it difficult to control the steadiness of my voice.'[7]

It was during Hoggart's evidence that the idea of Lawrence's puritanism was introduced.

> JEREMY: The book has also been described as little more than vicious indulgence in sex and sensuality. In your view is that a valid description of this novel?
> HOGGART: I think it is invalid on all three counts. It is not in any sense vicious: it is highly virtuous and, if anything, puritanical.
> JUDGE: Did you say 'virtuous and puritanical'?
> [Even on the page, one can hear the judge's barely suppressed astonishment at Hoggart's answer.]
> HOGGART: Yes, My Lord. I think there is no vicious indulgence in sexual activity. The sexual encounters, the parts in which we have

descriptions of sexual life, are all carefully woven into the psychological relationship, the context of the two people, and the natural
flow from this as part of an attempt at explaining their outlet,
either physical or spiritual. The third word of the statement is?

JEREMY: 'Vicious indulgence in sex and sensuality'.

HOGGART: The book obviously includes sensual passages because
they are part of the relationship, but certainly not indulgent and
certainly not vicious. I thought, taken as a whole, it was a moral
book.

JEREMY: We know one of the complaints is that it uses four-letter
words. What exactly do you mean by saying that, taken as a whole,
you think the book is a moral book?

HOGGART: I mean that the overwhelming impression which comes
out to me as a careful reader of it is of the enormous reverence
which must be paid by one human being to another with whom
he is in love, and in particular, the reverence towards one's physical
relationships. Physical relationships are not matters in which we
use one another like animals. A physical relationship which is not
founded in a much closer personal respect is a vicious thing and
this spirit seems to me to pervade *Lady Chatterley* throughout, and
in this it seems to me that it is highly moral and not degrading
of sex.

. . .

JEREMY: It is said that the descriptions of sex that follow have no
variation and no difference except in the place that they take
place. What would you say about that?

HOGGART: I would deny that absolutely. Again it is a gross misreading
of the book. I don't know how many times sexual intercourse
takes place in the book, perhaps eight or ten times; and any good
reading of the book, I don't mean a highbrow's reading, a good
decent person's reading of the book, shows that there is no one
the same as the next; each one is a progression of greater honesty
and greater understanding. If one reads them as being a series of
acts of sexual intercourse, one is doing violence to Lawrence's
whole intention, and not reading what is in the text.

JEREMY: By the time you have reached the end of the book, have
those two persons, in your view, found some true and real contact,
as opposed to all those at the beginning of the book?

HOGGART: Yes, I think the ending of the book has a result which
one can hardly find in literature now. He is able to say things in

the letter he writes at the end, the very last page, 'Now is the time to be chaste, it is so good to be chaste, like a river of cool water in my soul.' This is the writing of a pure man. 'I love the chastity now that it flows between us. It is like fresh water and rain. How can men want wearisomely to philander', that is, to be promiscuous . . . This seems to me a resolution which establishes that the book has moved through a whole cycle.

. . .

JEREMY: In your view is there anything more in this book than, at the end, two people finding a state of satisfactory sexual relationship?

HOGGART: There is not only more in it than that, but one could say – although it sounds paradoxical – one could say the physical side is subordinate. I am sure it was for Lawrence. He said more than once that really he is not interested, not unduly interested, in sexual acts. He is interested in a relationship between people which is in the deepest sense spiritual. This includes a due and proper regard for our sexual and physical side. I believe in this book what he said is, 'I must face this problem head on, even at the risk of having people think that I am obsessed by sex.' But one realizes from this last letter that, between Mellors and Lady Chatterley, there will be periods of extraordinary chasteness; there will be moments of coming together in love which will be all the better because they are not using one another like creatures for enjoyment. It is a kind of sacrament for him.

JEREMY: I want to pass now to the four-letter words. You told the Jury yesterday you were educated at an elementary school. Where was it?

HOGGART: Leeds.

JEREMY: How did you start your life?

HOGGART: I was born into the working class and I was orphaned at the age of eight and brought up by my grandmother.

JEREMY: What is your view as to the genuineness and necessity in this book of the use of these four-letter words in the mouth of Mellors?

HOGGART: They seem to me totally characteristic of many people, and I would like to say not only working-class people, because that would be wrong. They are used, or seem to me to be used, very freely indeed. Far more freely than many of us know. Fifty yards from this Court this morning I heard a man say 'fuck' three times as he passed me. He was speaking to himself and he said 'fuck it, fuck, it, fuck it' as he went past. If you have worked on a building site, as I have, you will find they recur over and over again. The man I heard this morning, and the men on building sites, use the words as words of contempt, and one of the things Lawrence found most worrying was that the word for this impor-tant relationship had become a word of vile abuse. So one would say 'fuck you' to a man, although the thing has totally lost its meaning; it has become simply derision, and in this sense he wanted to re-establish the meaning of it, the proper use of it.

JEREMY: What do you say about the use of these words as they have been used in this book by the writer?

HOGGART: The first effect, when I first read it, was some shock, because they don't go into polite literature normally. Then as one read further on one found the words lost that shock. They were being progressively purified as they were used. We have no word in English for this act which is not either a long abstraction or an evasive euphemism, and we are constantly running away from it, or dissolving into dots, at a passage like that. He wanted us to say, 'This is what one does, in a simple and ordinary way, one fucks', with no sniggering or dirt. I remember when I first read it being shocked; and secondly I thought they are therapeutic, they sterilize themselves, and as I have re-read the book I think in a literary way they work very well. It is we who are wrong here.

When Griffith-Jones rose to cross-examine, he could not conceal his contempt. 'I thought I had lived my life under a misapprehen-sion as to the meaning of the word "puritanical". Will you help me?' Hoggart treated this as a genuine question:

Yes, many people do live their lives under a misapprehension of the meaning of the word 'puritanical'. This is the way in which language decays. In England today and for a long time the word 'puritanical' has been distended to mean somebody who is against anything which is pleasurable, particularly sex. The proper meaning of it, to a literary man or to a linguist, is somebody who belongs to the tradition of British Puritanism generally and the distinguishing feature of that is an intense sense of responsibility for one's conscience. In this sense this book is puritanical.

But there was also class indignation at work here. As he had explained, Hoggart had been born to working-class parents in Leeds. He had gone to an elementary school and had worked on a building site. He now taught at Leicester University. One detects in Griffith-Jones's questioning the sneer of a ruling class irritated that its assumptions are being contradicted. He accused Hoggart of giving lectures ('I would have thought that could be answered without a lecture. We are at the Old Bailey, not at Leicester University'[8]); he hectored Hoggart ('You are not addressing the university at the moment'); he then read out particularly 'purple' passages before demanding, 'Is that puritanical?' The final stage of the questioning ran as follows:

> GRIFFITH-JONES [quoting from page 180 of the novel]: 'Her hands came timorously down his back, to the soft, smallish globes of his buttocks. Beauty! What beauty! A sudden little flame of new awareness went through her. How was it possible, this beauty here, where she had previously only been repelled? The unspeakable beauty to the touch of the warm, living buttocks! The life within life, the sheer warm, potent loveliness. And the strange weight of the balls between his legs! What a mystery! What a strange heavy weight of mystery, that could lie soft and heavy in one's hand! The roots, root of all that is lovely, the primeval root of all full beauty.' Perhaps that is enough. That again, I assume, you say is puritanical?
>
> HOGGART: Puritanical in its reverence.
>
> GRIFFITH-JONES: What! Reverence to the balls? Reverence to the weight of a man's balls? [By this point Griffith-Jones was shouting, on one account actually screaming.]
>
> HOGGART: Indeed yes.

It is difficult to imagine a more extraordinary exchange in Court 1 of the Old Bailey. This was Griffith-Jones's general strategy throughout the trial. Tax a witnesses with a particular 'purple passage' and ask, sarcastically, whether it was good writing, or realistic. It was a tactic that had failed calamitously with Hoggart. Jeremy explains: 'A witness box in a courtroom is a lonely place and none more so than in the Old Bailey. Lies or insincerity will be exposed by a good cross-examination. Hoggart's obvious sincerity emerged triumphant.'

Of the authors, journalists and editors giving evidence, the best known were C. Day Lewis, Rebecca West and E.M. Forster. West argued that the 'story' of the novel, which the prosecution had dismissed as 'padding', was in fact an 'allegory' of 'a culture that had become sterile and unhelpful to man's deepest needs'. She continued: 'The baronet and his impotence are a symbol of the impotent culture of his time; and the love affair with the gamekeeper was a calling, a return of the soul to the more intense life.'

'What joy,' Jeremy recalls, 'to stand up in the Central Court and say, "Call Mr E.M. Forster!"' The jury listened as a list of the author's honorary degrees and publications was read out. When it came to *A Passage to India*, 'their heads turned in unison to the left, taking a fresh look at him.' Forster was the only witness who had known Lawrence personally. He described *Chatterley* as having 'very high literary merit'; and, continuing Hoggart's theme, spoke of Lawrence as a writer in the tradition of Blake and Bunyan, who shared a 'passionate opinion of the world and what it ought to be, but is not'.

The critic Dilys Powell gave evidence that she considered *Chatterley* to be 'an extremely moral book', in which sex is described as 'a basis for a holy life'. Her views were supported by the clerical witnesses. According to John Robinson, Bishop of Woolwich, Lawrence was attempting to 'portray the sex relationship as something essentially sacred' and as akin to an 'act of holy communion'. It was the bishop's view that *Chatterley* was a book Christians ought to read. (Griffith-Jones: 'Bishop, I don't want to be offensive to you, but you are not here to makes speeches.') Norman St John-Stevas, not a priest, but a practising Roman Catholic, agreed. In his view, 'every Catholic priest and every Catholic would profit by reading' the novel.

Jeremy's examination of Sir Allen Lane, founder of Penguin Books, shored up in the jury's minds the idea of the defendant company as an established publisher of unimpeachable reputation. Lane described his reasons for founding the company: to publish good books 'for the price of ten cigarettes', accessible to all. In the years of its life, Penguin had published 3,500 titles, and sold 250 million copies.

The appearance of Roy Jenkins MP had, it was observed, 'an effect out of all proportion to its brevity'. Jenkins had been the chief sponsor of the Obscene Publications Bill in its passage through Parliament. Evidence as to the intention of Parliament in passing a particular piece of legislation is inadmissible in court. Jeremy asked Jenkins only two questions. The first was: 'Are you the author of a number of books?' to which Jenkins replied in the affirmative. Jeremy then referred the witness to the preamble of the Obscene Publications Act, and in particular the words 'To provide for the protection of literature'. 'In your view,' Jeremy asked the witness, 'is this book, *Lady Chatterley's Lover*, literature?' Jenkins replied: 'Yes, it most certainly is. Indeed, if I may add, it did not occur to me in the five years' work I did on the Bill—' The witness was stopped by the judge: 'I really don't think we want to go into that.' C.H. Rolph, who was present in court, described what happened next: '"I'm so sorry, My Lord," said Mr Jenkins, who did not look sorry, and Mr Hutchinson sat down, looking satisfied.' In Rolph's view: 'Evidence had been given – and interrupted just too late – that the whole prosecution ran counter to the intentions of the legislator . . . The "intention of Parliament" had never been so skilfully put before a court.'[9]

The last witness was Bernardine Wall,[10] who was Gerald Gardiner's particular contribution to the evidence in the case. Briefed late in the day, Gardiner had endorsed the cadre of witnesses so carefully assembled by Jeremy and Rubinstein. He made only one suggestion, Jeremy recalls. Rubinstein must find 'a young woman, preferably under twenty-one, very beautiful, who has read the novel and finds it un-shocking'. Jeremy objected: the person described could not possibly pass as an expert. Gardiner replied: 'Find one who's done an English course at university.' Rubinstein found Miss Bernardine Wall, who possessed, to an exemplary degree, the characteristics required of her. She was twenty-one and beautiful; she had been educated at a convent, and had an English degree from Cambridge; and she was writing her first novel. Wall's evidence was that she had not been shocked by the use of 'four-letter words' in the novel because she already knew them. She made a 'deep impression' on the court.

Just prior to the examination of Bernardine Wall, Gardiner gave notice to the court that she would be his last witness. He would not call the 'thirty-six witnesses of the same character' who were waiting outside court. This followed Griffith-Jones's announcement that no evidence would be called for the prosecution, which elicited a 'gasp of surprise' in court. Gardiner explained his decision to call no further evidence on the grounds, first, that the prosecution was calling no evidence of its own, and, second, 'in view of the actual decrease in the amount of cross-examination'.

Of the thirty-five witnesses who gave evidence, only fourteen were cross-examined. As the trial progressed, Griffith-Jones cross-examined less and less. It was clear, from his dialogue with the witnesses he did examine, that he was inadequately prepared. He did not know *Chatterley* well enough. The text did offer opportunities for effective cross-examination, most of which he squandered. A well-prepared advocate should have been able to match the experts quote for quote: Griffith-Jones was unable to do this. Nor, it became apparent, had he considered the likely thrust of Penguin's case; and could not anticipate it. As the trial proceeded, Griffith-Jones's efforts to cross-examine became shorter and shriller. His voice became sneering. When his efforts to unsettle the defence witnesses came to nothing, the barrister was reduced to sarcasm.

The judge then summed up. No one could doubt where his inclinations lay when, having heard the thirty-five experts over the preceding days, he told the jury this: 'In these days the world seems to be full of experts. There is no subject you can think of where there is not to be found an expert who will be able to deal, or says he will be able to deal, with the situation. But the criminal law in this country is based upon the view that a jury takes of the facts and not upon the view that experts may have.' Jeremy gave a mental groan when it became clear that the evidence of the most eminent of the witnesses called by the defence, E.M. Forster, did not even merit a mention by the judge.

On the sixth day of the trial, 2 November 1960, the jury retired to consider its verdict. It is easy, looking back from the safety of the present, to assume that an acquittal was inevitable. But that is not how it struck contemporaries. Julian Symons attended the trial on behalf of the *Sunday Times*. Writing in the immediate aftermath of the verdict, he says that he was sure that the jury would return within half an hour with a guilty verdict. He interpreted Griffith-Jones's decision to stop cross-examining the defence witnesses as the complacency of a man who thought he had it in the bag rather than as a sign of demoralization. And, while the trial was ongoing, both Sylvia Plath and Philip Larkin recorded privately their view that the prosecution was likely to succeed.[11] Gerald Gardiner had similar worries. He was seen pacing the corridors of the Old Bailey vigorously smoking his pipe as he waited for the jury to return. Jeremy was equally nervous. His fear was that there might be a disagreement in the jury room. It only required one sturdy juryman, shocked by the book and unconvinced by the 'high-falutin rubbish' that had been spoken over the last week, to bring about a retrial, for which of course the prosecution would have been far better prepared. But then, two and a half hours later, the jurors returned to the courtroom. There was applause and cheering in the public gallery when the verdict was announced: 'Not Guilty!' The judge, his icy composure undisturbed, expressed his displeasure by refusing, without giving reasons, Gardiner's application for costs on behalf of Penguin. At the end of a trial it is usual for the judge to express his gratitude to the jury for their patience and attention. As he and Lady Byrne left court he merely stared at them.

From a personal point of view, the verdict was a triumph for Jeremy. It was recognized that his work had been key to the result. His examination of Richard Hoggart and Sir Allen Lane were widely remarked upon at the time. It was immediately seen that Hoggart's evidence was decisive. Jeremy still has the letters of congratulation he received in the aftermath. Peter Hall and Leslie Caron, then married, wrote from Stratford: 'A good clean fight well done.' Laurie Lee wrote: 'Congratulations, old boy, for having restored to us briefly, the short sharp vigour of the Anglo-Saxon monosyllable.' Jeremy took silk the next year and his reputation was sealed as the leading criminal barrister of the period.

The result was also a triumph for Penguin. *The Times* of 3 November 1960 reported that 'As soon as the result of the case was known, Sir Allen Lane . . . telephoned to his office to start distribution of the 200,000 copies stored in a warehouse in Harmondsworth.'

Sale of the book was deferred for a week; this was to allow all booksellers the chance to obtain a sufficient supply of copies. The novel was sold under the banner, 'Now you can read it!' The entire print run was sold on the first day of sale, 10 November 1960. By 31 December 1960, 2 million copies had been sold. A further 1.3 million were sold the following year. *Chatterley* brought Penguin, and Lane personally, huge financial reward. This has led some to question their motive in inviting the prosecution. As one critic put it: 'I can see no reason for Sir Allen's knight errantry unless he has a golden fleece in view.' Lane was a businessman, and he would have been aware of the phenomenal sales of *Chatterley* in the United States following the court's decision in the preceding year. But if financial reward was one of Lane's motives in publishing the novel, it does not follow that there were not others. The evidence of the Penguin archive suggests that Lane and his fellow directors acted as much on principle, as for gain.

Not everybody welcomed the verdict. *The Times* concluded its editorial of 3 November 1960: 'There is no appeal against the jury's verdict. But on the grounds of decency, and taste, and even morals, it is still possible to express dissent.' There was criticism of the handling of the prosecution case. In the same editorial, *The Times* averred that the 'parade of witnesses for the defence' could, and by implication should, have been matched by the prosecution 'bishop for bishop, and don for don'. That the prosecution had attempted to obtain expert evidence is evidenced by several letters of refusal from those approached, including individuals such as Noel Annan and Helen Gardner, who instead gave evidence for Penguin. In fact the recently opened records reveal an increasingly desperate search for witnesses who would speak for the prosecution (including a suggestion that Rudyard Kipling be approached[12]), contradicting the DPP's public explanation that the questions of whether the book was obscene and whether publication was justified were matters for the jury, on which expert evidence could not assist.[13] Notwithstanding the judge's direction, the absence of expert evidence was a mortal blow to the prosecution case. A jury member would have been entitled to conclude, and no doubt did, that a prosecution without evidence, in contrast to a defence with a superfluity of it, was of little merit.

That the prosecution had difficulties in obtaining expert evidence is testament, not merely to the inadequacy of their methods, but to the fundamental misconception of the prosecution itself. The purpose of the Act, as set out in its preamble, was to distinguish between literature and pornography, and to protect the former. *Chatterley* was precisely the kind of book that the Act was designed to safeguard. No doubt there were many bishops and dons who disliked the novel, and even those who considered it obscene; but few would have been foolhardy enough to challenge Lawrence's literary status. Moreover, as was referred to by Penguin during the trial, the novel in its unexpurgated form was generally available in the English-speaking world. It was a ridiculous situation that the only country in which it was not available was the author's own.

The example of the US, and the decision of Judge Bryan, should have been enough to deter prosecution. In March 1960, two months prior to Penguin's announcement of their intention to publish, the Second Circuit Court of Appeals in New York unanimously upheld Judge Bryan's decision of first instance. Chief Justice Charles Clark stated that Lawrence 'writes with power and indeed with moving tenderness which is compelling, once our age-long inhibitions against sex revelations have been passed'. The English *Chatterley* trial has been contrasted unfavourably with its American counterpart. Indeed it is difficult not to compare the judgements of the US courts, which present as a model of enlightenment, with the judicial pronouncements of Mr Justice Byrne. Byrne's summing-up to the jury, if not actually biased, left no doubt in the mind of the listener as to whose side the judge was on. There is little doubt that, absent a jury, Byrne would have convicted.

Charles Rebar, lawyer for the book's American publisher, Grove, in the US proceedings, has gone further. He criticizes the conduct of the defence in the English proceedings, which he describes as a 'caricature'. In Rebar's view, Penguin's witnesses were not 'experts' so much as 'lobbyists', who were 'not so much offering evidence as putting prestige into the claim that the book was innocent'. Rebar's claim that the defence was grounded on 'weight of numbers' is, at least, partly true. The quantity of witnesses called, and the symmetry of their evidence, must have had an overwhelming effect on the jury.

Technically, as Mr Justice Byrne advised the jury, the question of public good was a matter for them: they should give weight to the expert evidence put before them only as they thought fit. But how could an ordinary juror, of no particular literary training or expertise, realistically come to a conclusion different from the view expressed by thirty-five of the country's intellectual elite – with thirty-six more ready to support in the wings? To this extent, the jury was relieved, or deprived, of a crucial aspect of their decision-making function.

Rebar's criticism is unfair. Penguin, and its lawyers, had one purpose: to secure an acquittal. Penguin was entitled to call as many witnesses as it could, with the purpose of building as strong a case as possible. That it was able to muster so many witnesses, who together represented Britain's leading intellects, is a consequence of the idiocy of the decision to prosecute. If the evidence of the defence witnesses was overwhelming, this was, at least to some extent, the fault of the prosecution, who brought no evidence, and cross-examined ineffectively.

To describe, as some have done, the evidence given by the defence as 'cant' or 'humbug' is also unfair. There is no question as to the sincerity of the testimony. One could be forgiven, on reading a transcript of the trial, for concluding that one or two of the experts had read a different version of *Chatterley* from that commonly available. Sometimes, one might even think that the experts had read a literary critique of the novel, rather than the novel itself. The uniformity of the evidence given is also startling. But again, this is not a criticism of the defence. Rather it is testament to the fastidiousness with which the defence case was prepared.

The most sensational critique of the prosecution's handling of the case came from John Sparrow, Warden of All Souls College, in an article published in *Encounter* magazine in February 1962, entitled 'An Undisclosed Element in the Case'. The title refers to the seventh episode of sexual activity between Connie and Mellors, which Lawrence describes as 'a night of sensual passion'. Sparrow argues that the sexual act described on this occasion was anal intercourse. Scholars now agree that this is what is described. Indeed the passage lends itself to no other explanation.

Sparrow implicitly charges the defence team with duplicity in their presentation of the case. Since the meaning of the passage must have been apparent to them, he argues, it was wrong for defence counsel to argue, as they did, that the novel contained no 'perversion' (as this act would have been considered at the time). Further, Sparrow argued, the defence's claim that the graphic descriptions of sexual activity were necessary to further Lawrence's purpose of encouraging frank and open sexual relations was disingenuous. Lawrence's description of the sexual act in 'the night of sensual passion' is anything but frank and open. Instead, Lawrence proceeds here by veiled allusion and insinuation, laying down clues, some of which are found elsewhere in the novel.

Jeremy was fully alive to the meaning of the passage, and raised it as a potential stumbling block at a pre-trial conference with Gerald Gardiner and Penguin's principal witnesses, Graham Hough and Helen Gardner. They all three dismissed Jeremy's fears as unfounded. Did they perhaps see this as a typical view of a criminal practitioner at the Old Bailey's 'dirty mind'? While this might lead one to question how well these three key protagonists for the defence understood the novel, the important thing, as Jeremy put it, was that Griffith-Jones 'didn't twig it'. This point did not go unnoticed by others. Harold Nicolson was approached as a potential defence witness. In a letter to Jeremy he wrote:

> I thought at one time that I might be prepared to say that I was certain that Lawrence did not intend the book to be pornographic, but wished to write a lyrical essay on normal sex relationships. On reading it again, however, I realise that Lady Chatterley's relations with the gamekeeper were not any more normal than those which he had imposed upon his unfortunate wife. Rubinstein failed to notice this point and was rather shocked when I mentioned it. But I imagine that those whom the Attorney General has chosen to brief him will have caught on to the point, and that in cross-examination I should have to admit that the sexual relations between the hero and heroine were not in the least normal, and to that extent the book was 'liable to corrupt' within the meaning of the Act.

Nicolson was not called as a witness. But the cross-examination anticipated by him, and which Jeremy remained nervous of throughout the trial, never came.

Sparrow argues that the verdict might have been different, if Griffith-Jones had properly 'twigged' it. The 'night of sensual passion', as properly interpreted, provided almost boundless opportunity for cross-examination. Griffith-Jones squandered all such opportunities. His only reference to the scene was in his closing speech, when he quoted from the passage, and commented: 'Not very easy, sometimes, not very easy, you know, to know what in fact he is driving at in that passage.' According to C.H. Rolph: 'This unexpected and totally unheralded innuendo visibly shocked some members of the Jury.'[14] It is not surprising that they were shocked: at the time – indeed, until 1994 – heterosexual buggery was a crime in England and Wales, punishable by a maximum sentence of life in prison.

It subsequently became known that, having read the novel at the beginning of the trial, of the twelve jurors, nine were in favour of an acquittal, and three against. This polarity was maintained until the jury retired to consider their verdict, during which time the minority were persuaded to reconsider. Apparently they relented because of the sheer weight of the evidence called by Penguin. The requirement for a unanimous verdict had the consequence of making the views of every jury member of crucial and equal weight. Jeremy recalls how this fact preoccupied him during the trial. 'It only required one . . .' to stymie an acquittal. It is not difficult to envisage a scenario in which a detailed exposition of the 'night of sensual passion' tipped the balance, for at least one of the 'doubting' jurors, with the result that they stood firm against the blandishments of their fellows, and refused to acquiesce in the acquittal.

Geoffrey Robertson QC disagrees with Sparrow's contention that the jury would have convicted if they had understood 'the night of sensual passion'. In Robertson's view, the jurors still 'had to ask themselves the common-sense question of whether the publication as a whole would do any harm and, if so, whether its literary merit might redeem it'.[15] But a juror who found himself shocked and offended by Lawrence's 'paean of praise' of anal intercourse might conclude that publication of it was not in the public interest; or rather he might consider himself fortified to withstand the arguments of the literary experts who told him that it was.

F.R. Leavis's criticism of the trial took a different form. At the time, Leavis was the leading authority on Lawrence. Indeed, it was Leavis's critical support for Lawrence that had established the writer's reputation over the previous twenty or so years. Leavis attacked those (he was referring to T.S. Eliot in particular) who, having reviled Lawrence when he was unfashionable, now found it convenient to change their minds. In Leavis's view, the enthusiasm of these recent converts to Lawrence's work lacked appropriate critical rigour. However, Leavis's principal criticism of the *Chatterley* trial was that it associated Lawrence's name with his most unrepresentative work. He refused to countenance that *Chatterley* was great literature, or even a good novel; in his seminal book *D.H. Lawrence: Novelist*, *Chatterley* is not even discussed. Leavis's concern for Lawrence's memory was prescient. Today, it is arguable that the novelist is associated uppermost in the public mind, not with the delicacy of description of *The Rainbow* or *Sons and Lovers*, but with *Chatterley*, a famously 'salacious' novel.

A critical factor in the decision to prosecute seems to have been the price at which Penguin was proposing to sell the novel. It was one thing for the intellectuals and upper classes to be able to read *Chatterley*, quite another for it to be available generally. Consider Griffith-Jones's suggestion to the jurors, in opening, that they might consider it likely that *Chatterley* would corrupt 'many of the persons who are likely to buy it at the price of 3s 6d'. Penguin wanted to make *Chatterley* available to all. Was it this that made publication dangerous? No doubt the plot of the novel contributed to the anxiety of the prosecuting authorities. Had Connie chosen a lover of her own class, then perhaps Lawrence's description of their sexual activity may not have had such a tendency to deprave and corrupt.

In closing, Griffith-Jones tried to take the initiative on class, by portraying Penguin's experts, 'lecturers, bishops and so on', as out-of-touch elitists. Penguin's lawyers had anticipated this charge and made strenuous, and largely successful efforts to rebut it, for example by asking the witnesses about their families, their background, their education. It is significant, however, that it was Richard Hoggart, the least 'elite' of the literary academics, and a working-class boy in Lawrence's own mould, who was the most effective of Penguin's witnesses.

The outcome of the trial saw the establishment made a laughing stock. In a 'them and us' trial, 'us' had won, albeit a somewhat rarefied version of 'us'. The predominant, but by no means universal, mood of the press was one of contempt. Robert Blake suggested that the prosecution would surely go down as one of the most asinine ever brought. A further blow had been dealt to the culture of deference. The cartoonists were provided with their best material in years: Timothy in the *Sunday Times* has a well-padded publisher informing a sheepish-looking author: 'Sorry, my boy – we'll never get a prosecution with this rubbish.' Belsky in the *Daily Herald* has a beatnik girl languorously telling her friend, who is holding a copy of the novel, 'Not as exciting as the trial, I thought.' Osbert Lancaster in the *Express* shows a lady telling a bookseller: 'It is odd that now one <u>knows</u> that it is profoundly moral and packed with deep spiritual significance a lot of the old charm seems to have gone.'[16] And yet an acquittal was not a foregone conclusion. Had the jury delivered a guilty verdict, the cultural and social history of Britain over the next half century might well have been markedly different.

John Sutherland perceives a further significance. The *Chatterley* trial sparked the beginning of what he describes as the 'paperback revolution'.[17] Publishers now openly published in softback a whole spate of novels that would never before have been considered except in expurgated editions: works by Henry Miller, J.P. Donleavy, James Baldwin and Simone de Beauvoir. It is notable that when, in March 1963, Mervyn Griffith-Jones's opinion was sought by the DPP in relation to the threatened publication of *Tropic of Cancer* he advised against a prosecution: 'In my opinion the book *Tropic of Cancer* is not obscene . . . It is an unpleasant and disgusting book but the manner in which it is written is quite unlike any other book which has been the subject of proceedings over the last few years . . . Moreover, even if the book should be considered by some to be "obscene", I think it is extremely doubtful whether a conviction would be obtained.' It is difficult to imagine that Griffith-Jones's advice would have been the same had a conviction been obtained in *Chatterley. Tropic of Cancer* was duly published, as was Miller's entire *oeuvre*. In such incremental steps does social change occur.

But it was not only highbrow literature that benefited. As Sutherland puts it, there was inaugurated a new mode of hard-boiled bestsellers exploiting to the uttermost post-*Chatterley* freedoms. The bestseller of the early 1960s was Harold Robbins's *The Carpetbaggers*. The *Chatterley* trial did not just usher in freedom of expression for avowedly literary books.

I conclude with two contrasting responses to the trial. Barbara Barr, Lawrence's stepdaughter, summed up the feeling of many: 'I feel as if a window has been opened and blown fresh air through England.' By contrast, in a House of Lords debate the sixth Earl of Craven complained:

> I made a trip on the M1 the other day, on my way to Manchester, and stopped at Forte's restaurant . . . It was the day that *Lady Chatterley's Lover* was on sale to the public and there, at every serving counter, sat a snigger of youths. Everyone had a copy of the book held up to his face with one hand, while he forked nourishment into his open mouth with the other. They held the seeds of suggestive lust, which was expressed quite blatantly, by glance and remark, to the girls serving them. That I saw with my own eyes . . . Purity is sacrificed on the altar of promiscuity as woolly-headed intellectuals pour their vociferous sewage into the ears of the public.[18]

5

'Exciting, bawdy, extrovert'

R v Gold (Mayflower Books intervening) (1964)

ALTHOUGH THE LADY *Chatterley* trial and its outcome may be said to have produced a minor revolution in the collective British mind, that revolution, like all moral upheavals, would take many years to work its course. There were many who remained committed to a rearguard action against the forces of liberalization and, in the moral panic that followed the Stephen Ward trial and the publication of the Denning Report on the Profumo affair,[1] the establishment decided once again to go on the offensive. In its flailings, it alighted upon a charming and, to modern eyes, inoffensive piece of eighteenth-century erotica.

John Cleland wrote *Fanny Hill, or the Memoirs of a Woman of Pleasure* while languishing in a debtors' prison. The novel, a high-spirited epistolary account of the sexual adventures of a young courtesan, was published in two instalments in November 1748 and February 1749. Cleland was released shortly afterwards. He had raised sufficient funds to redeem his debt through a book whose immediate purpose was to raise quick money. However Cleland was no businessman. For writing *Fanny Hill* he received 20 guineas; the publisher is said to have made £10,000. But Cleland's misfortunes were not over. As the author of what was said to be an obscene work, Cleland was soon after prosecuted for 'corrupting the King's subjects' and the book was officially withdrawn from publication.[2] Nonetheless, for over two centuries *Fanny Hill* enjoyed a vigorous underground existence as, so it was billed, the first erotic English novel. Given its contents it is not wholly surprising to find that it was the first novel ever to be prosecuted, in 1821, for obscenity in the United States. But it is remarkable that a novel written in 1748 should, over 200 years later, have been the subject of judicial proceedings brought in London with the purpose of its immolation.

It was in the *annus mirabilis* of 1963 that Mayflower Press, sensing perhaps the change of mood later celebrated by Larkin, and inspired by the acquittal of Penguin Books in the *Chatterley* case, decided to publish openly an unexpurgated edition of *Fanny Hill*. This would be the first since the original publication in the 1740s. An American edition had been published a few months earlier and had survived a ban on appeal. Publication was greeted by Marghanita Laski,[3] writing in the *Guardian*:[4]

> what takes place is sex as we all know (or believe) it to be, and, which I found especially pleasing, with a full acceptance of women's equal desire and pleasure. 'How often, when the rage and tumult of my senses had subsided . . . have I asked myself . . . if it was in nature for any of its creatures to be so happy as I was?' Many writers have tried to describe a woman's sexual feelings; this one succeeds . . . Of course it is pornographic in that it rouses feelings of sexual desire, but it does so directly and straightforwardly, without any possibility of confusing these feelings with others, and usually without any aftertaste of disgust.

Laski then raised the issue that had exercised the court in *Chatterley*: 'But with a cheap paperback edition we do have to ask what we feel about it in the hands of the young. There is a lot to be said for self-denial, and I do feel that on the whole young people are as well-advised not to read about sex, beyond essential physiological information, before they encounter it, as they are not to look at photographs of Venice before they go there.' Nonetheless she was inclined to think that *Fanny Hill*, 'with its emphasis on sex as thoroughly enjoyable, might well be a better, healthier guide than the self-conscious, self-righteous, painfully frank instruction manuals of our own times.' Wayland Young, writing in the same newspaper,[5] was unwilling to grant *Fanny* a place at the top table of literature but nonetheless greeted the book for what it was, an energetic paean to sexual adventure: 'A lyrical time is had by all, kindness and a most amiable sensuality prevail, and no harm could come to anyone from reading the book, unless of course, one is to regard sexual excitement itself as harmful; but that is like banning salt . . . Compared with the best social-content novels of its own time and language it is a soap-bubble for a lonely afternoon. Only vacuous sentimentality could value such a book highly, but only withered bigotry could wish to suppress it.'

Worthy sentiments from reputable writers in an enlightened newspaper.[6] But the publication was also advertised by Ralph Gold,[7] a bookseller who ran the Magic Shop, a sort of joke shop that also purveyed a few risqué books, in the Tottenham Court Road. 'Just out Fanny Hill, banned in America,[8] 3s 6d', said the notice. When the Vice Squad learned of this, 171 copies of the book were seized just prior to the publication date, which had been set for 8 November 1963. Unlike in the *Chatterley* case, the authorities proceeded not against the publisher itself, but rather against Mr Gold the bookseller. He was summonsed before the Bow Street Magistrates Court under section 3 of the Obscene Publications Act 1959 to 'show cause' why copies of the novel that had been seized should not be forfeited.[9] Under this section the question of obscenity would be decided not by a jury but by a magistrate, a man or woman rather less likely to be susceptible to the new mood of the times or the silken oratory of defence counsel.

Remarkably, at the same time another publisher, the Luxor Press, published in England a 'de luxe' edition of *Fanny Hill*, selling at very much more than the Mayflower paperback. This edition escaped seizure or prosecution. *The Times* reported, on 30 November 1963, the proprietor of the Luxor Press's statement that the book 'was selling well', although a number of West End bookshops were not displaying copies openly. Still the authorities took no action. Clearly Mayflower Press's and Mr Gold's crime, in the eyes of the Director of Public Prosecutions, was not the publication of *Fanny Hill* per se, but the publication of a venerable piece of erotica at a price that the hoi polloi could afford: what is more, at the very same price that Penguin had proposed to sell its paperback of *Lady Chatterley's Lover*.

The further oddity of the proceedings against the hapless Mr Gold was that a conviction would not make it generally illegal in England to publish or sell *Fanny Hill*. The court's ruling could only extend to its own jurisdiction, which was confined to central London (where *Fanny Hill* was both written and set). When Roy Jenkins raised this point in the House of Commons[10] the Solicitor General, Sir Peter

Rawlinson's, response, reeking with sententious piety, was to the effect that it had been considered that a prosecution of the publisher under section 2[11] (the section under which Penguin Books had been prosecuted) would be 'oppressive'. Yet the publishers themselves had made it quite clear that they would prefer, indeed welcomed, a trial by jury. In a letter written by Mayflower Press's solicitors, they stated that the decision to publish *Fanny Hill* was their client's alone and Mayflower felt strongly that the responsibility should accordingly be borne by it alone; Mayflower also felt, so the letter continued, that 'one of the objects of the Obscene Publications Act 1959 was to enable the propriety of such a publication as this to be determined by the verdict of a jury representing public opinion at the time, who would decide not only whether the book taken as a whole was obscene but whether under s.4 of the Act, the publication was justified as being for the public good upon the grounds set out in that section.'

It was pointed out that copies of the book had been widely distributed throughout the country to many booksellers of repute and therefore Mayflower might be faced with a multiplicity of appearances in other magistrates courts whatever the outcome of the Bow Street proceedings, without any of such proceedings ever achieving the finality of a verdict of a jury, by which verdict Mayflower would abide. In conclusion, continued Mayflower's solicitors, they were instructed to ask that proceedings be brought against Mayflower Books under section 2. It is clear from the terms of this letter that any suggestion that a prosecution under section 2 was considered 'oppressive' was pure humbug. Rawlinson also let slip in his answer to Roy Jenkins that the DPP had taken counsel's advice on the proper manner of proceeding. As we shall see, it is almost certain that that counsel was none other than Mervyn Griffith-Jones. One can well imagine what that advice was. Griffith-Jones, his memories of the *Chatterley* trial still fresh, must have realized that the prospects of a conviction before a jury were negligible; whereas before a 'sound' magistrate those prospects rose to a near certainty.

With the trial looming, Jeremy was retained by Mayflower Books, who had intervened in the case to lend assistance to Mr Gold and defend their edition from destruction. The Christmas of 1963 was spent busily reading up on the book and contacting witnesses who might be prepared to stand up in court and defend it. A note written by Jeremy's junior at the time sets out the state of play: John Freeman, of *Face to Face* fame, declined ('I'm no expert'); as did Sir Stanley Unwin ('I'm too old') and A.P. Herbert ('I've a weak heart'). Raymond Mortimer, one-time lover of Harold Nicolson and the embodiment of Bloomsbury values, had also been asked to give evidence. His letter to Jeremy was especially disheartening: 'The book seems to me more entirely pornographic than I remembered from a reading of it in French many years ago. I think that its author obviously had a gift for writing, but that here this is used merely to excite sexual desire, and that the book has no remarkable value as literature.' On the other hand a clutch of intellectuals *had* agreed to give evidence in support of *Fanny*, including Bernard Levin (who was concerned that he might 'create a bad impression'), Peter Quennell, H. Montgomery Hyde and Kenneth Tynan, as well as Marghanita Laski and Wayland Young.

The summons was to be heard at Bow Street Magistrates Court, the court where Henry Fielding, himself a celebrant of 'direct and straightforward' sexual desire, had sat as Chief Magistrate while Cleland wrote his novel at the Marshalsea. In this court now sat Sir Robert Blundell, the Chief Metropolitan Magistrate, a man whose practice at the Bar had been undistinguished, his judicial career similarly so. He had already read, and judged, *Fanny Hill* when, the previous November, he had granted the warrant to the police to raid the Magic Shop in the first place. This was not an auspicious start. (It was perhaps similarly inauspicious that Mandy Rice-Davies was quoted on 1 January 1964, at the launch of her memoir *The Mandy Report*, as saying that she might be starring in a film version of *Fanny Hill*.) But what equally worried Jeremy was the fact that this case might not be just an enquiry into the merits – or lack of them – of *Fanny Hill*, but rather a judgement on the Magic Shop itself. Finally, although the bulk of the book deals with joyous lovemaking, there was one scene that would create forensic difficulties for the defence: a scene where Fanny has to flagellate an elderly client.

And so, on a grey morning in January 1964, an English court

embarked on an enquiry into whether *Fanny Hill* was obscene. The tiny press gallery of Court 3 was packed with murmuring newspaper reporters seeing in this case the potential for a rerun of the *Chatterley* trial and all the marvellous copy that had produced. It was reported in the *Daily Mail* that the public gallery mainly contained young people, 'including one wearing a beard', and the former Lady Rothschild – in fact Jeremy's sister, come to give moral support. The case was opened by Jeremy's old adversary from the *Chatterley* case, Mervyn Griffith-Jones, who had also been Reginald Manningham-Buller's junior in the Blake case and, just six months earlier, had prosecuted Stephen Ward. His career stands as a sort of sanctimonious rebuke to that of Jeremy, and yet, Jeremy recalls, they always got on well outside court. 'I think that Mervyn Griffith-Jones was a man who was genuinely horrified by the onset of the permissive society and saw himself as a foot soldier in the fight against degeneracy. For all his stridency he was utterly sincere.'[12] In a lecture Griffith-Jones gave much later, after he had become a judge, he advised prosecutors against acting 'as second defending counsel as some young men seem to think they should do in order to be fair'. This was not a man who was going to hold back.

In a voice replete with moral outrage[13] Griffith-Jones enunciated before Sir Robert Blundell the now familiar test of obscenity: articles should be deemed to be obscene if the effect taken as a whole was such as to tend to deprave and corrupt persons who were likely, having regard to all the relevant circumstances, to read the matter. He then handed the magistrate a photograph of the Magic Shop, calling careful attention to the fact that half the premises were used for selling books, of a particular kind, and the other half for selling jokes and tricks.

Just as in the *Chatterley* trial, the prosecution offered no evidence other than that of the police officer who had purchased a copy from the Magic Shop: no doubt Griffith-Jones counted on the good sense of Sir Robert Blundell. Something that Detective Inspector Webb was careful to emphasize in his evidence was that when he entered the Magic Shop he saw, on either side of the cash register, a pile of books. The shop assistant, without Webb having said a word, took a copy of the novel, placed it in a bag and handed it to him.

The innuendo was clear: middle-aged men only came to the Magic Shop for one purpose, and that was not to purchase whoopee cushions. After Webb had been cross-examined, Griffith-Jones then re-examined him on a remarkable basis. He showed the bemused policeman a book entitled *A Critical Dictionary of English Literature and British and American Authors*, published in 1859 and referred to the entry on Cleland – which included the phrase 'Several works give him no credit'. The prosecutor continued: 'There is no mention of *Fanny Hill*, unless it be covered by that phrase.' The good inspector agreed. How the oblique views of the editors of an almanac published in 1859 could be of any conceivable relevance to a trial in 1964 was unclear; but no doubt Sir Robert nodded vigorously.

Jeremy then rose. He drew attention to the fact that the prosecution had chosen to bypass section 2 of the Act: one of the objects of the 1959 Act had been to enable the propriety of a publication such as *Fanny Hill* to be tested by a jury's verdict representing public opinion at the time. He referred to section 3 in withering terms – this 'ridiculous section' – which had been deployed to evade a jury.

Jeremy called first Peter Quennell, the well-known author and editor of *History Today*, who had written an introduction to the Mayflower edition. Quennell described *Fanny Hill* as Cleland's claim to 'a modest immortality'; although it was no masterpiece it had literary and historical merit; it was certainly literature as distinct from pornography. Its moral was that love was the justification and crown of sexual activity. It was the literary equivalent of Hogarth's *Harlot's Progress*. Jeremy read aloud from Quennell's preface: 'We escape the nauseating modern mixture of sexual appetite and criminal violence . . . Fanny Hill would have shuddered at Lady Chatterley.'

> JEREMY: Is that your view?
> QUENNELL: I think she would have been horrified . . . Fanny is an advocate of the pleasures of straightforward sex and when she describes deviations she makes clear that she does not approve of them or considers them inferior substitutes for straightforward enjoyment.

Indeed, Quennell continued: 'I suppose that Fanny's insistence on her own pleasure, quite apart from that of her lover's pleasure, is in its way rather revolutionary. It represents perhaps a step in the emancipation of the opposite sex . . . In a curious way there is always respect for the individual.' There remained that tricky flagellation scene: 'She describes it as something she deplores and does not understand.'

Mervyn Griffith-Jones's cross-examination of Quennell was laden with his usual brand of haughty contempt. As anticipated, Griffith-Jones was keen to enquire into the Magic Shop, though it must be doubted whether Peter Quennell had ever found himself passing through its doors:

GRIFFITH-JONES: Do you think any person who went into that shop would do so for any reason other than to get a kick out of reading about sexual encounters?
QUENNELL: I don't know anything about that class of reader.
GRIFFITH-JONES: But with your knowledge of the world?
QUENNELL: I think their motives might be a bit suspect.

However, although the customers of the Magic Shop might have bought for the wrong motives, Quennell said, 'it was quite possible that they would receive some historic instruction as they go along.' It was at this point that Sir Robert Blundell made one of his few, and characteristically opaque, interventions: he was interested that Fanny 'never seemed to leave the house in the book'.

At the adjournment of the first day of the trial Griffith-Jones invited Quennell to write out a list of passages that he thought of historical interest. When the trial resumed a week later Quennell said that he had identified forty such passages. But, as if this were apropos of anything at all, Griffith-Jones was scornful of the notion that any purchaser at the Magic Shop would be buying *Fanny Hill* for reasons of historical research. Calling attention to one lengthy passage in the book he asked:

GRIFFITH-JONES: Those six pages are what the purchaser at the Magic Shop might regard as 'fairly good stuff' are they not?
QUENNELL: I cannot imagine a reader at the Magic Shop with any exactitude [and one could certainly accept that evidence], but I can imagine that he or she would find that part more interesting than I would find it interesting.

Griffith-Jones then referred to Barvill, the character in the novel who delights in flagellation, and the passages in the book that told of how Fanny was dressed – in the finest linen, white uniform gown, petticoat, stockings and satin slippers, with her hair in dropped curls – before 'being led like a lamb to the slaughter to some horrible brute who could not have sexual intercourse unless he was whipped first'. Quennell's answer was ironically amusing, though it is doubtful it amused Sir Robert Blundell: 'The description of the dropped curls was interesting from the point of view of ladies' hair styles of the period.' Mr Quennell then commended another passage which provided a good description of a public house in Chelsea in the 1740s. Griffith-Jones: 'And to get to that snippet on page 40 there is another act of intercourse, an act of lesbianism and another act of lesbianism.' What a palaver!

Apart from his obsessive interest in the clientele of the Magic Shop, Griffith-Jones's other hobby-horse, and one that he returned to time and again, was the fact that Fanny's world was one of 'laughter and pleasure, wealth and happiness'. There was no refer-ence to venereal disease. The characters were, well, simply enjoying themselves too much. And here we have, as it were, a kind of fierce light being shone on to the Griffith-Jones cast of mind. The main objection to this book was the very characteristic on which Marghanita Laski and Wayland Young had founded its charm and delightfulness: sex is fun and a book that celebrates that is a Good Thing. And so the trial proceeded as a two-way conversation between interlocutors speaking two different languages, neither understanding the other's.

In re-examination by Jeremy Mr Quennell commented that *Fanny Hill* was one of the first novels to say that women enjoyed sex. Jeremy then said: 'It was put to you with horror that these girls had enjoyed sex immensely. Does that horrify you?' Mr Quennell: 'It horrifies me less than it does Mr Griffith-Jones.' Again it is doubtful that this sardonic response impressed Sir Robert. It impressed Griffith-Jones even less. He rose in protest: 'I am sure that Mr Hutchinson and the witness realise that counsel have work to do and that these personal comments have nothing to do with the matter. It is most undesirable that this should become or tend to become a personal matter.' The level of self-deception contained in this rebuke here is notable: rarely has counsel so identified himself with the case he is presenting.[14]

H. Montgomery Hyde, the next defence witness, was a former Ulster Unionist MP and author of a forthcoming book on the history of pornography. He praised the way that Cleland depicted the 'gusto, directness and straightforwardness' with which Fanny and her companions engaged in sexual encounters with men. But here was Griffith-Jones back prowling about on the Tottenham Court Road. Again it is doubtful that Hyde, then residing at Lamb House, Rye,[15] was especially familiar with the Magic Shop, but nonetheless he was taxed with the question: 'There was in the Magic Shop a notice saying "Just published – banned in America"; do you think that that would encourage any ordinary person's curiosity as to the history and manners of the middle of the eighteenth century?'

Marghanita Laski then gave evidence that the book made her feel 'very cheerful'; it was a 'gay little book'. She also noted that *Fanny Hill* provided sixty or seventy words and phrases for the *Oxford English Dictionary*, including 'teatime', 'mock modesty' and 'dumb waiter'. Professor Iain Watt was the next witness. The author of *The Rise of the Novel*, and an expert in eighteenth-century fiction, said that the book would 'on balance, increase the understanding of gaiety and pleasure in the world', although he thought that the average reader might not be able to get through the book because there was a need for a relatively high literary understanding; to which Griffith-Jones responded, if that was so, why had 100,000 copies been printed? By this time Sir Robert Blundell was becoming exasperated by this parade of literati purporting, as he no doubt saw it, to tell him his business. He told Professor Watt, who had spent three years as a prisoner of war in Changi prison working on the construction of the Burma Railway, to 'stand up straight and put those notes away', as if he were reprimanding a witness to a pub brawl in Brixton. Yet even the literary critic of the *Sunday Express*, not a newspaper known for its tireless promotion of pornography, testified to *Fanny*'s literary and historical merit, and compared it favourably to the treatment of sex in *Lady Chatterley*.

Jeremy had called an impressive array of witnesses from all walks of intellectual life: to be able to call a former Unionist MP and a *Sunday Express* journalist in defence of *Fanny* showed that it was not only dangerous libertarians and wayward professors who were prepared to defend the book. But it is doubtful that Sir Robert was paying much attention. He had read the book and no doubt spluttered over the scenes of eighteenth-century bawdy. Nonetheless Jeremy made a valiant closing speech. He argued that the forfeiture procedure adopted by the prosecution was quite inappropriate and that it was never designed to test the obscenity of a single book where the defence was that the book was literature and not pornography. He then took issue with the prosecutor's central strategy, which was to concentrate on the likely motives of purchasers finding their way to the Magic Shop in the Tottenham Court Road. Griffith-Jones had conjured up before the magistrate an unpalatable vision of the pervert in the proverbial dirty mackintosh poring over what he so charmingly described as 'fairly good stuff'. This, argued Jeremy, was a fundamental misconception of the law; the court had to consider the book as a whole and not the motives of people who might buy it.

> If you start from the premise that sex is dirty and in itself depraved, then of course you speak, as Mr Griffith-Jones has done, of the 'kicks' in the book and 'hot passages' and so on. This book is about sex, which is a most absorbing subject – always has been and always will be – and it has never been part of the defence that people should read it in a high-minded way, bearing in mind its place in literature, as a social or moral tract. All the witnesses have said that it is exciting, bawdy, extrovert, gay; sometimes sombre and sometimes hilariously funny. But if in fact the book is written in a very excellent way and has historical interest and is a child of its age, then all those matters indicate that the book finds its place in the history of literature and not in the history of smut. It matters not at all from the point of view of this court what is the motive of anyone who buys it. That is entirely irrelevant. The only evidence called by the prosecution has been directed to the shop. Not one witness has been called by them with evidence directed to the book. One might think that they were discussing here whether the Magic Shop is on trial rather than the novel by John Cleland. Just because the novel was being sold with the notice 'Banned in America', just because a bookseller thought

he could puff a book by affixing to it an entirely misleading notice, does not make that book obscene. If *Madame Bovary* is brought out with a lurid cover with 'Sex! Sex! Sex!' printed on the outside it does not make Flaubert's novel obscene merely because that was how somebody wanted to dress it up.

Jeremy noted that, just as had occurred in the *Lady Chatterley* trial, the prosecution had called no evidence at all to challenge the merits of the book or the statutory defence that had been set up. 'Out of the whole length and breadth of this country, not one single person qualified to speak has come forward to go into the witness box and say that this book is not literature.' By contrast here 'eighteen individuals of the highest possible reputation had all spoken of the book's literary merit.'

Griffith-Jones had called attention to the price of the edition: 3s 6d – available to the student, the manual worker, the housewife, God forbid, and even the hard-pressed married couple. It was a similar strategy to his catastrophic submission in *Chatterley*. But no doubt he took the view that conjuring up a horrifying vision of the commonality being able to leaf through the pages of *Fanny Hill* would appeal to Sir Robert Blundell, even if it had not appealed to a jury. Jeremy dealt with this point: 'Are we to say that contemporary literature is to be measured by what was suitable for a fourteen-year-old schoolgirl to read? If the book is literary and not pornographic or not literary and not obscene, who is to say in the name of the law that the book should be rationed by price? To say that the price of a novel was relevant to its obscenity was the voice of the censor and not of the judge.'

The answer, unfortunately, was that Sir Robert viewed his role precisely as that: a censor of what the people could or could not read. On 11 February 1964, after two and half minutes' careful reflection, he declared Cleland's jolly novel obscene. 'I have come to my decision on what I have heard in the witness box and such exhibits as I have seen . . . doing the best I can in the circumstances I have no hesitation in saying that the order should be made.' He also said that in deciding that *Fanny* was obscene he had regard to a 'due sense of the realities'. What Sir Robert meant by this phrase will for ever remain unexplained; it is one of those phrases judges like to use to provide cover for gut instinct masquerading as objective reasoning. This then was the sum total of his reasoning; this was the end product of almost four days of evidence and argument. The result was that he ordered the 171 paperback copies confiscated from the Magic Shop to be forfeited. Mayflower's managing director drew attention to the absurdity of the situation: 'So far as I know, there is nothing to stop a bookshop in Scunthorpe or Glasgow or even Chelsea from selling the book. There might be another court action, but another magistrate might take a different view.'[16]

And so the trial ended. It had been a shabby and dispiriting affair in a court more used to the prosecution of midnight affrays than the proscription of eighteenth-century literature.[17] Montgomery Hyde sent a letter of commiseration to Jeremy: 'I think you put up a wonderful defence. I was in Oxford speaking to the University Law Society the other day and everyone there was loud in your praises.' Jeremy's junior, Dick Du Cann, also wrote to him: 'I shall cherish, in a strictly professional sense, Fanny Hill, for a long time to come and should like you to know how grateful I am [to you] for making it possible for me to join you in the case. Today's papers provide warming reading. We have the press even though we could not win over Blundell. That we have that much is due to your patience and perseverance, for Cox[18] and Mayflower in fact contributed little enough – except some good lunches at Boulestin. For my seat at both tables thank you again.'

The result was too much for certain liberal members of Parliament. An all-party motion was tabled by Tom Driberg on 13 February 1964 criticizing Sir Robert Blundell's decision, urging the DPP not to undertake any further prosecutions in respect of *Fanny Hill* and asking the Home Secretary to encourage chief constables not to waste the time of the courts any further. Roy Jenkins was a signatory. The motion noted that the decision was contrary to all the evidence given by expert and reputable witnesses and considered it anomalous that there was no seizure and forfeiture of a more expensive edition of the book, a form of rationing (Jeremy's phrase) that discriminated 'insultingly' against students of eighteenth-century manners who might only be able to afford to buy the cheap edition. Lastly the motion noted the further anomaly that the cheap edition could still be sold in the majority of bookshops in Great Britain.[19]

The battle might have been lost but a larger war had been won, or nearly so. There was a general sense of embarrassment and uneasiness following the end of the trial; a collective 'what have we done?'[20] In proceedings before the Commons Standing Committee on the Obscene Publications Bill later that year the Solicitor General, Sir Peter Rawlinson (he who had earlier upheld the propriety of proceeding under section 3), gave an assurance that where a publisher indicated that whatever the outcome of forfeiture proceedings it would continue to publish, then the Attorney General would only proceed by way of a prosecution under section 2. This was an important concession. And the prosecution of *Fanny Hill* was to prove to be the penultimate state-sponsored prosecution of a novel purporting to have literary merit.

The last 'literary' prosecution for obscenity to be brought in England occurred two years later. Hubert Selby's *Last Exit to Brooklyn* was published in England by Calder & Boyars in January 1966, to generally positive reviews. A shocking account of street violence and sexual sadism in contemporary New York, it was described in the *Spectator* as 'the end of the pitshaft. There is no lower level to be probed.' Nonetheless the DPP declined to proceed against it. Tom Driberg tabled a motion in the House of Commons, this time congratulating the DPP on his restraint. Sir Cyril Black, Conservative MP for Wimbledon, was riled by Driberg's provocation. Months after the publication date, and after many thousands of sales, he instituted a private prosecution. The summons was again issued under section 3 of the 1959 Act and was heard by none other than Sir Robert Blundell. It will come as little surprise that Sir Robert enthusiastically granted the search warrant that allowed copies of *Last Exit* to be seized from any bookshop within the jurisdiction of the court, which extended to Soho and the area around Shaftesbury Avenue. Only three were found. The case to decide the fate of these three copies was heard a few weeks later. This time the prosecution itself called an array of witnesses in support – including now Montgomery Hyde, who had testified two years earlier in favour of

Fanny Hill, and a certain Robert Maxwell MP. The magistrate held the book to be obscene and the three copies were duly burned. But the publishers vowed to keep selling.

This time the DPP was roused to action and brought a prosecution of *Last Exit* before a jury. Jeremy was approached to act as counsel for the publisher. On this occasion, much as he deplored the idea that the book should be banned, he felt that, given the shocking nature of some of the material, he could not properly defend it. He explains: 'It is sometimes painful enough to utter the words of a defendant in a criminal case. But obscenity cases are matters of opinion rather than fact and so it is almost impossible to persuade a jury with any conviction of your client's case if your own personal opinion is contrary to it. I could not stand up and read out the account of the rape scene in *Last Exit* and say persuasively that there was nothing depraving about it. My heart would not be in it. So, unlike in all other criminal cases where your personal opinion is totally irrelevant and must never be disclosed, I suggested to the publisher that he would do better if he found someone else. Nevertheless, if he wished me to continue with the case of course I would do so.'[21] In the event the publisher turned to John Mortimer – later to be branded 'the Devil's Advocate' by Mary Whitehouse. Although the trial was lost the publishers appealed and won before the Court of Appeal. Soon after, the loophole in the 1959 Act under which private prosecutions could be brought was closed. And with that a new era began: never again would an avowedly literary work be prosecuted, whether by the state or by a private individual, for obscenity.

Finally in 1970 an unexpurgated *Fanny Hill* was published again.[22] There was no prosecution; there were no protests; not even Peregrine Worsthorne sounded the alarum of the imminent collapse of Christian marriage. In 1985 *Fanny Hill* finally received the imprimatur of publication as a Penguin Classic.

Let the last word go to *Fanny*. Mayflower Press brought out a new edition later in 1964, expurgated of the scenes that had so offended Mr Griffith-Jones. At the end of the edition there was a final and new letter that Fanny had apparently written.

Letter the Third

Madam,

I will not conceal from you the gratification, of which I was fully sensible, that my case was being heard, albeit in the smallest and meanest court at Bow Street, by no less a dignitary than Sir Robert Blundell, the Chief Metropolitan Magistrate, who occupied that rhadamanthine chair, where I remembered Henry Fielding, the genial author of a bawdy and liquorish book, 'Tom Jones', which my dear Charles forbade me to read, and by a prudent parental care withheld from the eyes of our young son.

Nor can I deny the hopes with which I was upheld when I learned that the worthy Sir Robert had been schooled, like Mr Cleland, the author who recorded my adventures, at Westminster, and that he advised the world at large, in the pages of 'Who's Who', that his recreation is deipnosophism, or the art of dining.

I was foolishly filled with the expectation that so rational a pleasurist, a kindly bachelor of some sixty years, would view with indulgence the story of the scandalous stages of my life after my safe coming home to port and the paths of Virtue.

I will not weary you with the details of a case encouraging in its progress as it was disappointing in its outcome, save to express my surprise that I was tried summarily, like a common street player, and not before a judge and jury like Lady Chatterley, who showed such a want of delicacy in the use of those vulgar expressions which I was so solicitous to avoid.

But what woman could not but be flattered by the approbation of my little work, of its historical interest and its literary merit by witnesses of the highest learning and distinction?

Under the skilful guidance of my silver-tongued advocate, Mr Jeremy Hutchinson, they spoke, as one, of the merit of my work. Some passages, indeed, they found as disagreeable to read as they were to experience, but they testified that even these painful incidents had not the power to disaffirm the moral of my little tale: that it is Love and Marriage alone which sanctify pleasure. They told Sir Robert of lubricious works lacking all decency and the simplest elements of literary artifice which were everywhere on sale to the common reader.

None were put out of countenance nor were deflected from their firm conviction that the place of my memoirs was 'in the history

of Literature and not in the history of smut', by the rigorous examination and the withering scorn of the unbending advocate of the
Police Commissioner, Mr Griffith-Jones, who could find no witness
throughout the length and breadth of the land to speak against me.

I felt a warm and lively appreciation directed towards me from
the journalists and the few members of a curious public, gathered in
positions of pinched and cramped discomfort, as Mr Hutchinson rose
to address the magistrate. In a speech in which reasoning vied with
eloquence to make an equal match, he seemed to carry all before
him: nor did it seem possible, as he argued, that my memoirs, which
may be freely read in the American and Canadian colonies, should
be proscribed in that very district which was the scene of many of
my adventures.

Judge then of the general amazement and the perturbation into
which I was thrown, when the good Sir Robert, with scarcely a
minute for reflection, pronounced against me.

I look, to see you soon, and, in the meantime, believe me ever,
MADAM,
Yours, etc., etc.

6

Decline and Fall

R v Kypreos (1971)

THE MOUTH AND *Oral Sex* was first published in 1969. Its author, Paul Ableman, was very far from being a salacious pornographer. Born in Leeds into an unconventional Jewish family, his first novel, *I Hear Voices*, a fragmented account of a man's dissolution into mental illness, had been published by Maurice Girodias's Olympia Press. Ableman's next three novels all received notices, albeit mixed, in the *Times Literary Supplement*. While he was extravagantly proclaimed as the heir to Sterne, Joyce and Beckett, his work was also noticeably suffused with erotic sentiment. Reviewing *Vac*, published in 1971, the *London Magazine* credited it with 'doing for Hampstead what Henry Miller's *Tropic of Cancer* did for Paris'. Perhaps for that reason WH Smith refused to stock it. Ableman was proud of having won the *Transatlantic Review*'s annual erotica competition in 1962 with his short story 'The Bay Area'. A committed member of the literary avant-garde, Ableman embraced the mental and sexual revolution of the 1960s with proselytizing gusto.

The Mouth is a book that typifies that period. It is impossible to think of it as having been published – or written – in 1959; and it would have seemed dated and at odds with the times by 1979. But the book proved a good fit at the end of the 1960s, when old taboos were under concerted assault by the libertarian vanguard. *The Mouth* not only dealt with a controversial subject, but also transgressed established genres: at once a protracted essay on what Ableman describes as 'oral sexuality'; a psychological history of the mouth, from conception to adulthood; and a sort of user's manual on the art of oral sex.

The text is heavily laden with quotations from writers as diverse as Freud, Wilhelm Stekel, Margaret Mead, Frank Harris and Havelock

Ellis, as if Ableman were concerned to ward off charges of indecency by wearing his learning on his sleeve. This concern seems also to have informed the illustration of the book: there are images from the likes of Magritte and Utamaro (but no bespoke 'educational' illustrations as later deployed in *The Joy of Sex*). *The Mouth* was a commission, and, as it proved, an inspired one, but Ableman warmed to his subject with the enthusiasm of the butterfly-collector or the railway-modeller. He could not entirely paper over the reality – that he was a diligent amateur in the area, writing at speed. One imagines him sitting at his typewriter dashing out text, surrounded by dusty volumes written by Viennese sexologists (in homage to Jack Kerouac's composition of *On the Road*, he would compose on a single continuous sheet of paper, as if a roll of lining paper were being spooled through his typewriter). But he achieves a tone of honest enquiry, intermingled with an ingenuous and artless delight in his subject.

The Mouth was both commissioned and published by Christopher Kypreos, an American poet who had arrived in London in 1966. Kypreos had initially been employed by Bob Guccione writing an art column for *Penthouse* magazine. Supplanted by Lynn Barber, he went on to found an underground magazine, *Running Man* (contributors to its first number included Stokely Carmichael, Patrick Leigh Fermor and Al Alvarez), before starting up a publishing house of the same name. Running Man Press specialized in erotic publications sold via catalogues and mail order. *How to Achieve Sexual Ecstasy* was a signal early success. With *The Mouth* Kypreos followed his usual modus operandi: he issued nearly 100,000 leaflets soliciting orders. Initial business was brisk and some 2,000 copies of the book were ordered.

Then, in December 1969, Kypreos's offices were raided by twelve members of the 'Dirty Squad'. Apparently there had been complaints from recipients of his mailing and a number of leaflets had been addressed to schoolchildren. Kypreos was suspicious that he might have been set up. He had recently employed a man who had co-written the copy for the leaflets in provocatively suggestive terms and would soon disappear for good. The mailing lists he used had been purchased with guarantees from the vendor that the names were appropriate for adult material. He recalls ruefully: 'A shady character who called himself Parker had sold me mailing lists, supposedly of bona fide adult book buyers. But the lists were padded out with minors and those of the great and good, and even included royalty.' Kypreos's flat was also raided. His secretary hastily ripped up innocuous correspondence he had received from Maurice Girodias, publisher of *Lolita* and *The Naked Lunch* (Girodias had declined to publish *The Mouth* in the United States because he said it was 'too tame'). 'She threw the confetti out of the window. Two police climbers were sent to gather the shredded letters from neighbouring balconies. The police inspector in charge later presented them to me, pasted on to a board, with a touch of irony as well as a good deal of pride in the efficiency of the police.'

Kypreos was prosecuted under the Obscene Publications Act 1959, and a separate charge of 'sending through the post indecent circulars' was thrown in for good measure. It was the first prosecution of a mainstream book since the trial of *Last Exit to Brooklyn* in 1967. As we have seen, Jeremy had been briefed to defend *Last Exit* but in the end John Mortimer had taken over the defence. However when instructed in 1971 to defend Kypreos for his publication of *The Mouth*, he had no compunction. He threw himself into the case with alacrity. 'How could this inoffensive little book be held to be corrupting? There was nothing "dirty" about it at all.' Still, Jeremy was worried that a jury, guided by a hostile judge, would take umbrage at Ableman's unashamed frankness. 'Judges especially were horrified by the idea of oral sex even in the 1970s.' Confirmation of this aversion can be found in Geoffrey Robertson's groundbreaking book *Obscenity*, published in 1979. Robertson records the judge's remark in the *Oz* case, tried a few months later: 'I wonder how many of you, ladies and gentlemen of the jury, had heard words like cunnilingus before you came into this courtroom?' Robertson mentions another case where, having been informed that oral sex was widely practised in Britain, the stipendiary magistrate remarked ruefully: 'If that is really so, then I am glad I do not have long to live.'[1]

The prosecutor was Jeremy's fellow member of chambers and friend Kenneth Richardson (Mervyn Griffith-Jones had by this time been safely packed off to the bench). What was the theme of *The Mouth*? Richardson asked the jury. 'Lust,' was his monosyllabic answer. Indeed, it was only 'old fuddy-duddies who engaged in normal sex who were regarded by the author as abnormal'. He continued by saying that the words 'deprave and corrupt' as they appeared in the 1959 Obscene Publications Act meant that a book could be held to be obscene if it made a significant number of readers feel 'less good'. The jury should consider whether the book made sex 'more beautiful' or 'ugly'. Jeremy recalls: 'I was sitting there listening to all this. I looked over at Kenneth and thought, This is not the man I know. But prosecuting obscenity cases did odd things to normally rational men. They suddenly became rabid moralists.'

The newspapers from the time report a marvellously vigorous response from Jeremy:

> Mr Richardson is absolutely wrong. The law has gone out of its way to show us that, if you feel 'less good', that is absolutely not the test on which this very important matter of whether the book is obscene is to be decided by twelve people in this country today. For that to be a criminal offence is almost unbelievable as a suggestion in this country in 1971. Mr Richardson's interpretation amounts to nothing less than censorship . . . the meaning of 'to corrupt you' is to cause you to do something wrong or criminal or in some way to blur your perception as to good and bad. Members of the jury, you won't find this a dirty book . . . You won't find it the sort of book that you see in dirty bookshops in Soho. It is a well-written book, not a book which has just been scribbled up by some purveyor of pornography.

Nevertheless *The Mouth* was far removed from the literary high ground occupied by *Lady Chatterley's Lover* or *Fanny Hill*. This time the prosecution had come armed with expert evidence to denounce it. Mr David Holbrook, Fellow of Jesus College, Cambridge, and author of *Sex and Dehumanisation*, gave evidence that the book was 'propaganda for perversion' and 'dressed-up pornography'. But, under cross-examination by Jeremy, he overplayed his hand. It became clear that Holbrook was a campaigner on a wider moral crusade: 'There is an ostensible theme, the mouth. There is, I think, also another kind of theme, which I will describe as belonging to the pursuit in the book of a certain kind of justification or vindication of oral perversion.' Jeremy probed him about his attitude to various recent publications and plays – including Kenneth Tynan's nude revue *Oh! Calcutta!* Holbrook answered: 'A great mistake had been made in tolerating that play's production. You see, one incident leads to another. If one fails to assert a view in one area then other things follow.'

Jeremy proceeded to call a phalanx of expert witnesses testifying to the virtues and beneficial uses of *The Mouth*: writers, doctors, sociologists and psychiatrists. Dr Ann Evans, a GP, explained that she thought that some of her patients would be helped by reading *The Mouth*. The coverage was, rightly, 'comprehensive'. Dr Leopold Field, a consultant psychiatrist, thought that the book had significant medical value. But it had all got too much for the judge, Judge King-Hamilton QC, who intervened:

> JUDGE: Have you read the *Decline and Fall of the Roman Empire*?
> DR FIELD [no doubt somewhat surprised]: No.
> JUDGE: But you know the view has been held that ancient Rome fell because of many years of decadence and immorality. Do you agree that in this country in recent years there are also signs of increasing decadence and immorality?
> DR FIELD: Yes.
> JUDGE: One has only to look at the increasing number of illegitimate births, abortions, cases of venereal disease and increasing homosexuality.
> DR FIELD: I think I would agree that the public has become increasingly decadent during the last decade.
> JUDGE: Is this book *The Mouth and Oral Sex* likely in your opinion to continue that process?

Extraordinarily, before Jeremy could get up to object to this question, the prosecutor himself took objection; and so the jury never found out whether Dr Field thought that *The Mouth* was continuing the process of the decay of Western civilization.

The star witness called by Jeremy was the young novelist Margaret Drabble. Jeremy explains: 'We needed a young woman, preferably with children, who would lend literary respectability to the book and its author. Maggie had written some marvellous novels and had three young children. She played her part to perfection.' Drabble praised the book's clarity and lightness of touch: 'I found it readable, entertaining and well written, although not a very serious medical work.' Richardson then cross-examined her:

RICHARDSON: In a book which deals frankly with sex, does it not surprise you that there is not a word about what old-fashioned people call love?

DRABBLE: This book is not dealing with romantic love. It is dealing with sociological ideas, but it contains more tenderness than some.

The judge then intervened to provide perhaps the comedic high point of the trial:

JUDGE: Why is it important to read about oral sex now? We have managed to get on for a couple of thousand years without it. [The witness paused.]

JUDGE: Witness, why do you hesitate?

DRABBLE: I'm sorry, My Lord, I was just trying to remember the passage in Ovid.

Jeremy stood up to re-examine Drabble. He asked solemnly, taking up the judge's point: 'Is it the case that people have got on perfectly well for 2,000 years without sexual matters being discussed?' Drabble: 'Jonathan Swift lived more than 200 years ago and was extremely neurotic because these matters were not discussed.' What a shame that the court was not then provided with a critical analysis of Swift's excremental verse. Margaret Drabble recalls leaving the witness box with a sense of *esprit d'escalier*. 'I cursed myself for not having reminded the judge of a passage in *The Taming of the Shrew*.' Let us make up for that now:

PETRUCHIO: Who knows not where a wasp does wear his sting? In his tail.

KATHERINA: In his tongue.

PETRUCHIO: Whose tongue?

KATHERINA: Yours, if you talk of tails: and so farewell.

PETRUCHIO: What, with my tongue in your tail? Nay, come again, good Kate; I am a gentleman.[2]

In his closing speech Jeremy told the jury emphatically that 'disgust is not enough – it is not enough for the Crown to show that the

176

book would horrify, shock, disgust or nauseate. In a free society people are allowed to experience all those things without a book being obscene.' John Mortimer would later tell the story that in his speech Jeremy added: 'The poor judge. The poor, poor judge. Gone without oral sex for 2,000 years.' In fact the real thrust of his attack was on the judge's ill-concealed suggestions to the jury that Britain was in terminal decline, and a principal cause of its undoing was too much sex. 'I just felt that he should not get away with this nonsense and so I decided to confront it head-on.'

> Members of the jury, was it permissive books that brought the Roman Empire down, or was it something more important, something called Christianity? Was it an Empire which we would all want to preserve? People held in bondage without any rights, without any freedom? It is terribly easy to think of the past as better than the present and that everything has gone to the dogs. But, in Victorian times, what was the position? . . . There were industrialists going to church, very proper and moral, when in their factories children were working fourteen to sixteen hours a day at the age of ten. You had judges of the greatest possible rectitude who were in fact hanging people for stealing and were later happily sentencing people to the cat-o'-nine-tails and transportation. In Leicester Square − you talk now about prostitutes − there were hundreds of prostitutes outside the theatres when the gentlemen came out of their reputable and honourable clubs in the evening. Why were all those prostitutes there?
>
> When it is said that now we are decadent, it is being said that therefore you, the jury, should stand up and find this gentleman here guilty of publishing this book, not because of the book's obscenity but because it will be in some way a protest against the decadence of our society. I ask you, first, not to act on that basis and, secondly, not to accept what is perhaps the inference that this world we live in, in England, is in fact more decadent than it was a little while ago.

Christopher Kypreos's experience of the trial was a strange one. In advance he had toyed with using the trial as a platform for a sort of counter-cultural circus, just as was to happen a few months later when the *Oz* trial got under way. At the time he was in therapy with R.D. Laing, who advised him to keep his head down. 'If I found myself with a tribe of cannibals dancing round a boiling pot, I'd paint myself and start dancing.' Ignorant of Laing's role, Jeremy had given similar advice. Kypreos looks back: 'I was ordered to get a short-back-and-sides, which my solicitor still thought too long. He sent me back to the barber. In the end I'd anticipated John Lennon's seventies hairstyle by six months.' Laing also counselled a 'conservative, even drab, and not particularly well-cut suit, perhaps dark blue would be the right colour. The jury would be less likely to convict someone dressed like them, because they would identify with the accused. He warned me to take particular care in choosing cuff links. For some unknown reason, he told me, people were exceptionally conscious of them.'

In this new, incongruous, look Kypreos sat in solitude in the dock staring straight at the jurors, the embodiment of an aspirant headmaster. Jeremy had told him that he was to have no active role in the trial. He was not called to give evidence. Kypreos recalls that he became more and more detached from the court proceedings. 'I was like an observer looking in on something unconnected to me.' But it was comforting to be entirely passive. 'Jeremy just took over. I felt everything was being taken care of. He lent a cachet of eighteenth-century gentility to the proceedings, as if waving an embroidered handkerchief to clear the air of the prosecution's noisome bigoted arguments.'

The jury spent six and a half hours deliberating. In his summing-up to the jury Judge King-Hamilton, his mind perhaps still clouded by dark images of the fall of Rome, had given them the clearest indication of his own view: 'In a civilised society, such as we like to think ours is – although sometimes one begins to doubt it – there must be a line of conduct below which behaviour is regarded as abnormal or perverse and above which it is regarded as normal. There must be a line below which things are regarded as obscene.' But the jury was unmoved by this plea. When they returned to give their verdict, another blow for freedom of expression had been struck. Kypreos was acquitted of the more important charge of 'having in his possession for publication for gain an obscene work' (i.e. *The Mouth*). But the brochure that he had sent out was too much for the jury and Kypreos was convicted of 'sending through the post indecent circulars'.

The judge made his true feelings known as he imposed a £250 fine on Kypreos:

> Whatever view one may take about the book, and obviously the jury have taken a different view about it, the majority of them had no doubt that it was all about the brochure. It was compiled by you and I think one cannot have any doubt that it was compiled to excite the interest of those who would be affected by or be curious about pornography. I say that without expressing a view as to whether the book is pornography or not [judicial code for saying that he had a very clear view of the nature of the book], because Mr Ableman has said he thought the brochure was unfair to his book. You did that quite deliberately to reach a market which you hoped would be interested in filth because that is the message of the brochure.

Paul Ableman, while not a defendant to the prosecution, had a close interest in its outcome. He emerged from the Old Bailey triumphant: 'I am absolutely delighted. I am weeping. The verdict justifies everything I ever felt about England. I think we will rush out a paperback edition. I think we deserve that after fifteen months' delay.' A paperback edition duly came out, published by Sphere Books. With the benefit of the publicity given to the trial, it may be supposed that it sold in very large quantities. Its front cover rather belied the high-minded tone of the book endorsed by Margaret Drabble: it shows a close-up of a young woman's face, full rouged lips puckering around a cigarette, in a look of orgasmic rapture. For Kypreos the acquittal was not such a cause for unalloyed celebration. The police had seized his mailing lists back in 1969 and his publishing business was effectively kept in suspense while the case came on for trial. The financial blow was irreversible.

Margaret Drabble herself looks back on the case as one of 'some hilarity', and undoubtedly it was. But Jeremy recalls that at the time he had no sense that an acquittal was a foregone conclusion. Fast in the wake of the 1960s revolution came a backlash against what even liberal sympathizers saw as the excesses of an endemic libertarianism. The production of *Oh! Calcutta!* made many of those who had previously supported the passing of the Obscene Publications Act feel distinctly queasy. By this time the prosecuting authorities had shifted their gaze away from 'serious' literature and were concentrating on the underground 'Yippy' press. *The Little Red School Book*, a manual for children with chapters on sex and drugs, was successfully prosecuted in 1970 for obscenity. *International Times*, the counter-cultural newspaper, was convicted because of the gay contact ads it contained in its back pages. And, most notoriously, the *Oz Schoolkids edition* was prosecuted in July 1971 in what was to be the longest obscenity trial ever. The defendants, Felix Dennis, Jim Anderson and Richard Neville, had been anxious for Jeremy to represent them, but unfortunately he was already booked – defending the notorious fraudster T. Dan Smith (Jeremy remembers that although he won the case this was the first and only time in his career when he was not paid; a substantial blow given that that trial lasted four weeks). Thus did the 'cab-rank'[3] rule prevent him from appearing in the most notorious obscenity case of the 1970s.

In the long run Jeremy regards this as a happy escape. Mortimer's celebrated defence in the *Oz* case marked him down as the 'pornographer's friend' and much of his life at the Bar thereafter was devoted to trailing round the country with what Mary Whitehouse described as his 'travelling circus' of experts, defending what could not be dressed up as anything other than turgid pornography. The mantle of defender of free speech, albeit free speech of a different timbre to what had gone before, had been passed to Mortimer. But it was a mantle Jeremy was happy to give up. Defending magazines called *Spank*, or films entitled *Toilet Orgy*, was not his idea of noble endeavour. Nor, in fact, was it particularly tasteful to John Mortimer, who wrote later: 'I started off defending works that had some value, but then got down to some pretty worthless things. I found it easier to defend books if I hadn't read them . . . One's only argument would be that people should not be censored.'[4] (Mortimer and Jeremy remained close friends. They retired from the Bar in the same year and would meet annually for lunch at the Garrick Club, where they would raise a joyous carefree toast to 'No more cases'.)

For Jeremy the remainder of the 1970s would be a working decade of great diversity, and his cases extended to bank robbers, journalists charged under the Official Secrets Act, and drug smugglers. But he also went on to appear in two of the most memorable obscenity trials of the 1970s and 1980s. In each case it was for what he felt was a worthwhile cause: the defence of *Last Tango in Paris* and *The Romans in Britain*.[5]

The jury's verdict that *The Mouth* was not obscene was a milestone. Serious, or even semi-serious, writing about sex was now set firmly beyond the reach of the prosecuting authorities. *The Joy of Sex*, complete with its famous drawings illustrating the various acts described, was published the next year without interference. It would become an international bestseller. There would only be one further obscenity prosecution of a book. *Inside Linda Lovelace*, a 'memoir' about a woman who discovers that her clitoris is to be found in her throat, was hauled up before the courts in 1976. That prosecution failed, John Mortimer having somehow managed to wheel out a charabanc of experts to speak to its literary and societal merit. The authorities subsequently took the view that if Linda Lovelace's ghosted memoirs were not beyond the pale then nothing was.

Judge King-Hamilton went on to try the blasphemy case brought by Mary Whitehouse in 1977 against *Gay News* and its editor Denis Lemon. The poet James Kirkup had written a poem – 'The Love that Dares to Speak its Name' – about the sexual longings of a Roman soldier over the dead Christ. Margaret Drabble again gave evidence in support of the defence, but this time, to King-Hamilton's enormous and undisguised satisfaction, a conviction was obtained. King-Hamilton published his autobiography in 1982, entitled, perhaps a trifle unoriginally, *And Nothing But the Truth*. The book is full of jaunty common sense. He relates the stories of many of the famous cases he tried while a judge of the Old Bailey – the *Gay News* case, Emil Savundra, Peter Hain, Janie Jones. But he finds no room for any mention of *The Mouth and Oral Sex*.

PART III

Eccentrics and Folk-Heroes

7

The 'Theft' of the Duke of Wellington

R v Bunton (1965)

IN 1812, AFTER his entry into Madrid in the course of the Peninsular War, the victorious Duke of Wellington sat for a portrait by Francisco Goya. It is a penetrating characterization. The heat of Spain and the weariness of battle are hinted at in a face that is slightly flushed but also imperious. Although Wellington wears his full dress uniform and regalia, there is a sense of his private character having been, almost despite himself, revealed.[1]

In 1960 the painting was purchased at Sotheby's in London by an American art collector, Charles Wrightsman, for the then stupendous sum of £140,000. Uproar ensued. Could such a national treasure, which had long been in the family of the Duke of Leeds, be permitted to cross the Atlantic? Wrightsman graciously agreed to sell the painting to the nation at the price he paid and, between them, the Wolfson Foundation and the Treasury funded the purchase. Britain's greatest warrior was saved and henceforth would be on public display to the nation.

Wellington went on show at the National Gallery in London, with considerable fanfare, on 2 August 1961. Just nineteen days later it went missing.[2] Dumbfounded security guards could offer no explanation and no clues pointed to the painting's whereabouts. This was the first time that a painting had ever been stolen from the National Gallery and there was consternation at the highest levels. The National Gallery's director offered his immediate resignation. The theft prompted an official enquiry into security at all of Britain's national galleries and museums, leading to far-reaching improvements – no longer would open windows lead to such easy pickings. A reward of £5,000 was offered for the return of the painting. The newspapers reported that the investigation into the missing picture apparently extended, through Interpol, across the world. Trains were stopped; aircraft and ships searched; hundreds of people were interviewed.

It was assumed that this was the work of a professional art thief until an anonymous letter was received by a newspaper demanding a donation of £140,000 to charity and an amnesty for the perpetrator in exchange for the painting's return. 'This act is an attempt to pick the pockets of those who love art more than charity,' the letter explained. This odd but intriguing offer was declined. There followed a number of further letters making similar demands. The National Gallery received a letter assuring it that 'The picture is not and will not be for sale. It is for ransom. £140,000 to be given to charity. If a fund is started it should be quickly made up and on the promise of a free pardon for the culprits the picture will be handed back. None of the group concerned in this escapade have any criminal convictions. All good people are urged to help this affair to a speedy conclusion.' The National Gallery remained unmoved, despite the offer of 'three pennyworth of old Spanish firewood in exchange for £140,000 of human happiness'. Then the *Daily Mirror* received the following note, headed 'Goya Com 3' carefully printed in capitals:

> The Duke is safe, his temperature cared for, his future uncertain. The painting is neither to be cloak-roomed or kiosked as such would defeat our purpose and leave us forever open to arrest. We want pardons, or the right to leave the country – banishment? We ask that some non-conformist type of person with the sportitude of a Butlin[3] and the fearless fortitude of a Montgomery should start a fund for £140,000. No law can touch him . . .

Unfortunately, no such non-conformist came forward and the trail otherwise went cold.

Nonetheless, public interest as to the whereabouts of the picture remained intense. The theft even hit the big screen: in a scene from *Dr No*, made in 1962, James Bond, walking through his adversary's lair, encounters *Wellington* propped up on an easel. Bond pauses and remarks in the trademark Connery deadpan: 'So there it is.'

Ever since its mysterious disappearance, the *Daily Mirror* had been conducting a vigorous campaign for the return of *Wellington*. In June

1965 its efforts were rewarded. Its editor received an anonymous communication enclosing a left luggage ticket issued at Birmingham New Street railway station. *Wellington* was rediscovered, rolled up and frameless, in this rather prosaic repository. It was swiftly returned to the National Gallery and its relieved director. The picture was back where it should be; but the mystery had hardly been solved.

A few weeks later, on 19 July 1965, a certain Kempton Bunton — so named because his father had apparently had a big win at the races there — surrendered himself to the police and confessed to being the culprit. Bunton, a sixty-one-year-old retired Newcastle bus driver,[4] and a figure about as far removed from the characterization of Dr No as it is possible to imagine, said that he was concerned that, after a few too many pints at his local, he had 'let something drop and was anxious that the reward of £5,000 should not be collected by a certain person . . . I thought that with a price on my head someone would squeal. To stop that I decided to give myself up . . . You would never have found it in eight hundred years. I put it at the back of my wardrobe and boarded it up.' Such was the confession that Detective Chief Inspector Weisner solemnly noted down.

The police were initially reluctant to credit Bunton's confession. Here was a man well into late middle age, upwards of six feet tall and weighing more than eighteen stones. How could he break into the National Gallery unnoticed? But Bunton was insistent. He told the incredulous officers that he had taken the painting as a protest against the imposition on poor pensioners of a mandatory television licence fee; he had presumably viewed the partly state-funded purchase of *Wellington* as a particularly acute example of false priorities. In fact, throughout the early 1960s Bunton had conducted a very public campaign against the licence fee and had twice been sentenced to short stretches in prison for his refusal to pay (his defence that he had altered his television set so that he could not receive BBC having failed to impress the Newcastle magistrates).[5]

Fantastical as it seemed, Bunton's story was supported by the forensic scientists and fingerprint experts who were called in to check it. A handwriting test confirmed his authorship of the ransom notes. Bunton also explained his methodology to the police. He had learned, from indiscreet remarks made to him by gallery guards, that the electronic security system was turned off every morning to allow the cleaners to do their rounds. During a visit to the gallery, he had opened a window in a lavatory which he was then able to climb in through the following morning, taking advantage of a ladder for-tuitously left by builders. While the guards were playing cards he removed the painting, still in its frame, from the wall and made his escape through the same window.

Bunton's confession was leaked and he was soon being lionized in the press as a particular example of the English underdog hero – 'a dreamer in a crumpled suit'. His photograph is ubiquitous in the tabloids of the day: a tall, ungainly, lumbering sort of man, pipe in hand, a jocular face sporting those round bakelite glasses that seem to have been standard issue in the early 1960s, to bus drivers and politicians alike. Bunton's wife was on hand to say her piece: Kempton was 'a clever man and a deep thinker', who had 'absolutely no regard for money. He would go a whole week with a halfpenny in his pocket providing he got his meals. He doesn't drink and would share his last pipe of baccy with anyone who had none.' It also turned out that he had written several plays, articles and even a novel: but none had ever been published. Having served as an air-raid warden in the war Bunton had then had a series of casual jobs. But, his wife continued ruefully, he would always leave after 'rowing with his boss over a matter of principle'.

The authorities were not so mesmerized by this unlikely star. Bunton was prosecuted for theft, making demands with menaces, and causing a public nuisance. The last charge was founded on the accusation that, by removing the painting, Bunton had 'deprived people of their enjoyment of it'. The trial came on at the Old Bailey in November 1965 before the Recorder of London, Judge Aarvold.[6]

Jeremy had been retained as leading counsel for Bunton. He decided to put forward a simple but ingenious defence. The defin-ition of theft at that time required that the defendant should take property belonging to another person with the intention of perman-ently depriving the owner of it. Jeremy would contend that Bunton could not be guilty of the offence of theft because he had never intended to deprive the owner – the National Gallery – of the painting permanently. He had merely intended to 'borrow' *Wellington* to draw attention to what he considered to be the 'outrageous' sum of £140,000 paid for it 'when so many old-age pensioners could not even afford a television licence'. Jeremy recalls: 'The judge was absolutely furious when he came to realize what the defence was. The idea that Bunton would plead "not guilty" did not occur to him.'

The trial started with the heavily guarded painting being shown and identified to the jurors by Michael Levey, then assistant keeper of the National Gallery.[7] Jeremy vigorously cross-examined Levey about the painting. He had, he recalls, an ace up his sleeve in the form of the pronouncements of a past president of the Royal Academy, Sir Gerald Kelly, who had questioned the authenticity of the painting, calling it 'slick, incompetent and vulgar'. Jeremy slowly built up the point. Was not the Royal Academy an august institution of artistic learning? Yes. Were not presidents of that institution only appointed on account of their eminence in the field of art? Yes. Had not Sir Gerald publicly questioned *Wellington*? Flustered, the hapless Levey admitted that there had been controversy concerning the authenticity of the painting; and that Sir Gerald might have said something to the effect that the painting was incompetent and vulgar. Jeremy continued. There were those, were there not, besides Mr Bunton, but also respectable figures in the art world, who thought that £140,000 was an outrageous sum to pay for this picture? Well, admitted Levey, there had been a certain amount of criticism. When the prosecution objected to this line of questioning as irrelevant, Jeremy robustly asserted that the issue of authenticity was relevant to the charge against Bunton that he had caused a public nuisance: 'If you are stopping someone going to see an old bit of canvas with a piece of paint slapped on it there might be some difference between that and a painting worth £140,000.' The judge interjected to say to Jeremy that whether *Wellington* was 'a genuine picture or rubbish it would still be a picture of interest to the public'. If he was going to try to prove during the trial that *Wellington* was a fake 'I shall be interested but I doubt whether I shall allow it.'[8]

Jeremy then challenged Lord Robbins, the chairman of the trustees of the National Gallery – who had made the ultimate decision to purchase this 'old bit of canvas' – on the authenticity of the painting and the price paid. Robbins, a much admired acquaintance of Jeremy, unlike Levey found Jeremy's questions rather more congenial and could not suppress a half-wink from the witness box. By this time the judge was becoming thoroughly agitated with Jeremy's questions concerning the painting's provenance. 'Mr Hutchinson, I do not want this trial to be a debating forum on the qualities of this picture. I rule the question irrelevant.' But the damage had been done to the prosecution case: the jury were left with the suspicion that not only had the state paid a very large sum of money for a painting – money that could perhaps have been used to assist deserving pensioners struggling to pay their television licences – but it might have bought a dud. Might Bunton have a point?

Meanwhile, Lord Robbins was enjoying his jousting with Jeremy. He was asked whether he had ever said that if the painting were returned the National Gallery would not treat it as a criminal matter. Lord Robbins's response was that he would never say that: 'It would have been an open invitation to any flighty minded person to borrow a Michelangelo or the *Virgin of the Rocks* and say for £500,000 to be given to the Boy Scouts it would be returned and there would be no offence.' Jeremy then, with the air of making a casual aside, asked Lord Robbins whether he felt at all alarmed when he had received Bunton's letter of demands. A conviction on the second charge would require evidence that the victim was caused some fear or apprehension by the menaces made. Lord Robbins retorted, 'No of course not.' That put paid to that charge.

Kempton Bunton then lumbered into the witness box. It was his turn to explain himself. In answer to questions put to him by Jeremy, he confirmed that when he had read about the price paid for *Wellington* he considered that the £140,000 'could be better spent in buying television licences for old-age pensioners'. When he came to London he 'had the idea of taking this picture from the National Gallery. On arriving I had a very bad dose of flu and the whole thing was rather hazy, but I had a job to do and I did it.' When he got home he had put the painting in a cupboard in his bedroom; he had not told his wife because 'the world would have known if

I had done so'. Bunton then, with a naivety which must have won over the jury, said that he had assumed that after his first ransom letter there would be an 'immediate collection for the picture as the money was to go to charity'. But he was insistent that he always intended to return the painting and never wanted any money for himself. 'It was no good to me otherwise. I could not have hung it in my kitchen.' Jeremy remembers what a charming character Kempton Bunton was and how his performance clearly endeared him to the jury. Here was 'sportitude' in the flesh.

The growing smiles on the jury's faces encouraged Jeremy to launch an attack on the whole prosecution. The authorities, he suggested, were desperately anxious to 'get the man who removed the £140,000 Goya portrait convicted of something. Maybe those concerned were irked that the wrong charges had been framed . . . But nothing in this country is a crime unless it is expressly forbidden by law, however inconvenient and unfortunate that might be.' Certainly it was 'not a crime in law to remove a picture from an art gallery, provided there was no intention to keep it permanently . . . You may think,' Jeremy told the jury, 'the law is stupid about this. If someone goes into your house and takes your television set because he wants to watch a football match and then keeps it, it is extremely irritating and annoying but it is not stealing. It is not stealing if you take your neighbour's lawn mower and forget all about it. If at the time the television set or the lawn mower was taken there was no intention of keeping it permanently you may have caused annoyance and intense irritation but it is not theft.'

Whether or not the jury was swayed by this argument or whether it was simply charmed by Bunton's gumption will never be known. But it acquitted Bunton of all charges, except that of theft of the frame of the picture, which Bunton said he had left in a King's Cross boarding house four years earlier and which he had been unable to locate. This frame was valued at £100, a drop in the ocean compared to the value of the painting itself. 'He had no idea it was even so valuable as that,' pleaded Jeremy. Nonetheless the judge sentenced Bunton to three months in prison. In his sentencing remarks the judge could not hide his irritation at the jury's leniency: 'The jury have accepted that at the material time you intended to return this picture and they have accepted that you made no demands for money with menaces for yourself or for charity as such. I, of course, accept the jury's verdict on these matters,[9] but motives, even if they are good, cannot justify creeping into art galleries in order to extract paintings of value so that you can use them for your own purposes. This has got to be discouraged.' Jeremy's reaction to the sentence passed on Bunton was that 'the judge committed a serious offence under section 1 of the Dirty Tricks Act.'

As for Bunton, he remained, as the *Daily Express* put it, 'bulkily impassive' as he heard the sentence being pronounced. Perhaps surprisingly for a man so garrulous in his ransom notes, it is reported that, after sentence had been passed, he merely declared, 'I have nothing further to say', before marching away to the cells, 'pausing only to smooth the creases from his cheap, crumpled suit'.

That was not the end of the matter. The authorities had taken note of Jeremy's arguments and the sympathy they had apparently elicited from the jury. In the National Gallery's biannual account of its activities, published in early 1967 it was complained: 'To most of the world it was a shock to read that it is not against the English law to climb into a public gallery at dead of night, remove a national treasure, keep it hidden for several years and meanwhile attempt to extort ransom money from the public for whom it had just been acquired . . . Bunton's trial has had the unfortunate result of informing the world that deeds like his can be performed in England with impunity – provided the perpetrator is more careful about details than Bunton was over the frame.' The response was a swiftly introduced change in the law. Section 1 of the Theft Act 1968 now read as follows: 'A person is guilty of theft if he dishonestly appropriates property belonging to another with the intention of permanently depriving the other of it; and "thief" and "steal" shall be construed accordingly.' But, by section 6 of the same Act the phrase 'with the intention of permanently depriving the other of it' was now elaborately defined: '(1) A person appropriating property belonging to another without meaning the other permanently to lose the thing itself is nevertheless to be regarded as having the intention of permanently depriving the other of it if his intention is to treat the thing as his own to dispose of regardless of the other's rights; and a borrowing or lending of it may amount to so treating it if, but only if, the borrowing or lending is for a period and in circumstances making it equivalent to an outright taking or disposal.' The sheer density of this drafting is surely a legislative attempt to prevent a future Bunton from getting away with it. On a belt and braces basis the Act also contained a wholly new provision at section 11: 'where the public have access to a building in order to view the building or part of it, or a collection or part of a collection housed in it, any person who without lawful authority removes from the building or its grounds the whole or part of any article displayed or kept for display to the public in the building or that part of it or in its grounds shall be guilty of an offence.'

One prominent legal commentator explained that this section had been inserted in response to 'public indignation at the outcome of the *Goya* case'.[10] While it cannot be doubted that Bunton's acquittal led to a change in the law, whether the reference to 'public indignation' is accurate is open to question. Bunton has taken his place as a minor member within a peculiarly English gallery of demotic hero-villains. Robin Hood is its honorary president and notable members include Captain Blood, who stole the Crown Jewels, and Jack Sheppard, the famous eighteenth-century thief, whose hanging at Tyburn drew a crowd of 200,000. I suspect that Bernard Levin, writing in *The Times* in 1972, captured the public mood more closely: 'The splendid Mr Kempton Bunton . . . was railroaded to jail in a very shabby manner; since he had constantly proclaimed his wish and intention to return the picture he could not be charged with larceny . . . So he was charged with stealing the frame, and imprisoned for that.'

The law may have been quickly changed, but it took Bunton rather longer to achieve the aim of his protest. Free television licences for the over-75s were only introduced in 2000.

There is an intriguing postscript to the case. After Bunton left prison in early 1966 it was reported that his son had distributed letters to the press inviting sealed bids for the full story 'plus film rights', and including the tantalizing suggestion that his 'defence advisors knew as little about the truth as you do'. It is not clear whether any bids were forthcoming, but certainly no film was made. However, in 1969 it was reported that a man from Leeds had apparently taken responsibility for the 'crime'. Nothing further came of that, but many years later, in 2012, the National Archives released a confidential file from the Director of Public Prosecutions dating from 1969, in which it appeared that the 'man from Leeds' was none other than Bunton's son, who had himself apparently confessed to the police that he – not his father – had taken the painting, in exactly the way Bunton had described to the police in 1965, to draw attention to his father's campaign against the television licence fee. Having crawled through the lavatory window, he had then given the painting to Bunton Snr. The policeman who had taken down Bunton Jnr's confession believed it. He reported:

> At the time of the offence, Kempton was 57 years old. He is a tall heavily built man, who now weighs somewhere in the region of 18 stones, and it is extremely unlikely that he would have had the agility to scale the outer wall and make his way unaided to the toilet window. He would also in my view have been incapable of returning to the wall and climbing over it, without causing some damage to the painting, whereas his son, John, who at that time was only 20 years of age, is still of good physique and would have been quite capable of taking the painting in the manner in which he describes.[11]

Nonetheless, bruised by the result in the first trial, the authorities decided to take the matter no further. The police's original doubts about Bunton's ability to squeeze through a first-floor lavatory window may have been justified after all.

So far as I know, the authenticity of Goya's *Wellington* has not since been questioned. It remains on view in Room 39 at the National Gallery.

8

'Like a Boeing 707'

R v Keating (1979)

THE TOM KEATING story started in July 1976 and, for the next few years, exercised a mesmeric fascination over the nation. Its beginnings were mysterious and hesitant, its denouement dramatic, and its consequences far-reaching.

On 16 July 1976 *The Times* published a lengthy article, written by its Sale Room Correspondent Geraldine Norman, about a spate of drawings that had, over the last five years or so, come on to the market, apparently by the early nineteenth-century visionary painter, Samuel Palmer. A follower of William Blake, Palmer had produced, while a young man living at Shoreham in Kent, a series of landscape drawings of luminous and mysterious beauty: a kind of artistic equivalent of one of Keats's odes. He had then married and, as the years went by, his style had shifted to a more recognizably Victorian mode of painting. On Palmer's death in 1881 his son, having inherited much of his work, had destroyed many of the Shoreham drawings, dismissing them as meretricious juvenilia before his father found his mature, if conventional, style. This act of destruction would make Palmer's Shoreham *oeuvre*, small in number but uncertain in extent, all the more prized in the more receptive twentieth century. And so, possibly, all the more susceptible to the forger's art.

Geraldine Norman's thesis, produced after a protracted and in-depth investigation,[1] which had included discussions with a number of academics and curators, was a startling one. It was clearly stated in the opening words of her article: 'The surmise that a forger has been at work imitating Samuel Palmer's Shoreham period drawings has only recently begun to crystallise towards certainty in the minds of those most interested in Palmer's work.'[2] Five of the drawings identified by Norman had come from the same source, a certain Jane Kelly, who had claimed that they had been sent back from Sri Lanka on the death of her grandfather, the drawings having apparently been originally owned by an ancestor who travelled to the East in the 1860s to become a tea planter. There they had apparently remained ever since. Four of Kelly's Palmers had been acquired by the Leger Galleries of Bond Street and one had since been sold at Sotheby's at a record price for the artist. But a phalanx of leading experts now cast doubt on their authenticity.

Close analysis revealed that the brushwork was unlike other undisputed works and the paper had constituents consistent only with manufacture in the twentieth century. It had also been noted that the questioned drawings seemed to contain various references to other genuine Palmers. Norman had undertaken a considerable amount of research on the questioned Palmers and the article had been published despite warnings from Leger's solicitors that its publication might provoke a libel writ. Norman recalls going with her editor, William Rees-Mogg, to see a libel silk in the Temple who advised that if any claim were brought the prospects were 60/40 in favour of *The Times*; but that if the Leger succeeded damages would be likely to be heavy, over £100,000. That was good enough for Rees-Mogg: he agreed to publication. Yet the missing link was Jane Kelly. She was nowhere to be found – although it was thought that she might now be somewhere in either North or South America. Norman's article ended with the words: 'Somewhere there is a talented painter at work, and I would love to meet him.'

The article provoked an angry response from a director of the Leger Galleries. In a letter to the editor[3] he robustly asserted the authenticity of the drawings. There followed a vigorous correspondence played out in the letters page of *The Times* from a variety of correspondents, either supporting or denouncing the forgery charge.[4] It was made known that the British Antique Dealers' Association was convening an urgent meeting on the question.

Norman's article also elicited more elliptical interest. A few days later Norman received an anonymous phone call. A nameless voice at the end of the telephone, having lowered his demand in a matter of minutes from £5,000 to £150 for the information, told her that Jane Kelly was a picture restorer who had, a few years earlier, been living in Suffolk with a painter twice her age called Tom Keating. Norman realized she might be getting closer to the truth. A trip to East Anglia finally led her to a small and isolated cottage in Dedham and to Keating's door. It was opened by a garrulous man in his sixties, sporting a full white beard and sparkling eyes. 'I thought I had met Father Christmas.' Norman was led into a room where was hung a version of Constable's *Hay Wain* over the mantelpiece. Keating offered Norman a cup of Nescafé, apologizing that he could not afford whisky, and poured out his life story. He was forthcoming on all subjects except two: Jane Kelly and Samuel Palmer. But, as Norman recalls, 'his laughing eyes belied his reticence.'

Further attempts by Norman to meet Keating were stymied by information that he had hurriedly departed on a protracted motor-cycle tour of West Country churches. Nonetheless, on 10 August Norman decided to make a positive identification. The story she now described was an extraordinary one. She positively identified the 'masterly imitator of Samuel Palmer' (she did not use the word forger) as Keating and the man she now described was a true original.

Born in a slum in Forest Hill during the Great War, one of seven children, Keating had left home at fourteen and worked in almost every kind of job imaginable before finding himself, a stoker in the navy, in Singapore when the Japanese invaded in 1941. His life after demobilization had been one of hardship. Having failed to obtain a diploma in art at Goldsmiths College (while scoring high marks for 'painterly technique', he fell down on 'original composition'), he was thwarted in his ambition to become an art teacher and an original artist. Instead he had taken up picture restoration and had developed, at the instigation of restorers for whom he worked, a facility for creating pastiches of old masters and Impressionists. The clear implication of Norman's article was that Keating had put into the market huge quantities of 'pastiches' of such masters as Degas and Constable, and the Canadian genre painter Krieghoff.

His life had been chaotic, moving from place to place, obtaining work where he could get it, a man liked by all who came into contact with him, but with no apparent facility, or interest, in making money. 'One gets the clear impression,' Norman wrote, 'not of a calculating man, rather of one who is a painter first and a picture restorer second, but has a facility for imitation.' But he was a man with a grudge against the art establishment. His diatribe against art dealers was 'littered with expletives'.

Meanwhile the art world against which Keating railed was in frenzy. Committees were formed to investigate. There were demands for formal enquiries. Resignations were threatened. The search for Keatings mistaken for the works of others began in earnest. By contrast, after their initial very public assertion of the authenticity of their disputed Palmers, Leger Galleries went particularly quiet. No writ was issued. It transpired that they had agreed to take back a drawing that they had sold to a private collector.

The elusive Tom Keating had read from his West Country fastness the article that had named him as the master 'imitator'. He telephoned Geraldine Norman. A dinner at Odin's restaurant on Devonshire Street in London was convened and Keating cut short his church tour. By the end of a lengthy supper next steps had been resolved. Geraldine and her husband Frank, the novelist and playwright, retreated to a Georgian manor in Berkshire – which the Normans had borrowed from a friend for their summer holiday – with Tom Keating in tow. The next two weeks were spent extracting Keating's life story in a series of marathon interviews, shaded from the heat of the hottest summer of the century by a magnolia tree, and lubricated by copious quantities of red wine. Geraldine may have 'outed' Keating, but now she, with her husband, were to be his biographers and collaborators. Frank Norman was himself a Barnardo's boy turned Soho bohemian who had made a success out of writing about cockney life. He had had a huge hit a few years earlier with the musical *Fings Ain't Wot They Used T'Be*, and the two men immediately realized they had much in common.

From Berkshire Keating now wrote his own letter to *The Times*,[5] letting loose a broadside against the art establishment. 'I have just returned from the hallowed ground of Glastonbury to find that my activities in the field of art have caused some consternation in artistic circles (though not half as much as my amateur activities as a motor-cyclist created on the busy by-ways of our lovely land – apologies to the policemen on point duty in Bath last week).' So began his

letter, and in that single paragraph the quiddity of Keating's personality was perfectly demonstrated. Keating then addressed the central
charge made against him. 'It seems that I am held responsible for
the making of pastiches in the style of Samuel Palmer, the French
impressionists, German expressionists etc over the past twenty-five
years. I do not deny these allegations. In fact, I openly confess to having
done them.' Keating defended himself vigorously. He explained that
under his oil paintings he had written his own name, or the word
'fake', or a rude word. He had also, when producing his pastiches,
intentionally used paper that was not contemporary with the artist
being imitated; this was to 'ensure that the work could not possibly
long be taken for the master in question'. Keating then set out his
core position (which would, a couple of years later, form the main-
stay of his defence in the trial he had to face):

> I cannot imagine how anyone could begin to believe that the crude
> daubs being marketed as Samuel Palmer's were authentic. Anyone
> with a true love of this kindly, generous and devout artist (who was
> unable to afford a pinch of snuff in his declining years) will know
> that he could not possibly have done this work, even on an off day.
> I flooded the market with the 'work' of Palmer and many others,
> not for gain (I hope I am no materialist), but simply as a protest
> against merchants who make capital out of those I am proud to call
> my brother artists, both living and dead.

Keating refuted any suggestion that he had intentionally duped
anyone. 'I have never sold directly to anyone who was not aware of
the nature of the work or made any secret of my imitations.'

Rarely has a letter to *The Times* created a greater sensation. The
newspapers were agog. One dealer immediately offered Keating his
gallery for an exhibition of his imitations. During his Berkshire
retreat, while press reporters engaged in desperate searches to find
him, Tom now revealed all to Geraldine and Frank Norman. His
faker's art had been learned working for a picture restorer and had
inexorably progressed from restoration to imitation. A seminal experience had been when he saw one of his imitations, which he had
produced at the request of his employer, in a window on Old Bond
Street with the signature of the painter he had sought to pastiche

painted in. 'I wondered, as I stood there, how many other dealers in the West End went in for this kind of deception.' These paintings were never strict copies of existing works, rather they were based on and in the manner of the work of masters from the past. He claimed that he had produced between 1,000 and 2,000 pastiches, or 'Sexton Blakes' as he described them,[6] over a period of some twenty-five years. This apparently included about eighty Palmers. Geraldine Norman was immediately taken with the idea of a further project: to produce a form of anti-catalogue raisonné of Keating's output. But it soon became apparent that such a project was foredoomed. Tom's mode of production and distribution was chaotic: he would give them to friends, use them to pay off minor debts, place them randomly in country auctions, provide them to friendly dealers to see if they could sell them. They had gone out into the world; except for the tiny proportion whose location was known, where they were now it would be impossible to determine.[7]

Terms were swiftly hammered out with the publishers Hutchinson and Co.,[8] and on 27 August, barely six weeks after the 'Samuel Palmer affair' had broken, Tom Keating made his first public appearance before an intrigued world. There is a charming photograph of Tom, standing before one of his own pastiches, the *Hay Wain* in reverse, beneath which Geraldine Norman had drunk her instant coffee a few weeks earlier, arms open and grinning broadly, seeming to revel in his sudden notoriety, as fifty photographers clicked away and a hundred journalists asked their questions. Tom proved as garrulous in person as he had been on paper. He again spoke of his dislike of the art establishment. 'My aim was never to make money but to make the art world look foolish.' And yet already the ambiguity in Tom's position was becoming apparent. Who was exploiting whom? He explained that he had started making pastiches because he had been conned by the art world but 'some of my pastiches were purchased by gentlemen, if that's what I can call them, from the art world for sums of about £20. They would end up being sold on the art market after false signatures had been painted on them by a man known as "Jim the Penman".' And, as if indifferent to the consequences, as if the very force of his joviality and lack of *savoir faire* would see him through, he continued his self-revelatory correspondence to *The Times*. In one letter[9] he proclaimed: 'I have made dozens of pastiches in the style of Palmer, mostly quick sketches. I signed those I felt might reach an avaricious hand with "not S Palmer" (the not being hidden under the slip of the frame); I also signed my own name in the bark of a tree, etc or I wrote "S Palmerer", the last two letters being hidden under the slip on the right hand side. When marouflaging paper to panel I often used modern synthetic gum and signed my own name or whatever words came to me at the time, i.e. "fake", or "God Bless" or "why be greedy" – but never swear words as Palmer was a religious man.' A trip to Canada saw him treated like a celebrity as he appeared on television shows and visited museums with journalists in tow, in search of his fakes. Tom Keating may have suddenly become famous, but the attention now focused on him was a strain; his health suffered and he was unable to work.

The Fake's Progress ('Being the cautionary history of the master painter and simulator Mr Tom Keating', as it was subtitled) was published a few months later in 1977, with Tom Keating and Geraldine and Frank Norman all billed as authors. As well as offering an account of his picaresque life, the book purported to explain his reasons for producing his pastiches. What emerged was a complex tangle of motives – hinted at during his press conference the year before – that were not all consistent one with the other. His fakes were not exact copies of existing paintings, but, wrote Tom, they were 'maybe close enough to the original for someone to take it for the real thing'. The resentment against the art world was palpable and 'Getting my own back on dealers who exploit people in this way is one of the reasons I started doing Sexton Blakes . . . It seemed disgraceful to me how many [artists] had died in poverty. All their lives they had been exploited by unscrupulous dealers and then, as if to dishonour their memory, these same dealers continued to exploit them in death. I was determined to do what I could to avenge my brothers . . .' But a few pages later Tom spoke of his desire to do 'homage to the old masters' and was insistent that he had no intention to deceive anyone. 'No matter how clever a Sexton may be it will always show up if you put it alongside a genuine picture or have a genuine picture still fresh in your mind.' Hence on one occasion, he tells the reader that, having consigned a Krieghoff pastiche to auction he was greatly relieved when it only achieved a small sum. And 'I have never made any secret of the fact that I do Sexton Blakes.' A few pages later: 'Auctions are always a gamble and I've never minded all that much if my Sextons have got on to the market in this way, because at least the buyer has a sporting chance. But whenever I've had any say in the matter I've always tried to stop people that I've been associated with from selling them directly to dealers.' And yet later Tom is recalling a story of a large Muller canvas being taken to Sotheby's and it being rejected because painted in acrylic: 'You can't win them all I suppose.' Where did artlessness turn into artfulness? What could not be denied, however, was that if Tom's purpose had been to deceive, it certainly had not been to make himself a rich man. He displayed an almost wilful inability to turn a penny. As he said in a BBC programme broadcast just before the book's publication, 'If I'd wanted money, mate, you'd never have heard of me.' This was an attribute noted by Geraldine Norman: 'He did not like having money and when he got it he would give it away as if keeping it somehow corrupted him. He identified with poverty. With his facility, he could have been rich years earlier, but he needed this grudge against the world which poverty allowed him to maintain.'

Tom Keating might describe his pastiches as 'crude daubs', but, in fairness to the directors of the Leger Galleries, they had taken in many other experts. The red faces extended to Sotheby's and Colnaghi's as well as the keeper of the Department of Prints and Drawings at the British Museum, who had verified one Palmer drawing before its purchase by a local museum. The same drawing had even been included as part of the established *oeuvre* in a recently published book on Palmer.

Then things turned sour. It emerged that some years earlier the Redfern Gallery, at that time one of the leading dealers in modern art, had purchased a large collection of (so it now appeared) pastiche German Expressionist paintings from friends of Keating's, who had acted as informal agents for him. In keeping with Keating's lack of commercial nous, the sum paid by Redfern had been derisory. Yet some of these had been sold on as genuine. The Redfern had made a complaint to the police. They were followed by the Leger Galleries. A prolonged investigation ensued and Tom was interviewed four times by Scotland Yard. Keating was defiant. An article in *The Times* described him, 'tumbler of alcohol in one hand and homemade cigarette in the other', dismissing any worries at the rumoured prospect of arrest. 'I am a little guy who likes to creep round corners, look at the birdies and the flowers and have a quiet noggin.' One detects in this bravado a slightly forced tone. Tom may have enjoyed his notoriety, but the ongoing police investigation was oppressing him. Faithful to his principles of fecklessness, fame appears to have brought him no financial security and by June 1977 it was reported that he was 'stony broke'. Some comfort came in the form of an anonymous patron – a 'Medici without a dagger' in his lovely description – who offered him sanctuary in the grounds of his Suffolk castle.

This show of sanguinity proved misplaced. At the end of July 1977, just a month after the publication of *The Fake's Progress*, Keating was charged with nine offences of conspiracy, criminal deception and inducing people to sign cheques by deception, the majority relating to the Palmers. The essence of the charges was that Keating had passed off his Palmer pastiches as genuine, using Jane Kelly, his former girlfriend, as his fence. There can be little doubt that the decision to charge was hastened by the revelations that emerged with the imprimatur of having actually come from the man himself. An arrest warrant was also issued against Jane Kelly, now living in Toronto. She was eventually extradited back to England, to be charged alongside Keating.

With his background it was inevitable that Jeremy would be retained as Keating's counsel. 'I met Tom Keating a number of times before the trial and I came to like him enormously. He was as close to an anarchist as any man I ever met. He seemed to have this hatred for art dealers and the art establishment, which he felt had excluded him and exploited him for so long. So, he wanted to undermine this whole market in art which he despised by infiltrating it with fakes. The result was that in some cases the market in particular painters was actually deflated because of the perceived risk that any painting might be a fake. This served Tom's purpose – it made art more affordable and also undermined dealers' profits. And it also went some way, as he saw it, to creating a kind of democracy of painting ownership. Nonetheless, Tom assured me that, when putting a work into auction or offering it to a dealer, he had never made a false pretence as to its authorship, but had always left it to the auctioneer or dealer to make his own assessment. The real problem came when the first of his Palmer pastiches was sold at auction to the Leger Galleries for the extraordinary sum of £9,400. It was then that Jane Kelly went down to see Harold Leger in London and suddenly substantial sums were being paid out.'

The principal charges against Tom Keating were that he had conspired with Jane Kelly intentionally to mislead the Leger Galleries, as well as a Suffolk gallery, into believing that works by him had in fact been painted by Samuel Palmer. Jeremy saw that the only way to handle the case was to 'arouse in the minds of the jury a suspicion that the greedy dealers were well aware that the works might not be genuine, but that the possibility of making a substantial profit overcame their scruples, operating as they were in a dubious market. If there was doubt about deception that should be an end to the case. There remained, of course, the distasteful vision of the perpetrator of the fakes apparently seeking to save his own skin by putting the blame on his young lover. Yet Tom's engaging personality and determination to disrupt the dodgy goings-on of the art trade might, I felt, win the day. But it was going to be a very difficult defence. As I read *The Fake's Progress*, it was like an albatross round my neck, one vastly long, if opaque act of self-incrimination which the prosecution could make hay with against Tom.'

The trial started in January 1979 and was expected to last four weeks. Jeremy's habit was to arrive in court early to arrange his papers and compose himself for the battle ahead. Trials are events which, however formal their physical locations, are in the end examinations of human behaviour in all its contingency and waywardness. They can throw up the unexpected at any moment and barristers guard themselves against that by rituals of organiza-tion: the pens placed just so, the notebook in just such a place on the desk, and so on. Alone in the courtroom that morning, Jeremy discovered an intriguing package on his lectern. 'I opened it and found a delightful Sexton Blake by the artist Constantin Guys. In my chambers, hanging behind my chair, was a drawing by Guys of two ladies of the town. When Tom came for consultations with me I would often notice, while I was expostulating on the law, he seemed rather more occupied drawing in his notepad. He had obviously spotted it. Both pictures are hung in my study, side by side, to this day.'

By now Jane Kelly had herself pleaded guilty to obtaining money by deception, and had agreed to give evidence for the prosecution against her former lover. The prosecutor, David Tudor Price, a colleague in Jeremy's chambers, told the jury that Keating had exercised a 'Svengali-like' influence over her. She had sold on his behalf four 'false Palmers' to the Leger Galleries in 1970 and 1971 for a total of £20,750. Leger had then sold those Palmers for £40,500 over the next two years. Keating had claimed that he had not benefited at all from the sales, something Kelly described as an absolute lie. She told a rather different story to the picture painted by Tom Keating of himself as an ingénu who despised money: 'After I got the money from the first sale of a Palmer pastiche to the Leger Galleries, we took the cash home and spread it all on a large table in the sitting room. Tom said he had always hoped that one day he would be able to cover the carpet with bank notes.' Jeremy remembers how difficult it was to cross-examine Jane Kelly. 'Tom had loved her dearly and could not bear the thought of challenging her in court. At one stage he had contemplated pleading guilty to save her. And I was very worried that attacking her credibility in the witness box would be very dangerous. After all she was decades younger than Tom and had first met him when she was sixteen. Was it credible that he, the faker, was the one being taken in, rather than the other way round? But Tom's version of events was that she had conned him about the money she got from selling his Palmers. He had seen hardly any of it. But what was interesting is that the judge seemed to have rather taken to Tom.' Sir James Miskin, the Recorder of London, intervened in Jeremy's cross-examination:

JUDGE: In layman's language, in many of your conversations with
Mr Posnett [one of the directors of the Leger Galleries] you were
lying like a trooper?
KELLY: Oh yes, I lied about the origins of the paintings.

The prosecution's next witness was David Posnett, a director of the
Leger Galleries, who complained that Keating had made Leger a
'laughing stock of the trade'. Later to become one of London's most
eminent dealers, Posnett was at the time a young man with a peri-
pheral involvement in the purchase of the pastiches by his gallery.
He was called to give evidence because it was to him that Jane Kelly
had provided the false provenance surrounding the pastiches and it
was he who had written out the cheques on behalf of the Leger
Galleries. As Jeremy recalls, the Gallery's 'position was difficult for
the prosecution. Harold Leger's original purchase of a Palmer fake
had been at a Suffolk auction in 1970 when they paid £9,400. Days
afterwards an art dealer, David Gould, had written a letter to *The
Times* questioning the painting – in particular the "somewhat unusual
bats". But Leger had nonetheless put it in their exhibition as a
genuine Palmer at a price of £15,000, and sold it, at a profit. They
then bought three more of these Palmers from Jane Kelly, and sold
each one for a profit.' The gallery had, after all, made a substantial
profit on the Palmers they had purchased. Jeremy exploited Leger's
position (in a manner, as his solicitor remembered, which was 'almost
intimidating in its charm and courtesy'):

JEREMY: When you read Mr Gould's letter in *The Times* did you
make any further enquiries into the painting's authenticity?
POSNETT: No. It caused us to think but we did not seek further
expert opinion.
JEREMY: Look please at the painting of *Sepham Barn*.
POSNETT: Yes, I see it.
JEREMY: If this picture turned out to be a pastiche you would have
lost your £9,400 and the profit you hoped to make.
POSNETT: I am well aware of the pitfalls of art dealing.
JEREMY: Do you see the so-called bat hovering by the setting moon?
POSNETT: Yes.
JEREMY: It looks more like a Boeing 707, does it not?
[Laughter.]

POSNETT: It did not cause me to doubt the picture's authenticity.

JEREMY: And the paintings subsequently brought to you by Jane Kelly, you believed that they were all genuine Samuel Palmers?

POSNETT: I did.

JEREMY: You genuinely believed that this cornucopia of Samuel Palmers suddenly appearing was really happening . . .?

POSNETT: I did, sir . . . If I thought for one moment that any of these pictures were wrong, I would not have bought them; my firm would not have bought them; and if we thought the picture we already had was wrong, we would never have offered it for sale.

By now the jury were beginning to enjoy themselves and showing signs of amusement. And so it went on. The *Observer* described the trial at the Old Bailey as 'the best show in town, where they have been packing them in for the past two weeks for the trial of artist, eccentric and bon viveur, Tom Keating'. Meanwhile Keating himself spent his time in court drawing. It was reported that he had already accomplished seven sketches of faces in court and that the 'policeman whose job it is to make sure he doesn't make a bolt for it was full of admiration for his work'. The newspaper also noted something that Jeremy was conscious of in court: 'Even though Jane Kelly and Tom were now on different sides of the court, and I was having to attack her evidence, she and Tom would look at each other, as if remembering the old days and their past love.'

David Gould, who had first challenged the authenticity of a Keating pastiche, himself gave evidence. He was shown *Sepham Barn*, the earliest of Keating's versions of Palmer to be sold to the Leger Galleries. Asked by Jeremy if he needed time to consider it, and to further laughter, he declined: 'That is unnecessary. This is an appalling little piece of rubbish.' Jeremy asked him to look at the bat in flight. Gould responded, 'Ah this is your infamous Boeing 707.' Jeremy (amid further laughter): 'I have never been so strongly supported before.' Jeremy notes: 'Our defence, as so often, depended on belittling the ability of the defendant. We had to show that there was at least reasonable doubt that no serious art dealer or expert could have mistaken Tom's daubs for the genuine product.' On the other hand another witness, wriggling with embarrassment, testified to having included three

Constable pastiches, which Jane Kelly had offered to him, in his book on Constable. In the book he had described the ostensible Constables thus: 'His work comes through to the viewer like a familiar voice.' And, as he explained with some pathos, even now, knowing what he knew, they still did.

The highlight of the trial was of course the arrival of Tom Keating into the witness box. Was he a money-hating innocent who knew nothing of what became of his pastiches after they left his studio, or was he a scheming duper who was doing his best to bamboozle the art world to make some cash? Jeremy recalls: 'I felt sure he was the former but the problem was that his book and his public pronouncements allowed for both interpretations.' There was no doubt that it had been Jane Kelly who had dealt with the various galleries and auction houses, and a critical question was Tom's knowledge of her conduct. He was asked what had happened to the £9,400 made from the sale of the first Palmer. 'We rowed about it for days. Jane argued that it did not matter whether it was 30 shillings or £30,000: the dealer ought to have known what he was buying. My own feeling was that it would be wonderful to give back the money and show this fellow what he had bought. Jane said that I had been exploited all my life – "let this pay for all the years you have worked". In the end I agreed. It was a Robin Hood, Maid Marion thing if you like.' Jeremy asked him what had happened to the money? 'I probably had some, she probably had some, and lots of other people probably had some. My family would have, I have always sent them money. My children, my mother. Other odd people. I doubled the salary of the cleaning lady. The only thing I bought for myself was a moped for £93.'

Then he became more lyrical. 'Sometimes my pastiches were so good I can say with all due modesty that I think there was some curious combination with the old master himself. Some painters say it is spiritualism. I am not a spiritualist, but there were times when the master came down and took over the painting and it was terribly difficult to tell the difference between his work and my own.' But, on the other hand, one of the Palmers sold to Leger was, he said, an obvious fake. 'It certainly isn't Palmer. It is far too woolly. Even the sheep are woolly.' Jeremy recalls: 'Tom came out of the witness box largely unscathed. For all the contradictions in his case, the sheer force of his personality had somehow ploughed through the difficulties. He had charmed the whole court.' The final witness to give evidence for Tom was Brian Sewell. Sewell looks back on the case with amusement: 'My role was to pour cold water on the art establishment. As far as I could see, it was the establishment which should be in the dock, not Tom Keating, for being so credulous and setting themselves up as experts when they had been so easily seduced. One of the Leger directors was so cross with me that when we next met, as I was walking down Bond Street on a rainy afternoon, he started belabouring me with his umbrella. I had to take refuge in a tobacconist's shop.' John Ford, Tom Keating's solicitor, recalls an extraordinary day in court: 'I have never seen a witness enjoy giving his testimony so enthusiastically. In order to show the obvious falsity of a subscription supporting a provenance of *Sepham Barn*, for example, which read *Mr Palmer Gilt. Mt. send Thurs. 3/–*, Sewell pointed out that three shillings was an absurdly large sum for a mount. He drew attention to a letter from the Shoreham period in which a journey to Devon is mooted, and Palmer says that he can take a ship from London to Plymouth for five shillings. Sewell also commented that the word "mount" did not start being used in connection with picture framing until some fifty years later. I am left with the abiding memory of Brian Sewell holding forth while striding up and down the large witness box of Court no. 1, and keeping his audience in rapt attention.'

Jeremy's own take on Sewell is similar unalloyed pleasure. 'I can still remember Sewell, in a soft-collared cream silk shirt and knitted black tie, walking proudly up to the witness box. I had asked my solicitor to see if he could find an expert who could lift the lid on the practices of the art world. As Sewell came into court, I leaned over to John Ford and whispered "perfect". I asked him a question along the lines of, "Can you tell the jury something about what happens in a gallery in Cork Street?" And he turned to the judge and said "My Lord, may I answer that?" And the judge said, "Yes, Mr Sewell, go on, you may." I said something like, "For instance, I think you overheard a telephone conversation with your boss about the restoration of a particular painting?" And Sewell replied, "Yes,

I did." I asked, "Well, what did he say on the telephone?" "My Lord, may I actually use the words I heard?" The judge: "Yes, Mr Sewell, get on." Of course the jury were twittering with pleasure. And Sewell then gave a wonderful description of a conversation between this dealer and the restorer where the dealer was telling the restorer [perhaps it was 'Jim the Penman'] "strengthen the signature, just strengthen it", the implication being that there was a certain amount of dressing up of a particular picture.'

Events then took a dramatic turn. While riding his moped (cost £93, as it was now known) on Sunday Keating skidded on ice and his leg was badly injured. The judge was surprisingly sympathetic: 'It is terribly important that anybody charged should give their evidence feeling on top of the world.' Although Keating struggled on in court for a couple of days, he then had a seizure and had to be rushed from the Old Bailey to St Bartholomew's Hospital. The trial was adjourned to see how Keating's recovery progressed. Two weeks passed and it took a turn for a worse. The jury was discharged. Jeremy went to see the Attorney General, Sam Silkin, and placed the medical evidence before him, which cast doubt on Keating's ability to withstand another trial. A week later the prosecution announced that it was dropping the charges. Jeremy looks back: 'The case had been going on, in fits and starts, for several weeks. It had taken an enormous toll on Tom's health. It can be a great strain knowing that the whole apparatus of the law has convened to consider your behaviour; that everyone in court is there effectively looking at you. I wondered at the time whether the prosecution's decision to abandon the case altogether was really inspired by concern for his well-being, or whether it flowed from the reluctance of the prosecution witnesses to go once again into the box and face further cross-examination. But although there were laughs to be had out of some of the art expert witnesses, I could not help feeling some sympathy for the Leger Galleries. The pastiches were, in fact, very fine indeed, for all Tom's self-deprecation, and they were provided with a most elaborate, but false, provenance.' Brian Sewell elaborates: 'It is a well-known phenomenon in the art world that a dealer or curator can become fixated on the idea that they have discovered a long lost work of a master. Once one has convinced oneself it is right, it becomes psychologically impossible to reject that conclusion and accept it is wrong.'

After the case Keating made a partial recovery. His fame only increased. His pastiches were to be found emblazoned on London buses advertising Hennessy cognac. In 1982 Channel Four put him on mainstream television and, each week in the early evening, he could be seen explaining to his audience how to paint in the manner of Constable or Turner, or Goya or Degas. *Tom Keating on Painters* proved to be phenomenally successful and garnered awards.[10] Magnus Magnusson noted that 'Tom Keating was almost on a par with art historian Kenneth Clark and his pioneering 1969 BBC television series *Civilisation.*'[11] In an article published after the trial, Frank Norman described him as the most famous painter in England.[12] An exhibition of his 'step-by-step paintings' showing the techniques of the old masters opened at the Barbican. At an exhibition at the Tate Gallery (held during Jeremy's tenure as chairman and much to Jeremy's delight), sponsored by Winsor & Newton, on artists' materials, he gave demonstrations of his technique. Brian Sewell, also invited to give lectures, remembers that Tom's was 'by far the most popular marquee, but by lunchtime, drunk, he was no longer capable of holding a brush and the Winsor & Newton men were blushing at his vocabulary'.[13] Christie's sold Tom's paintings – both his fakes and those bearing his signature. A pastiche known to be by Keating, rather than thought to be by an earlier master, became a valuable object in itself. Geraldine Norman was able to report in December 1983 that £72,000 had been spent on Keatings at the Christie's South Kensington sale. She may have been the cause of his prosecution, but she was also the cause of his fame – and, one hopes, a certain financial security. He was reported to have responded to the sale by saying that 'he could now afford to buy a little cottage'. Perhaps he had learnt a certain financial continence. It was fitting that at the sale there was hardly a dealer in sight: the buyers were almost exclusively private purchasers.

His final triumph was summed up by the fact that in 1981 it was reported that the Cecil Higgins Museum, which had shamefacedly taken down an alleged Samuel Palmer after it had emerged a few years earlier that it had been painted by Tom Keating, had now put it back on display because more people wanted to see the Keating than had ever wanted to see the Palmer. *The Times* noted sagely: 'Surely their instinct was a surer one than that of the Roman cognoscenti who were furious once to discover that a marble cupid, sold as antique by the young sculptor (who had artificially discoloured it to make it look old) was not antique at all, but only a Michelangelo.'[14] Keating had unwittingly managed to take some steps in democratizing the art world and extending its reach to the television-viewing masses.

Yet Keating's triumph was tinged with a certain tragedy. For all his desire to be recognized as a painter in his own right, his status was achieved only through the imitation of others. His original work is forgotten. Tom Keating was only able to enjoy his new-found fame and fortune momentarily: the years of smoking and drinking, and breathing in the fumes of a fuggy studio, had taken their toll. He died in February 1984.

9

Brotherhood of Love

R v Marks (1981)

SCHOLAR. EVANGELIST FOR mental enlightenment. Cannabis smuggler. Hipster. Raconteur. Author. Jester. Howard Marks is a man of multitudes. In the 1970s he became an accidental anti-establishment folk-hero, a position he has managed to maintain, navigating and overcoming various setbacks, ever since. Perhaps this is why Jeremy and he were drawn together, to participate in one of the most famous set pieces of courtroom establishment tail-tweaking of the 1980s. The trial was later enacted in the film version of Howard's famous memoir *Mr Nice*, and Jeremy found himself portrayed on screen for the second time.[1]

The son of a merchant navy captain and a teacher, Howard was born in the Welsh village of Kenfig Hill in 1945. Through a combination of brilliance and blagging, he found his way to Balliol College, Oxford, in 1964 to read physics. His shaggy, easy-going Welsh exoticism ensured him early celebrity status among the rather more buttoned-up undergraduates of the university and he became the darling of the upper-middle-class girls who invited him to tea and oftentimes more. One woman who did not forget her encounter with him was the 'rivetingly glamorous Lynn Barber'. Throughout his life Howard has exercised his mesmeric charm on men and women alike.

It was the era when middle-class England discovered drugs and Howard enthusiastically assisted it in that discovery. The shape of his university days became indiscernible through a fug of cannabis smoke while his rooms became the favoured hangout for his confrères. He graduated from beatnik drainpipes to hippy flares accompanied by the soundtrack of the Rolling Stones.

The sight of the corpse of his friend Joshua Macmillan, grandson of the former Prime Minister and former heroin addict, being carried down from his college rooms following an overdose of valium and alcohol caused him to swear off anything harder than cannabis. But about cannabis he was, even then, evangelical.

Through a concerted effort of concentration, somehow Howard managed to gain his degree, and for the next few years floated between Oxford, London and Brighton, studying at various universities and confronting the familiar postgraduate predicament: what to do with one's life. Indecision was made easier by a heavy hashish intake and an all-enveloping obsession with the Japanese board-game Go.

On the surface Howard's post-Oxford life seemed to belie his early promise. He eventually abandoned a doctorate at Sussex University in the philosophy of science and then, according to a later police report, 'dabbled in a number of small firms of interior decorators, property speculators and stamp dealers without a great deal of financial success, finally ending up as a director of an Oxford boutique called "Annabelinda"'. But beneath the surface Howard's life was becoming very interesting indeed.

Through old Oxford connections he gravitated into the then nascent world of international cannabis smuggling. His friend and fellow Go player Graham Plinston had become a dealer with connections to exporters in Lebanon and Pakistan, but had been busted and incarcerated in Germany. Plinston's supplier needed a replacement dealer to sell hashish in London. Howard agreed to help out and so gave up a life of contemplation for a life of action and risk-taking. Now he was experiencing 'religious flashes' and 'asexual orgasms' as he successfully crossed European borders with stashes of hashish stowed in the doors of the car. 'Trading in cannabis would remain my active profession for the next 18 years.'[2]

Suddenly Howard was rich and the 'small firms' the police described were the businesses through which he laundered some of his cash. Through fits and starts the operation became more sophisticated. The real money was to be made in arranging for the importation out of Lebanon, Afghanistan or Pakistan rather than simply receiving the hash in London. The solution was found in the person of self-proclaimed IRA gun-runner James McCann. McCann, aka the 'Kid', aka 'the Shamrock Pimpernel', was a legend of his own making. Remanded on suspicion of throwing Molotov cocktails at Queen's

University Belfast, he had made a Houdini-like escape from Crumlin Road prison and set himself up as a chaos-bringer, poet and nationalist. But, for all his self-avowed republican credentials, he was not averse to making money out of drug smuggling. He also had a good friend at Shannon Airport who was corruptible and was led to believe that the shipments from Kabul, Karachi or Beirut to 'Ashling Distribution Services' were of arms for the republican struggle. By 1971 Howard was air-freighting hashish to Shannon by the tonne. It would then be driven over into England in inconspicuous beaten-up cars by a small army of old friends, informally described by Howard as the 'Tafia', all on his payroll.

In late 1972 Howard had a call from an old university friend who was not on his payroll. Hamilton Macmillan (no relation to the former Prime Minister) had never entered into the full hippy spirit of mid-sixties Oxford and had perhaps thereby marked himself out as a man who could be trusted for government work. He now told Howard that he was employed by MI6 and would like to recruit Howard as an agent. The exact nature of the work that it was envisaged Howard would undertake remains obscure. There was talk of Howard opening branches of Annabelinda in Iron Curtain countries to act as a front to employ MI6 agents. What we do know is that he was initially asked to seduce a Czech Embassy employee suspected of working for the KGB. This assignment foundered when she failed to show up at the party that Howard had been instructed to attend, in his full seduction suit. Howard speculates that it was simply a test of his patriotism.

MI6's real interest seems to have been in McCann, the Irish gun-runner and dope smuggler, and, over drinks at the Pillars of Hercules in Soho with a senior MI6 figure known only as 'Donald', Howard was tasked with gathering information about him. Howard immediately informed McCann of his mission. If MI6 knew that McCann was in the hashish business then so would the puritanical Provisional IRA, who would be likely to take a dim view of McCann's sideline. It is not clear that Howard was of any real use to MI6 during his brief stint, although Howard made claims that he had lured McCann into various traps, including attempting to entice him to Germany, where McCann was wanted on suspicion of planting a bomb at a NATO base.

By mid-1973 it had become public knowledge that MI6 had used a convicted robber called Kenneth Littlejohn to attempt to infiltrate the Provisional IRA. Littlejohn had been convicted in Dublin for the largest armed robbery in Irish history and during the trial had loudly protested that he had been set up to do it by the British. Amid the cacophony of public outrage it seems that Hamilton Macmillan thought it best to bring MI6's brief association with Howard to a swift end. Whether or not a residual link remained is unclear. But Howard was not reticent about bruiting an embellished version of his involvement in MI6 to anyone who cared to listen. Many listened carefully, and remembered.

It is clear from the various accounts of Howard's life that the cannabis smuggler of the 1970s (and perhaps of any age) had to be steeled for sudden and heavy reverses. An importation might be intercepted and bang would go £100,000 of profit. The haul might be stolen along the way by a member of the operation. There was the ever present risk of arrest. And then there was the unexpected. An attempt was made to import 700 pounds of cannabis from Beirut to Italy by boat. En route the haul was stashed on a remote Greek island. A herd of goats unearthed the hashish, which was then discovered by some Greek sponge fishermen and merrily flogged by them in Crete. But against all that was the possibility of making vertigo-inducing profits.

Howard found that, despite the success of the Shannon Airport scam, working with the unstable McCann was tiresome and unnerving. (At one stage McCann conceived a violent dislike of John Lennon – apparently because the by now ex-Beatle had reneged on a promise to play a free concert in County Derry – and attempted to burn down Lennon's Weybridge house.) Howard decided to diversify his importation methods. He branched into the United States market, through a system that would later be described by an impressed policeman:

> Musical instruments and amplifiers for a pop group were purchased, specially made to have concealed places for hashish. A non-existent pop-group [initially known as 'Laughing Grass'] was formed with offices in London. Customs carnets were obtained from London for the alleged movement of those musical instruments from the Continent of Europe

to the United States, allegedly for the performance of this non-existent pop group. The instruments would be driven by a minor member going to say Italy, where at an arranged house they would be packed up with up to 1,000lbs weight of hashish worth several million dollars. They would then be air freighted to an American city, say Chicago, where they would be collected by a minor member of the American gang and driven to California where the drugs would be unpacked and disposed of by an American West Coast criminal organisation believed to be called the 'Brotherhood of Love'.[3] The empty instruments and recorders would then be air freighted back to a European country, moved to a second European country, filled with hashish and air freighted again to the United States, returned and so on. About 7 trips were made by this method involving the importation of some 12 million dollars' worth in drugs.

A chance sniff by a chance sniffer dog unravelled the US importation scheme. Howard was arrested in Amsterdam and extradited back to England to face charges of conspiracy to export cannabis from the continent of Europe to the United States of America. He was granted bail with sureties of £50,000 and ostensibly returned to Oxford to engage in quiet study. With a trial at the Old Bailey looming, and the evidence against him stacked high, Howard decided to skip his bail. He did it artfully; he procured an associate to show up at the house where he was staying and announce himself to the landlady as from 'Customs and Excise'. Howard went to the door, looking suitably pale and nervous, and departed with the mysterious figure, mumbling that he would be back as soon as he could. The wheeze worked. Police investigations soon picked up the stories of Howard's MI6 involvement that he had disseminated to his Oxford friends. Instead of concluding that Howard had simply decided to abscond they admitted the possibility that he had been kidnapped by the IRA or the Mafia, and possibly murdered. The usual consequence of flitting bail was forfeiture of the sureties, which had been put up by Howard's father and a family friend. Given the murky circumstances the judge showed mercy. They got their money back. The legal adviser to MI6, interviewed during the police investigations, demonstrated perspicacity: he voiced the fear that Howard would 'use his small but true involvement with MI6 as his defence from his criminal activities in smuggling drugs'.

When, on 30 April 1974, Howard failed to show up for the first day of his trial he became instantly famous. His connection with MI6 had been leaked to the press and the front page of the *Mirror* screamed out: 'Where is Mr Marks?' The *Evening News*'s front page proclaimed 'London Drug Trial Man in IRA Riddle'. Howard now found himself referred to as 'Mr Mystery'. One supposition was that, having infiltrated one of its gangs, Howard had been abducted and murdered by the IRA. Others suggested that Howard had been abducted by the Mafia, concerned that he would spill too many beans at his trial. In fact Howard was hunkering down with a friend on the Isle of Dogs while cultivating an elaborate moustache and planning a new life abroad. He then slipped quietly away to Italy, where a Winnebago awaited him.

Howard managed three itinerant months before the pull of England overcame him. He returned and for the next six years continued his old life with one difference: now he was a man on the run. And yet the only organization that seemed to be actively interested in his whereabouts was not the British police but the *Mirror* newspaper. Another IRA informer working for MI6, Kenneth Lennon, had been found shot in a ditch in Surrey and perhaps the thought of Howard being put on trial and trumpeting his own MI6 connection was not attractive to the authorities. On one occasion in 1975 Howard had to make a hasty exit from his Regent's Park penthouse as four journalists barged into the entrance lobby. The next day the front page carried a photograph of Howard, bewhiskered and sporting unlikely glasses, with the headline 'The Face of a Fugitive'.

Within four days Howard and his girlfriend had set themselves up in an obscure Liverpool terrace and were remaking their lives. The deals continued, the money flowed in and the false identities multiplied. By 1978 Howard had acquired his most notorious moniker, Donald Nice, borrowed from a released murderer who had no interest in foreign travel. In 1974 a police report had described Howard as a 'scruffy, semi-hippy type of individual, highly educated and intelligent with little physical courage, a Walter Mitty type of character who revels in intrigue'. By 1980 he was living in Hans

Court in Knightsbridge, breakfasting on caviar omelettes whisked up at the Caviar House and ostensibly acting as manager for the rocker P.J. Proby.

The intricacies of Howard's life during the 1970s are told in supercharged gonzo prose by David Leigh, investigative journalist extraordinaire and Howard's first semi-official biographer, in his book *High Times*,[4] and later, and more sedately, by Howard himself in his bestselling autobiography *Mr Nice*. Not for one minute does Howard countenance any notion that what he was doing was morally objectionable. Technically in contravention of the law, yes, but Howard could see no rational arguments against the importation of a drug that, in his eyes, was an unmitigated boon for humanity. But he drew a sharp divide between cannabis and hard drugs and, apart from some early experiments with LSD, he never involved himself in anything other than cannabis, whether as a user or an importer.

In 1979 Howard decided to undertake an importation of breathtaking proportions, which was to be celebrated by David Leigh as the 'Great Big Monster Scheme'. According to his girlfriend (and soon to be wife) Judy this was intended to be his last job, and he hoped to net £1 million, enough to retire. The plan was to import fifteen tonnes of Colombian 'weed' into Britain. It was loaded on to a salvage tug off the coast of Colombia, which inconspicuously chugged its three-week journey across the Atlantic. Two yachts, *Bagheera* and *Salammbo*, then quietly slid out of the inlet of an island off the west coast of Scotland, met the tug and offloaded the cannabis. Fifteen tonnes was worth £20 million. It would fill a thirty-eight-tonne articulated lorry. It was the largest importation in British history. As Howard later put it, it was enough for every person in Britain to get high at the same time.

The cannabis was then distributed to a series of storage sites across the country, including a baronial mansion at Fort William that Howard had rented on the pretence of shooting a film. But Customs and Excise were on to him. The Americans who had funded the deal – apparently a collection of New York vegans – were agitated that the cannabis was not being sold quickly enough. They suspected skulduggery and sent over two factotums, the delightfully named Mr Joel Magazine and Mr Walter Nath, to make an inventory and see that there had been no leakage. This duo checked into the Dorchester and made rather too much commotion as they pursued their investigations. The authorities caught wind of their enquiries, and started a protracted surveillance operation. The trail led to the cannabis, and also to Howard, who was arrested in May 1980 in the Swan Hotel in Lavenham, just after he had ordered an incongruous glass of sherry at the bar. While being questioned, Howard solemnly informed Customs officers: 'My work is of a secret nature. I work for MI6. It is difficult to resist when you have been flattered into believing your country needs you.'

Unsurprisingly, Howard was refused bail. In a classic piece of Marksian bravado, while on remand he managed to talk his way out of Brixton prison for the day to attend his wedding to Judy, now five months pregnant, at the Basil Street Hotel in Knightsbridge. The white Cadillac that carried the bride and groom was notable for also having a prison guard as a passenger.

Howard's solicitor for the 1974 trial, which he had successfully evaded, was Bernie Simons, a partner in the fashionable Soho firm of Simons Muirhead & Allan. Simons was an executive member of the National Council for Civil Liberties, and distrusted by the police for his regular defence of alleged IRA bombers (though many of his clients were in fact policemen). It was to Simons that Howard turned once again after his arrest. Having instructed Jeremy a few years earlier in the *ABC* case (see Chapter 12 below), Simons knew there was only one man who could extract Howard from his predicament. The trouble was that Jeremy was now in semi-retirement from the Bar, his life largely taken up with House of Lords work and chairmanship of the Tate Gallery. Simons nonetheless gave it a go and called Ronald, the legendary (and to Jeremy much loved) clerk of Queen Elizabeth Building. 'Well Mr Simons, you do know that Lord Hutchinson isn't really practising much any more . . . but I will ask him . . . and if the fee is right, who knows?' (In fact Jeremy was notorious for his languid indifference to the fees that his clerk dutifully negotiated for him. It has long been a tradition at the Bar to 'mark' the barrister's brief with the fee agreed for a trial or hearing, and it was a longstanding joke in his chambers that this was always the last page he turned to. In a speech in the House of Lords Lord Mishcon would later generously say of Jeremy's reputation at the Bar that he 'would accept a case if he possibly could, regardless of the amount on the brief'.[5])

Ronald called Jeremy at the House of Lords. 'Mr Jeremy, I am sure you won't be interested, but Howard Marks's solicitor has just phoned and would like to know whether you would be willing to act for him in his trial . . .' (Although it was virtually unheard of for clerks to address barristers other than by their surname until the 1990s, Jeremy was throughout his career referred to as 'Mr Jeremy' in deference to, and to distinguish him from, his late father, who was 'Mr Hutchinson'. This was notwithstanding that he joined his father's chambers five years after Mr Hutchinson's death.) Jeremy instantly knew that this would be a fascinating case. 'Of course I'll do it!' he intoned down the phone.

Jeremy and his junior, Stephen Solley,[6] a rising young barrister, would visit Howard in Brixton prison regularly in the run-up to the case to discuss Howard's defence. Jeremy recalls that Howard had somehow managed to get himself appointed to the post of tea-boy to his wing. 'Congratulations, Howard, that is the best job in prison, is it not? How did you manage that?' 'Well, Lord Hutchinson, the screws just seem to like me.' Stephen Solley recalls that even in those days it was rare for QCs to go to the bother of seeing their client before or after the trial, especially if they were on remand in prison: 'I remember in one murder case the silk who led me didn't even go to see his client after he had been convicted. It was left to me as the junior to go to the cells to discuss what had happened. Jeremy was the exact opposite. He rolled his sleeves up and got completely stuck in, even though he was at the time the leader of the criminal Bar.'

These were the days when a remand prisoner (that is a prisoner charged with an offence who had yet to be tried and sentenced) was allowed to wear his own clothes and bring in his own provisions. Solley remembers lunches shipped in from Fortnum & Mason fortified by bottles of vintage wine. 'One of Howard's favourite tricks was to give me a glass of wine and ask me to guess the year.' Lunches over, there remained the business of trying to work out Howard's defence.

Howard explained why he was not guilty:

I was recruited by MI6 to infiltrate an IRA arms and drug smuggling business. My main mission was to track down James McCann, a notorious IRA gun-runner and entrap him through dope deals. But then I was arrested in 1973 and put on trial and my role as an MI6 agent came out. Later MI6 put me on to the Mexican secret service, who were also interested in McCann. I continued to keep track of McCann but each time he evaded my grasp. The Mexicans then tasked me with the job of working undercover – I had to infiltrate the Colombian drug world. I was given false identities and passports. The Mexicans were convinced that a Marxist terrorist organization – the September 23 Communist League – were financing their activities by importing drugs. I was the Mexicans' inside man in the UK importation – I was trying to find out the people behind the operation and how the cash was getting to the terrorists. I was getting very close when I was arrested.

Howard later recalled Jeremy's own reaction to this story.[7] 'That is your defence, Howard?' (Howard remembers Jeremy gasping with astonishment as he said this, although Jeremy insists otherwise: 'In fact I have never gasped at anything any client ever told me.')

'Yes. Why? What's wrong?'

Howard's account is that Jeremy replied: 'That is, absolutely without doubt, the most ridiculous defence I have ever heard in my entire life.' (Jeremy demurs. 'I am sure I said words to the effect of "Howard, we will have great difficulty in getting a jury to accept all this unless you can get a witness from the Mexican intelligence to support your account."')

'You mean you don't believe it.'

'Belief is not a factor, Howard. I am obliged to be your voice in court, even if your defence is idiotic.'

'Almost all of it can be backed up with evidence, Lord Hutchinson.'

'It is a pity, Howard, that no one from the Mexican secret service is prepared to come to London to testify that you did work for them.'

'Actually, Lord Hutchinson, my immediate superior, a man called Jorge del Rio, a member of the Mexican government, is only too happy to help.'

For almost a year and a half Howard had sat in his cell on remand in Brixton practising yoga, meditating, and plotting his defence. The masterstroke would be the calling of a member of the Mexican secret service to give evidence for him, supporting his story that, far from being a hardened drug smuggler, he was a valiant warrior in the fight against terrorism and organized crime.

Jeremy ruminated on this promise: it did not seem to be one that Howard was likely to be able to make good on. Howard's story as a whole seemed a tall one. But it is a critical part of the barrister's ethical code that he must not prejudge his client's case. The barrister's opinion of the truth or falsity of his client's account is irrelevant. Similarly, however distasteful the barrister may find his client (and in this instance Jeremy found him very congenial indeed) that cannot come in the way of his defence of that client. Jeremy would recall how during his career at the Bar he had often been stopped in the Temple by senior judges who would address him along the lines, 'I was very surprised to see you mixed up in a case like that.' 'That was still the attitude of so many members of the judiciary and of laymen at that time, illustrative of the low status in which the criminal Bar was then held.' He expressed the point some years later in a speech made in the House of Lords:

> At the very basis of our freedom lies the knowledge that in the criminal courts, however unpopular your cause, however hopeless, however unlikely, however seemingly overwhelming the pressure of the state upon you is as an individual, you can obtain an independent, professionally dedicated advocate to undertake and argue your case and to argue it before a tribunal which is presided over by an equivalently independent judge. From then on the advocate must fearlessly promote by all proper and lawful means that person's interest without regard to his own.[8]

It was these sentiments that John Mortimer put into the mouth of Horace Rumpole in *Rumpole and the Age of Miracles*: "'A barrister is an old taxi plying for hire. So it is my sacred duty, Mr Morry Machin, to take on anyone in trouble. However repellent I may happen to find them." "Thank you, Mr Rumpole." Morry was genuinely grateful. "Think nothing of it."'[9]

Howard didn't bother to apply for legal aid. A few days before the trial started a man who said he was from the Mexican Embassy appeared at Bernie Simons's offices with a suitcase. Inside was £50,000 cash.

The prosecution against Howard, along with those of his supposed accomplices who had not already pleaded guilty (and there were many who had), finally got under way in September 1981 at the Old Bailey before Judge Peter Mason QC.[10] This was to be one of the longest trials of Jeremy's career. In all it would run for two exhausting months. But, as he sat with his ancient, yellowing wig perched precariously on his head, surveying the packed court through his owlish glasses, he was happy to be back in the Old Bailey.

The case against Howard was nothing less than that he was the mastermind behind the biggest ever importation of drugs into the UK. For all his bravado Howard was unnerved. He decided he would consider pleading guilty if the judge would guarantee a sentence of seven years or under. Jeremy went to see the judge 'in chambers' (it was permissible for defence counsel to go to see the judge, accompanied by prosecution counsel, to ascertain the likely sentence in the event of a guilty plea, so as to save the time and expense of a long trial and receive the benefit of a reduced sentence). The expression he wore on his return did not suggest that the meeting had been a successful one.

'I am afraid the Judge takes the view that it's a serious case. If you go down then I fear he will sentence you to a far longer stretch than seven years.'

'Old Bastard. I was offering him a really good deal.'

Jeremy paused. 'You know what they all call Mason?'

'No, what?'

'Penal Pete.'

'Oh, terrific!'[11]

Howard decided to take his chance.

First, there was the question of the jury. Jeremy wished to ensure that as many young women as possible sat as jurors. The psychology was perhaps crude but he thought that they would be drawn to Howard, and inclined to sympathize. At this time both the defence and prosecution were entitled to challenge up to three jurors without giving reasons. After a number of objections the jury was constituted: eight men, four women, two of them young and attractive. But as it turned out, according to Stephen Solley, the female gaze became as much focused on Jeremy as Howard as the trial continued. He remembers that there was one juror, who regularly wore a jumper speckled with knitted strawberries, who seemed mesmerized by Jeremy's mellifluous intonations. And she was not the only one to be charmed. In her own autobiography Judy Marks recalls her first meeting with the great advocate. 'I looked up into intelligent, kind eyes framed by laughter lines that contradicted the lines of concern on his brow. His face was thin, gentle. The night before I had lain in bed tossing and turning, dreading today. I felt strangely reassured by him.'[12] Jeremy was never one to stand on ceremony. Greeting her warmly on the first day of the trial he asked her to 'Call me Jeremy'.

A problem for the prosecution was the tendency, especially among the young, to regard possession of cannabis as not really something that was criminal. This difficulty was compounded by the fact that in the dock sat a man who exuded an aura of mystique and a kind of rangy charm, a combination which undermined the idea that he might be guilty of a serious offence. Undeterred, the prosecution counsel, John Rogers QC, opened the prosecution case in slow and grave cadences. Now and then he would attempt to leaven the atmosphere with a joke.

'So it was that the Isle of Mull, which was once the scene of Sir Compton Mackenzie's great, hilarious novel *Whisky Galore*, once again hit the headlines. You can guess what the press did with it. They called it "Cannabis Galore".'

Judges love to display superior knowledge to everyone else in court, and Judge Mason was no exception. He piped up: 'I must interrupt you, I'm afraid, Mr Rogers, but *Whisky Galore* was in fact set on the island of Barra.'

Rogers ploughed on in his comedic furrow. 'And I must tell you the name of the place on the foreshore where most of the bales of cannabis were washed up. It was called . . . Grass Point.'

And so it went on.

'Members of the jury, Mr Marks had so many identities one wonders how on earth he remembered who he was at any given point of time.'[13]

The prosecution then engaged in a piece of courtroom theatrics that was intended to bring home to the court the full magnitude of the smuggling operation. They had had brought to court, with considerable security fanfare, a sack of the confiscated cannabis. It was solemnly handed to Judge Mason. No child of the age, Mason prodded it gingerly. 'Er, how is it ingested?' It was then passed to the jury. Jeremy noted that a number of them sniffed deeply and smirked. Some made scooping hand movements, as if pretending to pocket some of it. This was a good start . . .

The trial continued and a seemingly never-ending stream of police and Customs witnesses paraded in and out of the witness box. The evidence mounted up. What emerged was a smuggling operation of astonishing professionalism. Once the cannabis arrived ashore it was stored in a variety of 'warehouses' across the country, presided over by various quartermasters. These were not men one would normally associate with drug smuggling. One was the brother of a well-known QC; another the son-in-law of a High Court judge; each presiding over a remote farmhouse in Inverness, a barn in Essex, a falconry in Northamptonshire, each with tonnes of cannabis stashed under the rafters. By the time Customs swooped, over half had been sold. But what was left was taller than the Customs officer who posed, perhaps betraying a hint of a grin, for the photographs that the jury were solemnly shown; and it was more than the total amount confiscated by Customs officers in the previous two years. As regards Howard, the evidence against him seemed overwhelming: found in his possession were papers detailing, in his own handwriting, the various quantities, values and destinations of the cannabis, as well as a key to the falconry. Thirty thousand pounds in cash had been discovered stowed in a bedside table.

Customs Officer Stephenson claimed that he had seen Howard meeting with the two Americans at the Dorchester Hotel. Jeremy subjected him to a scathing cross-examination:

JEREMY: How did you know it was Mr Marks in Mr Nath's hotel room?
STEPHENSON: I viewed him through the keyhole.
JEREMY: Ah, so you recognised him by his knees, Mr Stephenson.

Judy Marks, sitting in the public gallery, was loving every minute of it ('I started to hero-worship Lord Hutchinson'). As were the jury; she recalls that one of the jurors laughed so vigorously that she started choking and an adjournment had to be ordered.[14] In fact, for all the ease and humour that this excerpt of cross-examination suggests, Stephen Solley adds a valuable corrective: 'It was crucial that Stephenson's account be discredited. We wanted to show that he could not have seen Howard at the Dorchester. I remember that Jeremy and I paced around the corridors of the hotel, drawing up plans and taking measurements. A great cross-examination is not just conjured out of thin air. It requires intense preparation.'

Jeremy recalls that the mood again changed as he cross-examined one of the last witnesses, the police officer in charge of the investigation.

'It is right, officer, is it not, that Mr Marks worked at one time as an agent for British intelligence?' Jeremy points out that the phrase 'at one time' was crucial. It could mean one week, it could mean three years.

> POLICE OFFICER: Well, I am not sure I can really—
> JEREMY: No, officer, would you just answer the question?
> POLICE OFFICER: [A pause] Well . . . yes, he did, but it was only for—
> JEREMY [cutting him short]: Thank you, officer, that is all I wanted to know.

The jury leaned forward. In criminal trials there can be moments where suddenly the mood changes. What seemed an open and shut case can, with one answer, founder. A new fact may emerge that entirely unbalances assumptions. This was such a climacteric.

Then Howard gave evidence. Out came his story, slowly extracted by Jeremy. The jury listened intently as his Welsh intonations flowed. It was pitch-perfect. So complex was Howard's narrative of intrigue, so densely populated was his account with agents and double-agents, that the judge threw up his hands in despair. 'Mr Marks, I find it extraordinarily difficult to follow your evidence. I am getting lost in a mass of detail. How the jury copes I just do not know.' This was all part of Howard's plan: could such a story all be just one huge bluff?

Then it was the prosecutor's turn to cross-examine. But one thing

Howard forgot to do was to wipe the hint of an ironic smile off his face. The judge commented on it.

'Mr Marks, both I, and I am sure the jury, cannot fail to have noticed that you cannot stop smiling so much while you give evidence. Are you smiling in contempt of us?'

It was a potentially very damaging intervention. The judge's remark entirely bamboozled Howard. Stephen Solley remembers that for the next hour or so Howard seemed knocked for six. It was a relief when the judge adjourned for lunch (witnesses, like boxers, often need time out of the ring to recover). Howard did a lot of thinking in that precious hour before the court resumed at 2 p.m. Before Rogers could continue his onslaught Howard made a short statement to the judge. 'My Lord, the remark you made this morning has troubled me greatly. I am fully aware I must establish my innocence or I face many years' imprisonment with considerable distress to myself and my family. But I still try to smile, although I have spent the last eighteen months in prison. It is the only way I have to deal with adversity and it in no way indicates smugness or contempt.'

Jeremy sighed in relief. It was a brilliant speech. Howard had regained his composure. The woman in the strawberry jumper looked suitably sympathetic.

Howard walked serenely from the box, the picture of injured innocence.

Jeremy's other potential trump card was the long-promised Mexicans. The days passed and still they did not come. The other defendants gave their evidence and the case was drawing to a close. Still no sign of them. Stephen Solley looked gloomily at Jeremy. 'It looks like the star witnesses are going to be a no-show.'

That night, as Jeremy lay asleep, he was woken by a telephone call. 'Jeremy, it's Bernie.'

'Bernie, it's one in the morning. What's happened?'

'They've arrived.'

'Marvellous.'

Jeremy hastily threw on his suit. Within half an hour he, Stephen Solley and Bernie Simons were sitting in the bar at the Sheraton Hotel in Knightsbridge. Jeremy remembers: 'It was extraordinary. There were two Mexicans wearing what looked like sombreros

and dark glasses.' The promised intelligence officers, whose presence had been nervously awaited for days, had finally arrived. 'We
sorry. Difficulties getting here,' one of them told him. They
explained that as members of the President's inner security circle
they had only been able to get away after the end of a key Latin
American summit. They then confirmed, in monosyllabic answers,
Howard's role in the Scottish importation. It is a longstanding rule
of the Bar that in criminal cases counsel do not take statements
from witnesses. That is a matter for the instructing solicitor. But
this was a moment where the rules had to be broken. It was an
emergency. An hour later, the three lawyers emerged into the
autumnal London night. Stephen Solley recalls: 'We just could not
believe the experience we had had. It was this extraordinary piece
of real-life theatre that we had been involved in. And here was
the evidence which could turn the case.' But, notwithstanding the
bizarreness of that night, it was anchored in firm reality.
Accompanying the Mexicans was a dapper, grey-haired Englishman
who confirmed that he worked for British intelligence.

The next day Jeremy strode back into court, feeling apprehensive
yet buoyant. There is always the worry the barrister has to face
when he calls a witness. How will the witness come across? Will
he crumble under cross-examination? But his hesitant optimism
was short-lived. The Mexicans were not there. Bernie Simons
explained that the Mexican Ambassador had apparently forbidden
them from giving evidence and withdrawn their credentials.
However the mysterious Englishman was there. Another day passed.
The Mexicans were waiting outside the courtroom. It seemed
that the Ambassador had somehow relented. One of the Mexicans
told Jeremy: 'I only testify in private. I won't do it in public.
Secret matters.'

Jeremy decided to whisk up some theatre. 'My Lord, the next
witness I propose to call is giving evidence on matters of a very
delicate and secret nature which justifies the application which I
now make, that his evidence shall be heard in camera.' To his surprise
the judge agreed. The court was cleared and the public and journalists trooped out. The jury looked terribly interested. This was the
second climacteric of the trial. Jeremy remembers: 'The whole court

seemed to wake up and pay attention. There was a sense that something enormously serious was about to occur.'

Jeremy put on his most solemn voice.

> JEREMY: The court has been cleared of the public and the press, do you understand?
> MEXICAN: [in a heavy Mexican accent] Yes.
> JEREMY: What is your name?
> MEXICAN: [The witness shook his head.]
> JEREMY: Are you prepared to write it down?
> MEXICAN: Yes.
> [A piece of paper was handed to him. The witness scrawled something.]
> JEREMY: Is what is written on that piece of paper, as regards your name, correct?
> MEXICAN: Yes.
> JUDGE MASON: Lord Hutchinson, should not the jury see it as well, now that the court has been closed?
> JEREMY [very solemn indeed now]: I think he would rather not.

The Mexican was proving every bit as monosyllabic as he had at the Sheraton. Jeremy could not afford to ask him too many questions. He pointed at Howard.

> JEREMY: Do you know this man?
> MEXICAN: [A nod]
> JEREMY: Have you ever worked for the Mexican intelligence?
> MEXICAN: [Another nod]
> JEREMY: Do you still work for the intelligence?
> MEXICAN: Yes.
> JEREMY: Did you know Mr Marks in the context of your job?
> MEXICAN: Yes.

A few more questions elicited that Howard had a connection with the Mexican intelligence and had received large sums of money from them. That explained the £30,000 found at Hans Court.

How to cross-examine such a witness? John Rogers QC, the prosecuting counsel, had no material at all on which to found an attack other than sheer incredulity.

ROGERS: Why did you provide Mr Marks with cash?

MEXICAN: I cannot answer. Secret.

ROGERS: What opportunity can you afford me to check your credentials?

MEXICAN: None.

ROGERS: Well, how am I to determine that you are who you claim to be?

MEXICAN: There is no way.

JUDGE MASON [unable to contain himself]: Mr Rogers is saying that you might be anyone, do you follow that?

MEXICAN: Yes, I could be anybody.

Whenever any party at a trial calls a witness to give evidence for him, he has the right to re-examine that witness after the end of the cross-examination. The art of re-examination requires utmost care. One of its aims is to try to undo damage inflicted on a witness in cross-examination. But if the witness continues making damaging statements under re-examination then the harm to the case he is supposed to support is magnified before the jury. And the problem is that a witness is often so punch-drunk after an effective cross-examination that he does not know what he is saying. Advocates therefore often have to resist the temptation to ask a witness too many questions in re-examination.

Jeremy slowly rose to his full height and asked the Mexican one question only:

JEREMY: Can I ask you – in view of that – Are you *ever* . . . [the word was very heavily emphasized and carried all the dignity of a pre-war Oxford education] allowed to show your credentials to anyone?

MEXICAN: No, sir.

JEREMY: Thank you, I have no further questions.

Jeremy sat down hastily. And with that the surprise witness disappeared from the court, never to be seen again. But the jury looked impressed. Presumably a member of the Mexican secret services was obliged to maintain absolute secrecy about his identity. But for all his outward display of serenity, Jeremy had found the Mexican's brief sojourn in the witness box a nerve-racking one. The question of whether to call the Mexican to give evidence at all had been a difficult one. In the event he had sustained an air of total credibility. There was then the question of how to refer to the Mexican agent in submissions. The judge suggested that he be described as 'Mr X'. 'I always think Mr A sounds less sinister,' drawled Jeremy. 'Mr A it shall be,' assented the judge.

Jeremy's other trump card was the MI6 connection. Fortunately the *New Statesman* had published an article in 1979, before Howard's arrest, about that very question. Drawing heavily from a leaked police report prepared after Howard's 1974 disappearance, the article told a tangled story of intrigue, which included a claim by James McCann that Howard had set up an attempt by British intelligence to assassinate him. It also suggested that Howard may have been blackmailed by MI6 into working for them. This was heady stuff. Against that background the prosecution had had to admit that Howard had been an agent who had worked for MI6. But while they insisted that Howard's involvement had lasted just a few months, Howard's evidence was that it had lasted much longer. The problem for John Rogers was that he had called no witnesses to contradict Howard's account of this intelligence work, or to question the identity of the Mexican witness. In contrast the defence had Howard's sworn version of events and had at least called an independent witness testifying to Howard's involvement with the Mexican intelligence service. This was a state of affairs that Jeremy exploited to the full as he made his final speech:

> Mr Marks was used by MI6 to infiltrate the IRA. Three times he traced James McCann, but three times he [McCann] managed to slip away. But British intelligence would not come into this court and admit, as the prosecution did, that Howard Marks was working for them. They just sit up in the public gallery here. You can see them up there, members of the jury, I'm sure. [Jeremy gestured with a roll of the hand up to the public gallery.] Instead Mr Marks was left out in the cold. That is the code of the intelligence services. They say, as is the way of the security services, 'You are on your own, old boy.' Members of the jury, you may remember the cases of those Russian spies, not only Kim Philby but Anthony Blunt. It appears that British intelligence can grant immunity from prosecution to spies who have

acted against this country.[15] But not so, it would seem, when they have actually been acting on behalf of this country.

The wait for the jury to return was agonizing. Only after they had been safely housed overnight in a London hotel to continue their deliberations, did the jury come to their decision. Everyone returned to court for that sweaty prelude before the jury foreman says either one word or two.

'Not guilty.'

Howard grinned at the jury. But there was one charge he could not evade. Howard had also been charged with making false passport applications. Given that he had been found with a handful of false passports in his possession – most notoriously one for 'Donald Nice' – the Hutchinson charm could do little to get Howard out of that particular bind. But there still remained the mitigation.

> It is perfectly clear from Your Lordship's summing-up that you have formed an adverse opinion of my client. But the jury have acquitted him of the drugs charges and it is Your Lordship's duty to pay attention to the jury's views and loyally accept them. The question of the passports is entirely divorced from any allegation of drug smuggling and there is not the slightest sign that they were used for committing any crime. In fact my client needed those passports because of his intelligence work trying to track down McCann, the IRA gun-runner. McCann learned that my client was giving information to the British intelligence and had publicly stated that he was 'after' him. My client had the strongest possible reason for changing his identity – fear.

The judge testily replied, 'I hear what you say, Lord Hutchinson.'

Jeremy's answer, remembered to this day by a young barrister, Christopher Sallon,[16] who was present in court on behalf of another defendant, was devastating: 'It is apparent that Your Lordship hears what I say, but equally apparent that Your Lordship has not understood a word of it.' Sallon recalls Judge Mason as 'like a rabbit frozen in the headlamps of a steadily approaching Rolls-Royce'.

Nonetheless, 'Penal' Pete, furious at Howard's acquittal, sentenced Howard to two years on the passports charge – the maximum available. But Howard had the last laugh. Jeremy went straight to the Court of

Appeal, which quashed the sentence. A plea bargain was negotiated in respect of the 1973 charge and Howard was released early in 1982. Having spent almost two years in Brixton prison he was a free man. He and Judy celebrated with Jeremy, Bernie Simons and Stephen Solley over dinner at the Dorchester. 'A grand idea,' Jeremy quipped, 'given that you have never set foot in the place before.'

Stephen Solley, who himself later became a leading criminal silk, looks back on his time working with Jeremy with delight and awe. 'I have never seen a trial so completely dominated by the personality of one man. Jeremy's charm and humour entirely won over the jury and eclipsed the prosecutor.' A telling vignette that is lodged in his memory is of Jeremy's reaction when John Rogers passed photographs of the yachts up to the jury. 'Jeremy, an ex-naval officer and small-boat sailor, and counsel for another defendant engaged in a protracted stage-whispered conversation about the qualities of the yachts. The jury were more interested in what they were talking about than the prosecution opening.' Solley also recalls the sheer amount of hard work put in by Jeremy during the months of the case.

In truth Jeremy was exhausted. He was going to turn sixty-seven in March 1982, just three months away. In that month he appeared in the *Romans in Britain* trial, which garnered as much publicity as the Howard Marks case.[17] It would be his last Old Bailey trial. He finally retired in early 1984.

In Jeremy's archives there are various letters from solicitors pleading with him to come out of retirement to fight particular cases. One struck me especially. In July 1984 Clive Ponting, a senior civil servant, sent documents to Tam Dalyell MP concerning the sinking of the *General Belgrano* during the Falklands War. This led to the most famous Official Secrets Act trial of the 1980s, presided over by my father-in-law, Mr Justice McCowan. Jeremy pondered hard whether to accept the invitation. In the end he decided not to. His retirement was final.

As for Howard Marks, I have it on good authority that the Younger Society, the Balliol College law society, seriously contemplated asking him to present a lecture on 'trial by jury'.

PART IV

The Secret Society

10

'Would you press the button?'

R v Chandler and Others (1962)

A S 1962 DAWNED the Cold War was reaching its most menacing
phase. Political relations between the West and the Soviet Union
were at their nadir. Against this gloomy backdrop Jeremy returned
to the Old Bailey to represent six nuclear-disarmament campaigners
charged under the Official Secrets Act. The trial was the most politically charged case of the year, perhaps of the decade, and engaged
the pressing ethical questions of the period. How should the
individual respond to the threat of nuclear apocalypse? Are they
entitled to act on their own moral convictions, and against the
law of the land, if they perceive that the government is following
a policy that threatens the future of their country, and the world?
Who is the final arbiter of the public interest – the state or the
jury? It is testament to the seriousness with which the establishment treated this case that ranged against Jeremy in court were
the heaviest guns in the prosecution armoury: his old adversaries,
Sir Reginald Manningham-Buller, the Attorney General,[1] and
Mervyn Griffith-Jones.

The six defendants were leading members of the Committee of
100, an organization founded in April 1960 to campaign for unilateral
nuclear disarmament by means of non-violent civil disobedience.
The offences related to a demonstration held at Wethersfield Air
Base, in Essex, on 9 December 1961. Wethersfield was one of several
air bases in East Anglia used by the US Air Force under the auspices
of NATO. It was admitted by the defendants that their plans for the
demonstration had included the entry on to the airfield of selected
individuals, who were to sit on the runway and thereby prevent
planes taking off.

The trial that followed was a cause célèbre. To the modern reader, for whom the existence of nuclear weapons now may seem of little moment, it provides a fascinating insight into the preoccupations and responses of the generation who first learned to live with the risk of imminent mass destruction.

The story of the Committee of 100 is rooted in the development of atomic and nuclear weapons in the years following the Second World War. The use of atomic bombs at Hiroshima and Nagasaki had shown, with devastating clarity, the immense destructive potential of nuclear warfare. When it became clear that the US was not prepared to share its know-how with the United Kingdom, development of a British atomic weapon began secretly in 1946 under the aegis of the Atomic Weapons Research Establishment. Clement Attlee revealed the existence of a nuclear programme in a speech to Parliament on 12 May 1948. It was uncontroversial. In July 1954, under the auspices of a Conservative government, work began on a British thermonuclear weapon, or H-bomb.

Justification for the development of nuclear armaments was set out in a government white paper of 4 April 1957, which provided for a massive scaling back of conventional forces in favour of the development of a nuclear capability. The thrust of the argument was the perceived threat of the Soviet Union to the security of Europe, and the widening numerical superiority of Soviet conventional forces over those of NATO. Since, it was argued, a Soviet invasion of Europe could not be repelled by conventional arms, a nuclear deterrent was the only means of safeguarding European security: only the threat of nuclear destruction would deter the Russians from contemplating an invasion.

The rationalization for a specifically British nuclear deterrent, as distinct from a deterrent that was solely American but under which Britain took shelter, was more complicated. An internal government report of 1957 stated that a nuclear weapons programme was necessary to 'retain our special relation with the United States, and through it our influence in world affairs and, especially, our right to have a voice in the final issue of peace or war'.[2] The desire to retain great power status, at a time of obvious national decline (acutely felt after the humiliating debacle of the Suez crisis of 1956), was a significant factor. As Churchill put it, nuclear weapons were a price worth paying for a place at the 'top table'.[3]

The perennial concern for the stability of the US 'special relationship' was also important. Conversely, the idea of the fragility of that relationship, or at least the danger of over-dependence on America, was also seen as a justification. The leader of the Labour Party Hugh Gaitskell, then in opposition, explained prior to the publication of the white paper that 'Our party decided to support the manufacture of the hydrogen bomb . . . because we do not think it right that this country should be so dependent . . . upon the US.' There was, furthermore, the danger that the US might retreat to its old isolationist ways, and it was certainly possible to envisage a situation, like Suez, in which the interests of America and Europe did not coincide, or in which US interests were not sufficiently at stake to risk intervention.

The British nuclear deterrent of the 1950s was designed to be delivered by the RAF's fleet of Victor and Vulcan bombers. With the launch of Sputnik in 1957, it became clear that the USSR was (or would shortly be) capable of delivering a nuclear warhead anywhere in the western hemisphere by intercontinental ballistic missile, against which there could be no effective defence. The nuclear bomber would soon be obsolete. A scramble to close the so-called 'missile gap' ensued. While the US forged ahead, British attempts to build an independent ballistic delivery system were shelved after the crippling costs of the 'Blue Streak' rocket project proved to be insupportable. It was apparent that a British nuclear deterrent could not be developed independently of its American counterpart, and that Britain was destined to play the role of nuclear client, rather than nuclear partner, to its superpower ally. In May 1957 Eisenhower and Macmillan agreed to the stationing of US-built Thor intermediate ballistic missiles in bases in Britain. The Mutual Defence Agreement of 1958 provided for the exchange between the two countries of classified information relating to 'atomic weapon design, development and fabrication capability', but this was really one-way traffic. In March 1960 the US government agreed to the purchase by Britain of the American-built long-range Skybolt missile. In return, the US required, and was given, permission to use Holy

Loch on the Firth of Clyde as a base for submarines carrying the new underwater-launched Polaris nuclear missiles. There was no requirement for Washington to seek the permission of, or even consult, the British before launching a nuclear strike from the Polaris submarines stationed on the Clyde, notwithstanding that such a strike would have been likely to provoke a retaliatory attack on Britain of devastating proportions.

From the late 1950s, there began to be opposition to the presence of nuclear weapons, and in particular US nuclear weapons, on British soil. The Campaign for Nuclear Disarmament was founded in November 1957 to further the cause of 'unilateral disarmament' – the idea that Britain should voluntarily renounce its nuclear weapons, with a view to persuading other nuclear powers, by her example, to follow suit. The same idea, or hope, of Britain as a still influential world power lay behind the unilateralist argument, as had supported the case of the proponents of the British deterrent.

Five thousand people attended the inaugural meeting of CND at the Methodist Central Hall in Westminster on 17 February 1958. 'Celebrity' support for the venture included E.M. Forster, Doris Lessing, John Arlott, Edith Evans, Henry Moore and Jeremy's wife Peggy Ashcroft. The octogenarian mathematician and philosopher Bertrand Russell was appointed president. The cause quickly attracted mass support. A march from Trafalgar Square to the Atomic Weapons Research Establishment at Aldermaston over Easter 1958, organized by a disarmament protest group known as the Direct Action Committee,[4] attracted immense publicity. The march was adopted by CND and became an annual event, albeit from then on the direction of travel was reversed. In 1959, 60,000 people took part; in 1961 and 1962, 150,000 did. Jeremy, never a unilateralist himself, participated in one of the marches partly out of loyalty to his wife, although, he admits, he only joined at Turnham Green. The Aldermaston Marches, the slogan 'Ban the Bomb', and the ubiquitous CND symbol became defining images of the age.

The catalyst for the inception of CND had been an article in the *New Statesman* of 2 November 1957 by the playwright J.B. Priestley, in which he had criticized Aneurin Bevan, the left-wing firebrand of the Labour Party for his decision to renounce unilateralism. From the start, the disarmament movement's relationship with the Labour Party was troubled. CND's founding members had anticipated that the organization would work independently of, but in harmony with, the Labour Party to achieve its objectives. That this was not a workable scenario soon became apparent, not least because of the internal divisions within the party. Hugh Gaitskell, leader of the party from 1957, publicly supported the nuclear deterrent. The high-water mark of CND influence on national politics came at the 1960 Labour Party conference when delegates voted in favour of unilateralism.

Success was short-lived: at their party conference of the following year delegates voted to overturn their previous decision. It was this vote, and the failure of the Labour Party to win the general election of 1959, that persuaded many in the disarmament movement that support for the unilateralist cause could only be generated by extra-parliamentary means.

In July 1960 a young American left-wing activist called Ralph Schoenman, then a postgraduate student at the London School of Economics, approached Bertrand Russell with an idea for a pressure group committed to publicizing the unilateralist cause through a campaign of civil disobedience. Russell was receptive. In his auto-biography, the philosopher explained that at the time 'it seemed more than ever as if new methods must be sought to impress upon the public the increasingly precarious state of international affairs . . . [Schoenman] acted as a catalyst for my gropings as to what could be done to give our work in the CND a new life.'[5]

Schoenman's original model for his committee[6] was that it should use 'big names' as a catalyst to stimulate publicity and public support. Protest, in the form of non-violent civil disobedience, had to be 'mass'. It was later agreed that a 'sit-down' would not take place without prior pledges of support from at least 2,000 people.

Schoenman and Russell had chosen an apt moment for founding a disarmament pressure group. The 'precarious state of international affairs' referred to by Russell was a reference to the build-up of East/West tension in early 1960. On 1 May 1960 an American U-2 spy plane was shot down in Soviet airspace. The pilot, Gary Powers, survived and revealed the purpose of his mission to his Russian interrogators. Assuming that Powers had died, the US government initially publicly denied espionage, and was then forced to backtrack. Eisenhower and Khrushchev had been due to meet at a summit in Paris on 15 May. The talks were doomed, and broke up in an atmosphere of mutual recrimination.

Schoenman and Russell spent the summer of 1960 soliciting the backing of celebrities known to support the unilateralist cause. These included the playwrights John Osborne, Arnold Wesker, Shelagh Delaney, John Arden and Robert Bolt, the theatre director Lindsay Anderson, the writers John Braine and Sir Compton Mackenzie, and the painter Augustus John. These were the 'big names' that were to be the catalysts for the movement.

The inaugural meeting of the Committee of 100 was held on 22 October 1960 at the Friends Meeting House in the Euston Road. Russell became president of the committee (he had resigned his presidency of CND the previous day) and Michael Randle its secretary. The meeting was gripped by a sense of urgency and purpose. It was agreed that the perilous state of international relations, and the nuclear threat, demanded immediate action. The purpose of the committee was to awaken the country to the perils, and imminent danger, of nuclear war. According to the committee's manifesto 'Act or Perish', their purpose was to 'form a body of such irresistible persuasive force that the present madness of East and West may give way to a new hope'.[7]

The committee conceived of itself as an alarum, whose purpose was to wake the nation from its slumbering refusal to acknowledge the imminent danger of nuclear catastrophe. Civil disobedience was adopted as a strategy because it guaranteed publicity, and because the lawful methods preferred by CND had, it was thought, failed. As Russell put it, in an interview in *Encounter* magazine given shortly after the inaugural meeting of the committee, civil disobedience was the only means of 'breaking through the barrier of silence and deceit by means of which populations are being lured to their doom'.[8]

The committee's first demonstration took place in Whitehall on 18 February 1961. The date was chosen to coincide with the expected arrival of the US Polaris submarine tender vessel *Proteus* in the Clyde. Led by the eighty-eight-year-old Russell and his wife, several thousand demonstrators marched in silence down Whitehall and sat for two and a half hours outside the Ministry of Defence. As Russell attempted, like some modern-day Luther, to nail a declaration to the ministry door, a civil servant opened it and handed him a roll of Sellotape. The declaration demanded the 'immediate scrapping of the agreement to base Polaris-carrying submarines in Britain' and 'the complete rejection by our country of nuclear weapons and all policies and alliances that depend upon them'. The sit-down was described as 'the quietest, most orderly, most impressive mass demonstration senior police officers could recall'.[9] There were no arrests. This represented something of a disappointment for the committee leaders. 'We do not want for ever to be tolerated by the police,' Russell lamented.[10]

His anxiety on this score was short-lived. At the next committee demonstration, on 29 April 1961, there were 826 arrests. Over 2,000 people marched down Whitehall from Trafalgar Square and sat down in Parliament Square. Police tactics were notably different on this occasion. Some 3,000 officers had been drafted into central London, and they worked effectively to restrict the movement of the demonstrators within the square. Officers worked in pairs to lift individual demonstrators into police vans. The majority of those arrested were fined £1 in the local magistrates court. John Neville and Vanessa Redgrave managed to leave court in time to appear in the matinee performance of Ibsen's *The Lady from the Sea* in Shaftesbury Avenue.

The demonstration in Parliament Square generated mass media coverage, and the committee's star was high. Support for the movement received an extra fillip as international relations deteriorated further. During the summer of 1961 Soviet and US tanks faced each other in a stand-off over the closure by the East German government of the border between East and West Berlin. This was followed by the East Germans' start of the construction of the Berlin Wall in mid-August. Notwithstanding the existence of a joint moratorium, the USSR resumed nuclear testing on 31 August, and the US followed suit on 6 September. In London, mindful of the increase in support for the committee's activities, the government changed tack. In the first week of September 1961 thirty-six members of the committee, including Lord and Lady Russell, were arrested and charged with incitement to commit breaches of the peace. At Bow Street

Magistrates Court, those charged were given the opportunity to bind themselves over for a year to keep the peace, but most, including the Russells, refused. Russell was sentenced to two months' imprisonment. The result was a government own-goal. In court, there were shouts of 'fascists' and 'poor old man'. The magistrate later reduced Lord Russell's sentence to one week, after having been shown a medical certificate.[11]

The arrests had been intended to undermine the demonstration planned by the committee for 17 September 1961. Instead, the suggestion of government heavy-handedness fuelled support for the cause. The Trafalgar Square sit-down of 17 September 1961 represents the high-water mark of the committee's activities. Some 12,000 people took part in the demonstration, and there were 1,314 arrests. ITV cancelled all its regular afternoon programmes to provide live coverage of the demonstration. On the very same day there was also a successful demonstration by the Scottish Committee of 100 at the Polaris Base at Holy Loch. Despite appalling weather 500 people attended, of whom 350 were arrested.

The very success of the 1961 demonstrations proved the committee's undoing. The government took fright at the committee's potential to create mass disorder, and began taking steps to diminish it. Further, the committee, sensing that it was on the brink of a genuinely mass movement, overreached itself. Activists were faced with the dilemma of how best to follow up on the success of their recent protests. Rather than try endlessly to repeat or extend the successful formula of the London demonstrations, the committee decided to refocus its efforts on disruption of the military apparatus. Here was a major step-change. The purpose of this new-style protest would be not simply publicity for the cause, but immobilization of military bases such as Wethersfield, Ruislip and Brize Norton. This was a logical extension of the committee's long-term goal, at least as viewed by its more radical members, namely the obstruction of the state's capacity to wage war.

The radicalization of the committee had proceeded apace following the early demonstrations. The majority of the 'big names', with whose aid the movement had started, had by this time fallen by the wayside, often in response to this very radicalization, to be replaced by younger and more politically engaged activists. The imprisonment of many of the more senior and experienced members of the committee following the Trafalgar Square demonstration had had a profound impact. The working group of the committee was now dominated by what was described as 'a group of teenagers'. Meetings were anarchic and increasingly revolutionary in tone.

Demonstrations at several air bases, including Wethersfield, were fixed for 9 December 1961. The plan was for a large mass of demonstrators – the aim was for as many as 50,000 – to arrive at the bases and stage a sit-down around the entrances, while a smaller group would try to penetrate the perimeter and stage a separate sit-down on the runway, so as to ground aircraft and immobilize the airfields. Wethersfield was a US Air Force base, and it was suspected that the aircraft located there carried nuclear weapons.

It soon became apparent that the committee's new focus was over-ambitious. The logistics of transporting demonstrators to relatively inaccessible locations in the middle of winter were almost insurmountable, and it proved impossible to attract large-scale support. Meanwhile, the government, alive to the radicalization of the committee's methods and objectives, threw its weight behind efforts to stymie the demonstrations. A fleet of buses commissioned by the committee to transport protesters to Wethersfield was put out of operation. Government preparations for the demonstration at Wethersfield included the erection of a twelve-foot wire fence around the perimeter of the airfield. All police leave was cancelled, and 3,000 civil and military officers were scheduled for duty. A local secondary school was turned into a makeshift courthouse, ready to dispense summary justice to demonstrators.

The government's *coup de théâtre* was the arrest on 8 December 1961, in anticipation of the demonstration on the following day, of five leading members of the committee: Michael Randle, Trevor Hatton, Terry Chandler, Ian Dixon and Helen Allegranza. A sixth member of the committee, Pat Pottle, for whom a warrant had also been obtained, evaded arrest by going into hiding. Two days previously, on 6 December 1961, Special Branch had raided the headquarters of the committee, and searched the homes of those subsequently arrested, removing papers relating to the demonstration at Wethersfield.

This notwithstanding, the demonstration at Wethersfield and else-where went ahead and an overall turnout of 5,000 people was achieved, in spite of dismal weather. Michael Randle records his sense of disappointment that only 600 went to Wethersfield.[12] Unable to get anywhere near the base, they milled around in the next-door village. Film footage of the demonstration shows crowds of duffel-coat-wearing young men and women being pursued by camera crews and journalists while the incongruous figure of Randolph Churchill, son of the former Prime Minister, berates them and records his bizarre advice that 'they should have borrowed their baby brother's Aquascutum knickers to keep their bottoms dry.' Churchill told one journalist that 'They merely bore the police and put a lot of extra money on the shoulders of the rate payers – I don't know how many of them are rate payers in this county.' There were 850 arrests across the country.

At the previous Committee of 100 demonstrations, participants had been charged with relatively minor public order offences. Now that the committee had redirected its focus to military bases, the response of the authorities was to up the ante. Notwithstanding the relative failure of the Wethersfield demonstration, the fear was of a continuing concerted effort at disabling military facilities. A hammer-blow had to be inflicted. Accordingly the 'Wethersfield Six' were charged under section 1 of the Official Secrets Act 1911. So far as relevant this piece of legislation provided that '(1) If any person for any purpose prejudicial to the safety or interests of the State (a) approaches . . . or enters any prohibited place within the meaning of this Act . . . he shall be guilty of felony.' The maximum sentence for such an offence was fourteen years in prison. The defendants were charged on two counts: of conspiring or agreeing with others to commit a breach of section 1, by entering Wethersfield Air Base on 9 December 1961; and second, of conspiracy to incite others to do likewise.

The Wethersfield Six welcomed the prosecution: Michael Randle writes that 'we decided that our best hope at this point was to turn the forthcoming trial into an indictment of government policy.'[13] It was of course admitted that the defendants had planned to approach and enter the Wethersfield Air Base (which was a 'prohibited place' under the Act) and had incited others to do likewise. In fact the defendants publicly proclaimed that fact. Instead the trial was to hinge on the meaning of the crucial phrase 'for any purpose preju-dicial to the safety or interests of the State'. As far as the defendants, and a large proportion of the population, were concerned it was in fact the policy of maintaining 'bombed-up' planes on constant battle-readiness at an Essex airfield that was prejudicial to the safety and interests of the state. Any attempt to disable that battle-readiness could only benefit the state. The question was how to convert that political and humanitarian belief into a legal defence.

Michael Randle recalls that Jeremy was the obvious choice of leading counsel to defend them at the trial.

> We had all followed the Blake case which had happened a few months earlier. Whilst I had no sympathy for Blake's conduct I, like many others, had been appalled by the sentence meted out to him. I read the newspaper reports of Jeremy's speech on behalf of George Blake and was particularly struck by his description of the forty-two-year prison sentence as 'so inhumane that it is alien to all the principles on which a civilized country would treat its subjects'. I agreed and felt that Jeremy had the skills, and sympathies, required for our case.[14]

The trial of the Wethersfield Six began at the Old Bailey on 12 February 1962 before Mr Justice Havers. It was barely two months after the demonstration. Jeremy recalls: 'The trial came on with almost indecent haste before a weak judge, who was prone to wavering.' Pat Pottle had come out of hiding six days earlier and stood trial alongside his comrades. With Reginald Manningham-Buller and Mervyn Griffith-Jones as the formidable counsel team assembled for the prosecution, this was very much a re-match of the Blake case. But this time, although there was no dispute on the facts, the defendants were not pleading guilty. Their defence was a bold one. It involved a simple, but highly contentious proposition: that it was for the jury, not the government of the day, to decide what the 'interests of the State' were and that, in arriving at that decision, jurors could take account of evidence concerning the risks inherent in the UK's nuclear policy and the likely effects of nuclear war.

Jeremy remembers vividly that crisp first morning of the trial.

I had now been in silk for almost a year and felt much more comfortable in my new role. Every new silk feels a slight sense of being a fraud, but thankfully that had left me. After the Blake case, I no longer felt overawed by the Attorney General. I was exhilarated at the thought of what was bound to be a fascinating and hard-fought trial at which such deeply held convictions were at stake. I also wanted to take the opportunity to question the use of section 1 of the Official Secrets Act by the government to suppress civil disobedience. What then happened was unique in all my experience of criminal trials. As I left the Old Bailey robing room I was surprised to find the great hall of the building crowded with demonstrators carrying banners, some bearing the words – to my horror – 'Hutchinson v Manningham-Buller', and all seeming to be chanting and singing and distributing leaflets – in which again my name featured prominently. This was a scene never seen before in the august Central Criminal Court of the capital. I hastily retired to Court 1 where I found the Attorney General looking at me in a sort of apoplectic fury – as if I had orchestrated the demonstration myself!

The Attorney General was certainly not amused. He opened proceedings by handing to the judge one of the leaflets published by the Committee of 100, which had been thrust into his hands by a protester as he strode into court. Jeremy still has one of the leaflets. It includes a list of the current members of the committee (it is notable that a lot of the 'big names' no longer featured), a map of the Wethersfield base, and the following rousing statement: 'We on the Committee are all responsible for the Wethersfield demonstration. We do not apologize for the demonstration which challenged the right of the Government to prepare to kill millions of people. We are proud of it and are determined that this kind of resistance shall continue on a still greater scale. It is the Government which is on trial charged with preparing to commit mass murder.'

'My Lord,' intoned the Attorney General, 'this . . . pamphlet [he could hardly bring himself to refer to it] is nothing less than an attempt to interfere with the course of justice.' Mr Justice Havers nodded gravely and agreed, threatening dire sanctions on any further distribution. Both Manningham-Buller and the judge were looking at Jeremy with an air of veiled accusation. 'Not only Manningham-Buller, but the judge also seemed to think I had been party to the distribution of this pamphlet.' The newspapers reported the following response from Jeremy: 'I think it right that I should say at once that neither I nor my learned junior, nor my instructing solicitor, has seen this document or heard of it. If we had seen it and had known it was going to be published we would have taken the strongest measures to see that was not done.'[15] Bail was granted to the defendants for the duration of the trial only on the condition that they refrain from participation in any demonstration and distribution of leaflets in the precincts of the court. According to Michael Randle, the defendants agreed to this 'with some misgivings'. There was further 'off-stage' business as various other members of the committee, furious at what they saw as the victimization of the Wethersfield Six, attended at police stations across London on the first day of the trial, demanding to be arrested and tried alongside their colleagues. Bewildered police officers advised that they attend at the Old Bailey and 'surrender' to Jeremy. As he left the Bailey on that first day Jeremy was taxed about this by a *Daily Telegraph* journalist who reported his response: 'I don't know why they have been advised to surrender to me – I can't do anything!'

The judge then required that each member of the jury be questioned as to whether they had seen or read the leaflet. It appeared that none of them had. Manningham-Buller objected to three jurors, and Jeremy to six, and they were replaced. As Jeremy explains, the empanelling of the jury was an anxious time for the defence. At this time a unanimous verdict was required to convict or acquit (the majority verdict was introduced some years later), so the individual juror wielded power to scupper both conviction and acquittal. Counsel would anxiously scour the expression and demeanour of the putative juror, trying to discover where his or her sympathies might lie.

Manningham-Buller opened the case for the Crown by denying that the prosecution was politically motivated. Given that, as Attorney General, Manningham-Buller was a government minister and chief legal adviser to the Crown, this was a difficult proposition to swallow. The defendants, he said, were being prosecuted for their conduct, and not for their political views. Referring the jurors to the relevant section of the Official Secrets Act, the Attorney General stated that it was the Crown's case that Wethersfield Air Base was a 'prohibited place' within the meaning of the Act. To prove that the defendants had intended to 'enter' Wethersfield, and had incited others to do so, Manningham-Buller put before the court the evidence obtained in the course of police raids on the committee headquarters and the defendants' homes.

The evidence included minutes of meetings, leaflets and corres-pondence. From this, according to the prosecution, it was clear that the defendants had planned a five-hour sit-down at the two entrances to Wethersfield. It was also the committee's intention that 'a number of trained people' would break away from the main demonstrations and enter the base. Once inside, they were to attempt to lie down on the runway. The prosecution produced a letter from Michael Randle to a friend at Cambridge in which he stated that it was intended to 'immobilize' the base.

On day two of the trial, just as the prosecution was due to start calling its witnesses, it was announced that Pat Pottle had decided to represent himself. As Jeremy recalls, the decision was made following discussions between Pottle and himself in conference. 'If the judge ruled that some or all of the evidence we wished to call was not admissible, I as professional counsel would have to accept that ruling. Pottle then decided that he would represent himself and exploit the greater freedom traditionally granted to a layman conducting his own case.' This proved to be exactly what happened.

The prosecution then called its principal witness, Air Commodore Graham Magill, Director of Operations at the Air Ministry. Magill told the court that on 9 December of the previous year, the RAF air base at Wethersfield was being used by squadrons of the US Air Force, under the command of the Supreme Commander, Allied Forces in Europe. The squadrons were vital to the defence of Britain and Western Europe, said Magill. The aircraft were 'combat ready', at constant alert, and ready to take off at any time. It was his view that, in the event of an emergency, any interference with the aircrafts' ability to take off would gravely prejudice the nation's defences.

It was in relation to Magill's evidence that the fundamental battle-lines of the trial emerged. What Jeremy wanted to do was to ask him about the government's nuclear policy and its dangers. More broadly he wanted to put his clients' case to Magill: namely that the immobilization of Wethersfield was in fact beneficial to the interests of the state. As he warmed to this theme the judge realized the implications of this line of questioning, predicated as it was on the notion that what the 'interests of the State' were was a matter for the jury to decide. The judge demanded that Jeremy clarify his clients' case. His response was reported in the newspapers:

JEREMY: The question in issue for the jury to decide is, first, what was the purpose of the accused in going to Wethersfield. Was that purpose or intention prejudicial to the interest of the state? In coming to that decision the jury must hear evidence about it. They have heard evidence from Air Commodore Magill on which the prosecution says there is evidence to show that the purpose of these persons was prejudicial to the interests of the state. The accused in their turn seek to adduce evidence that their purpose was not. The essential basis of my clients' defence is that this aerodrome was one of the places where there were nuclear bombs and what they will put before the jury is that in the circumstances which obtained at the time it was not in the interests of the state to have aircraft so armed at that time. The defence of my clients is that they went to this airfield not for a purpose prejudicial to this country.

JUDGE: What sort of evidence can you tender to prove that?

JEREMY: I shall tender the evidence of the accused and the evidence of other persons who are experts.

JUDGE: Experts in the science of readiness for war?

JEREMY: Yes, certainly.

JUDGE: Supposing the evidence shows conclusively that the intention was to enter and immobilize and block the airfield and prevent aircraft taking off, can you then disagree when the air commodore says any interruption of their ability to take off would be prejudicial to the interests of the state?

JEREMY: That is a question which the jury will have to decide.

JUDGE: You are saying it would be far better if the aircraft remained on the ground.

JEREMY: One might go as far as that, certainly. It is for the jury to decide why these defendants went to the airfield. It is also for them to decide whether they went for a purpose prejudicial to the state.

JUDGE: You are asking the jury to say that notwithstanding the fact that the effectiveness of the airfield might have been completely destroyed it still was not prejudicial to the security of the state.

JEREMY: In the view of the defendants it was beneficial.

Here lay the crux of the case. The purpose for which the defendants agreed to enter Wethersfield was not, as argued by the prosecution, prejudicial to the state, but rather to its benefit. This was because the actions that the defendants intended to take there, for example sitting on the runway, would prevent, for that period of time, one or more aircraft carrying nuclear weapons from taking off. The defendants' case was predicated on their belief that nuclear weapons posed a threat to the very existence of humanity, so that any act that prevented them being used was of benefit to the state. Jeremy said that he intended to call evidence to prove the catastrophic effect of a nuclear explosion, the danger of an aircraft accident causing such an explosion, the possibility of a mistaken radar reading, and the certainty of a devastating retaliation if a nuclear weapon was used. 'I also wanted to show that the defendants' belief that the state would in fact be safer by removing these potential dangers was honestly held, and reasonable, and their purpose was therefore beneficial rather than prejudicial to the state. To prove this we had lined up a formidable battery of witnesses, which included Bertrand Russell and Linus Pauling, both Nobel Prize winners, as well as the former Archbishop of Bombay and the actress Vanessa Redgrave.'

If Jeremy could question Magill in the way he proposed, and if he could call his expert witnesses, then did that not mean that the jury did have the function he proposed – that is to decide themselves what were 'the interests of the State'? Did it not also mean that the prosecution, to obtain a conviction, had to show an intention on the part of the defendants to prejudice the state, so allowing the defendants to give evidence as to their subjective motives? These were the incendiary propositions that the judge now considered.

Having heard extensive legal argument, he ruled against the defendants. First, he decided that the subjective motives of the defendants were irrelevant. All that needed to be proved was that the actions of the defendants were, objectively considered, prejudicial to the state. And in proving prejudice to the state, all that mattered was current government policy. Those responsible for the national security of the realm must be the sole judges of what national security required.

This was the determinative ruling of the case. The defendants were precluded from arguing that they had intended benefit, rather than prejudice, to the state. They could not give evidence explaining why they had done what they did. Further, they were precluded from calling evidence relating to the dangers of nuclear weapons, which would have been necessary to show that their intentions had been reasonable and that what they had done was, as a matter of fact, *beneficial* to the state.

The judge's ruling effectively destroyed the defendants' case, and with it, as Jeremy recalls, all real hope of an acquittal. It also seriously curtailed the defendants' ability to turn the case into an enquiry into the merits of the government's nuclear policy. The rest of the trial would be a game of cat and mouse: how far could the defendants seek to evade the judge's strictures and widen the scope of the proceedings?

Air Commodore Magill returned to the witness box. Bound as he was by the judge's ruling on the admissibility of evidence, Jeremy's attempts to cross-examine the air commodore proved fruitless.

> JEREMY [to Magill]: Would I be right in thinking that it is quite obvious that the American authorities did not consider this sit-down demonstration was such that it would put aircraft to any prejudice?
> JUDGE: I do not think you can put that to him.

A few more questions met with the same fate. Jeremy recalls:

> It was terribly frustrating. The defence had been neutered at an early stage. However, because Pat Pottle was representing himself, he was also entitled to cross-examine the prosecution's witnesses after I had

sat down. He showed little concern for the judge's ruling. His questioning of Magill was remarkable – both for its tenacity in the face of repeated judicial intervention, and its cheerful disregard of the judge's clear guidance on what was allowable. Pat still saw the trial as a potential opportunity to publicize the unilateralist cause, and he made full use of it. The high point of the trial soon came.

Pat Pottle stood up. After some preliminaries he jumped in at the deep end:

POTTLE: Have you read the facts about the nuclear bombs on Hiroshima and Nagasaki?

JUDGE: Do not answer that.

POTTLE: Is there any official order from the government that you could not accept?

JUDGE: He is an officer in Her Majesty's forces.

POTTLE: So there is no decision that you would not accept?

MAGILL: It is my duty to carry it out.

POTTLE: Would you press the button that you know is going to annihilate millions of people?

Pottle's co-defendant Michael Randle recalls that, as Pottle asked the question: 'I held my breath . . . willing the judge not to intervene. I think most of the people in the public gallery of the court were holding their breath too.'[16] In the event, the judge was not quick enough off the mark. The defining statement of the trial, and to many a horrifying answer, was elicited.

MAGILL: If the circumstances so demanded it, I would.

This response inspired Pottle to continue in more emotive vein: 'Would you slit the throats of all the two-year-old children in this country, Air Commodore?' The judge was now rather more swift in his interventions. He told Pottle, 'I think you must stop all that.' And so it went on, the judge preventing an answer to each question. But he could not stop the questions being posed and the newspapers noted them down: 'You have said that you would accept any order from the state that was given to you. Eichmann's defence was—' Again the judge intervened: 'You cannot mention him in this case.'

The questions kept coming: 'Air Commodore, do you agree with

[Winston Churchill's] statement, "We must not forget that by creating atomic bases in East Anglia we have made ourselves the target and perhaps the bull's-eye of a Soviet attack"?' and 'Do you agree with the statement made by Mr Duncan Sandys in 1957, when he was Minister of Defence, when he said bases cannot defend people?' The judge prevented Magill from answering on both occasions, but as Michael Randle pointed out, 'Even the disallowed questions made their point.'

With Magill's evidence finished that was the end of the prosecution case.

Jeremy opened the case for the defence by calling Michael Randle. Jeremy remembers him as a man of seriousness and conviction (he would later become a Fellow in the Department of Peace Studies at Bradford University). These qualities were demonstrated by Randle in the course of his testimony, which though measured in tone, was as effective as Pottle's in publicizing the disarmament cause. He was assisted in this by Manningham-Buller, who, in the course of cross-examination, quoted at length from a Committee of 100 policy memorandum justifying civil disobedience. The Attorney General's insistence that Randle divulge his personal beliefs on the subject of pacifism was an own goal as it now made it possible for Jeremy to ask Randle about his beliefs in re-examination, and in particular in relation to the genocidal potential of nuclear weapons, notwithstanding the judge's earlier ruling. To a question about his reasons for wishing to enter the air base, Randle replied: 'I helped organize it to prevent the murder of millions of people.' On what, Jeremy asked, was his decision to act based?

> RANDLE: On the fact that atomic weapons, megaton bombs, can kill millions of people. They can knock out a whole city.
> JEREMY: Was it on the official figures in relation to the effect of the [Hiroshima] bomb that you based, among other considerations, your personal views?
> RANDLE: It was indeed, yes.

Randle concluded his testimony on the morning of the fourth day of the trial. He had scored one other point during his evidence. It is an acute insight into the period that Manningham-Buller had addressed him during cross-examination by his surname alone, exhibiting a kind of class prejudice that still persisted at this time. Randle had insisted to the judge that the Attorney General refer to him as 'Mr'. He got his way.

Jeremy then advised the court that he would not be calling the four remaining defendants to give evidence on their behalf, as they would simply reiterate what had been said by Randle. Instead Terry Chandler, Trevor Hatton, Ian Dixon and Helen Allegranza would each make an unsworn statement from the dock. In the course of their statements, all four defendants accepted their share of responsibility for the protest at Wethersfield. Trevor Hatton stated that the object of the demonstration had been to 'bring home to the people of this country the dangers of the use of the nuclear deterrent'. Ian Dixon told the jury that 'there are some things which even a democratic society may not do . . . one of them is to consign millions of human beings to death.'

'Sir Robert Watson-Watt, the inventor of radar, a former archbishop, an actress and a doctor were called at the Central Criminal Court yesterday,' announced *The Times* of 16 February 1962. Following the conclusion of the case for the five defendants represented by Jeremy, Pat Pottle began his own defence. To the delight of the newspapers and the public gallery, his witnesses included Vanessa Redgrave and three Nobel laureates. All these witnesses were to have been called by Jeremy, but he was precluded from doing so by the judge's ruling. But Pat Pottle might have a better chance of getting their evidence before the jury.

Sir Robert Watson-Watt had flown from California in order to give evidence. He had been patiently waiting at court since the start of the trial. The relevance of Watson-Watt's expertise to the issues of the trial was somewhat tenuous, but this proved to be of little importance, as he was not allowed to answer most of the questions that were put to him. He was able to respond to Pottle's question: 'Is it possible to tell the difference between a missile and a flock of geese on the radar systems which are in use in this country and America?' in the affirmative. But Pottle's question: 'If the Committee of 100 had got on to the runway at Wethersfield on December 9 would the emergency operations have been able to go off as planned?' was disallowed, as was a series of other questions. Watson-Watt was stood down after only twenty-two minutes in the box.

Other witnesses called by Pat Pottle included Dr Roberts, a former Roman Catholic Archbishop of Bombay, who gave evidence concerning whether civil disobedience could be morally justified when it opposes policies approved by the majority. He agreed with Pottle's assertion that Christian martyrs had broken the law and that the majority opinion of the time condemned them for doing so. Meanwhile, 'We, in our day, are asked to acquiesce passively if not actively in actions leading to tyrannical brutalities compared with which all former horrors sink into insignificance.' Pottle's question: 'Do you feel, Archbishop Roberts, that there is justification for some more Christian martyrs?' was disallowed.

Both Vanessa Redgrave and Bertrand Russell also gave evidence. They testified that they bore equal responsibility with the defendants for the demonstrations at Wethersfield. Redgrave explained that she had been a member of the committee since the previous September and, in response to Pottle's question, 'Did you, Miss Redgrave, conspire with others to incite people to go on to the Wethersfield base?' Redgrave replied emphatically, 'I did.' At that point the judge intervened: 'Before you answer that, it is my duty to warn you that you are not bound to answer any questions which you think may tend to incriminate you.' Pottle repeated his question, and Redgrave gave the same reply. Redgrave agreed that it was her intention to block and immobilize the base. Bertrand Russell then took to the witness box. Jeremy remembers how the now eighty-nine-year-old philosopher and Nobel laureate for literature stood in the witness box. 'His reed-like frame was ramrod straight.' Russell declined to take his oath on the Bible and refused the chair that was offered to him. 'No thank you, I prefer to stand.' He too gave evidence of his foundation of the Committee of 100 ('to try to avoid the extermination of the people of this country and of many millions elsewhere') and his involvement in the Wethersfield demonstration. Again the judge warned him of his right not to incriminate himself.

RUSSELL: Have I not the right to incriminate myself?
JUDGE: My duty is to warn you, the same as for witnesses who might
    not know. You are perfectly entitled to incriminate yourself.
RUSSELL: Well, I do.

The same spirit that, in 1917, had seen Russell imprisoned for his advocacy of pacifism, was still burning bright. Russell was able to explain that his purpose in attempting to occupy Wethersfield was based on his belief that he had a duty to make known the dire peril in which the world found itself – before his evidence was ruled irrelevant. Finally Professor Linus Pauling, Professor of Chemistry at the California Institute of Technology, and the recipient of the 1954 Nobel Prize for chemistry, attempted to give evidence. The judge again prevented him from answering most of the questions put to him.

The evidence, such as it was, was now over and the case moved towards its finale. In his closing speech to the jury, Manningham-Buller repeated his earlier denial that the prosecution was politically motivated: 'I should make it clear that this is not a prosecution by the government.' The prosecution had been brought, he said, because the accused had deliberately broken the law.

> It is clear, is it not, from the evidence of Mr Randle [note the use of Mr!] that the Committee of 100 and the accused have sought to arrogate to themselves the right to seek to break any law which they consider relevant and immoral. They seek, do they not, to put themselves above the law and I ask you to consider for one moment what would happen if other bodies or persons, perhaps with very different views, adopted the same course. If that happened, if many other bodies did this, if they succeeded in their efforts, it would be an end to the rule of law. It would lead to the end of democracy, to anarchy, and possibly to dictatorship in this country.

Jeremy recalls that in constructing his own closing submissions he had been deprived of any evidential basis for presenting his clients' case. 'I decided to try to use this to the defendants' advantage and challenge the judge's ruling':

> Why did the Attorney General ask Mr Randle about civil disobedience? What has it got to do with the case if the only question for you

to decide here is: did they stop the planes, or mean to, and was it prejudicial . . .? What has civil disobedience got to do with it? It has a vast amount to do with it, of course, if their intentions and motives and aims *are* relevant; of course it has, because the Attorney General said to you over and over again that these defendants have set out to break the law, and if that is said, then surely to goodness, they are permitted to tell you why? How on earth in all common sense – and for goodness' sake let's apply some – can you consider the purpose of anybody without looking at their views on which the purpose is founded? It doesn't make any sense at all. It is cloud cuckoo-land to try to decide this case on the grounds that their views, intentions, aims are utterly irrelevant and you haven't to consider them at all.

You may recall, members of the jury, that I asked Mr Randle, 'Did you intend to do anything prejudicial to the interests of the state?' Immediately the Attorney General objected and said that was a question for the jury to decide. Where indeed have we got to if a man in the No. 1 Court at the Central Criminal Court is not allowed to answer 'No, I didn't' or 'Yes, I did' because it is a question for the jury . . . It is the easiest thing to say that these people are a nuisance. Of course they are a nuisance to the authorities, and a great many people. They are an irritant to the authorities and you may think they are an irritant to the consciences of a great many people as well.

(A year later, in a profile of Jeremy in the *Evening Standard*, the writer Edgar Lustgarten described his style of advocacy: 'He can, on apt occasions, suddenly lower the temperature with a flash of humour, but his characteristic gift as a defender is the maintenance and mounting of intensity. Nothing to make light of here. Nothing could matter more.')

The judge in summing up told the jury that 'No one in this country, however strong and sincere are his convictions, and however honourable he might be, had the right to arrogate to himself to decide which laws were bad laws.' It is notable that, as these words were spoken, Adolf Eichmann's appeal against the death sentence passed on him in Jerusalem was about to be heard. It was an appeal founded upon Eichmann's defence that he had been obliged to follow orders.

The jury retired at 12.40 p.m. on 20 February 1962. The judge had in truth given them no option but to convict. Nonetheless, the jury struggled with their verdict for more than four hours. Returning to the court at 4.55 p.m., the foreman of the jury pronounced a verdict of 'guilty' on both counts against all defendants. But he added this rider: 'It is our unanimous decision that we would like the court to consider leniency.' Before sentencing, the judge turned to Jeremy and said: 'Even at this late hour it would affect my mind in considering what the appropriate sentence should be if these accused were to tell me that they now realize that however honest and sincere their convictions, they were completely misguided.' According to *The Times*, the judge's remarks elicited laughter from the public gallery. Unperturbed, the judge carried on: 'If the defendants would assure me that they would give up this campaign of civil disobedience and . . . not commit any more criminal offences' he would consider leniency.

Having taken instructions, Jeremy informed the judge that: 'None of my clients is able to give Your Lordship the undertaking that you ask for. Although my instructions were to add nothing to the facts that you know, I might add just this, that I know you will take into account the long period which the jury took to come to a conclusion about this matter and the recommendation they have made.'

Through their moral honesty, the defendants had sealed for themselves a significantly longer sentence than would otherwise have been passed.

The five male defendants were sentenced to eighteen months in prison. (As we have seen it was while in prison that Michael Randle and Pat Pottle met George Blake.) Helen Allegranza received the lesser sentence of twelve months, on account of the supposed fact that she had 'played a far less active part than the others' (she cried out at this moment, 'With respect, My Lord, I wish to be considered equally guilty with my friends'). The judge stated that, in passing sentence, he had taken 'fully into account that you are persons who hold strong views and honestly and sincerely believe in those views'. 'It may well be,' he continued, 'that you came under the influence of Lord Russell.' As to Russell: 'He is certainly old enough to know better than to incite a lot of young people to break the laws of this country.' *The Times* reported that after sentence had been handed down there were cries of 'Shame, Shame' from the public gallery, then shouts of 'Ban the Bomb!'

The verdict was upheld in the Court of Appeal. However the Lord Chief Justice certified that the case raised a point of law of general importance concerning the construction of section 1 of the Official Secrets Act and so the case progressed to the House of Lords for a final appeal. By the time the case reached the House of Lords, Jeremy had been replaced as leading counsel by Sir John Foster QC, Fellow of All Souls, a leading constitutional lawyer and Conservative MP. The Wethersfield Six were embarrassed about replacing Jeremy and sent him letters from prison explaining their decision. Trevor Hatton wrote: 'We hope sincerely you understand why we finally decided to instruct John Foster for the forthcoming appeal to the House of Lords. It was a most difficult decision to make and we should hate you to think that we were in any way dissatisfied with your own conduct of the trial and the appeal [to the Court of Appeal]. Personally, I thought you were superb . . .'

Jeremy bore no hard feelings. 'I was a very young silk with no experience of appearing in the House of Lords and I could see that they needed a more senior counsel with long experience of advocating before that august tribunal.'

The decision of the House of Lords in *DPP v Chandler and Others*[17] has become a landmark of the criminal law, studied by all law students. In the course of his judgement in the House of Lords, Lord Radcliffe distinguished between the defendants' direct purpose – to enter and immobilize the base, which was the purpose relevant to section 1 of the Act – and their indirect purpose, or motive – to reduce the risk of nuclear catastrophe, which was not. In his opinion, evidence relating to the defendants' motive had been properly excluded. This was because matters of national defence depended on the exercise of the royal prerogative, which could not be questioned in a court of law. Only those who were responsible for national security could determine what that security required. In Lord Radcliffe's view, 'the question whether it is in the true interests of this country to acquire, retain or house nuclear armaments depends on an infinity of considerations, military and diplomatic, technical, psychological and moral, and of decisions, tentative and final' and was, for this reason, untriable. Lord Devlin, the only judge in the House of Lords with extensive criminal experience, whilst agreeing in the result, was rather more exercised by the questions raised by the defendants' appeal:

> The Attorney General submitted that, while it is a question of fact for the jury whether the entry was for a purpose prejudicial, once it was proved that the purpose was to interfere with a prohibited place and to prevent its operating, then a judge should be entitled to direct a jury to return a verdict of guilty. With great respect I think that to be an unconstitutional doctrine. It is the conscience of the jury and not the power of the judge that provides the constitutional safeguard against perverse acquittal . . . [As Lord Mansfield said:] 'It is the duty of the judge, in all cases of general justice, to tell the jury how to do right, though they have it in their power to do wrong, which is a matter entirely between God and their own consciences' . . . The servants of the Crown, like other men animated by the highest motives, are capable of formulating a policy ad hoc so as to prevent the citizen from doing something that the Crown does not want him to do. It is the duty of the courts to be as alert now as they have always been to prevent abuse of the prerogative . . . the arguments put forward in this appeal . . . have embraced big constitutional questions concerning the right to trial by jury and not by judge, and the extent to which the courts can question statements on political matters by the executive. All such questions which concern the liberty of the subject need great care in their consideration. It is to me a special inducement to the exercise of care that these appellants have not traded their liberty for personal gain but for what they sincerely, and however mistakenly, believe to be the safety of the world. Furthermore (their own expressed determination to break the law notwithstanding), it is the duty of this House to see that men and women who have a creed they want to preach in no case pay any penalty for their faith unless they have taken themselves out of the protection of the law by doing that which the law forbids.

Jeremy had known, when he was first retained, that an acquittal was very unlikely. The judge's ruling on the exclusion of evidence destroyed what case he had, and with it any residual hope of avoiding a guilty verdict. The views of the individual jurors are not known. The fact that they took several hours to consider their verdict, and then tempered it with a unanimous appeal for leniency, suggests that they were sympathetic to the defendants' commitment, if not their cause. It was, of course, open to the jury to flout judicial guidance both as to the proper construction of the Act, and the interests of the safety of the state, and acquit. But for the jury in the Committee of 100, regardless of their sympathies, this was a step too far.

By the time of the determinative hearing in the House of Lords in May 1962 the Committee of 100 was in decline. As a result of the trial, six of the leading figures of the movement were in prison. The failure of the Wethersfield demonstration and the trial itself had a demoralizing effect. Support dwindled. The committee's demonstrations in 1962 were lacklustre affairs in comparison with the triumphs of the preceding year. By early 1963 the committee had become, in the view of one commentator, 'a small, crankish group of young extremists who were hardly taken seriously even by many who were sympathetic to unilateralism'.[18]

The committee suffered this deterioration of fortune notwithstanding the Cuban missile crisis of October 1962, by general consensus the moment when the world came closest to nuclear war. The Cuban crisis did not, contrary to what might be supposed, coincide with an increase in support for disarmament. If anything, the period witnessed a general falling off of commitment to the unilateral cause. Support for unilateral disarmament in the general population hovered about the 25 per cent mark for much of the period, rising to a peak of 33 per cent in April 1960 before declining again. To achieve their stated ends, the unilateralists would have had to turn minority support into majority, but this they signally failed to do.

One of the frustrations of the movement was that while the general populace might care about the risk of imminent nuclear annihilation, they did not care about it enough. A Gallup poll of late 1959 found that only one person in fourteen listed the international situation, the Cold War, or the bomb among their major political concerns. For many in the unilateralist movement this was evidence not so much of indifference, as of ignorance. The fault lay, according to Bertrand Russell, in a conspiracy of silence instigated by government and connived at by a subservient press. In his view, only the shock of civil disobedience could break through 'the barrier of silence and deceit by means of which populations are being lured to their doom'.[19]

In fact most people were aware of the realities of nuclear warfare. A Gallup poll of 1958 recorded that four out of five Britons believed that less than half the population would survive a nuclear attack. The reason that people worried less than activists thought they should about nuclear attack is, simply, that they had more pressing things to worry about, or took the view that Armageddon was best averted by the maintenance of a nuclear deterrent. It was as incomprehensible to the anti-nuclear campaigners of the 1960s, as it is to the climate change activists of today, that the majority of the population should show such perceived indifference to the imminent destruction of their planet. Yet for most people the realities of everyday life, and perhaps the blandishments of the consumer society (which the Conservative government had done so much to foment), left little time for anxiety over a theoretical future, over which they could have slight, if any, control. It is noteworthy that disarmament activists were generally middle class and reasonably affluent. The unilateral movement never generated significant working-class support, and here lies one of the central reasons it failed.

Moreover, by the early 1960s it was increasingly clear that, given the declining status of Britain as a world power, and the comparative insignificance of the British nuclear arsenal, unilateral disarmament, even if it succeeded, would have little or no effect. As the historian A.J.P. Taylor remarked: 'If we threw away our bombs, who'd notice?'[20]

The Committee of 100 is chiefly remembered for its espousal of civil disobedience, which set it apart from CND. Bertrand Russell adopted such methods because they attracted publicity. For many in the movement, however, the use of non-violent resistance was an aspect of what they considered to be their moral obligation to prevent genocide through nuclear war. At the trial, Pat Pottle and Michael Randle both drew comparison between their own sense of moral obligation, and that incumbent on Germans at the time of the Holocaust. In an exchange with the judge, Randle argued, 'There were people in Germany during the Nazi regime who were ordered to commit what have since been defined as crimes against humanity. They would have been going against the law of their country by disobeying their orders. I feel they had a moral duty to disobey that orders in that situation.'

Until the Trafalgar Square demonstration of 17 September 1961 the civil disobedience practised by the committee constituted little threat to the social or political system. Indeed in the early stages of their campaign 'the Committee's conception of civil disobedience was not at odds with Britain's prevailing democratic norms.'[21] The radicalization of the committee's methods and objectives during the autumn of 1961 took them beyond it. It is no surprise that the government responded firmly to the planned entry of Wethersfield. At stake was not only, as had been contended at trial, the security of Britain and Western Europe. The committee's plans threatened the very military organization of the country.

The trial of the Wethersfield Six stands as testament to the spirit of the principled activist who, in pursuit of his or her convictions, and in the face of general apathy and political hostility, risks their own freedom for what they consider to be the good of mankind. As Christopher Driver has remarked: 'If an Englishman in 1961 genuinely thought that the only way to preserve the world from nuclear annihilation was to trespass upon Wethersfield base at the cost of a few months in jail, he was surely as right to do so as the judge was right to impose the specified penalty.'

I I

'Much ado about nothing'

R v Cairns, Aitken, Roberts and Sunday Telegraph Ltd (1971)

T HE EVENING STANDARD published an article about Jeremy in the 1960s. It was headed 'He lived down the curse of a brilliant father'. That father, St John Hutchinson, had himself been one of the legendary criminal defenders of the 1930s and it was his father's former chambers that Jeremy joined in 1946. St John had died suddenly four years earlier, in 1942, but 1 Garden Court was a set still haunted by his beneficent ghost. Jeremy remembers that the warmth and benevolence of his father's personality even after his death continued to infuse the atmosphere of his chambers. 'The whole character of what became Queen Elizabeth Building[1] seemed to have been set by him. It was a chambers without rancour or professional envy, which is unusual because life at the Bar can breed jealousies. His spirit still lingered even when, forty years later, I retired.'

As the years went by, Jeremy could not help sensing multiple parallels between his own life and that of his father. Just like St John, Jeremy would become a great Old Bailey defender. His father became the Recorder of Hastings and would spend several weeks a year trying criminal cases at the seaside town. Jeremy himself became Recorder of Bath. In the last weeks of his life St John, passionately interested in modern art, became a trustee of the Tate Gallery. Jeremy would do likewise in the 1970s before eventually becoming chairman. His father was a close friend of D.H. Lawrence and, in 1927, defended the gallery that had exhibited his paintings for alleged obscenity. As we have seen, Jeremy would later defend Lawrence's writings against similar charges.

When Jeremy took his seat in Court 1 of the Old Bailey on 12 January 1971 to start the trial in the case of *R v Cairns, Aitken, Roberts and Sunday Telegraph Ltd* he thought again of his father. On

12 January 1933, exactly thirty-eight years earlier, St John Hutchinson had sat in the same court as counsel for the novelist and writer Compton Mackenzie, who had been brought before the Old Bailey as the first author charged under section 2 of the Official Secrets Act 1911. His alleged crime was to have written a book, *Greek Memories*, drawing on his experiences working for the intelligence service in Athens during the First World War. What riled the authorities was that Mackenzie had quoted from various official telegrams passing between London and Athens, which showed senior members of the secret services in a poor light, and had named various individuals connected with it during the war. This was categorized as 'a most dangerous disclosure, because it might be necessary to use them again in the event of another war'.

During the committal proceedings, deploying a tactic that would become a stock-in-trade in such prosecutions, the prosecutor had informed the judge, 'I am now going to call as a witness a present member of the secret service. And although we are in camera I am going to ask you if he may keep his name secret and that he be alluded to as Major X.' St John Hutchinson rose to cross-examine Major X, armed, as Mackenzie later recorded in his memoirs, 'with all the information supplied by myself about the dozen or so alleged ex-members of the Secret Service whose future careers I was supposed to have imperilled'.[2] It turned out that of these one had died ten years earlier; one was the Consul-General in Alexandria and listed his work in the wartime intelligence in his *Who's Who* entry; and one was Deputy Keeper of the Victoria and Albert Museum. In the event, notwithstanding the manifest absurdity of the charges, Mackenzie reluctantly pleaded guilty on the promise of a derisory fine. Years later Mackenzie would score a minor revenge by quoting in full St John's wonderfully sarcastic cross-examination of the hapless Major X in his memoirs.

The case was castigated at the time as a political prosecution 'brought either for the settlement of scores or to warn off more eminent Crown servants from making unauthorized disclosures about their wartime activities'.[3] It was said that the two most eminent figures whom Mackenzie's conviction was designed to silence were Lloyd George and Winston Churchill. Indeed Churchill – who would later remark of the Official Secrets Act that 'It ought not to be used to shield Ministers who have strong personal interests in concealing the truth about matters from the country' – was apparently sufficiently unnerved that he burned a number of documents retained from his period in office during the First World War.

Now, thirty-eight years later, Jeremy was sitting in the same court representing a seasoned and universally respected journalist, Brian Roberts, and the newspaper of which he was editor, the *Sunday Telegraph*, on charges brought under the same section of the same Act. Again, the Act had been misused by an administration wishing to punish writers and journalists – this time for seeking to expose government hypocrisy and double-dealing. The trial that followed was as much a human drama of misunderstandings, fiercely held convictions and broken friendships, as it was an indictment of governmental misconduct.

The *Sunday Telegraph* case had its origins in the ethnic and political tensions of post-colonial Nigeria. Decolonization had exposed the profound divisions between the predominantly Muslim Hausa people of the north, and the Christian Ibo of the south-east. On 30 May 1967 Colonel Ojukwu, the military governor of the Ibo-dominated part of the country, declared the secession of the region from Nigeria, and the formation of the independent Republic of Biafra.

In the civil war that followed, the Nigerian Federalists, who sought to return the Biafran state to the federation of Nigeria, enjoyed a considerable superiority in both weaponry and manpower. It was thought that the war, and the Biafran secession, would be short-lived. However the tenacity of the Biafran rebels frustrated Federalist hopes for an early victory, and by early 1968 the conflict had reached a stalemate. Then, between April and June 1968, a Nigerian offensive succeeded in encircling the Biafran heartland, which was cut off from the outside world. As supply routes became impassable, the Biafrans accused the Federalists of using starvation and genocide as weapons of war. Shocking photographs of starving Biafran children were flashed across the world, and the extent of the humanitarian crisis consequent on the blockade became a cause exciting condemnation worldwide.

The Labour government under Harold Wilson supported the Federalists, motivated by a desire both to preserve the integrity of the Nigerian federation, which had been created by the post-colonial settlement, and to protect significant British economic interests in the country. As it became clear that the 'short surgical police action'[4] promised by the Nigerian leader General Gowon had mutated into a prolonged military impasse, opinion divided between those who supported the continuing supply of British arms to the Nigerian government (on the grounds that this was the best way to ensure an early Nigerian victory, and through it an end to the humanitarian crisis); and those who considered that supplying weapons to the Federalists was morally reprehensible, given that they were participating in the effective genocide of the Biafran people.

For liberal-minded onlookers, the Biafran cause embodied a kind of heroic romanticism and it attracted the support of many prominent figures in England and elsewhere. Jonathan Aitken was one of them. At this time he was a glamorous young journalist and author specializing in international affairs. He was also the prospective Conservative parliamentary candidate for the constituency of Thirsk and Malton in Yorkshire. He had taken a particular interest in the plight of the Biafrans and, in September 1969, visited Nigeria and Biafra at the instigation of the London *Evening Standard*, who had commissioned him to write a series of articles on the war. Aitken was greatly affected by what he saw in Biafra, which hardened his opposition to the supply of British arms to the Federal forces. The strength of his feeling is clear from the following contemporaneous entries in his notebook: 'We want to bring to Brit people that greatest moral int crime since Hitler ext jews now going on here . . . Nigerians more interested in civilian targets that military ones. This war would be over in a few weeks if Brit would stop arms supplies.'

In the course of his visit Aitken met two men who were to figure largely in the subsequent trial. The first was Colonel Douglas Cairns, a retired army officer and now an employee of Barclays Bank, who had obtained an ad hoc role as the senior British representative on an international team of military observers set up at the instigation of the Nigerians to monitor the behaviour of their own Federal forces. Aitken had brought with him a letter of introduction to Cairns from

Major-General Henry Alexander, Aitken's neighbour in Yorkshire, with whom he was on friendly terms. Alexander was also to play a leading role at the subsequent trial. According to Aitken, Cairns proved an 'exceptionally helpful and agreeable expert on the war'.[5]

Second, Aitken met the Defence Adviser to the British High Commission in Lagos, Colonel Robert Scott. Scott gave Aitken an extensive briefing on the military situation which suggested that, despite the fact that the Nigerian Federal Army was riddled with incompetence and wastage, the Biafran military situation was bleak.

On his return to London, Aitken recounted what he had seen in Biafra in a series of impassioned newspaper articles and radio and television broadcasts. His criticism of the Labour government's policy of continuing arms sales to Nigeria brought Aitken into close contact with the parliamentary 'Biafra Lobby' – a cross-party grouping dedicated to changing government policy on the war. Its leading members included Hugh Fraser, a dashing and maverick Conservative MP (he had previously been Secretary of State for Air in the Macmillan government), who lobbied tirelessly in support of the Biafran cause. As the war continued, and public awareness of the dire humanitarian situation in Biafra grew, support for the Biafra Lobby intensified. By December 1969 over 150 MPs across the political spectrum supported the cessation of arms sales to Nigeria.

On 21 December 1969 Jonathan Aitken attended a dinner party at the Old Rectory in Brandsby in Yorkshire, the residence of General Alexander, whose letter of invitation he had used to contact Colonel Cairns in Nigeria. Alexander had recently retired from the army after a career of notable achievement. At one time the youngest Major-General in the British peacetime army, Alexander had served in seven countries and won the DSO and an OBE. He had been seconded to the Ghanaian Army as President Nkrumah's Chief of Defence Staff, and had also latterly served as the British representative on the international team of observers in Nigeria, the post that was subsequently filled by Douglas Cairns.

Alexander lived a few miles from Aitken's Yorkshire cottage and was an active member of the local Conservative Association. It was in this capacity that the two men met. They quickly discovered a common interest in the Biafran conflict. Alexander was well informed on the military situation in West Africa, and prior to Aitken's visit to the region provided him with information on the current status of the war as well as helpful contacts. On Aitken's return to Britain, Alexander continued to brief him on the conflict. According to Aitken, there was a clear understanding between the two men that he could use whatever information Alexander provided to him, on the condition that Alexander would not be named as the source. As Alexander supported the continuing supply of British arms to the Federal Army, which he saw as necessary to hasten the end of the war, Aitken considered that Alexander's motive in briefing him so generously was, at least in part, to try to persuade Aitken to his own point of view.

Aitken's fellow guests at this convivial dinner – which would give rise to much controversy – included Colonel Geoffrey Preston, an old army friend and neighbour of the host, and his wife Daphne, and the Alexanders' son David. A local landowner, Tony Cliff, whom Aitken knew in Cliff's capacity as former chairman of the local Conservative Association, and his wife, also joined the party.

The ladies retired after dinner (such was polite Yorkshire life in the 1960s) and the men remained at the table drinking port, in high spirits. According to Aitken's account of the evening,[6] the conversation concentrated first on domestic political affairs, before turning to Africa. Alexander criticized what he considered the lack of understanding of the situation in Biafra displayed in the speeches of MPs supporting the Biafra Lobby, some of whom had claimed, in a debate on the subject in the House of Commons on 9 December, that the Federalists could not win the war. Aitken, who had helped prepare Hugh Fraser's speech for that very debate, defended the assertions of the Biafra Lobby. Aitken remembered that he said words to the effect that 'Your Federals are nowhere near winning this war.' The general's response, Aitken recalled, was dismissive. 'You're talking rubbish. I've just had a report come in from Lagos, which proves the Nigerians are going to finish this war off very soon. I'll let you see it.'

At this point, the men joined the ladies in the drawing room, where the guests stayed talking and drinking until about eleven thirty. By then, only the Cliffs, Aitken and the three Alexanders remained. Aitken recalled that he was sitting on a sofa talking to Mrs Cliff, when General Alexander entered the room carrying some papers. Alexander handed them to Aitken, saying that this was the report that he had mentioned earlier. There was then, according to Aitken, a 'very brief exchange of conversation', between the two men, 'largely on the subject of when I would return the document, and including the phrase "You see it's marked confidential".'

The document that Alexander gave to Aitken was a report entitled An Appreciation of the Nigerian Conflict. Its author was Colonel Scott, whom Aitken had met during his time in Nigeria a couple of months earlier. Scott had drafted the first version of the report in early 1969, at the request of the British government, in preparation for Harold Wilson's visit to Lagos in April 1969. The document obtained by Alexander was an updated version, completed by Scott only days before. The object of this version of the report was stated to be to 'examine whether either side in the Nigerian civil war can reach a successful conclusion before the end of the present dry season' (that is, April 1970). It comprised an appraisal of the military capability of the opposing factions in the conflict, and an assessment of the future course of the war. Fifty-one copies of the report, each marked 'Confidential', were distributed to officials in London and Lagos. Recipients also included the Australian and Canadian High Commissioners, the Defence Attaché to the US Embassy, and the two British representatives on the international observer team, Colonel Cairns and a Major Gray.

On 6 December 1969 Scott had held a press conference at which he briefed British and foreign journalists on the current state of the conflict. In the course of the subsequent proceedings Scott admitted that as he had just finished writing the report, it was uppermost in his mind when he gave the briefing, and he quoted, or at least referred to, large sections of it during the course of the conference.

Colonel Cairns had provided invaluable assistance to Scott in the preparation of the report. As Scott was largely confined to Lagos, he had relied on Cairns for information from the front line, and Cairns had also helped in compiling the document. In this capacity, and as senior British member of the observer team, Cairns was an obvious recipient of a copy of the finished document. In turn, Cairns quickly sent on a copy to General Alexander in England. Cairns had worked as Alexander's deputy on the international observer team, and after Alexander had returned to Yorkshire from Nigeria,

Cairns had promised to keep him up to date with what was happening in Nigeria. Cairns did not ask Scott's permission to do this and, in his covering letter, Cairns asked Alexander not to mention to Scott that he had received a copy. These were words that would later excite suspicion and Cairns would explain that, out of common courtesy, he had wanted to inform Scott first.

As we have seen, Alexander, though formally retired from the military, remained actively interested in the Nigerian conflict. He was briefed by the Foreign Office, and lectured on the war from a pro-Federalist standpoint, with the government's unofficial blessing. Cairns provided Alexander with observer reports and other non-classified information. At the trial, Cairns would say that it did not occur to him that he was doing anything wrong in sending the Scott report to Alexander. The general was a trusted colleague, with impeccable military credentials, who was using the information provided by Cairns to further the work undertaken by him with the unofficial, but real, support of the British government. Besides, both men had signed, and were bound by, the Official Secrets Act. It did not occur to Cairns that the general might use the report for an unauthorized purpose.

As Jonathan Aitken eagerly read the Scott report on his return home, late in the evening of 21 December, what struck him most forcefully was the disparity between Scott's estimation of the number of British weapons supplied to the Federal Army, and the figures previously stated by the British government. On 10 July 1969 the Foreign Secretary, Michael Stewart, had told the House of Commons that the arms currently being supplied by Britain equated 'broadly both in quality and quantity' to those it had supplied before the war. On 9 December 1969 Stewart had told the House that British arms sales amounted to 'about fifteen per cent by value' of the total arms purchased by Nigeria. In contrast, the Scott report indicated that the British were supplying a minimum of 70 per cent of Nigerian arms purchases, and that they were supplying vastly more than they had done before the war. The Scott report revealed in the plainest terms the existence of government duplicity.

On the morning of 22 December 1969 Aitken attended a long-standing appointment with Michael Deakin, a senior documentary producer with Yorkshire Television, at his offices in Leeds. Aitken had worked for Yorkshire since 1968 in various roles including writing scripts and presenting a regional news programme. He and Deakin were at the time discussing with the company a possible documentary about Biafra. Aitken took the Scott report with him when he attended the meeting in Leeds. Deakin read it and agreed that it would be useful. He had six photocopies made. In his evidence at trial Deakin said that the decision to copy the document had been his, as he needed it for the purposes of the documentary. Aitken took the original and four of the copies away with him, and Deakin retained two. That evening Aitken went to the Old Rectory at Brandsby to return the original to Alexander. The general was out, and Aitken left the document with a member of his domestic staff.

While at the offices of Yorkshire Television, Aitken had telephoned Hugh Fraser to tell him about the report. Fraser saw the potential to embarrass the government, and asked Aitken to provide him with two copies. This Aitken did when he went to stay with Fraser, and his wife Lady Antonia Fraser, at their house in Inverness-shire over the New Year. (Here was another parallel with the Compton Mackenzie case. It was in Fraser's house in Scotland, Eilean Aigas, that, forty years before, Mackenzie had written *Greek Memories*.) Aitken and Fraser studied the report at length and discussed how it could best be used. As Aitken recalls, 'Hugh Fraser and I both felt a passionate indignation over this evidence that ministers of the Crown had been making misleading statements about the British Government's Nigeria policy. Over a war in which two million people had died, the apparent ministerial deceit seemed unpardonable.'[7] The plan of action adopted by Aitken and Fraser involved publishing the report in the press, in coordination with a concerted parliamentary campaign.

It was decided to offer the report to the *Sunday Telegraph*. The newspaper had previously adopted a pro-Biafran stance in its editorials and had dispatched Frederick Forsyth to cover the war. Neither Aitken nor Fraser had any contacts on the paper, so they agreed to use a literary agent, Graham Watson of Curtis Brown, as a conduit. Aitken sent the report to Watson following his return to London on 8 January 1970, together with some notes summarizing its contents.[8] Watson forwarded the report to the *Sunday Telegraph*, where the editor, Brian Roberts, asked his assistant editor, Gordon Brook-Shepherd, to check its authenticity. Events then started to move very fast.

Watson had not told the *Sunday Telegraph* how he had obtained the report, but he had referred the newspaper to Aitken and Fraser as experts to whom the paper could turn on matters such as provenance and authenticity. At some point on 9 January, Brook-Shepherd phoned Aitken and Fraser for confirmation of the authenticity of the document, which was given. According to Aitken, he was careful to protect Alexander, and referred to the report as being obtained from a 'military source'. On the same day, Brook-Shepherd had lunch with Johann Welser, who worked in the Information and Research Department of the Foreign Office, and whom he knew socially. They discussed the report, which Brook-Shepherd had brought with him. Welser expressed some doubt about the authenticity of the document, adding that 'if it was genuine, it would be much better if it was not published.' He agreed to make further enquiries at the Foreign Office, which he did that afternoon.

At four o'clock that day, Vice-Admiral Sir Norman Denning, the Secretary of the D-Notice Committee,[9] telephoned Brook-Shepherd, at the latter's instigation, to discuss the report. Brook-Shepherd gave Denning a summary account of the report, and Denning agreed to make enquiries. At 4.30 p.m. Welser telephoned Brook-Shepherd and told him that, further to the enquiries he had made at the Foreign Office, the report was genuine.[10] This satisfied Roberts, and at 5 p.m. the *Sunday Telegraph* agreed to purchase the report for a fee of £500 – which Aitken donated to a charity providing relief to children in Biafra. Although Aitken would later be accused of highly dishonourable conduct, it was never suggested that his behaviour in this episode was motivated by anything other than deeply held conviction.

An hour later, Admiral Denning telephoned Brook-Shepherd and told him it was his view that the report did not involve national security and would not therefore attract a D-Notice. According to Denning's evidence at the trial, he added that if the report was an official confidential document it would nonetheless be subject to the Official Secrets Act.[11] As Brook-Shepherd seemed to be in a quandary as to how to proceed, Denning said that he would mention the matter to Sir Edward Peck, Deputy Secretary at the Foreign and Commonwealth Office, who was the Foreign Office representative on the D-Notice Committee. Sir Edward Peck did not contact Brook-Shepherd directly, but does appear to have spoken to Johann Welser. At about 7 p.m. Welser had another conversation with Brook-Shepherd during which, according to Welser's account, he told Brook-Shepherd that the report was almost certainly a copy of an official document and that it should not be published.

Having considered the information received that day, the editor of the *Sunday Telegraph*, Brian Roberts, decided to run the story of the Scott report. Two days later, on 11 January 1970, a lengthy article setting out its contents appeared under the headline 'Secret Biafra War Plan Revealed'. Subheadings included 'Muddle, Corruption, Waste, by Federals', 'Map of Operations' and 'Order of Battle'. However the scoop was overtaken by news received in London in the late afternoon of the same day that the Biafran line had broken and its army was in flight. In the later editions of the *Sunday Telegraph*, the Scott report headline was juxtaposed against another: 'Biafra About to Collapse'. On 13 January the Biafran Army surrendered; a few days later the Federal forces advanced into the remaining Biafran-held territories with little opposition. Scott, the author of the report, was swiftly expelled from Nigeria by a government seemingly incensed at the revelation of his trenchant views about its military forces, as set out in detail in the *Sunday Telegraph* splash.[12]

It was not only the Nigerian authorities who were agitated. The publication of the Scott report had seriously embarrassed the British government and, so it was feared, might throw a spanner into Anglo-Nigerian relations. In London a full-scale investigation into the circumstances of the leak was immediately ordered by the Foreign Office, under the direction of Detective Chief Superintendent Kenneth Pendered of Special Branch.

In a letter to Aitken on 19 January 1970, General Alexander was already showing signs of panic. He queried who could have leaked the report to the *Sunday Telegraph*, and asked Aitken not to disclose that he had been lent a copy. In reply, Aitken promised a 'grave-like silence'.[13] Alexander's agitation was exacerbated when the police arranged a meeting with him. He now wrote to Aitken stating that he felt obliged to inform them that he had shown a copy of the report to Aitken and demanded Aitken's permission to reveal his identity. Later, on 28 January, Alexander attended Scotland Yard on his own initiative and gave a statement describing the circumstances of his loan of the report to Aitken. Meanwhile, on 27 January, Special Branch officers interviewed Brian Roberts and obtained the copy of the report that had been sold to the *Sunday Telegraph* by Graham Watson. Analysis of that document showed that it was a copy of the version in Alexander's possession.

The channels of communication from Colonel Cairns through to the *Sunday Telegraph* had now been identified. Aitken was interviewed, and, on advice from his lawyers Lord Goodman and Basil Wigoder QC, declined to answer any questions. Goodman proffered the firm view that any prosecution would be a blatant abuse of the law for political purposes; and in any event he was sure that Harold Wilson would not wish to risk, at this late stage of the current Parliament (the election that would be held in June 1970 had already been planned), another Vassall-like rumpus with the press.[14] Comforted by this advice, from a man who knew Wilson better than most, Aitken was sure the brouhaha would blow over and flew off to India and Australia on reporting assignments.

On the face of it, Aitken had good reason to take a sanguine view of the situation. After all, the Scott report involved no issue of national security and related to matters that had been decisively overtaken by the tide of events. At the very moment of publication the information revealed became irrelevant except as a demonstration of ministerial mendacity. But Aitken's confidence proved to be misplaced. He was summoned back to England by an urgent telegram informing him that police officers had arrived in Yorkshire and were conducting extensive enquiries. All the guests at General Alexander's dinner were interviewed and, for no obviously sensible reason, the police showed a particular interest in Aitken's relations with his local Conservative Association (which was now, so Aitken was told, in a state of 'near hysteria'). Events had taken a serious turn. The investigations seemed to the beleaguered Aitken to have taken on the air of a state-sponsored witch-hunt.

On the morning of 11 March 1970 Aitken telephoned Alexander and asked if they could meet. Aitken had heard that Alexander was relating to senior members of the local Conservative Association a version of events concerning the Christmas dinner party that was highly discreditable to Aitken: in short, that he had provided the report to Aitken in the strictest confidence, which confidence Aitken had betrayed. Aitken, fearful of the consequences for his candidacy, was anxious to smooth things over with the general. Alexander invited him over to tea. They met that afternoon in the library at the Old Rectory in Brandsby. Aitken recalls that when he arrived a log fire was blazing, and the accoutrements of fox-hunting, from which activity the general had recently returned, lay about the room. There was, as Aitken concedes, an aspect of farce about the encounter. By this time the men were, in Aitken's words, 'wary antagonists', both equally set on the task of avoiding prosecution. 'To this end,' according to Aitken, 'we had both prepared separate and mutually hostile strategies which we were now putting into effect beneath the veneer of a mutually friendly conversation.'[15] What Aitken did not know was that Alexander was secretly taping their conversation. One particular exchange would later prove especially difficult for Aitken, as it gave a partially false account of his own role in proceedings. Alexander had turned the conversation to how the report had found its way to the *Sunday Telegraph*:

> AITKEN: Well from you to me, from me to Hugh Fraser, Fraser to the *Sunday Telegraph*. As you know, things just spiralled totally out of control.
> ALEXANDER: Who did the copying?
> AITKEN: The copying was done by an innocent third party – at Hugh Fraser's direction.

Aitken later explained in his account of the case that Hugh Fraser had specifically asked him to shift the blame to him (Fraser) so as to try to save himself, given that he was on the brink of commencing his political career.[16]

On 17 March 1970 Cairns, Aitken, Brian Roberts and the *Sunday Telegraph* itself were all charged under section 2 of the Official Secrets Act 1911. The decision had been approved by the Labour Attorney

General, Sir Elwyn Jones, whose consent was required under the Act. It was the first occasion in living memory that journalists had been charged under the Act, and the decision prompted almost unanimous protest from the press. *The Times* thundered that section 2 'is so broad a clause that any newspaper is likely to be in breach of it in the ordinary course of its business perhaps several times a day. We all sometimes have a public duty to act in breach of it. Any official information which is given to a newspaper by any servant of the Crown, high or low, without an authority or a duty to communicate could in theory lead to a prosecution.'[17] Motions were tabled in the House of Commons questioning the decision to prosecute.

The eccentric selection of the defendants who were charged also attracted the opprobrium of the press. It fuelled the suspicions of the many who saw in the prosecution a blatant act of intimidation against journalists who were unsympathetic to the present government (with Cairns unfortunately swept along with them) and seeking to hold the administration to account. If Cairns was deemed worthy of prosecution for having handed a copy of the Scott report to his old and trusted friend General Alexander, why was not Alexander also in the dock? Why was Cairns more culpable than Alexander? And why was Hugh Fraser MP not a defendant, given his intimate involvement in the decision to pass the report to the *Sunday Telegraph*? Or Deakin for copying the report for circulation? Most remarkable of all was the decision to prosecute Brian Roberts. When he learned of the summons against Roberts, Lord Hartwell, the then editor-in-chief and proprietor of the *Sunday Telegraph*, dispatched a letter to the Attorney General assuming full responsibility for the decision to publish the contents of the report and, in effect, demanding to be prosecuted alongside his editor. Hartwell received an inconsequential reply and was not proceeded against. No answers were ever provided to any of these questions.[18]

But precisely what crime was it alleged that the defendants had committed? At the time, section 2 of the Official Secrets Act created two principal – and highly convoluted – offences. The first concerned the communication of information, which had been obtained by a defendant in his capacity as an employee or contractor of the state, or which had been entrusted in confidence to him by such a person, and which he communicated to a third party who was not author-ized to receive it, or to a person to whom it was not in the interests of the state for the defendant to communicate it. This was the 'communication' offence. The second offence involved the receipt of information in circumstances where, at the time the information was received, the defendant knew or had reasonable grounds to believe that it was communicated to him in contravention of the Act. This was the 'receiving' offence. The crucial word 'informa-tion', which was common to both offences, was not defined. On its face, it was not restricted to information that was secret or confi-dential or that could be harmful to national security. As was often said, it could include the menu in a civil service canteen.

Jonathan Aitken, Brian Roberts and the *Sunday Telegraph* were all charged with the 'receiving' offence: Aitken in respect of his receipt of the Scott report from General Alexander, and Roberts and the *Sunday Telegraph* in respect of their indirect receipt of the report from Aitken. Douglas Cairns was charged with a 'commu-nication' offence, for sending the report to Alexander. Aitken, Roberts and the *Sunday Telegraph* were also charged with the 'communication' offence, in each case in respect of their publication of the report.

The committal proceedings were fixed to take place in April before the magistrate and Jeremy was instructed on behalf of Brian Roberts and his newspaper. Now in his mid-fifties, Jeremy was generally recognized as the leading criminal silk at the Bar. But still, given his known leftist leanings, he was an interesting choice of counsel for the *Sunday Telegraph* and its highly conservative editor. (Lord Hartwell would later recall that, as editor, Roberts 'had to be weaned from the idea that as a Tory his business was to attack the Labour govern-ment on every issue'.) Roberts had been appointed editor in 1967 and brought to the task a form of downbeat professionalism. It would be said of him that he inspired respect, if not love, from his staff. Jeremy remembers meeting a small, slight and rather hunched man, utterly unlike the stereotype of the rumbustious Fleet Street editor. 'He was a very retiring, quiet man. It was a shocking event for an editor to be prosecuted at all, let alone in a case which eventually wound up in a four-week trial at Court 1 of the Old Bailey, but he

bore the ordeal with immense calm and a kind of bleak wit.' Roberts
was certain the prosecution was motivated by political revenge. He
would later write that, while the Nigerian government was 'hyster-
ically infuriated' by the publication and no doubt pressed for action,
he suspected that Michael Stewart, the Labour Foreign Secretary, and
the Foreign Office mandarins 'needed no incitement to try to punish
the newspaper and its editor'.[19] In fact subsequently declassified Foreign
Office documents provide no support for the suggestion that it was
the Nigerian government that goaded the British authorities into
action. Roberts's darker suspicions appear to have been justified:
recent research suggests that the prosecution was driven by Wilson
and Stewart. Their motives appear to have been a mix of agitation
at Aitken's and Roberts's conduct in exposing their falsities; the desire
to 'neutralize' a recent prosecution of a Labour MP, Will Owen, who
was accused of spying for the Czechs, by showing that conservatives
were also capable of breaching the Official Secrets Act; and a residual
urge to appease the Nigerians.[20]

As the prosecution case was unveiled before the magistrate, it
became clear that the person most directly in the Crown's sights was
Aitken. He was accused of having 'deliberately dishonoured a promise'
made to General Alexander concerning his use of the report and
having told a 'deliberate and dishonourable lie' in his dealings with
Alexander. Aitken later recorded that he felt 'personally shattered'[21]
by the onslaught against him. Jeremy recalls: 'Jonathan Aitken was
the most vulnerable of the defendants and I think the prosecution
saw that in undermining him, they could somehow catch Cairns
and Roberts in the same net.'

Yet a few days into the proceedings a proposal was made by the
prosecution that sat strangely with the purported gravity of the case.
Having had the full might of the law launched upon them, the
defendants were offered an accommodation whereby, in return for
pleading guilty, the prosecution would not press for the case to be
sent to the Old Bailey. This was significant because, whereas judges
of the Bailey could impose a sentence of up to two years in prison
and an unlimited fine for a conviction under section 2, the magistrates
court could only impose a fine of up to £50 and a three-month
prison sentence. Roberts and the *Sunday Telegraph* were presented

with a dilemma: Roberts was convinced that the decision he had made to publish the contents of the Scott report was the right one. But he faced the prospect of a lengthy trial, with no guarantee of victory. So widely was section 2 cast that it embraced activity that could not be characterized as blameworthy in any sense recognizable by a non-lawyer. And there was a real risk of imprisonment if the verdict was one of guilty. Jeremy remembers the agonized discussions that went on long into the evening. As he notes: 'I always found it very difficult to advise a client who was being offered a plea bargain. Does one buy off the cost and risk of a lengthy trial in return for what will still be a criminal conviction?' Meanwhile, Jonathan Aitken was having similar discussions with Lord Goodman and his counsel. It looked as if the case might fizzle out with the humiliation of guilty pleas, a token fine, and the ineffable annoyance of seeing an over-bearing state apparently vindicated.

What saved Roberts and Aitken from this fate – and from having to make a final decision on the prosecution's offer – was the fortitude of Colonel Cairns. The hoary warrior was damned if he was going to plead guilty on any basis! Besides, as an employee of Barclays Bank, any form of criminal conviction would almost certainly lead to his dismissal. The offer made by the prosecution could be accepted by all the defendants, or none of them. With Cairns holding firm, the deal collapsed and the case was sent for trial at the Old Bailey. The most immediate consequence was that Jonathan Aitken felt obliged to resign his candidacy in the forthcoming general election. He mentally prepared himself for the possibility of conviction and a resulting prison sentence. It would be another four years before he became a Member of Parliament.

This, then, was the convoluted background to the trial that opened at the Old Bailey on 12 January 1971 before the amiable figure of Mr Justice Bernard Caulfield (Jeremy wryly notes that he had got to know Caulfield 'rather well' when they had argued an eight-day appeal in the House of Lords on a buggery case a few years earlier).[22] A journalist sitting in the press gallery noted that Caulfield was a man who moved briskly into his work with a quick glance up to the public gallery 'as if to assess the size of the day's house'. The idea of this trial being a protracted theatrical performance was one that would be picked up again later in proceedings.

By this stage, the general election had brought in a Conservative government, headed by Edward Heath. Jeremy explains: 'I assume that the new administration were hardly enamoured of the prosecution, but what could it do? It could not be seen to be interfering with the due process of law.' But he notes that, whereas usually the Attorney General or Solicitor General prosecute in Official Secrets cases (as he knew only too well, given his experiences of the early 1960s), for the trial sitting in prosecution counsel's bench was John Mathew, senior Treasury counsel. 'I think Peter Rawlinson and Geoffrey Howe [who were then the government's law officers] left it to John Mathew, the fairest and most accomplished prosecuting counsel at the Bar.' Alongside Jeremy in the defence benches were two other legendary defenders, Basil Wigoder QC for Jonathan Aitken and James Comyn QC for Colonel Cairns. Jeremy recalls the delight of appearing with these outstanding advocates. Jeremy and Wigoder had a particularly close association, as they had helped found the Criminal Bar Association in 1969 and were now its chairman and vice-chairman respectively.

Sitting in the vast dock of Court 1, thought Jeremy, were a decidedly odd combination of men.

There was the tall and debonair Aitken, then only in his late twenties; the stooped Roberts, by now in his mid-sixties; and the thickset and bluff Cairns. Apart from a brief meeting between Cairns and Aitken in Nigeria, none of them had known each other before the case was brought and yet they were all part of a chain of events which had led to the publication. I think there was a certain cool camaraderie between them, notwithstanding that their individual positions were very different. They sat on these ghastly little chairs which had been in the dock for as long as I could remember. (I recall Brian Roberts complaining what an indignity it was to be sitting in the same chair that had been occupied a couple of years earlier by one of the Kray twins.) Worse, although they were of course all on bail, the defendants had, each day, to go through the humiliating ritual of being taken down to the cells below just before the court day started, and then being brought back up a hidden staircase that led from the bowels of the Bailey straight into the dock as the warder shouted the words 'Bring up the prisoners.' It was moments like these that strengthened my conviction that the whole concept of the dock, which singled out the defendant from the rest of the court, was completely outmoded and should be abolished.

A journalist who attended the trial noted that it was 'a classless trial in that both accusers and accused are of the same social class. There are nearly as many bowler hats in court as lawyer's wigs, which, with three defence counsel, one prosecuting counsel and an impressive back-up force of junior counsel for each, means a lot of bowler hats.'[23]

In his opening remarks at the earlier committal hearing, John Mathew had claimed that the unauthorized publication of the Scott report had led to serious consequences, including a rift in Britain's diplomatic relations with Nigeria. His opening at the trial was far milder in tone. Rather than referring to any specific repercussions consequent on the exposure of the report, Mathew now couched his case in more general terms. He was particularly concerned to explain why it was important that confidential documents, such as the Scott report, should be protected from unauthorized publication of the kind prohibited by the Act. 'In the submission of the Crown,' Mathew argued, 'it is most important that the preparation of uninhibited reports and assessments by representatives of the British Government in other countries should be one of the functions of diplomacy, and if reports from overseas provided by diplomats were made available for publication, the system of diplomacy . . . would break down. This applies even to facts in a report which had already been matters of general speculation.'

Mathew also set out the prosecution case in respect of what was conceded to be an essential ingredient of each offence, namely a 'guilty mind'. In the case of Cairns, it was argued that he was an employee of the Crown, who had signed the Official Secrets Act and knew its ramifications. By asking Alexander not to tell Scott that he had sent him a copy of the report, had not Cairns demonstrated that he knew that what he was doing was wrong? Outlining the case against Aitken, Mathew argued that the journalist knew as a result of what was said by Alexander at the December dinner party that the report was secret and confidential, which was enough to impute to him a 'guilty mind'. This was shown, Mathew contended, by Aitken's subsequent conduct. He had, for instance, copied the report in what was described as an 'underhand way', and had, by various means, attempted to conceal what he had done. Brian Roberts and the *Sunday Telegraph* likewise had guilty minds, Mathew argued, because they had been warned by Johann Welser and Admiral Denning that publication of the report might represent an infringement of the Act.

Colonel Robert Scott, the author of the report, appeared as the first prosecution witness. At the committal hearing Scott had been cross-examined for two and a half days by Basil Wigoder, Jonathan Aitken's counsel, who had taken him through the report, paragraph by paragraph, in an attempt to prove that the facts it contained were, with very few exceptions, public knowledge prior to publication. This forensic assault had proved very effective, and at trial Scott now conceded that the report's factual contents were widely known. Scott said that he would not have authorized the communication of the report to Alexander, who, he said, was too 'remote from the scene'. However he was later constrained to admit that he himself had sent a copy of the report to an individual who was even more remote from the scene, namely the British Ambassador in Rio de Janeiro and former High Commissioner in Lagos, Sir David Hunt. Defence counsel were at pains to obtain Scott's admission that such confidentiality as the report had once possessed had been blown following his briefing of British and foreign journalists on 6 December 1969. Jeremy then stood up.

> JEREMY: We reach the position, do we not, that as far as the contents of the report are concerned, they cease to be confidential when they are conveyed to the press.
>
> SCOTT: Under their name but not under mine.
>
> JUDGE: The point Mr Hutchinson is making is this: That information once disclosed to the reporter ceases to be confidential and becomes public knowledge.
>
> SCOTT: Certainly.
>
> JEREMY: Thus what was confidential on Monday and subject to the Official Secrets Act becomes public property.
>
> SCOTT: That is so.

JEREMY: As far as the *Sunday Telegraph* was concerned, a number of copies were in circulation to members of the public before it published its story.

SCOTT: Correct.

JEREMY: And if that document was going to be raised in the House of Commons the very next day by a Privy Counsellor [i.e. Hugh Fraser], the whole thing clearly would not be confidential?

SCOTT: I could not agree more.

These concessions were devastating to the prosecution case.

Next into the witness box was Alexander, who cut a somewhat Edwardian figure with his splendid moustache. Here was the linchpin witness for the Crown. His position was exquisitely equivocal. Jeremy remembers the atmosphere in court as febrile as Alexander sought to explain his conduct. On the one hand, he had received the report as a favour from Cairns and, by showing it to Aitken, had placed Cairns in the dock. (Cairns had every reason to feel indignation against Alexander, which was unlikely to have been mellowed by the tone of a letter Alexander had later written to him: 'However bitter you may feel, surely you must remember that I got you into Nigeria in the first place.') And yet, on the other hand, Alexander was seeking to defend his conduct by now maintaining that he had given Aitken the report at the December dinner on three specific conditions: that the report was secret and confidential; that Aitken could read it as background material, and in strict confidence; and finally, that he, Alexander, did not think he himself should be in possession of it anyway. He added: 'I had a special relationship with Aitken. I was not dealing with him as a second-class journalist, but as a prospective Conservative candidate and a friend . . . I considered Aitken to be a trusted friend. I had helped smooth his path when there were difficulties about his nomination as the Conservative candidate for my constituency. He had accompanied my daughter to a dance.'

By the time that Comyn, Wigoder and Jeremy had finished their cross-examinations of the general, this evidence had been very seriously undermined.

The evidence of Alexander's son, David, another guest at the dinner, was considerably less dogmatic. His recollection in relation to the crucial exchange was that his father had told Aitken that he 'could have the document for his own information as someone interested in the Nigerian situation'. Mrs Cliff, who had been sitting on the sofa with Aitken when Alexander handed him the report, would later give evidence that, as far as she could recall, the general had said, 'This is the paper I thought you would be interested to see, you see it is marked confidential, and I'll be pleased to have it back as soon as possible.' Tony Cliff remembered that the general had handed the report to Aitken 'quite openly'; in fact he had flourished it 'like one might wave a race card'.

The next witness, Graham Watson, gave evidence that prior to offering the report to the *Sunday Telegraph* he had consulted Hugh Fraser MP, and having learned that the report was going to be raised by him in Parliament, had concluded that everything was above board. Jeremy recalls that Watson was one of the most pre-eminent agents of the period and establishing his rectitude was crucial.

> JEREMY: Was anything said by Mr Fraser which caused you to think that you might be committing an offence against the Official Secrets Act if you offered the report to the *Sunday Telegraph*?
> WATSON: No, rather the contrary.
> JUDGE: When you offered the report to the *Sunday Telegraph* you felt you were doing nothing wrong.
> WATSON: That is so.

These answers went a long way to spelling the end of the 'receiving' charge against Roberts and his newspaper. On that basis, how could they have received the document 'knowing or having reasonable grounds for believing that it had been communicated in contravention' of the Act?

Johann Welser of the Foreign Office gave evidence as to the communications between him and Gordon Brook-Shepherd, the assistant editor of the *Sunday Telegraph*, on 9 January 1970, when the decision to publish was made. Despite the best efforts of Mr Mathew, Welser did not repeat his earlier claim to the effect that he had warned Brook-Shepherd that the report might be subject to the Official Secrets Act.

Vice-Admiral Sir Norman Denning from the D-Notice Committee, in giving his evidence as to what had transpired on 9 January, averred that, although there was no issue of national security at stake, he had warned Brook-Shepherd that if the report was a genuine official document it would be covered by the Act. This was evidence heavily relied upon by the prosecution because it suggested that the *Sunday Telegraph* published with knowledge that it was infringing the Official Secrets Act. But, cross-examined by Jeremy, Admiral Denning conceded that he could not speak for the government on the question of whether the report fell within the ambit of the Act. He also accepted that he told Brook-Shepherd that he would inform Sir Edward Peck, the Deputy Secretary of the Foreign Office and its representative on the D-Notice Committee, of the situation, so that the Foreign Office could notify the paper of any concerns they might have over the proposed publication of the report. Yet neither Peck nor any other representatives of the Foreign Office had communicated with anyone at the *Sunday Telegraph*.[24]

> JEREMY: If Sir Edward Peck of the Foreign Office took the view that publication might involve a breach of the Act, he could be expected to get in touch with the editor and tell him so?
>
> DENNING: Yes indeed. I could only inform him and leave him to take such action as would be necessary, but I had expected him to get in touch with the editor.
>
> JEREMY: Because for the editor to make that difficult decision it is vital that he should be given, as fully as possible, the official reasons for requiring suppression.
>
> DENNING: Most certainly. Within my own sphere, I have never asked for anything to be suppressed. I have been able to adjust the article so that the sensitive part is omitted or otherwise so that no damage is done.

With that, Jeremy sat down. He recalls that, given the evidence of Watson, Welser and Admiral Denning, it was difficult to see how his clients could be convicted. Accordingly, in conjunction with the other defendants, he now launched into a 'submission of no case to answer' – that is, he invited the judge to dismiss the prosecution as wholly ill-founded without the requirement of the defendants calling their evidence. There then followed what Jonathan Aitken would later describe as a 'titanic legal battle between prosecution and defence counsel'. Two and half days of legal submissions followed, concerning the interpretation of section 2 of the Act, and the evidence given for the prosecution. Aitken listened, fascinated, throughout. Writing immediately after the trial he noted: 'These submissions, in the view of some observers, were directly responsible for the part of the judge's final summing up in which he urged that Section 2 of the 1911 Act should be "pensioned off". Indeed it is not too far-fetched to say that the impetus for the present [Conservative] government's desire to change the law springs more from those two and a half days of esoteric intellectual argument than from half a century of popular agitation by aggrieved Official Secrets Act victims.'[25]

Speaking recently, Aitken recalled a donnish atmosphere, in which Jeremy dominated the debate. 'The judge seemed to treat Jeremy's submissions with an almost deferential air.' It came as a surprise and disappointment to the defence when, having listened patiently for so long, the judge confined himself merely to stating that there was a proper case to go to the jury. Jeremy thinks that the judge felt that a case of this importance was 'better decided by the jury rather than by an intervention from on high'. The defence's attempt to have the case dismissed had failed. But the intense dissection of the Official Secrets Act, its scope and true interpretation, was the foundation on which the judge would later make his strongly expressed criticism when he came to sum up.

Opening the evidence for the defence, Colonel Douglas Cairns stood stolidly in the witness box. It must have been extraordinary for this exemplary officer to find himself having to give evidence in his own defence, in the foremost criminal court in England. And yet Jeremy remembers a man who showed not one iota of nerves or prevarication. Cairns explained that he had considered Alexander's loyalty as absolutely unquestioned, and that it had never crossed his mind that he might be breaking the Official Secrets Act when he sent the general – his former senior officer – a copy of the report. In fact, he had considered it his positive duty to do so: 'I thought he was an unofficial envoy of the Foreign Office and of the government.' Cairns explained that he had not contemplated that Alexander would pass on the report to anyone else. Cross-examining a man of such obvious integrity was a very difficult job for John Mathew, not helped by the sympathies of the judge, which he did nothing to hide:

MATHEW: Who were you to decide that you could send this report
   to General Alexander?

JUDGE: Throw your shoulders back, Colonel, and tell the jury who
   you were.

CAIRNS: I was the senior British member of the international observer
   team.

JUDGE: And you thought you were doing your duty in sending the
   report?

CAIRNS: Yes, My Lord.

Brian Roberts was listening to all this very carefully. He later observed
that, while John Mathew had conducted the prosecution with 'scru-
pulous fairness', the prosecutor 'appeared to become more and more
depressed' as the proceedings went on: 'He had been given a wretched
brief and I think he knew it.'[26]

Nonetheless, Jonathan Aitken was in the witness box for six long
hours of gruelling cross-examination at his hands. For Jeremy, Aitken
was always going to be the wild card witness. 'I was concerned
because his position was the most equivocal of the defendants. There
was this fundamental dispute between him and General Alexander
as to the terms on which the report had been handed over. And
there was this very difficult tape recording in which Aitken had not
been wholly truthful with the general. Yet in the event he gave his
evidence with absolute conviction and sangfroid. I was very relieved.'
Under sustained questioning by John Mathew, Aitken categorically
denied that he had been given the report subject to the three conditions specified by Alexander in his evidence. His version of events
– which was supported by the other guests – was that there had
been a brief exchange chiefly relating to when Aitken was to return
the document. The general had drawn his attention to the fact that
the report was confidential, but had not laid down any conditions.
Aitken denied that he knew, or had any reason to believe, that the
report was being given to him in contravention of the Act. 'If I had
thought I had been given the document in confidence, I would not
have passed it on or copied it.'

The tensest moment in Aitken's evidence came when the court
was provided with a transcript of the taped conversation between
him and Alexander at Brandsby on 11 March 1970. This threatened

Jeremy becomes a QC, 1961. Two years later he was profiled in the *Daily Express*: 'The jury sees a handsome man of forty-eight, his powerful features beneath the high-domed forehead set in forbidding lines: a face to fit a judge. Now and again the tension he has built up is relieved by a sudden smile. But all the time he is building the wall of doubt to clear the man in the dock.'

Sportitude in the flesh. Kempton Bunton, 'a dreamer in a crumpled suit', confesses to removing – but not stealing – *The Duke of Wellington*, August 1965.

Goya's *Portrait of Field Marshal Arthur Wellesley, 1st Duke of Wellington*, 1812–14. It disappeared nineteen days after it had gone on show at the National Gallery in 1961.

Tom Keating greets the world's press, standing before his pastiche of Constable's *The Hay Wain*, August 1976.

Two Ladies of the Town, by Constantin Guys. It hung behind Jeremy's desk in chambers for thirty years.

Tom Keating's pastiche of Guys, which he gave to Jeremy on the first day of his trial.

Tom Keating imitates Samuel Palmer. *Sepham Barn* was sold for £15,000 in 1971, a record for Palmer. At the trial Jeremy described the hovering bat at the top of the picture as 'looking more like a Boeing 707'.

Bertrand Russell stages a sit-down in Whitehall, February 1961. The following February, at the trial of the Committee of 100, he insisted on standing.

Committee of 100
13 GOODWIN STREET, N.4   ARC 1239

OLD BAILEY

FEBRUARY 12, 1962

REGINA

V

The Committee of
100

UNDER THE OFFICIAL SECRETS ACT

We are all on trial

The leaflet distributed outside Court 1 of the Old Bailey. The judge seemed to think that Jeremy was somehow involved in its production.

The Wethersfield Six (together with Anne Randle) in defiant mode outside the Old Bailey, February 1962.

Colonel Douglas Cairns, Brian Roberts and Jonathan Aitken savouring their acquittal on Official Secrets Act charges, February 1971. Jeremy noted 'a certain cool camaraderie between them'.

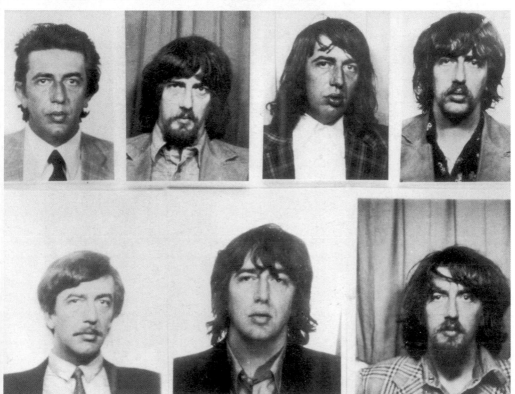

The many faces of Howard Marks. The prosecutor advised the jury: 'Mr Marks had so many identities one wonders how on earth he remembered who he was at any given point of time.'

The ABC defendants, Duncan Campbell, Crispin Aubrey and John Berry arrive at Court accompanied by their supporters, September 1978. The prosecutor described Campbell as 'a thoroughly subversive man'.

Jeremy's attack on jury-vetting attracts the attention of JAK in the *Evening Standard*.

"M'lud, I have reason to believe the SAS have sneaked another juror in!"

The Festival of Light in Trafalgar Square, September 1971. Mary Whitehouse sings a duet with Judy Mackenzie in protest against moral pollution.

Romans v Celts, centre stage at the National Theatre. *The Romans in Britain* was described as 'Not Suitable for Children'. Mary Whitehouse believed that it was not suitable for anyone.

The original poster for *Last Tango in Paris*. When the British Board of Film Censors granted it an X certificate, Mary Whitehouse called for the resignation of every member of the board on the grounds that their decision was evidence of a 'collective madness'.

Jeremy in 2013, aged ninety-eight.

to undermine Aitken's credibility, as it exposed him telling a number of untruths in what appeared to be an attempt to save his position as the local Conservative candidate. Fortunately, when Hugh Fraser MP stepped into the witness box, still fresh notwithstanding having come straight from an all-night debate at the House of Commons, he agreed that he had told Aitken that 'he could put the blame on me'.

Now came the most turbulent episode in the trial. Under fierce attack by John Mathew, Fraser asserted that the Labour government had brought the prosecution for political purposes, and had abused its powers under the Official Secrets Act. He told how he and Aitken had worked in tandem to publicize the report. Fraser explained why he had done so: 'I wanted a change in government policy. I believed it was in the interests of Parliament that they should know the truth.' Finally, Aitken was fortunate in being able to call, as a character witness, the Speaker of the House of Commons and former Chancellor of the Exchequer, Selwyn Lloyd, whose private secretary he had been between 1965 and 1966. The Speaker described Aitken as a man of 'the highest integrity'.

It was now Jeremy's turn to get up and make his opening speech for Roberts and the *Sunday Telegraph*. He explains: 'I was quite determined to ensure that my clients were not somehow caught up in the wider imbroglio of the relationships between Cairns, Alexander, Aitken and Fraser and the broader politics of the Biafran situation. Brian Roberts knew nothing of any of this complex backstory. He was presented with a report by Graham Watson, knowing nothing of its source, and he decided to publish it.' So Jeremy told the jury:

> You have been taken through the realms of politics, dinner parties, port, Federal and Biafra lobbies, Yorkshire Television, Hansard and the House of Commons. Now I ask you to come back to the realities of the workings of an efficient and successful Sunday newspaper and to consider the basic allegation – namely that Mr Roberts and the *Sunday Telegraph* acted in a criminal manner during January 1970 . . .
>
> The *Sunday Telegraph* is not the political poodle of either Mr Aitken or Mr Fraser. It is now clear that the newspaper was quite innocently caught up in the tangled political web which these gentlemen had woven in Yorkshire, Scotland and London.

And what of Roberts's state of knowledge at the time?

> The paper knew nothing of course of these goings-on. The docu-
> ment had already gone to many other people before it was published,
> and this coloured everything in the mind of the editor . . . If the
> Foreign and Commonwealth Office thought publication would
> embarrass this country's relations with Nigeria and would therefore
> be against the interests of the state why did it not say so at the time?
> Why did not one of its senior officials pick up a telephone and say
> to the editor: 'Please do not publish because it is not in the interests
> of the state that you should.'

He then addressed the potentially compromising fact that the newspaper had, in its presentation of the Scott report, made much of its
supposed 'secrecy'. This could be said to constitute a recognition of
the illicit receipt of the report: 'The report was of course dressed
up for the paper's readers. Maybe it was overdressed, but the document was full of great stodgy passages and you may feel a suet
pudding is very much improved by a dash of golden syrup, but not
in this case with Aitken and Fraser as the manufacturers.'

In his evidence for the defence, Gordon Brook-Shepherd, assistant
editor at the *Sunday Telegraph*, asserted that 'Had even an under-
secretary telephoned and spoken on behalf of the Foreign Office it
would have put a totally different complexion on the matter.' Brook-
Shepherd denied that he had received any official warning as to a
possible infringement of the Act. Admiral Denning 'did not mention
the Official Secrets Act' but had merely said that it was an official
document and suggested that we should get permission to publish
it. 'We never received any official warning.' It remained one of the
difficulties of the prosecution case that it was unable to offer any
explanation as to why nobody from the Foreign Office had contacted
the newspaper to warn it off publishing the report.

The final witness was Brian Roberts. The sixty-four-year-old
veteran of Fleet Street gave his evidence with quiet dignity. He
affirmed that if the Foreign Office had considered publication of
the report to be detrimental to the national interest, he would have
expected communication from them at the very highest level. 'I
thought that possibly the Permanent Secretary, Sir Denis Greenhill,

or the Foreign Secretary, Mr Michael Stewart, would telephone Lord Hartwell or myself and say, "Look, publication of this report will damage national interests. We will tell you off the record why." When Jeremy asked him about his reasons for publishing the document Roberts stated: 'The task of the press is the disclosure within the law of matters of public interest. This report, when I read it, dealt with matters which at the time were of intense public interest, and this document having been cleared on the grounds of public security, I thought that publication was within the law. At no time did it occur to me that publication of the document would be an infringement of the law.' Roberts continued: 'Whatever confidentiality might have originally existed in this report, it was entirely negatived by the knowledge that it was in the hands of MPs and others and that questions were going to be tabled in the House of Commons.'

Now came the turn of the defendants' counsel to make their closing submissions. After many days of evidence, which had seen the prosecution case irreparably wounded, here was an opportunity for some high-flown oratory from the three silks. It was not an opportunity that any of them wasted, as they lambasted the decision to prosecute and slighted the might of the state. Even now, reading the words on the page raises the hairs on the back of the neck. James Comyn QC, representing Douglas Cairns, told the jury that they should not be tempted into convicting the colonel for what had been portrayed by the prosecution as a 'tiny technical offence'. Conviction of a 'teeny-weeny little offence' such as that argued for by the prosecution was still a conviction.

> Members of the jury, you have listened for nearly three weeks to a multitude of words and you may think that this misconceived prosecution has crumbled and disintegrated against all four defendants. You may think that this whole case is much ado about nothing, but that is not how the accused look at it. Consider what the stain of a conviction would mean to Colonel Cairns. First there is his honour, which stands so high . . . This case is a farce and has had nearly a three-week run. It is high time the run finished, and let us hope it is not revived. On grounds of common sense, in law, and on any honourable approach I ask the members of the jury to find Colonel Cairns not guilty.

Basil Wigoder QC, closing for Jonathan Aitken, told the jury that if they accepted Aitken's contention that he passed the Scott report to the *Sunday Telegraph* because he considered it his duty to do so in the interests of the state, so that its contents could be placed before the British people, then they must acquit him. In a five-hour display of high-octane rhetoric, Wigoder argued that the prosecution was politically inspired. It had, he said, been instigated for the purpose of offering up 'sacrificial lambs' to appease the 'momentary indignation of some Nigerian officials'.

> This case has been called the Queen against Aitken. I am tempted to call it the Queen of Hearts against Aitken, for if ever there was an Alice in Wonderland trial then this is it. The prosecution's arguments have become, as Alice said, 'curiouser and curiouser' and now Mr Mathew has taken over the role of the Queen of Hearts, shouting 'Off with his head, Off with his head!', presumably in the hope that if this was said often enough then you, members of the jury, will come to believe that Mr Aitken has done something criminal.

As the courtroom echoed to Wigoder's fiery words, Jeremy finally got up to round off the defendants' closing speeches. He recalls: 'I wanted to be much shorter than Basil Wigoder and Jimmy Comyn – I did not want the jury to think that there was any difficulty at all in arriving at a not guilty verdict in respect of Brian Roberts and, again, I wanted to keep as much distance as possible from all the shenanigans between the central players. The central point I drove home was the total absence of any warning given by the Foreign Office to the *Telegraph* – a point never explained by the prosecution.' In these circumstances, he argued, the editor: 'exercising his responsibility and his honest appreciation of all the circumstances, decided to publish the report . . . What on earth more can a responsible newspaper do? One of the most astonishing facts of this case is that all the way through we have never heard a word from the Crown as to why no official word was passed to the newspaper and its distinguished editor. It has never been explained why it was wholly blanketed in official fog.'

With reference to a remark made earlier in the hearing to the effect of the Official Secrets Act circling like a vulture over Fleet Street, Jeremy concluded with his own vivid metaphor: 'You have heard of vultures in this case, but you may think that these gentlemen of the Foreign and Commonwealth Office acted like a lot of old hens, fluttering their feathers in their Whitehall coops, pecking away at their classifications, and that when the truth began to leak upon them, they ran to their traditional range, the deep litter house – the Official Secrets Act. And for all we know they are still there.'

Yet the most remarkable part of this remarkable trial was yet to come. Throughout the trial Mr Justice Caulfield had shown an increasingly overt sympathy for the defendants (Caulfield was clearly a man whose sympathies, when aroused, were firmly held ones. When, fifteen years later, he was the judge in the Jeffrey Archer libel trial, he would famously say of Mary Archer: 'Has she elegance? Has she fragrance? Would she have, without the strain of this trial, radiance?'). Now, in his summing-up to the jury, there came a prolonged savaging of the prosecution case. Jeremy explains: 'Usually a judge's summing-up attempts to be neutral in its marshalling of the evidence for the jury. Sometimes it leans in favour of the prosecution case and subtly invites the jury to convict. But I have never heard a summing-up more excoriating of a prosecution. It virtually required the jury to acquit.'

The judge began with a thinly veiled attack on what he appeared to have considered the real motive behind the prosecution: 'It may well be that prosecutions under this Act can serve as a convenient and reasonable substitute for a political trial, with the added advantage of achieving the same end without incurring the implied odium.' The judge did not hide his disquiet about the provisions of section 2 of the Official Secrets Act, which, in his view, affected 'the liberty of speech and communication of Her Majesty's subjects – a freedom all of us recognize as a basic freedom . . . If the press is the watchdog of freedom the fangs of a watchdog can be drawn and all that will ensue is a whimper, possibly a whine, but no bite . . . This case if it does nothing more may well alert those who govern us at least to consider whether or not section 2 of this Act has reached retirement age and should be pensioned off.' As regards Jonathan Aitken's prevarications in the taped conversation at the Old Rectory, Brandsby, the judge was dismissive of their significance. 'This case is not concerned whether the Crown have proved that Aitken did the dirty on General Alexander. He may well have done. The prosecution have to prove a crime, not merely a dirty act using ordinary language.'

The judge went on to direct an acquittal of Roberts and the *Sunday Telegraph* in relation to their 'receiving' charge, on the grounds that, as a matter of law, there was no evidence available on which to convict them. In relation to the second charge against Roberts and the *Sunday Telegraph*, the judge made it clear that in his view the editor and his associates had done everything they could to vet the report prior to its publication, and also that they had not, in publishing it, considered that they were doing anything unlawful.

While the judge was engaging in this fulsome exoneration of Brian Roberts, Lord Goodman, Jonathan Aitken's solicitor, sent a note over to Lord Hartwell, who was sitting in court, on which he had written the following words: 'I think your man is going to be given a medal. A.G.' Hartwell had the note framed for his editor, and it remained on his desk to the day of his death. By contrast, the prosecutor John Mathew sat 'slumped in his seat looking like a thundercloud' as he listened to the summing-up, Roberts recalled. (Mathew explains that he realized that the judge had taken against the prosecution case within minutes of the trial starting.)

The judge concluded: 'It may well be during the course of the case you have said to yourselves, "Well, really, we can't see the wood for the trees." Members of the jury, you might pause and ask yourselves whether there are any trees at all, and what you might have seen, when you look at the whole of the evidence and what you have been told in this case, is that really there is only a desert, a barren waste; and that this prosecution perhaps has been put before you in this way: that once a document emanating from an official source is stamped "confidential" that therefore anybody who handles the document is breaking the law. I hope I have explained to you in my directions in law that that is not the law.' Jeremy recalls: 'It was incredible to hear a judge speaking so plainly.'

The jury retired to consider their verdict on 3 February 1971. After the most perfunctory absence – a mere two hours and eleven minutes, after a trial lasting seventeen days – they returned and unanimously acquitted the defendants on all charges. In an unusual move, which no doubt reflected his distaste for the proceedings, the judge awarded the defendants their costs. It was said to be one of the most expensive criminal trials ever.

The trial and its verdict unleashed a frenzy of public debate. What had been the reason for the prosecution? What was the future of the Official Secrets Act? How could the government law officers have properly permitted a prosecution against a respected newspaper and its editor? These questions were raked over at length in the press. There was much criticism of the choice of the defendants, it being widely thought that the prosecutors had chosen the junior, and more vulnerable, recipients of the report: Cairns, Aitken and Brian Roberts, rather than their more powerful counterparts: Alexander, Hugh Fraser and Lord Hartwell. The *Evening Standard*'s leading article of 13 April 1971 is typical: 'The Government has chosen to prosecute under an antiquated section of an unsatisfactory Act, an editor rather than his editor-in-chief, a military adviser (a colonel) rather than a major-general and a junior Conservative candidate rather than a senior Conservative MP. When this case is settled, Parliament and the public will be entitled to the fullest explanation of why this revelation in particular was considered worthy of prosecution – and why these people were selected for summons.'

There were few who disagreed with the *Evening Standard*'s assessment of section 2 of the Act. The section was criticized in particular for the ambiguity of its drafting. According to the *New Law Journal*,[27] 'it is couched in such general terms that it is impossible to give the offence which it purports to create that strictness of definition that is essential to any acceptable criminal law.' The perniciousness of the clause had, prior to the present proceedings, been kept in check, argued the *Daily Telegraph* in a leader on 4 February 1971, by 'the good sense of the Law Officers of the Crown' who had known to prosecute only when 'information dangerous to national security' was involved. Given that it had never been suggested by the Crown that the Scott report proceedings involved matters of national security, the press would now have to look again at the risk posed to them by the Official Secrets Act. In the light of the recent prosecutions, this appeared to represent both an infringement of press freedom, and a shackle on the press's right to publish stories on matters of public interest.

The agitation against the prosecution and the all-embracing nature of section 2 led the government to institute an enquiry under Lord Franks, which reported in 1972, castigating section 2 as a 'mess' and unacceptably wide. Yet it was not until 1989, after a number of further high-profile prosecutions, that section 2 was repealed.

Jeremy looks back on the case as a classic illustration of the dangers of legislation designed to protect the interests and safety of the state being used for the political purpose of protecting the policies of government. He notes that 'it was also an outstanding example of the true independence of the judiciary (I contrast Caulfield with Lord Parker's conduct in the Profumo affair[28]), of the role of a courageous and principled newspaper editor, and the importance not only for the defendants but also for the judge to have the very best advocacy. It was a great example of how a judge can be assisted by the quality of the advocate. The higher the quality of the advocacy the higher the quality of the justice.'

As for the principal participants, Colonel Scott's career was blighted. An expected posting to Tokyo was cancelled. General Alexander's hoped-for recall to assist the Nigerian Army was not forthcoming. He remained in retirement in Yorkshire until his early death some years later. Colonel Cairns left court with his honour intact and his job at Barclays Bank secure. He was later awarded an OBE for his services in Nigeria. Thwarted in his attempt to be the member for Malton and Thirsk, Jonathan Aitken had to wait until February 1974 to enter Parliament, as the member for Thanet East. His book on the case, *Officially Secret*, written in the immediate aftermath of the trial, was widely noted and would inform debate on the subject for years to come. Aitken would eventually become Chief Secretary to the Treasury in 1994 before a second, less successful, encounter with the criminal law. Brian Roberts was awarded the gold medal by the Institute of Journalists for his defence of press freedom. He remained editor of the *Sunday Telegraph* until he retired in 1976, an unlikely icon of the cause of free speech.

12

'This raddled and discredited prima donna'

R v Aubrey, Berry and Campbell (1978)

B EING AN INVESTIGATIVE journalist under a Labour government
in the 1970s was not a safe occupation. At the time (and before),
there was a tendency among Labour ministers to try to forestall
suggestions that they were not as robust as their Tory counterparts
by over-compensating in their resort to the Official Secrets Act.
Denis McShane, then the president of the National Union of
Journalists (and later a Labour minister in the 2000s), could say, in
1978, that 'Anybody concerned about civil liberties will find it
difficult to campaign for a Labour Party that has one of the worst
records this century in defending journalistic freedom.'[1]

But, irrespective of the political complexion of the government,
there was an underlying culture of secrecy that permeated the state
apparatus in the 1970s, founded upon the twin assumptions that the
vast behemoth of government was there to benefit the people, and
that it was not for the people so benefited to question its mysterious
workings. It was certainly not for journalists to challenge those assumptions or to pry into those workings. Like a great octopus, the Official
Secrets Act 1911 smothered the state from the world at large, suppressing
public knowledge of its internal activities and warning off enquiry.

As we have seen,[2] Jeremy had, in 1971, successfully defended the
Sunday Telegraph and its editor, Brian Roberts, against charges instituted by the Labour Attorney General Sir Elwyn Jones in the dying
months of the Wilson government. Jonathan Aitken, a co-defendant
in the dock alongside Roberts, had ended his book on the trial,
Officially Secret, on a hopeful note that reform of the Official Secrets
Act was surely imminent: 'if the results of this one battle cause an
eventual victory in the war for freedom of speech against the dark
forces of bureaucratic over-secrecy then the ordeal will seem very

299

much worthwhile. For if meaningful law reforms of the Official Secrets Act are passed, no journalist or private citizen will ever again in Britain face criminal charges for publishing official information which is merely embarrassing or inconvenient to the government of the day.'[3]

This optimism was not to be borne out by events. The Franks Committee, which was established in the immediate wake of the *Sunday Telegraph* case, and tasked to conduct a review of section 2 of the Act, published its findings in 1972. Its report was greeted with platitudinous bromides from all parties about the 'need for reform', but duly gathered dust on Whitehall shelves. After the Labour victories in the February and October 1974 elections, the incoming administration, notwithstanding manifesto commitments, showed no inclination to enact its recommendations. Instead, in 1978, the then Attorney General Sam Silkin gave his fiat (a necessary precondition to any prosecution under the Act) to the institution of a prosecution that became one of the most notorious, and, as it proved for the government and security services, catastrophic proceedings ever instigated under the Act. It says something about the diverse targets of the secret state in this period that, whereas Jeremy appeared for a high Tory newspaper and its editor in 1971, on this occasion he was to defend a radical young investigative journalist in a case later described by Geoffrey Robertson as 'the trial which in the seventies had the most impact on law and on politics'.[4]

The targets of the secret state were not just impertinent journalists, agitators or those in the pay of foreign powers. In 1975 Silkin had brought a civil claim against the estate of his former colleague, the late Dick Crossman, for daring to seek to publish Crossman's diaries of his time in government in the early 1960s. The submission Silkin is recorded as having made to the court betrays the prevailing mentality: 'An important aspect of the present case is the intolerable effect of revealing the confidences of Cabinet discussion which was contrary to public interest. Confidentiality is an inherent and essential part of the administrative machinery of government. The principle of confidentiality is fortified by the provisions of the Official Secrets Act 1911 and the Privy Councillor's oath.'[5] (The judge dismissed the claim on the grounds that it was absurd to imagine that what had been discussed in Cabinet ten years earlier could conceivably be damaging to the state.)

The prevailing paranoia of the times extended wider still. In 1963 Jeremy had successfully conducted the defence of an Italian nuclear physicist, Giuseppe Martelli, accused of breaches of section 1 of the Act by attempting to supply information to the Soviet Union. Then, in early 1965 Jeremy had acted in the so-called Kodak secrets case, in which two Kodak employees had allegedly been engaging in industrial espionage on behalf of East Germany. Again, the result was an acquittal. Both cases proved to be serious embarrassments to MI5. Jeremy's involvement, as well as his earlier connection with Blake and Vassall and his perceived leftist credentials, led to him being the subject of an enquiry by the 'D' branch of MI5, perhaps the only occasion when an English silk has been investigated by an intelligence agency as a potential security risk. At the time, in the mid-1960s, all that alerted Jeremy to this possibility was the telltale click on the telephone line that suggested his calls had started being monitored. There was also the oddity that when Roy Jenkins, then Home Secretary, wished to appoint Jeremy as one of his legal advisers, the suggestion was mysteriously kyboshed by nameless civil servants.[6]

But some years later Nigel West confirmed the fact of the investigation to Jeremy. In his subsequent history of MI5, West explained that the enquiry yielded 'only three items of interest: that he [Jeremy] was acknowledged to be a brilliant barrister; that he was married to the actress Dame Peggy Ashcroft who was a well-known political left-winger; and that he had been a member of the Haldane Society',[7] an organization for socialist lawyers. These facts were presumably not considered sufficiently incriminating to warrant any further action.

The *ABC* case (so called after the first letter of each of the defendants' names) had its genesis in an article published in *Time Out* in May 1976. At that point *Time Out* was not only a London listings magazine, as it is today, but also a radical paper with a reputation for controversial journalism. Headed 'The Eavesdroppers', the article in question considered the subject of electronic surveillance. Signals Intelligence, or SIGINT, was a method of surveillance involving the interception and decoding of radio signals and other communications. Government Communications Headquarters – better known as GCHQ – in Cheltenham was, and remains, the headquarters of

UK electronic surveillance. In the 1970s thousands of state employees received, analysed and decoded electronic communications intercepted by UK surveillance stations across the globe. Intercept stations, coordinated by GCHQ, and manned by members of the armed forces and the civilian Composite Signals Organization, were located in countries in the Far and Middle East, Africa, Australia and Europe. UK SIGINT operations were carried out in close cooperation with, and as a junior partner of, its US counterpart, the National Security Agency (NSA). At the time the very existence of GCHQ and its SIGINT network was a closely guarded secret. 'The Eavesdroppers' disclosed their activities for the first time.

The article was co-written by Duncan Campbell and an American, Mark Hosenball, though it was acknowledged by both journalists that it was largely Campbell's work. Duncan Campbell was a young Scottish physicist with a flair for investigative journalism; since leaving Oxford, where he had taken a First, he had concentrated his considerable mental faculties on an investigation into the intricacies of national and international defence communications.

Despite its controversial subject matter, the official response to their article was, at least overtly, muted. In fact Campbell later learned that the reaction within Whitehall to the article was one of incandescent rage, which was only fanned by the legal advice later received that Campbell could not be prosecuted because the article had been composed using public sources and information provided by American ex-employees of the NSA, who were not bound by the British Official Secrets Act.

Six months later, on 16 November 1976, the Home Secretary Merlyn Rees announced that Mark Hosenball and his compatriot Philip Agee were to be deported. No reasons for the deportations were given other than that it was considered to be 'in the interests of national security'. Agee was an ex-CIA officer who, following his resignation from the service, had exposed many of its secrets and failings in his book *Inside the Company: A CIA Diary*. Published in 1975 the book became a bestseller and had created consternation among the intelligence communities on both sides of the Atlantic. There was no obvious link between Agee and Hosenball,[8] other than that they had both incurred the wrath of the CIA. In Hosenball's case this was because he had helped name

CIA officers employed, under cover, at the American Embassy in London, in another *Time Out* article in July 1975. Given that Agee's exposures had not involved the British security services, it is likely that the deportations were ordered, at least in part, as a consequence of US, and specifically CIA, pressure. In Hosenball's case, his joint authorship of 'The Eavesdroppers' is likely to have been a significant contributing factor. It would later be explained that Hosenball's deportation was in part justified by the preparation of material for publication that was 'harmful to the security of the United Kingdom'.

The proposed deportations provoked public protest among libertarians and the left, which coalesced in the formation of an 'Agee-Hosenball Defence Committee'. One man in particular was moved by the protests. This was John Berry, a social worker from north London and an ex-corporal of the 9th Signals Regiment stationed in Cyprus, whose work had included intercepting radio communications. Berry's military career had come to an end seven years previously as a result of a drunken prank. Since then he had travelled a long road of disillusionment with his former career. In February 1977 Berry wrote to the Agee-Hosenball Defence Committee expressing his concern over the operation of Britain's covert security organizations, of which he had once been part, and seeking guidance as to the existence of any 'medium' that might be interested in publishing his views. A few days later, Berry attended the defence committee's headquarters at the offices of the National Council for Civil Liberties in King's Cross, and, at the invitation of the committee, typed out a 300-word statement. He wrote: 'It appears to me that secrecy is one of the most important keys to power and the existence of an organization capable of spending vast sums of money in the total absence of public control should do much to dispel any illusion about the democratic nature of our government.'[9]

Berry's statement was forwarded to *Time Out*, the only publication that might be prepared to defy the D-Notice covering GCHQ, where it was picked up by a reporter called Crispin Aubrey. According to Aubrey, it was Berry's attitude to his former job, and his belief that 'the secrecy was merely a sham to conceal an illegal organization' that immediately attracted his attention. 'It was simply the beginning of a good story,' he recalled, and 'most importantly, it was directly linked to the deportations of Philip Agee and Mark Hosenball. This was what had motivated Berry to break his silence, this was the story which I, like many reporters, wanted to get to the bottom of.'[10] Aubrey had worked with Hosenball on the news desk at *Time Out* and was subsequently a committed member of the Agee-Hosenball Defence Committee, so his interest was also personal.

Berry agreed to be interviewed for *Time Out*. Aubrey's grasp of electronic communications was limited, so he asked Duncan Campbell (as we have seen, a SIGINT specialist and principal author of 'The Eavesdroppers') to assist. It was agreed that the interview would take place at Berry's flat in Muswell Hill at 6.30 p.m. on 18 February. In the event, both Aubrey and Campbell, who had travelled separately, arrived half an hour late. Lubricated by a bottle of Italian wine, the interview lasted three hours and was, as it turned out unfortunately for all of them, recorded on Aubrey's tape recorder.

As Duncan Campbell recalls, part of the interview concerned Berry's personal recollections, for example why he had joined up. He also explained what he knew of the operation of SIGINT in Cyprus, and gave 'a few, very general, examples of how SIGINT had succeeded, for instance in monitoring the planned sailing of the Turkish fleet towards Cyprus'. Campbell also remembers stories about intercepted messages from the 1967 Arab-Israeli Six-Day War. Later Campbell told Aubrey that Berry's recollections had 'added virtually nothing to what he already knew'.[11] What Berry had to say was interesting enough, but Campbell had no inkling that the three hours he had spent in Berry's company that winter evening would prove to be in any sense momentous. What was to happen next was to be both shocking and unexpected.

Aubrey recalled: 'Just after 10 p.m. we emerged into the cold February gloom. For a moment, Duncan and I stood by my car discussing whether I could give him a lift.' Suddenly, 'A group of men appeared dramatically from the darkness.' One of them spoke: 'We are police officers. We have reason to believe that offences have been committed under the Official Secrets Act.' The arresting party comprised no fewer than thirteen police officers from Special Branch – described by Campbell as 'fetchers and carriers for the secret agencies who lack police powers of arrest'. Campbell vainly showed his NUJ card, as if his status as a journalist would defuse the crisis.

How the police came to learn of the meeting in Muswell Hill was never officially explained: all that the officer in charge of the operation would say when later giving evidence was that he had been required to attend at Berry's flat two hours prior to the actual arrests. Campbell remains in no doubt that MI5 learned of the meeting through tapping his or *Time Out*'s phone line. In the face of Campbell's effrontery the state had not been entirely impotent. While researching 'The Eavesdroppers' article Campbell had telephoned GCHQ directly and posed various questions to its librarian concerning its workings. It was the first time anyone had ever done such a thing. Fewer than forty-eight hours later Campbell was awoken at six o'clock in the morning by a strange repeated 'pinging' emitted by his telephone while it remained on the hook. A telecommunications expert (Campbell had recently completed a book called *The British Telephone System*), he knew exactly what it meant. The security services always did their business before the regular telephone workers started in the morning. Just as Jeremy's had been a decade earlier, Campbell's phone was being tapped.

Berry, Aubrey and Campbell were arrested and taken to Muswell Hill Police Station where they were questioned and held without access to legal advice for forty hours. Their houses were searched, and in the case of Duncan Campbell's flat in Brighton, ransacked: a transit van carried away most of its contents, including 400 books (among them one dutifully noted down as '*The Female Unok*') and a filing cabinet filled with papers, the product of years of research. At 5 p.m. on the Sunday following the arrest the trio were charged with offences under section 2 of the Official Secrets Act.

We have seen how wide section 2 was in Chapter 11. The section technically precluded all government and state employees – approximately 2 million people in the late 1970s – from non-authorized discussion of their employment or any information learned during the course of their employment. There was widespread dissatisfaction with this 'catch-all' provision, especially in the wake of the *Sunday Telegraph* case. It was remarked that every day there must be thousands of technical breaches of this section, without any harm to anyone (telling your husband the colour of the carpet in a particular governmental department would theoretically be caught by section 2). In the light of the 1972 Franks Committee recommendations the incoming Labour government had indicated its willingness to effect reform. Therefore the decision to charge Berry, Campbell and Aubrey with section 2 offences in respect of a conversation was greeted in many quarters with derision and alarm.

Berry himself certainly had no realistic defence to a charge of unauthorized communication of information. He had signed the Official Secrets Act nine times during the course of his military career and could be in no doubt as to its meaning. But Aubrey claimed in the course of the subsequent trial that he had never in his 'wildest dreams' considered that a journalistic interview could be covered by the Official Secrets Act.[12] However, pursuant to the provisions of section 2 the Crown had only to prove that Aubrey and Campbell had, on an objective rather than subjective basis, 'reasonable grounds to believe' that Berry was speaking without authorization. Given that Berry was an ex-soldier, and was revealing information deemed by the government to be secret, this would not have been difficult to prove. Geoffrey Robertson, who acted for Duncan Campbell at the committal hearing and subsequent trial as Jeremy's junior, considered that 'none of the three had any apparent defence to the Section 2 charges',[13] so widely was section 2 drawn.

An indication of the seriousness with which the state treated the ABC defendants' alleged offences was given early on. Strenuous resistance was mounted to bail applications and Tottenham magistrates obliged by remanding all three to Brixton prison, where they were held in separate cells in the maximum security block. In the end it took a High Court judge to grant Campbell bail, mollified by the smooth tongue of John Mortimer QC, who appeared on his behalf, emphasizing that he had taken a good degree at Oxford ('Which college?' was the judge's immediate response). John Berry, who could not lay claim to an Oxbridge education, had to remain on remand for a good deal longer.

Three months later the case took a very alarming turn. Berry, Aubrey and Campbell were additionally charged with offences under section 1 of the Official Secrets Act. Section 1 is a draconian provision intended for the prosecution of spies (George Blake and

John Vassall had both been convicted under this section), and carried a maximum penalty of a prison term of fourteen years. As we have seen, a person is guilty of an offence under section 1 if, for any 'purpose prejudicial to the safety or interests of the State', he obtains, or communicates to another person, information that might be 'directly or indirectly useful to an enemy'. The defendant's purpose in doing so is deemed to be prejudicial to the safety or interests of the state, unless the contrary is proved. There was nothing in the conversation over a bottle of wine in north London that remotely justified the ABC defendants being bludgeoned with section 1. Indeed this was the first time any journalist had ever been prosecuted under it. Although John Berry's behaviour might have understandably vexed the secret services he in fact was not their real target. It was Duncan Campbell, the twenty-four-year-old physics graduate and putative nemesis of the secret state, who really frightened that secret state. It wanted Campbell put away for 'a very long time', as the prosecutor candidly told Geoffrey Robertson. Section 1 provided the potential route to a hefty term of imprisonment.

The original section 1 charges were brought in relation to Berry's interview with Campbell and Aubrey. Then, in August 1977, an additional section 1 charge was levelled against Campbell alone. This became known as the 'collection' charge, as it related to material – photographs, sketches, notes, articles – collected by Campbell in relation to defence establishments across the country in the course of his research into the workings of the secret state (and later used in his book *War Plan UK*), and seized by the police during their raid of his Brighton flat. Nine hundred pages of material were produced by the Crown in support of a charge against Campbell of 'collecting information concerning defence communications . . . which might be of use to an enemy'. This new charge – which was expressly sanctioned by the Attorney General – represented a terrifying development in the state's attempts to gag and destroy an investigative journalist unaffiliated to any political cause and motivated solely by the desire to shed light on the secret state. As Campbell later explained:

A Major-General, in charge of defence communications, viewed a selection of the material and vouched his 'professional opinion' that it might be 'directly useful to an enemy'. Very simply then, the elements of a new political offence were created. It was sufficient to possess information, of itself neither illegal, improperly obtained, official or even secret, if it constituted a 'collection' or 'jigsaw' from which an incomplete picture of 'secret' activities could be assembled. Since agents of a hostile power can safely do this exercise at their leisure, the offence here resides in the political idea which motivates such research.[14]

If convicted on all charges Duncan Campbell now faced a potential prison sentence of up to thirty years.

The committal was heard in November 1977 at Tottenham Magistrates Court. It quickly became obvious that Berry and Aubrey were bit-players in the case. The true target of the prosecution was Campbell, described as a 'thoroughly subversive man'. It was even alleged that his conversation with Berry could have put 'lives in Northern Ireland' at risk – an allegation never substantiated with a shred of evidence.[15] But, hyperbole apart, the committal proceedings were memorable in particular for the introduction of 'Colonel B' to the case: he would later become one of the trial's leading stars. Before the trial had even started he briefly became, by a supreme irony, one of the best-known men in England.

Colonel B, previously commander of the 9th Signals Regiment at Ayios Nikolaos, Cyprus, was called by the Crown to give evidence to the effect that the information communicated by Berry was sufficiently sensitive to be covered by section 1 of the Act. The colonel was required to be called B in court because the prosecution considered that his real name was too secret to be revealed to the world at large (although his name was grudgingly provided to the court and to the defendants' lawyers). Such was the hypersensitivity over secrecy that prevailed at the time. In fact Colonel B replaced 'Lieutenant Colonel A', whom the prosecution had originally wished to call to give evidence. Lieutenant Colonel A was only withdrawn as a witness when the magistrates refused the prosecution's application that his name be withheld from the court and the defendants, because of the risk 'to his own security and to national security'. So Colonel B was slightly less super-secret than Lieutenant Colonel A.

During cross-examination Colonel B manfully attempted to uphold the prosecution's absolutist world of necessary secrecy. But the indefatigable Duncan Campbell had been carrying out his own investigations even before the start of the committal proceedings or Colonel B's name had been confidentially disclosed. He had discovered that the secret colonel was not so secret after all. Colonel B admitted that his name, rank and number, and the date of his appointment, had been published in a number of publications, including an issue of the regimental magazine, the *Wire*, where he had been reverentially described as 'the don of the communications underworld'. This was a publication freely available in various London libraries and to which, needless to say, Campbell had his own subscription. After the court clerk, a stickler for legal formality, had insisted that the month and number of the relevant edition of the *Wire* be provided for his note, it did not take long for journalists who had been present in court to track down the relevant issue of the *Wire*, and the colonel's name, 'Colonel H.A. Johnstone MBE', was subsequently published in various radical journals, including *Peace News* and the *Leveller*. The heavy-handed response of the Attorney General to this disclosure was to institute proceedings for contempt of court against these magazines. This in turn inspired four MPs, furious at what they saw as an abuse of state power, to ask questions naming 'Colonel Johnstone' during Parliamentary Questions, to the squirming embarrassment of Michael Foot, then Leader of the House, who had to field them.

From that moment it was open season on the unfortunate Colonel Johnstone – who, as Duncan Campbell recalls, 'rapidly achieved the position of national figure of ridicule' – and also on the government-sponsored prosecution of the ABC defendants. Being constitutionally entitled to report parliamentary proceedings, the rest of the media was now given the opportunity to publish the colonel's name. Television networks and all the leading national newspapers did so, in defiance of the Attorney General, and his Director of Public Prosecutions, Thomas Hetherington, who had issued Canute-like threats to prosecute any further news organizations that named the colonel for contempt of court.[16] Naming Colonel B became a national pastime: at the NUJ conference being held at Whitby his name was etched into the sand in letters ten feet high (by the time the police arrived the tide had washed them away). Red balloons were released bearing his name outside court. Badges were issued bearing the words 'H.A. Johnstone I presume!' The government's attempts to keep the name of Colonel B secret had spectacularly backfired.

The case having been committed to be tried at the Old Bailey, in June 1978 Jeremy was approached to defend Duncan Campbell at what was guaranteed to be a very high-profile trial. The ABC Defence Committee, founded by friends and colleagues of the defendants immediately after their arrest, was phenomenally successful in generating publicity and support for their cause. As Aubrey recalled, it was not long before a 'small group of friends' became a 'long list of supporters' which comprised MPs (including Jonathan Aitken), journalists, trade unionists, lawyers and civil servants. A network of associated support groups was set up across the country. The campaign was directed not only to highlighting the predicament of the ABC defendants, but also to shining a spotlight on the secret state and its machinations. Thousands of leaflets, posters and petitions were printed and distributed. The campaign's stunts, which often accompanied the defendants' arrival for court appearances, were widely reported. These included a bound and gagged 'journalist' seated in front of a typewriter that he could not reach out to, a 'silly secrets' dragon, a huge 'Buzby' (British Telecom's orange talking bird, appropriated for the campaign), a supporter masquerading in military uniform as Colonel X, T-shirts with slogans such as 'Military Intelligence is a Contradiction in Terms' and 'Tell Me an Official Secret', and children wearing badges saying 'MI3' or 'MI5½', according to their age. Further afield, walks were organized around 'secret' sites, culminating in a march on GCHQ. It is no exaggeration to say that, even before the trial started, the ABC prosecution, and the public response to it, had made a significant contribution to the demystification of the secret state. That task would be continued by Jeremy within the wood-panelled walls of Court 1 of the Old Bailey.

Jeremy's junior, Geoffrey Robertson, recalls that he spent much of the summer of 1978 discussing tactics with the newly ennobled Lord Hutchinson of Lullington. He describes Jeremy in his account of the case as 'the most fearless and formidable advocate of the day'.[17] The irony was not yet apparent, but Jeremy would spend much of the autumn of 1978 denouncing a prosecution instituted by a government that had elevated him to the House of Lords just a few months earlier.

But before they got to the trial Jeremy found himself at a London dinner party fortuitously sitting next to a senior civil servant who asked for a quiet word. That quiet word was nothing less than an attempt to bring the proceedings to an end. If the defendants pleaded guilty to the section 2 charges the section 1 charges would be dropped. The approach was duly reported to Duncan Campbell. The year and a half since his arrest had been a difficult period for him. The terms of his bail required him to report to a police station every day, a tiresome and humiliating chore. Since the raid on his flat he had found it unsettling to live there, so for much of the time he slept on a friend's sofa. Finally there was the burden of preparing for the trial, and his preparations, as Jeremy was later to discover, were meticulous. This made it very difficult for Campbell to do any paid work, though eventually, after an incomeless year, he got a job on the *New Statesman*.

The stakes could hardly have been higher: if convicted of the section 1 charges alone Campbell faced a term of imprisonment of up to twenty-eight years. In addition there were the section 2 charges, which themselves carried a maximum term of two years. The precedent set by the sentences meted out to Blake and Vassall was not an encouraging one, and the prosecuting authorities did not seem inclined to give Campbell much credit for not being a Soviet spy. So a plea bargain along the lines being offered had its potential attractions. But, in unison with his co-defendants, Campbell decided he had to take a stand. The trial would have to take place. The ABC defendants' undoubted courage was laced with an element of foolhardiness. To Jeremy's chagrin they called a press conference publicizing, and denouncing, the plea bargain that had been offered. This only enraged the prosecuting authorities even further.

The trial of the ABC defendants was listed to start on 5 September

1978. In consultation with Jeremy, Geoffrey Robertson and his solicitor Bernie Simons the day before, Duncan Campbell expressed his distrust of the security services; he wouldn't put it past them to 'vet' the jury, he said – that is, to ask the security service, MI5, to identify any potential juror suspected of being a security threat. Jeremy dismissed this out of hand. There was no vetting of juries in modern England, he reassured his client.

That night he lay awake and thought about what Campbell had told him. Early the next morning, Jeremy recalls, he strolled into the office of the Chief Clerk of the Old Bailey, and asked, 'quite innocently', whether there had been any interest in the jury for the official secrets trial. The clerk, no doubt delighted to be conversing with the famous advocate, replied unguardedly that there had been no interest for six weeks, since John Leonard QC, counsel for the prosecution, had applied for, and been granted, the names and addresses of the potential jurors, so they could be vetted for the forthcoming trial.

Geoffrey Robertson recalls the scene in the robing room that followed. 'Would you believe it, Geoffrey – they've vetted the jury!' Jeremy, he remembers, was 'half-enraged at the prosecution's behaviour' and 'half-excited by the mischief he would cause when he stood up in court to reveal it'.[18] Jeremy expressed his indignation in court later that morning in an impromptu attack.[19] He was, he said, 'extremely unhappy that a panel of jurors should be examined to make some decision about their loyalty'.[20] In response John Leonard stated that the application had been made 'to complete the checks which are normal in cases of this sort. Anyone known to be disloyal would obviously be disqualified.' In the event it appeared that no juror had actually been excluded as a result of the vetting exercise, though there remained the fact that of the eighty-two members on the panel only seventy-one had actually attended for selection that day. What had happened to the missing eleven jurors Mr Leonard could not say.

But the trial judge, Mr Justice Willis, was keen to move on. The last thing he wanted was a constitutional crisis erupting in his court. He agreed that the checks were 'perfectly proper in a case like this', and the trial proceeded. But an important event had occurred. The prosecuting authorities had been forced to admit for the first time that the practice of jury-vetting took place. The judge did not ban press coverage of the fact that the jury-vetting application had been made. The issue was widely reported and provoked heated discussion and debate. Though John Leonard had asserted that checks were 'normal' in 'cases of this sort' it was clear that the practice had been kept deliberately secret, that it had a dubious legal basis, and that, in the view of many, it confounded age-old notions of the independence and representative character of the jury. Further, it was not at all clear what 'normal' and 'cases of this sort' meant. The issue of the jury would soon re-emerge to turn the trial on its head.

John Leonard opened the case for the prosecution. While admitting that the offences 'came at the lowest end of the Section 1 scale', he asserted that the 'prejudicial purpose' required by section 1 was made out in the form of Aubrey and Campbell's intention to publish or pass on Berry's information. As for the 'collection' charge against Campbell, Leonard asserted that the journalist's collection of documents relating to defence communications went 'beyond the ordinary inquisitiveness of a journalist'. Campbell, he went on, had 'taken the pieces of our defence jigsaw puzzle, and put them together'. Campbell's intention was 'to build up a complete picture as far as he could of the defence communications facilities operating in the United Kingdom'. While Leonard conceded that Campbell was not a spy and was not communicating with spies, nonetheless 'it was clear that he was willing to pass on his information.' It turned out that this willingness related to Campbell's correspondence with an Ampleforth College schoolmaster – and Benedictine monk – who had an enthusiasm for locating defence establishments in the Yorkshire countryside with various of his pupils.

Then, as Crispin Aubrey recalls, Jeremy 'launched his counter-attack', albeit one that was 'quiet, elegant and persistent'. His strategy was to show that the information collected by Campbell, far from being secret and potentially valuable to an enemy, as asserted by the prosecution, was in fact culled from published sources available to all. This would answer the charge, required for a conviction under section 1, that the material collected by Campbell, including that obtained in the course of his interview with Berry, was prejudicial to the safety or interests of the state, and useful to an enemy.

Jeremy remembers that his aim was to draw back what he described as 'the bogus shroud of secrecy' with which the prosecution wished

313

to bamboozle the jury. 'The nonsense of the situation was that Duncan Campbell was accused of having collected information concerning these secret bases and locations, and yet the existence and purpose of these places was public knowledge.' He achieved this purpose through a series of lethal cross-examinations of the litany of prosecution witnesses, mostly RAF officers (reading the transcripts one imagines them to be, to a man, bewhiskered) called to give evidence in relation to bases that Campbell had referred to in his research, or had photographs of. Time after time, the witnesses were forced to admit that the so-called 'secret' bases were in fact the subject of newspaper articles, or official maps or publications. Aubrey refers to the prosecution witnesses as the 'security system's worst enemies' as, one by one, they evinced the same 'tight-lipped refusal to answer questions'.[21] Witness by witness, Jeremy chipped away at the prosecution case, as, in a dogged display of forensic tenacity, he demonstrated that practically every piece of information in Campbell's files was available from published sources.

In an attempt to import an atmosphere of legitimate secrecy, the prosecution suggested that everyone in court should refer to each location by reference to an elaborate schedule devised by the Crown lawyers. John Leonard could not have made this proposition sound more reasonable. 'My Lord, it would be more convenient to talk about numbers in the schedule so that witnesses can be more frank in answering questions.' Jeremy's take on this was uncompromising: 'This was a trap which I was not going to fall into.' To the judge he was adamant: 'Unless Your Lordship rules otherwise I intend to read what is written publicly in documents and published articles and ask witnesses about them. To refer to X, Y and Z and schedule numbers gives a bogus atmosphere of secrecy.'

Wing Commander Evans gave evidence about an RAF establishment at Orford Ness in Suffolk, which Campbell had taken a photograph of. The exchanges between Evans and Jeremy capture the surreal quality of the trial.

JEREMY: Is it right that the Ministry of Defence organized a press visit to the station at Orford Ness?
EVANS: Yes.
JEREMY: Look at the photograph which it is alleged my client took. Is there anything remotely secret about it?

EVANS: I am not competent to answer that question . . . I was not
involved in the decisions that declared the work at Orford Ness
to be secret, nor do I know what factors had influenced that
decision.
JEREMY: You mean someone, somewhere, puts a stamp on something
which says 'secret' and as far as you are concerned it is secret.
EVANS: I have to do my duty.
JEREMY: Even though when you open your *Daily Telegraph* in the
morning it is there for hundreds of thousands of people to read.
EVANS: It can be very annoying but I have to do it.
JEREMY: Would you agree with me, speaking as a human being, that
that is absolutely idiotic?
EVANS: I agree with you.

Jeremy was doing his job of humiliating the prosecution case rather
too well. The atmosphere in court became increasingly fractious as
John Leonard accused Jeremy of 'abusing his position' by identifying
in court RAF communication and radar bases, notwithstanding the
fact that the way he went about identifying those bases, as he cross-
examined each RAF panjandrum, was to read out their names from
newspaper articles or books. Eventually the trial pitched over into
absurdity as the judge insisted that Jeremy could henceforth only
refer to these bases by numbers that accorded with the prosecution's
schedule. One of these was the Post Office Tower, or rather location 23 as it now had to be known. Campbell recalls: 'What Jeremy
did, which was both beautiful and infuriating, depending on which
side of the Court you were on, was to manufacture a stumble or
mini-stutter as he read up to the name in each publication, then
flap about a bit to get the schedule or get Geoff Robertson to pick
it up off the floor, etc. It was a classic iterative comedy act for the
jury, which he could not of course seem to be playing for laughs
although that (as everyone from the Bench down got) was precisely
what he was doing.'

And so, when Squadron Leader Oakes was called, Jeremy spent
half an hour referring to his base at West Drayton as 'blank' or
'number 48 on the schedule', notwithstanding that the base had been
named in the 1974 RAF Yearbook as the link between Britain's three
radar stations on the east coast and the six NATO air defence ground

environment stations. He ploughed on, reading out to each witness lengthy sections of books, newspapers, magazine articles and official documents, which demonstrated the imbecility of the prosecution against Campbell on the 'collection charge'. But Willis was not happy:

> JUDGE: This is the most extraordinary way of cross-examining a witness I have ever come across.
>
> JEREMY: This is the most extraordinary witness to bring in this case. There is no more harm in microwave spotting than train spotting.

The next day Squadron Leader Mactavish was hauled in to give evidence about another of Campbell's 'targets'. Jeremy was not going to be dissuaded by judicial pressure, and showed Mactavish articles and photographs about the radar station the witness had come to speak about from the *Sunday Times* and *RAF News*, which explained the defence function of the station.

> JEREMY: *RAF News* likens the station's operations to a 'possible electronic battle of wits as Russian aircraft probed our defences'.
>
> MACTAVISH: I am not permitted to comment on this.
>
> JEREMY: So we have a situation that this information has appeared in an official RAF newspaper, yet when an official officer comes here he is not allowed to speak about it?
>
> MACTAVISH: That is service policy.
>
> JEREMY: So this is a secret, is it?
>
> MACTAVISH: I do not wish to discuss whether this is true or not.

However well the cross-examinations were going in the eyes of Duncan Campbell and the packed press gallery, the jury were looking as stony-faced as the judge. It was not a good sign when certain members expressed concern in a note to the judge that they might themselves be committing a criminal offence merely by *listening* to the evidence in the case. It turned out that three jurors had signed the Official Secrets Act. They included a DHSS clerk, an ex-soldier and, most alarmingly for the defendants, a former member of the SAS who had seen active service in Malaya, Cyprus and Northern Ireland. The last of these had managed to get himself elected foreman of the jury and, so it later transpired, was overheard insisting to his co-jurors that Berry should have been subjected to a court martial: 'He should have had a military trial, straight in, fourteen years, straight out.' As for Campbell, the prosecution had introduced articles written by him that demonstrated that he was hardly a firm friend of the SAS. Notwithstanding the prosecution's protestations that no steps had been taken to alter the make-up of the jury, Duncan Campbell could not help but feel that it was a singularly unfortunate occurrence that his fate was now in the hands of such a man. It was a gloomy moment when Jeremy's application for the discharge of the foreman from the jury, on the grounds that his training, experiences and attitudes would preclude him from approaching the evidence with an open mind, was turned down.[22] What outraged Jeremy most was the fact that the prosecution must have been told in advance of the trial, through the vetting process, that one of the potential jurors was a former SAS soldier – 'what joy that must have brought the prosecution when they discovered the news'. This was a fact of course unknown to the defence.

But this was a case that had further twists in store. Mr Justice Willis had ordered that his ruling refusing to discharge the foreman should not be reported. This ruling was immediately flouted by Christopher Hitchens, then a journalist with the *New Statesman*, who, as a guest on an LWT chat show, *Saturday Night People*, hosted by Russell Harty, revealed, as 'news which you won't have read or heard', what had happened in court the previous week. Duncan Campbell confirms what really happened. He and Hitchens both worked on the *New Statesman*. Campbell had casually mentioned to his colleagues what had happened in court that week. Hitchens reacted by passing on that information to the world on the Saturday. The SAS man watched open-mouthed and, the next Monday, reported what he regarded as an outrage to the judge. Deploring Hitchens's disclosure as 'a quite lamentable piece of gratuitous journalistic gossip', the judge said he had no alternative but to dismiss the jury, and the trial was halted. A new trial was fixed to start in two weeks before a new jury. The ABC defendants had escaped an unsympathetic hearing.

As it turned out the early termination of the first trial had another significant consequence for Duncan Campbell. For all the harrumphing of the judge and prosecutor at Jeremy's relentless belabouring of the prosecution witnesses, it had had the desired effect. According to one commentator, John Leonard was overheard announcing 'in a distinctly audible *sotto voce*' that the prosecution would continue with the collection charge against Campbell 'over my dead body'.[23] A confidential Ministry of Defence document dated 18 September 1978 concluded as follows:

> On behalf of Campbell, Lord Hutchinson has cross-questioned the witnesses and has concentrated on drawing attention to occasions when details of establishments have been published either in the press or, more damagingly, in quasi-official publications like the Royal Air Force Year Book. Mr Leonard, the prosecuting counsel, has come to the view that there have been so many published references to the information Campbell has acquired and the conclusions he has drawn from it that the chances of success with [the collection charge] are not good . . . It is understood that, if the [collection charge] is proceeded with, Campbell will give evidence himself and that his defending counsel expects him to be in the witness box for up to a month. It seems probable that he will produce more and more published information in open court to demonstrate how much is already available. This has been the tactic of the defence so far. It could be that this will draw attention to more information about defence which we should prefer not to be given such a public airing.

The prospect of Jeremy questioning Duncan Campbell about UK defence establishments for over a month in Court 1 of the Old Bailey no doubt ranked high in the Ministry of Defence's pantheon of nightmare scenarios. Before the second trial started the collection charge was abandoned. As the *Sunday Times* put it later: 'it took Campbell's defence counsel, Lord Hutchinson QC, only six days of brilliant cross-examination of the Crown's expert witnesses, to show that every fact in Campbell's files was available or deducible from public sources.'[24] It was a humiliating climbdown. But it was a climbdown for which Jeremy gives his client Duncan Campbell full credit. 'Duncan was the most extraordinary client to have; I remember meeting him in conference before the trial and shaking my head about some aspect of the case. The next week he would come back to see me with armfuls of documents he had dug up proving that some alleged secret was in fact no secret at all. By the time we got to trial he had prepared volumes of material which allowed me to launch our attack on the prosecution witnesses.'

The new trial began in early October 1978. A new judge, Mr Justice Mars-Jones, was appointed to replace Willis, who had fallen ill. (The ABC defendants had sent a bunch of roses to his hospital bed, which elicited a response from Willis that he was glad that he would not be conducting the retrial as he had 'not been looking forward to passing the sentences'.)

Now that he had advance notice of the issue, Jeremy opened with an impassioned attack on the unconstitutionality of jury-vetting.

> The present panel of jurors, as I understand it, have been subjected to a process of vetting or screening by the security service, a process, we were told on the last occasion, to ensure that there is no doubt as to each juryman's loyalty, so as to be sure that it is safe to entrust him or her with knowledge of the material in this case.
>
> I wish to submit on behalf of my client an unqualified objection to the selection of a jury from a panel which has been subject to a secret and I would say unconstitutional process. In my submission the very basis of jury trial is that the jury should be impartial and should be anonymous to both the prosecution and defence, other than the bare information on the panel – their names and addresses.
>
> Your Lordship will remember that Blackstone in his Commentaries wrote that 'the liberties of England depend on the jury remaining secret and inviolate, not only from open attacks, which none would be so hardy as to make, but from all secret machinations.' To subject citizens to surveillance, to run their names through an MI5 computer and then on undisclosed criteria, via hidden methods, pronounce upon their loyalty, is, in my submission, to strike at the very heart of the jury system and does amount, indeed, to a secret machination. These jurors will know, because of the publicity that has already surrounded this case, that they have been screened and if unchallenged by the Crown they will know that they are regarded by the authorities as safe jurors, which, in my submission, is or could be a subtle form of intimidation. It might also appear that the defence, by challenging this procedure, would be put in the position of apparently wanting disloyal members of the public on the jury and therefore be looked upon with suspicion from the start . . .

> I end by saying that this submission is not an idle submission: it
> does involve a principle which I suggest extends far beyond this trial
> and my application to the court is no less than to ask Your Lordship
> to uphold and maintain this most precious bulwark of our liberties.

Jeremy's objection was dismissed by Mr Justice Mars-Jones. However
a significant concession was made to the defendants. They were
entitled to ask each juror, as he or she was sworn in, whether they
had handled secret material in the last fifteen years – to avoid another
SAS foreman scenario. One of the jurors answered in the affirmative,
and was rejected.

But there was an even more significant consequence of Jeremy's
broadside about jury-vetting. Under pressure from the media, which
had been stirred up into a lather of indignation against jury-vetting,
on 10 October 1978 the Attorney General Sam Silkin issued a statement: 'Guidelines on Jury Checks', which set out, for the first time,
the details of jury-vetting practice. Things were not going well for
Silkin: the judge had banned reporting of Jeremy's application and
Silkin's response was in itself a breach of Mars-Jones's order. A
grovelling apology was tendered, with the remarkable explanation
that Silkin had not been informed of the judge's ruling.

In a preamble, Silkin explained that the guidelines had been drawn
up four years earlier in an attempt to consolidate and clarify a practice
that had been carried on, in an unregulated way, for years. It had
been issued to all police forces. The guidelines open with a statement
of adherence to the principle that 'members of a jury should be
selected at random from the panel', but with the modification that
there are 'certain exceptional types of case of public importance' where
the safeguards provided by Parliament (for example, majority verdicts)
in respect of jurors who may be 'corrupt or biased' are 'not sufficient
to ensure the proper administration of justice'. It is, the guidelines
suggest, 'impossible to define precisely these classes of case', but 'broadly
speaking' they will be serious offences where strong political motives
were involved, 'such as IRA and other terrorist cases and cases under
the Official Secrets Act', where jurors may, 'because of extreme political
beliefs, be biased against either the Prosecution or the Defence', or
be susceptible to 'improper pressure'. In these cases, in order to ascertain
whether 'any of these factors might seriously influence a potential

juror's impartial performance of his duties', a Chief Officer of Police can apply to the Director of Public Prosecutions for permission to check police, Special Branch and CID records.

Criticism of the guidelines concentrated on the vagueness of the defining terms (e.g. what exactly is an 'exceptional' case?), the inherent contradiction between a professed adherence to the principle of randomness of juries and the procedure outlined, a lack of account-ability in relation to those responsible for the procedure, the fact that it was not debated in Parliament, and the fact that jury-vetting as prescribed undermines a founding principle of English law, namely that a person is tried by his peers, who are 'selected at random, without respect to their beliefs or opinions, and . . . subject to no influence of state'.[25] E.P. Thompson led the attack in a brilliant article in *New Society*,[26] 'The State Versus its Enemies'. 'Mr Attorney-General,' he declaimed, 'what precision is there in these "guidelines" you served out secretly to the police? What is a guideline? Is it a rule at law or is it a nudge-nudge-be-careful-how-you-go?' And later: 'Are our liberties to rest on "guidelines" privately delivered – and delivered to the police? Is the whole of our history to hang on "broadly speaking"? This is to break the bargain made between the people and the Law.'

The second trial began, as the first had left off, in what Jeremy described as 'a needless atmosphere of secrecy'. Although the trial had been narrowed to the information divulged in the now notorious conversation in Muswell Hill, the prosecution still insisted on the necessity of calling military bases by number or letter rather than name, despite the fact that their identity was well known. For example, the 9th Signals Regiment was referred to as 'Unit A', and its base at Ayios Nikolaos as 'Location 1' on the grounds, as the prosecution claimed, that disclosure of these details would embarrass the Greek Cypriot government. This was notwithstanding that the Press Representative at the Cypriot High Commission was prepared, with the backing of his government, to give evidence that the fact that the base was used for monitoring purposes was well known.[27]

Hence the following exchange between Jeremy and a Crown witness:

JEREMY [showing the witness a photograph of a sign at the entrance to a particular base]: Is that the name of your unit?
WITNESS: I cannot answer that question, that is a secret.

JEREMY: Is that the board that is up outside the door of your unit?
WITNESS: Yes.
JEREMY: Read it out to the jury.
WITNESS: I cannot do that, that is a secret.

The 'celebrated' Colonel B, as the *Guardian* described him, made a reappearance at the second trial, though now he was unclothed of his secret identity. He was called into the witness box as plain Colonel Johnstone to explain to the jury why the information provided by Berry to Aubrey and Campbell could cause 'exceptionally grave damage' to the national interest. The colonel was in the witness box over six days, being cross-examined by Jeremy. According to one commentator, the colonel 'exemplified what the defence castigated as an obsession with secrecy'.[28]

Jeremy's cross-examination of Colonel Johnstone again revealed the inconsistencies, and absurdities, of the prosecution case. In one exchange, Jeremy asked the colonel how secrets were classified, when so much classified material had already been disclosed.

COLONEL B: What remains secret is what is designated secret by whoever makes the designation.
JEREMY: You mean the rules that are laid down for what is, and is not, secret are themselves secret?
COLONEL B: Yes.

Jeremy's attritional approach to the prosecution evidence continued to bear fruit. In one exchange the colonel conceded that the name and location of the 9th Signals Regiment was not secret, though its 'strength' was. An issue of the *Wire* was handed to the witness, and he was referred to a particular cartoon. The caption read: 'With a strength of just over 1,000, 9th Signals obviously contains many characters.' Johnstone was also asked about a part of the Muswell Hill transcript where Berry discussed certain Turkish military manoeuvres. In his initial evidence to the prosecution Johnstone had insisted that this information could only have come from SIGINT: hence Berry was revealing to Aubrey and Campbell that the United Kingdom was spying on a NATO ally. Yet, as Jeremy was able to demonstrate, at the time of these manoeuvres Berry was in the UK and they were then mentioned in the *Daily Telegraph*. Campbell was delighted: 'Johnstone had given away the fact that the UK was spying on the Turks from his former base.' In another exchange the colonel described a letter published in the *Wire* as itself a breach of the Official Secrets Act. In the end he was reduced to accepting, in what one newspaper described as a 'moment of gloomy confusion', that 'To be frank, I am not certain what is a secret and what isn't.'

The prosecution had previously indicated that it intended to call another secret witness, to be known, inevitably, as Mr C, and whose evidence would have to be heard entirely in camera. After Colonel B's mauling Mr C was never again mentioned.

All this was having the desired effect on the judge. On 24 October Mr Justice Mars-Jones invited counsel to address him on the question of whether any of the section 1 charges should continue. The judge indicated that he was personally unhappy with what he described as an 'oppressive prosecution'. In his view, section 1 was meant for the prosecution of spies and saboteurs, not journalists. John Leonard responded that the Attorney General had authorized the prosecution. 'If the Attorney General can authorize the prosecution, then he can un-authorize it!' the judge expostulated. The following morning John Leonard told the court that he had taken instructions from the Attorney General, and the section 1 charges – the ones that carried a maximum sentence of fourteen years – were being dropped against all the defendants. Yet further humiliation was being heaped on the prosecution. For Campbell and his co-defendants the relief was indescribable. The slur of being labelled a spy had been removed.

Mr Justice Mars-Jones told the jury, 'We now have to decide how many of the documents before you can be put on the bonfire.' He then said something else that was even more welcome to Duncan Campbell. He indicated in open court to the defendants that, in relation to the remaining section 2 charges, whatever the outcome he would not be considering a custodial sentence. As technically there seemed to be no answer to the section 2 charges Jeremy asked Campbell whether he wished to pursue the case further. Aubrey, Campbell and Berry conferred together and decided to carry on. Aubrey recalls: 'We were on to a winning streak, and we were not going to stop now.'[29] They had little to lose, and the prosecution had now become little more than a continuing embarrassment to the government. Later the judge wrote to Jeremy about that decision: 'I quite understand your reasons for going on after my somewhat unconventional announcement. Although I hoped it would have produced guilty pleas, I was not entirely surprised to find it did not. At least it made life easier for the "terrible trio" – as their faces clearly showed.'

The trial limped on for another three weeks. The battle had been largely won, but nonetheless Jeremy delivered a high-octane speech pouring scorn on the prosecution. It was lovingly reported in the newspapers:

> Hundreds of Mr Campbell's documents were taken by the Special Branch from the fresh air of Brighton to the fetid atmosphere of Scotland Yard. These faceless men from MI5, armed no doubt with magnifying glasses and microscopes, with chemicals and crystal balls, calling on the GCHQ, the NSA, Comint, Elint, Radint and a squad no doubt of cryptologists from Bletchley and analysts from Ashford, led by Admiral A and General B, rummaged through Mr Campbell's innocent papers. After many days of unremitting effort by the defence we were able to establish the harmless quality of each and every item which had been collected with such loving care by the Special Branch.

This is the rhetoric of righteous indignation. Jeremy went on to criticize the decision to prosecute Campbell under section 2 of the Act:

> Section 2 has been thoroughly castigated several times. But it is still alive and, as far as Mr Campbell is concerned, kicking. Even in its death throes it has managed to take up many hours of court time. Perhaps November 1978 will be remembered as positively the last appearance on the public stage of this raddled and discredited prima donna. I hope no government impresario will ever call upon her seductive services again. Now only one charge is left, under an Act which has been described as a 'lawyer's paradise', if you are the sort of lawyer who can find heaven in a fog.

He argued that the prosecutions were entirely misconceived: it is the task of a vigorous, healthy press, he said, 'to examine, probe, question and find out if there are mistakes and abuses and to embarrass governments, of whatever complexion, and not just to accept handouts from people in high places and churn out what they are told to say'. It was a fine note on which to end the proceedings, but still Jeremy held out little hope that Duncan Campbell could avoid a conviction under section 2.

The jury took sixty-eight hours of soul-searching to come to their verdict. Day after day they would return to court to seek clarification on some point of law or fact from the judge. Jeremy remembers the days of waiting. 'I could see that the jury were wrestling between the strict wording of the Act and their loathing of the prosecution.' In the end, try as the jury might to find a way of bringing in acquittals, all three defendants were found guilty of the section 2 charges. None was sent to prison. Berry was sentenced to six months in prison, suspended for two years; Aubrey and Campbell received conditional discharges, the judicial equivalent of a very light slap on the wrist for those who have committed only a technical infringement of the law. The sentences were greeted by the ABC campaign with wild scenes of jubilation outside the Old Bailey. As Campbell puts it, it was the type of conviction one wears with pride. As Aubrey said: 'After a trial lasting on and off for two and a half months, a cost to the taxpayer of an esti-mated £250,000, it had ended in a whimper, not a bang.'[30] The outcome gave particular satisfaction to Jeremy, who had carried the burden of the defence throughout weeks of gruelling cross-examination. His client had been confronted with charges that could have seen him jailed for half a lifetime. Now he was walking free, exonerated.

Prominent among the guests at the celebration party, which was held at a London pub on the evening of the verdict, were members of the jury, apologetic that they had felt obliged to return convic-tions under section 2 (the judge's summing-up left them little choice) but wholly sympathetic to the defendants' cause. (When recalling this Jeremy was at pains to register his disapproval of fraternizing with the jury!) The press was unanimous in its denunciation of the prosecution: 'Sam Silkin's Whitehall Farce' read the headline in the *Sunday Times*.[31] The *Observer* noted that 'the government's ham-fisted attempts to silence radical journalists on the subject of electronic intelligence have ended with almost nothing salvaged from the wreckage . . . After the pompous declarations of endangered national security which began the trial more than two months ago, it was a feeble anti-climax to a disastrous sequence of mistakes.'[32]

Why then were the charges brought? There was clearly a sensitivity akin to paranoia in official circles in relation to public knowledge of the operations of GCHQ. Duncan Campbell was a new kind of post-Watergate investigative journalist never really seen before. He and his like posed a direct threat to the secret state. It seems that the security services had made up their mind to punish Campbell for his authorship of 'The Eavesdroppers' article. The Berry interview provided the perfect opportunity.

The Special Branch officers who arrested the participants can only have known of the time and place of the interview, and that it was taking place at all, because the telephones of the leading protagonists had been tapped. 'The real problem,' as Geoffrey Robertson succinctly puts it, 'was that Duncan Campbell was a prodigy.' Campbell's scientific expertise and brilliant forensic perspicuity made him a figure to fear in official circles, because he discovered things that were meant to remain secret, and appeared willing to publish them. In the two years previous to Campbell's arrest, American journalists, untrammelled by any equivalent to the Official Secrets Act, had probed deep into the activities of the US secret services, and in particular the CIA. Their exposures had been extensive and shocking. Those in this country with an interest in keeping the British secret services secret were determined to stop the same thing happening here. But it was a losing battle, and the bringing of prosecutions such as the *ABC* case only hastened a process they were designed to halt. By the end of the trial Britain was a less secret country. Jeremy looks back: 'The public became aware at last of what our potential enemies had known for years, that GCHQ at Cheltenham was the centre of a surveillance and intelligence organization with a global network of listening posts. From that moment it became clear that this institution could be misused and could give rise to the dangers of the "surveillance state", with the ever increasing power of intrusion into our private lives.'

PART V

Mary Whitehouse v Jeremy Hutchinson

13

Last Tango

R v United Artists Corp Ltd (1974)

JEREMY'S SUCCESSFUL DEFENCE of the publisher of *The Mouth and Oral Sex* in 1971[1] saw the end of any further attempts by the prosecuting authorities to proscribe books that had any claim to seriousness of intent. From now on prosecutions under the Obscene Publications Act 1959 were confined to genuine pornography and the underground press. This disinclination to confront 'highbrow obscenity' extended to the cinema, which in the 1960s had begun its own process of radical experimentation and handling of subject matters previously deemed off-limits.

Such tolerance by the authorities gave rise to a new phenomenon: the moral crusader, willing to assume the mantle of upholder and protector of traditional standards against the depredations of the 'permissive society'. The leading proponent of this movement was Mary Whitehouse,[2] but in her wake were many others, impelled by the passionately held belief that the world needed saving from a rising tide of depravity and blasphemy.

Last Tango in Paris was the cinematic event of 1972. It starred Marlon Brando as a middle-aged American who, following the suicide of his wife, engages in a series of anonymous sexual encounters with a young French woman, played by Maria Schneider, in a Parisian apartment over a three-day period. The film was directed by Bernardo Bertolucci, Italian *auteur* of critically lauded art-house pictures such as *The Conformist* and *The Spider's Stratagem*, who also co-wrote the screenplay. Bertolucci later claimed that the idea for *Last Tango* had developed from a personal sexual fantasy. He said that he had 'once dreamed of seeing a beautiful nameless woman on the street and having sex with her without ever knowing who she was'.[3] The film was shot in Paris, and draws inspiration from the paintings of Francis Bacon. The predominant colours, 'rich oranges, light and cool grays, icy whites and occasional reds',[4] were drawn from Bacon's work. One can see in the film echoes of the great triptychs of the 1960s that Bacon made of his lover George Dyer. During the shooting of the film Bertolucci reportedly took Brando to the Bacon retrospective that was being presented at the Grand Palais in Paris, so that he could model his characterization of Paul on 'the figures that obsessively return in Bacon: faces eaten by something coming from the inside'.[5]

Having been banned in Italy, *Last Tango* was released in France in late 1972 to critical acclaim. Queues formed outside the picture houses where the film was being shown. Such was the excitement generated by the film's release that thousands of Spanish filmgoers circumvented a ban on the film in their own country (then still under the ultra-conservative rule of General Franco) by crossing the border to cinemas in Biarritz and Perpignan, in some cases having travelled hundreds of miles. The film was next released in New York in October 1972. High controversy ensued, with denunciation of the explicit sexual content of the film jostling for position on the pages of newspapers and periodicals with critical enthusiasm for the film's artistic merits. Vincent Canby, writing in the *New York Times*, identified the sex in the film as an artistic expression of 'the era of Norman Mailer and Germaine Greer . . . porno films and revolutionary semantics'.[6] The influential film critic Pauline Kael called *Last Tango* 'the most powerfully erotic movie ever made . . . October 14 1972 should become a landmark in movie history comparable to May 29 1913 – the night *Le Sacre du Printemps* was first performed – in music history . . . *Last Tango in Paris* has the same kind of hypnotic excitement as the *Sacre*, the same primitive force, and the same thrusting, jabbing eroticism. The movie breakthrough has finally come.'[7] Director Robert Altman was overwhelmed: 'I walked out of the screening and said to myself, "How dare I make another film?" My personal and artistic life will never be the same.'[8]

In Britain, the task of appraising the film's suitability for general release fell to the British Board of Film Censors (BBFC). Their decision was anticipated by the editors of the tabloid press who ran sensationalist articles on the film, describing its sexual content in lurid and often inaccurate terms. According to one account, *Last Tango* comprised 'a series of blistering sequences, guaranteed to knock the bottom out of the backstreet porno market'.[9] In the event the BBFC was surprised by the lack of 'gratuitous nastiness'. One board member, Tony Kerpel, noted that the 'sex is exercised with great restraint, a little too much in my opinion'.[10] In the course of their deliberations, members of the BBFC expressed concern about only two of the film's scenes. One involved 'very explicit sexual dialogue'; the other, a graphic depiction of sexual activity 'in which two characters employ butter as a sexual lubricant' – this was a reference to the notorious scene of anal intercourse: perhaps the most infamous sex scene in cinema.

It was decided to leave the dialogue intact on the grounds that it was difficult to edit it down without 'damaging an important part of the film'. The board did however decide to cut the length of the sex scene, which, it was felt, could be done without compromising the integrity of the film. A cut of twenty seconds was suggested, but after an appeal by the director, and negotiations between the secretary of the board, Stephen Murphy, and the film's producers, the cut was reduced to ten seconds – during which Brando appears to smear butter on Schneider's anus. The film was passed by the board on this basis as an 'X' on 16 February 1973.[11]

It was later admitted that the cut had been made at least in part to appease critics of the BBFC's recent classification approach on films such as Sam Peckinpah's *Straw Dogs*, Stanley Kubrick's *A Clockwork Orange* and Ken Russell's *The Devils*. As a concession it did little to assuage the outrage of moralists, who greeted the board's decision with fury. Mary Whitehouse called for the resignation of every member of the board on the grounds that their decision was evidence of a 'collective madness'. Supporters of the Festival of Light orchestrated the campaign against the film. This was an organization set up in early 1971 with the stated aims of protest against 'sexploitation' in the arts and media, and a return to the teachings of Christ as a means of restoring moral purity to the nation. Influential members included Mary Whitehouse, Malcolm Muggeridge and Cliff Richard.

The movement's inaugural rally took place at Methodist Central Hall on 9 September 1971 (setting for so many momentous events in this period, including the first public meeting of the Campaign for Nuclear Disarmament in 1958 and the theft of the World Cup in 1966). It was invaded by members of the Gay Liberation Front whose contribution to the proceedings involved turning off all the lights, sounding horns, and releasing mice.

Seventy regional Festival of Light rallies followed. On 23 September local members lit beacons and bonfires across the country in support of the movement. Two days later approximately 400,000 Festival supporters thronged to Trafalgar Square (where, almost exactly ten years earlier the Committee of 100 had organized a sit-down) where speaker after speaker denounced the commercial exploitation of sex and violence and called for a return to traditional Christian values. Proceedings continued later that afternoon with a Christian music festival in Hyde Park with star guests including Cliff Richard and the Irish songstress Dana.

Following the decision of the BBFC to pass *Last Tango* as suitable for adult viewing, responsibility passed to local authorities to decide whether to license the film for screening in their area. Supporters of the Festival of Light lobbied hard to persuade authorities to refuse a licence. They obtained a script of the film and sent it, with the most salacious parts underlined, to sympathetic MPs. The success of the Festival's campaign was demonstrated by the fact that approximately fifty local authorities banned the film.

Supporters of the film rallied to its defence. Stephen Murphy, the secretary of the BBFC, sent copies of favourable press reviews of the film to local authorities. The near unanimity of critical opinion in support of the film explains in part why many authorities, and most importantly the Greater London Council, resisted the pressure of the Festival of Light and licensed the film. Coach tours of '*Tango* tourists' travelling from 'censored' areas to more liberal jurisdictions to view the film showed up the absurdity of selective banning of the film, and undermined the Festival's campaign.

Festival disquiet simmered throughout 1973 as *Last Tango* continued to enjoy critical and commercial success. The moralists' campaign against the film entered a new phase at the end of that year when Edward Shackleton, a leading figure in the movement, decided to bring his own private prosecution against United Artists Ltd, distributors of the film in the UK. Shackleton was seventy, a retired social worker and former sergeant major in the Salvation Army. In early life he had worked for the Colonial Service as a district commissioner in Kenya. Of these years, Shackleton later recalled: 'I got into evil habits, led an immoral life and was addicted to impurity.'[12] He had suffered a mental collapse and spent a year in hospital where he found faith. Following his conversion Shackleton determined to devote the remainder of his life to God. He served with the Salvation Army for thirty years, and since his retirement had run a workshop for alcoholics. (It is notable how many moral crusaders have themselves passed through redemptive crises. The most famous litigant of the period, Raymond Blackburn, whose name appears throughout the law reports of the 1960s and 1970s, had himself emerged from alcoholism, bankruptcy and imprisonment for fraud to become the scourge of the liberal society: perhaps his most prominent moment was his attempt to have the proposed entry into the European Common Market declared illegal.[13])

Shackleton levelled two charges against United Artists in respect of their 'contract of hire' of the film to the Prince Charles Cinema in Leicester Square, a venue notable for its dedication to upmarket erotica. The charges, which were brought under the Obscene Publications Act 1959, were that United Artists had an obscene article, namely the film *Last Tango in Paris*, for publication for gain, and that they had 'published' it by 'letting the film on hire' to the cinema. At the time that Shackleton instigated the prosecution the film had been running at the Prince Charles for eighteen months and had been seen, nationwide, by about 2 million people.

While the newspapers were eagerly predicting a trial on a scale to rival the *Lady Chatterley* trial of thirteen years earlier, Jeremy was instructed by the leading City solicitors Richards Butler and Co. on behalf of United Artists. Richard Du Cann, his junior in the *Chatterley* case, was also instructed. (Jeremy notes that almost fifty years earlier his father, St John Hutchinson, had led Du Cann's father in another famous obscenity case, against the self-styled Count de Montalk.[14])

Legally, this was undoubtedly a first. Never before had a film been prosecuted for obscenity under the Obscene Publications Act. The case accordingly involved questions of law and statutory construction as yet unresolved by judicial determination. Since it was also the first time that a prosecution had been brought against a film holding a certificate from the BBFC, and in respect of a film licensed by a local authority (in this case the GLC), the status and legal authority of these entities were also brought into question.

When we were discussing this case Jeremy pulled out a sheaf of legal judgements that were generated by this case. 'Strange to say, *Last Tango* took me deeper into black-letter law than almost any other case I did.' He explains:

> In the *Lady Chatterley* case the only questions were whether the novel was, taken as a whole 'such as to tend to deprave and corrupt persons who are likely, having regard to all relevant circumstances, to read' it; and whether, even if it fulfilled that test of obscenity, it could nonetheless be said to be justified as being for the common good. But for *Last Tango* there was this subtle legal point which, if correct, would knock out the whole prosecution. To found an offence under the Obscene Publications Act it is necessary to prove that the defendant has 'published an obscene article'. That sounds simple enough but the word 'publish' was fraught with difficulty. Section 1 provides a series of definitions of the key words used in the Act. The word 'publish' or 'publishes' is defined in section 1(3) as follows: 'a person publishes an article who . . . (b) in the case of an article containing or embodying matter to be looked at . . . shows, plays or projects it'. However, the section then continued: 'Provided that paragraph (b) of this subsection shall not apply to anything done in the course of a cinematograph exhibition within the meaning of the Cinematograph Act, 1952'.
>
> Now at the time the quaint phrase 'a cinematograph exhibition' essentially meant showing a film in a public cinema. The point I wanted to argue was that section 1(3)(b) stymied any prosecution of the cinema itself when projecting the film for its paying audience. This is because it was not deemed to be a publication. Of

course it was true that my client – who was the distributor of the film – did not actually show the film in the 'cinematograph exhibition'. It was the owners of the Prince Charles Cinema who did that. But, so I thought, it would be absurd to have a situation where a distributor could be convicted of publishing an obscene film, when the cinema who actually showed the film to members of the public, whose morals the Act was designed to protect, was immune. Besides, it was clear that the only person to whom my client, the defendant distributor, had 'published' the film was the licensee to whom the film was let on hire, and there was no suggestion that his virtue had been imperilled – not least because the film was delivered in a closed canister! What I wanted to get across, convoluted as the point was, was that the 'publication' which my client was responsible for was not publication to the cinema-going population, who arguably would be 'corrupted and depraved' by the film, but the management of the Prince Charles Cinema, who patently were not. This was important because under the Act an 'article', whether it was a book or a photograph or a film was not per se obscene or not obscene. It was only to be judged obscene by reference to its likely audience – or as the Act put it 'persons likely to read, see or hear the matter contained or embodied in the article'.

This was the point argued by Jeremy at the committal hearing at the Marylebone Magistrates Court on 28 March 1974. Jeremy explains:

Although it was a rather abstruse point of law, it had huge ramifications. If it was right then distributors could very rarely, if ever, be criminally liable for the obscenity of any films they distributed to commercial cinemas. But despite my best efforts to persuade the magistrate, Mr Phipps, a former member of my chambers who I always found rather a bore, that the prosecution should be thrown out on the law, he refused – although he gave the impression of being sympathetic to our view of the law. As a result he committed the case to the Old Bailey. But I was worried about this case going to a jury so we took the rather unusual step of having another go at having the prosecution dismissed. Although I admired the film, there was a particular passage in it where the character played by Marlon Brando whispers various fantasies involving degradation of his anonymous lover, which I was very fearful of. In the film, what Brando says is quite difficult to follow, but the jury would of course be given the transcript where it was all set down. I could just see the prosecution poring over these words and the jury being horrified.

We came before the Lord Chief Justice, Lord Widgery. In refusing our application, Widgery gave reasons that actually appeared to favour an interpretation of the relevant sections of the Act quite different to that argued by me! It was very dispiriting and alarming for the film industry generally. What it seemed to mean was that although the cinema showing the film could not be prosecuted, the distributor could. However, thankfully the Lord Chief Justice made it clear that the views expressed by him on the construction of the relevant sections of the Act were not binding on the trial judge who was free to come to his own conclusion. This left the door open for me to argue, yet again, for a different result at the trial.

Widgery's ruling, which opened the door to private prosecutions against distributors, caused wide anxiety. It suggested that the existing classification system was overlaid with a further layer of potential censorship in the shape of the Obscene Publications Act. Nicholas de Jongh, writing in the *Guardian*, reported that Widgery's ruling had caused 'concern and doubt in legal circles . . . It must allow the chance of a multitude of private prosecutions. Mrs Whitehouse could well apply to have an "X" film seized en route to the BBC where it was being shown on late night television.'

What these reverses meant was that Jeremy had to prepare for a full-scale trial. In these days before the video-recorder many hours were spent in a private screening room studying the film almost frame by frame. The copy of the transcript which he still has is overscored with a mass of handwritten notes on each scene. 'I had to feel that I understood the film as completely as possible.' It will be remembered that Jeremy had founded the defence of Penguin Books in the *Lady Chatterley* case on the evidence of well-known and distinguished experts, to the effect that the publication of the novel was justified 'as being for the public good'. Jeremy and his team now set about the same task of identifying experts to support *Last Tango*.

We started with a preliminary list of potential witnesses included directors François Truffaut, Lindsay Anderson and Tony Richardson; actors John Mills, Laurence Olivier, Richard Attenborough, David Hemmings, Michael Crawford, Robert Shaw, Sean Connery, Roger Moore and Diana Rigg; playwrights John Osborne and John Mortimer; critics Kenneth Tynan and Dilys Powell; journalists David Frost and Bernard Levin as well as a variety of writers and clerics. I then went through the list and considered who would or would not be suitable. Those who were approached were asked to provide their views in writing on *Last Tango*. It was fascinating to read their analyses of the film. I always remember that the Rev. Paul Oestreicher, then a vicar in Blackheath, described the film as 'a powerful parable about human alienation and a compassionate study of sadness . . . this film at its best is a powerful sermon about hell, about man's isolation from his fellow man and from his true social purpose, that of loving. At its worst the story is a parable about the dead-end of sex without love, relationships without caring.' I thought that was so accurate. I thought the film was really far removed from pornography. There is really not a trace of eroticism in it.

Meanwhile Jeremy was also in touch with John Mortimer, who provided his own suggestions – though he wrote: 'I expect you have all the Profs, Psyches, and Revs lined up.'

The trial opened at the Old Bailey on 25 November 1974 before Mr Justice Kenneth Jones. It was billed by the newspapers as the most important obscenity case since *Lady Chatterley*. Looking back, Jeremy is inclined to agree with that assessment: 'Of course the press like to blow up the significance of these kinds of cases, but my feeling at the time was that *Last Tango* was such a significant film, both in terms of its stature as a work of art and in terms of its handling of sexual behaviour, that whether or not a jury ruled that it was obscene could have had a profound effect on the cultural values of the period.' In its account of the first day of the trial, the *Evening Standard* reported that Jeremy had 'objected to a number of middle-aged and elderly people who had been selected for the jury'. In its final composition, the jury comprised 'nine men and three women, whose ages ranged from 25 to 40'. (Jeremy explains: 'I just couldn't see anyone over the age of about fifty being particularly well-disposed to the film.')

Edward Shackleton had appeared as a litigant in person before the magistrates. Now he had managed to bring together a professional legal team, led by Robert Harman QC, to represent him in the trial. In opening for the prosecution, Harman told the jury that the film, which they would be shown in due course, contained scenes that they might consider highly indecent, but that was neither here nor there unless they found the film potentially harmful. 'The prosecution,' he continued, 'submits that this film is obscene because of the sadistic approach to sex which the character portrayed by Marlon Brando inflicts with violence and bestiality on the body of the girl.'

> He is determined not to know the girl as a human being, but as an object from which to get his own kicks. She is of an age to have been his daughter and he treats her as a sort of prey for sex without love or emotion – a distraction from his personal despair and perhaps a boost to his vanity. They have intercourse together against the wall of an empty apartment. Thereafter they meet frequently in the apartment so that he can repeat and vary their anonymous sexual experiences. There is then an occasion when he performs an act of sodomy on her, making her repeat, while he assaults her, such blasphemies and obscenities which on the spur of the moment he imagines.

Edward Shackleton was then called to the witness box, and gave evidence that he had seen the film at the Prince Charles Theatre in October 1973, having travelled to London from his home in Swindon for that purpose, with a view to bringing a private prosecution. He said that the responsibility for the prosecution was entirely his own, but that he had written to the police and the Director of Public Prosecutions before seeing the film. Jeremy then cross-examined him. He recalls: 'Even though we were on opposite sides of the courtroom, I had enormous respect for Edward Shackleton. He was a man who had a set of very sincerely held beliefs.'

JEREMY: Would you agree that Mr Brando is one of the most outstanding film actors in the world?

SHACKLETON: This was in fact the first time I had seen Mr Brando act. I don't go to the pictures.

JEREMY: Do the films *On the Waterfront* or *Mutiny on the Bounty* mean anything to you?

SHACKLETON: No.

JEREMY: If I put to you the names of any of the distinguished people who took part in the creation of this film they would not mean anything to you?

SHACKLETON: They did not mean anything then. Since then I have become more familiar with them.

Jeremy looks back on those questions and answers with a certain amount of embarrassment. 'It sounds as if I was trying to look down on Shackleton. But I had to convey to the jury the idea that the man who had brought this prosecution really knew nothing about the subject.'

At this point, reported *The Times*, the jury 'were sent home for the day while the judge heard legal arguments'. Jeremy explains: 'This was now the third time I was to set out our legal argument as to why, irrespective of the contents of the film, the prosecution had to fail. But, after Widgery had knocked us back, I was apprehensive that our judge now would feel constrained to follow his reasoning. It would require a brave judge to rule that the Lord Chief Justice was wrong in law.'

There followed a day and a half of legal argument in the absence of the jury. Mr Justice Kenneth Jones then ruled, in accordance with Jeremy's own reasoning, and in contradiction to the views expressed by the Lord Chief Justice, that the defendant's provision of the film to the Prince Charles Cinema under 'a contract of hire' could *not* amount to an offence under the Act, regardless of whether the film was obscene, and that there was therefore no case to answer. The judge instructed the jury to acquit, and the trial ended without further consideration of the 'obscenity' or otherwise of the film. Jeremy's experts were not called upon. 'In one way I was delighted that we had not had to await the jury's verdict and the case had been put to bed. But, of course, had the trial run its course I really think that it could have had almost the same significance for the 1970s that *Lady Chatterley* had for the sixties. There was obviously a little disappointment in not being a participant in such a case.'

Still, the outcome was a triumph for Jeremy. He received letters from the various expert witnesses who had, in the event, not been called upon to give evidence in support of the film. Dilys Powell, herself a veteran of the *Lady Chatterley* trial, wrote: 'It is true that I felt some apprehension about making yet another appearance at the Old Bailey! I can stand making an ass of myself, but one doesn't want to let the cause down. But apprehension was mixed with a kind of fearful joy . . .'

The *Sun*'s headline on the day following the judgement was 'Porn Row as Last Tango is Cleared'. The paper noted that while Shackleton 'refused to comment on the ruling', veteran anti-porn campaigner Mary Whitehouse was not so reticent. According to the *Guardian*, Whitehouse wrote to the Home Secretary immediately after the trial, saying that the obscenity laws had been shown to be 'wholly inadequate in protecting against moral pollution'. Given that the Home Secretary at the time was Roy Jenkins, the architect of the Obscene Publications Act, she can have had little hope of any alteration of the law.

Jeremy returned to the obscenity fray the following year, when he defended Classic Cinemas against another private prosecution, this time brought by Raymond Blackburn, in respect of the Swedish sex film *The Language of Love*. As we have seen, Blackburn was a reformer in the same mould as Shackleton. Since his own rebirth from years of alcoholism, Blackburn had started a new career as a moral crusader, and worked closely with Lord Longford on an anti-pornography platform. Blackburn had successfully prosecuted *More About the Language of Love* (*Mera ur Kärlekens Språk*), the second film in *The Language of Love* trilogy, before turning his attention to *The Language of Love* itself. At the trial at the Old Bailey in July 1976, Michael Coombe, prosecuting, alleged that the film, which depicted various types of sexual activity including oral sex and homosexuality, was 'disgusting, revolting and shocking'. For the defence, Jeremy argued that *The Language of Love* was a sex-education film designed to help sexual problems, and was not pornographic. The jury agreed: they acquitted the defendant after considering their verdict for only seventeen minutes. The judge, in a mark of his displeasure at the bringing of the action, awarded the defendant company its costs, to be paid out of public funds.

Jeremy looks back: 'I think these cases really stopped the moral majority bandwagon. Both were essentially serious films.' But the really titanic struggle with Mary Whitehouse was yet to come. When it did come it related not to the cinema, but the theatre.

14

The Theatre of the Absurd

R v Bogdanov (1982)

OR JEREMY THE early 1980s were dominated by an obscenity prosecution that generated a maelstrom of controversy on a par with that produced by the *Lady Chatterley* case twenty years earlier. The newspapers were full of heated agitations for and against the central protagonists. Passions ran high and much ink was shed in anger. Indeed, judging by their letters pages, a significant portion of the theatre-going public was also drawn into the fray. This time the arena was not the printed word but the stage. But the stakes were equally high. The case set up a mirror to the cultural wars of the period just as the *Chatterley* case had done. But, before the curtain is raised, let us start with a short prologue.

The English theatre was, for many centuries, subject to its own special censorship rules. The effect of the Licensing Act 1737, which had been introduced in response to Henry Fielding's lampoons on the Prime Minister Robert Walpole, was to give to the Lord Chamberlain, a medieval royal office that can be traced back at least to 1399, the power to prevent, or impose cuts on, any proposed public theatrical production 'for the preservation of good manners, decorum or of the public peace'. A list of the Lord Chamberlains of the twentieth century gives an insight into the type of man who was charged with the task of theatrical censorship: the last to exercise these powers was Lord Cobbold, a former chairman of the Bank of England not renowned for his interest in the theatre or insight into public morals. The attribute enjoyed by these men that qualified them to decide what could and what could not be seen by English theatre audiences was not apparent during the period of their office and is still less apparent now.

The Lord Chamberlain's fate as national censor was finally sealed by the production, in 1965, of Edward Bond's *Saved*. The play, a sort of dissection of urban alienation, which includes a notorious scene of disaffected south London youths stoning a baby to death in its pram, was submitted for approval. Five weeks later Bond was informed that that scene would have to be removed entirely as a condition of a licence for production. Refusing to bow to the Lord Chamberlain's edict, the play was instead performed at a private 'theatre club', temporarily set up at the Royal Court (all that happened was that the audience joined up as members for the evening), a then standard way of attempting to evade the requirement for a public licence.[1] This device did not work; police officers managed to see the play and the director was prosecuted for publicly presenting an unlicensed performance. He was convicted, but the agitation that ensued over the long arm of the Lord Chamberlain stirred Parliament to action. It was in any case inevitable that this clanking relic of the past would fall victim to Roy Jenkins's new-broom programme of social reform in the 1960s. The Theatres Act 1968 abolished the Lord Chamberlain's role. Section 1 was headed in very clear terms: 'Abolition of censorship of the theatre'.

Although the Lord Chamberlain's sway was brought to an end, the 1968 Act did make it an offence to stage a performance of a play that was 'obscene'. The definition of that word derived from Jenkins's earlier Obscene Publications Act: 'a play shall be deemed to be obscene if, taken as a whole, its effect was such as to tend to deprave and corrupt persons who were likely, having regard to all relevant circumstances, to attend it.' And the defence of 'public good', which had been so successfully deployed in the *Lady Chatterley* case, together with the right of the defence to call experts to speak to the artistic, literary or other merits of the play in question, was imported into the later Act too. Apart from that, the Act ensured that all the old common law offences relating to the performance of plays that might be indecent, offensive, disgusting or injurious to morality were abolished. The Act went even further. By section 8 it required the consent of the Attorney General to bring any proceedings for obscenity.

In what was a final – if Canute-like – gesture of defiance, the Lord Chamberlain's last act before he was neutered as a public censor was to refuse a licence to 'The American Tribal Love-Rock Musical' *Hair*. Its eventual opening in London was delayed until after the passing of the Act, but it went on to have a London run of more than 1,700 nights. More than ten years of artistic freedom followed. There were virtually no prosecutions under the Theatres Act. It appeared that rationality had at last become embedded in the regulation of theatrical performance.

Then, in 1980, the National Theatre decided to perform a play co-written by the leading theatrical iconoclast, Howard Brenton, who had earned recent notoriety with his play *A Short Sharp Shock*, put on at the Royal Court in June 1980. An attempt at anti-Thatcher satire, one particular scene that had excited hostile critical reaction was of the ghosts of Airey Neave and Earl Mountbatten, both recently murdered by the IRA, appearing on stage 'clutching their *disjecta membra*'.[2]

This did not dissuade the National Theatre from commissioning Brenton's next play, to be staged in the most hallowed theatrical space in England, the Olivier. *The Romans in Britain* was primarily set in 54 BC, during the second incursion by Julius Caesar into England. A sprawling behemoth of a play, with roles played by thirty actors, the action jumps from Roman soldiers hunting out Celts, to the first Anglo-Saxon invasions in the early sixth century, and on to present-day Northern Ireland, the stage peopled by British soldiers and IRA Provos. The perhaps clunking premise was that each territory is a victim of colonial despoliation; the plight of late twentieth-century Catholic Belfast dwellers analogous to the indigenous Britons during the Roman invasion. Brenton explained that the idea for the play started with an image of Caesar walking towards a dead Celt with a knife in his hand. 'Just that.' He told Peter Hall his idea, and Hall commissioned the play. The thesis of the play was that 'all empire is bad. The Republican cause is just. The border is a crime.' Hall had slated himself to direct the play but, in the event, he was detained in New York with *Amadeus* and Michael Bogdanov, recently named Director of the Year at the Laurence Olivier Awards for his *Taming of the Shrew*, took up the reins.

Classified adverts that appeared in the newspapers in the days leading up to the first performance rather ominously noted 'Not suitable for children'. As it proved, in the eyes of many, this warning was couched too narrowly. *The Romans in Britain* opened on 16 October 1980 to the greatest furore in the National Theatre's history. There was almost universal opprobrium from the critics. The normally sympathetic Ned Chaillet, writing in *The Times* the next day, concluded that although there were ideas in the play that deserved an airing, 'there were so many misjudgements in the writing and the production that it was difficult to determine where things really went wrong.' Other reviews were more vitriolic. Milton Shulman, writing in the *Evening Standard*, urged the National to remove *Romans* from its repertoire as soon as was decently possible. The liberal-minded James Fenton, writing in the *Sunday Times*, described it as 'a nauseating load of rubbish from beginning to end'; it was not just unsuitable for children – 'it is unsuitable for anyone'. Michael Billington, temperamentally inclined to support Brenton's work, felt obliged to register his own disapproval in the *Guardian*: 'I accept totally that Mr Brenton finds the hunger for empire anathema; but in order to savage such a crucial historical phenomenon I suggest you first have to understand it.'

One scene that particularly mesmerized critics and audiences alike, was Act 1, Scene 3. Marauding Roman soldiers happen upon three young Celtic druids, skylarking after a swim. Two are killed by the legionnaires and the third – Marben – is attacked and knocked unconscious. He is held down by two of the soldiers and is subjected to an attempted buggery by the third, who is now naked. Michael Bogdanov explains:

> I staged the scene uncompromisingly, centre stage, in the bright white light of the midday sun. It was shocking, but it was meant to be. The issues were confronted, not fudged. After seeing a run-through of the play in its late stages, Peter Hall questioned Howard and myself on the wisdom of the staging. Could it be set upstage, in the leafy shadows behind one of the large trees constituting the forest clearing? We replied that to do so would make the scene more salacious and titillating, and would be dodging the issue – as if we were afraid of what was the most important scene in the play, its central metaphor. Peter accepted the argument, agreeing that it was fully justified in the context.

The precise actions on stage were to be controversial, but the script ran as follows:

> THIRD SOLDIER: Arseful of piles. Like fucking a fistful of marbles.
> I mean, what do they do in this island, sit with their bums in
> puddles of mud all year long?
> [He stands.]
> Huh.
> [He looks at himself.]
> And I'm covered in shit.

In all the attempted buggery lasted some thirty seconds in a play of almost three hours. But it was undoubtedly a harrowing scene. On one night a hapless woman in the audience was heard to cry out, 'Oh no, I can't believe it.'[3]

But it was not this scene that prompted the collective outpouring of critical venom. The point was summed up by Sheridan Morley, writing in the *International Herald Tribune*:

> What we have is a rambling three-hour catastrophe. The fact that
> the leader of the GLC has threatened a withdrawal of subsidy, thereby
> allowing the National's Sir Peter Hall to climb on a high horse
> labelled artistic freedom, disguises the true problem, which is that
> the play is shocking not sexually but theatrically. Scenes of nude
> homosexuality and rape are, in the end, less disturbing than the idea
> that a National Theatre Board of Management could seriously consider
> allowing a ragged and threadbare pageant of early British history (the
> kind that got school plays a bad name 30 years ago) to be loosely
> yoked to a superficial account of the current Irish troubles in the
> name of contemporary drama.

The play, and in particular Act 1, Scene 3, had attracted attention from other quarters. It was reported on 18 October that the Obscene Publications Squad was to investigate a complaint against the play made by Mrs Mary Whitehouse. Mrs Whitehouse's complaint was based solely on her reading of the London evening newspapers; she had apparently decided that it was out of the question to go to see the play itself. This intervention prompted John Mortimer QC, a member of the National Theatre board, and, as we have seen, ascribed by Mrs Whitehouse the moniker of 'the Devil's Advocate' (in honour of his reputation for stout defending in obscenity trials[4]), to state that a prosecution under the Theatres Act was unlikely and could not succeed: indeed Mortimer had advised the National in advance to the same effect.

It is difficult now to convey fully the extent of Mary Whitehouse's influence in the England of the 1970s. A former art teacher who had become concerned by what she saw as the pernicious influence of television on the moral compass of the young, she founded the National Viewers' and Listeners' Association (NVLA) in the early 1960s with a view to campaigning against the portrayal of sex and violence on screen and radio. Reviled and mocked by the liberal elite,[5] nonetheless her integrity of purpose cannot be doubted. Public support for her stand against what she saw as the erosion of traditional values attracted huge support.[6] Her most recent private prosecution had been against the editor of *Gay News* for publishing a poem entitled 'The Love that Dares to Speak its Name', which, as it was drily described in the law report, 'purported to describe in explicit detail acts of sodomy and fellatio with the body of Christ immediately after his death'.[7] The case had gone as far as the House of Lords and she had emerged triumphant. Notwithstanding that he was always sitting on the other side of the court from her, Jeremy himself had developed a certain affection for Mrs Whitehouse. He regarded her as a doughty opponent who retained a mischievous sense of humour. 'She always gave me a friendly smile when I came into court.'

Meanwhile the play encouraged a heated correspondence in *The Times*, with the forces of liberalism and conservatism struggling to outdo each other with displays of moral outrage, either in denunciation of the play itself, or of the attacks on it. Here was the chairman of the GLC, Sir Horace Cutler (who had made a great show of walking out halfway through the first night), making dark suggestions that it was inevitable that the GLC, which funded the National to the tune of a grant of £630,000 a year, should 'consider its position'. While he doubted 'whether anyone would seriously suggest that one lapse of judgment should condemn the National Theatre to eternal financial limbo', nonetheless 'short rations often clear the head'. This letter was apparently preceded by a telegram sent by Sir

Horace to his fellow knight Sir Peter Hall castigating the play as a disgrace. Edward Shackleton, leading member of the executive committee of the Festival of Light,[8] and unbowed by his failure to prevent the distribution of *Last Tango in Paris*,[9] wrote to 'absolutely deny the oft-repeated plaint that no one should criticize a play or film unless they have seen it'. Harold Hobson, the doyen of drama critics, then weighed in to deny categorically that there was anything in *The Romans in Britain* that was as revolting as what happened to Gloucester in *King Lear* or Oedipus in *Oedipus Rex* – 'Yet even schoolchildren are quite justifiably urged to see these plays.' Hobson concluded that the climax of the first act was as 'fine and thunderstriking' as anything seen or heard on the London stage for a very long time. The debate extended into Parliament. Norman St John-Stevas, author of the bill that became the Obscene Publications Act, and witness for the defence in the *Lady Chatterley* trial, was now Arts Minister. He found himself the subject of outraged questions from Tory backwoodsmen. Yes, he said, he found the play 'extremely bad, scatological and somewhat offensive', but he was against 'suppression and censorship'.

Needless to say, while the debate intensified (it was reported that the Festival of Light had even asked the Charity Commission to rule whether the National Theatre had broken its responsibilities as a charity), ticket sales were reported to be brisk. Touts were apparently able to achieve mark-ups of 100 per cent and more. The run was extended into December.

The police having proved supine, Mrs Whitehouse was prompted to take, once again, the law into her own hands. The standing counsel to the NVLA, John Smyth QC, was duly dispatched to put his own moral integrity in jeopardy by attending a performance; it survived and he was able to announce after the ordeal that he was in 'no doubt' that the play constituted a prima facie breach of the criminal law. Next, Mr Graham Ross-Cornes, Mrs Whitehouse's solicitor, and a foot-soldier in the NVLA, was sent to see the play, a visit that would later be subject to a detailed forensic investigation at the Old Bailey. A letter was sent by the NVLA urging Sir Michael Havers QC, the Attorney General, to take action against the play. John Mortimer's advice proved prescient: the DPP, Sir Thomas

Hetherington, announced that he had advised Havers that the play did not contravene the Theatres Act. No prosecution would therefore be brought under the Act for obscenity. This would not be the Attorney General's last appearance in the saga that was unfolding.

Mrs Whitehouse publicly ventilated her rage against Havers. 'Just what has got to happen on the stage before this man will act? What will be the next performance? Will it involve violation of children?' But she was not to be thwarted by the pusillanimity of the law officers. Fresh from the success of the *Gay News* case, she decided to re-enter the lists as a private prosecutor.[10] First, she was refused permission to bring a private prosecution for obscenity under the Theatres Act. This reverse did not dim Mrs Whitehouse's resolve. Rather, it prompted her to undertake some digging around in the statute book. She and her legal team happened upon a crime that had been created by section 13 of the Sexual Offences Act 1956: 'It is an offence for a man to commit an act of gross indecency with another man, whether in public or private, or to be a party to the commission by a man of an act of gross indecency with another man, or to procure the commission by a man of an act of gross indecency with another man.'[11]

It seemed that this offence had not been affected in any way by the Theatres Act, largely because it had been overlooked by the draughtsman; or more probably it had never occurred to him that it could possibly be applicable to a theatrical production of simulated acts. As one newspaper commented, it was a law that was meant to apply to homosexual behaviour in London's public lavatories, not to simulations of events from the Roman invasion on the stage of the National Theatre. Bringing a prosecution under this provision did not require any form of permission from the law officers. Mrs Whitehouse was free to proceed as a private prosecutor, without oversight. 'She found a little chink in the law, and, quick as a field-mouse, she nipped through it.'[12] Publicly stating that she considered it 'of the utmost importance that the courts should have the opportunity to adjudicate on the play', she issued a summons against Bogdanov in the Horseferry Road Magistrates Court. What she alleged was that he, as director, had, in the language of section 13, 'procured' an act of 'gross indecency' between two men, by directing the two actors playing the Roman soldier and the Celtic druid (Peter Sproule and Greg Hicks) to simulate an act of buggery on the stage of the National Theatre.

The absurdity of the situation was stark. Section 13 of the Sexual Offences Act had never been invoked against a play or against an act simulated for the purposes of an artistic production. The crime with which Mr Bogdanov was charged was one that could only be committed by a man. So, had the director been a woman no case could have been brought, regardless of the fact that the actual events on stage remained the same. Furthermore, the case could not have been brought had the simulated rape been a heterosexual one. Most worryingly, under section 13 the defendant had the benefit of none of the safeguards created by the Theatres Act: a prosecution did not require the permission of the government law officers and a defendant could not rely upon a 'public good' defence. But whatever the absurdities swilling around the prosecution, for Michael Bogdanov Mrs Whitehouse's decision was deadly serious. The maximum sentence, if he were to be found guilty, was two years' imprisonment.

Jeremy and Geoffrey Robertson were briefed as counsel for Bogdanov. Jeremy had attended the opening of the National Theatre in 1976 and had seen the first production ever put on at the South Bank, Beckett's *Happy Days*, in which his former wife, Peggy Ashcroft, had played Winnie. He knew Max Rayne, the chairman of the board of the National Theatre, and was an old friend of Peter Hall. More importantly Jeremy was, with John Mortimer, the doyen of obscenity cases. It was immediately agreed that Jeremy was the obvious choice of leading counsel to defend Bogdanov.

At that time the defence could require the prosecution to disclose its evidence at the committal stage. If it appeared unsatisfactory, whether on the facts or as a matter of law, the defendant could submit to the magistrate that the case should not be committed for trial at all. So, in Horseferry Road Magistrates Court on 29 June 1981, the committal proceedings against Bogdanov started. As the proceedings opened Michael Billington, writing in the *Guardian*, described the case as the most important of its kind since the *Saved* prosecution in 1966. Mr John Smyth QC opened Mrs Whitehouse's case. He described the offending scene and continued:

> We then come to the act of gross indecency alleged. The second soldier raises Marben's buttocks by putting his arms round his torso and raising him up in that way. The third soldier, who is completely naked by this time, turns somewhat away from the audience but can be seen quite clearly to be making masturbatory movements as he is turned away, and then he turns back to face the audience and he is holding his penis in an apparently erect position. He then goes to the back of Marben . . . He places his penis between Marben's legs from behind and makes a number of thrusting movements. This takes place in the bright light of centre stage and there is no doubt that an act of buggery is simulated.

The prosecution's only witness was Graham Ross-Cornes, who described what he had seen on stage on the night of 19 December 1980. Jeremy's cross-examination revealed the gulf between two world-views. What was painfully clear was that Ross-Cornes knew nothing about modern drama; knew nothing about Bogdanov's and Brenton's eminence, and virtually never went to the theatre.

> JEREMY: What you are doing, Mr Ross-Cornes, you and your client, is simply finding a way of circumventing [the prohibition contained in the Theatres Act]?
>
> ROSS-CORNES: No, sir. If this act took place in the street it would clearly be an offence and I cannot see that there is any difference that it takes place on the stage of the National Theatre . . .
>
> JEREMY: You would agree with me, would you not, that something might be unacceptable, indecent, in one context, and perfectly valid in another?
>
> ROSS-CORNES: No, sir.
>
> JEREMY: You would not agree?
>
> ROSS-CORNES: No, I think an act of gross indecency is an act of gross indecency wherever it takes place and in whatever context.

Jeremy decided to call Sir Peter Hall as a witness, to enlighten the magistrate as to the reasons for commissioning the play, the choice and status of directors at the National, and their role in the production of plays. This was important because a central element that the prosecution had to prove was that Bogdanov had actually 'procured' what the two actors had done on the stage. Hall explained to the magistrate the serious message of the play and that Bogdanov had been selected as a brilliant young director who had taken Hall's place when he found that he was required to be in New York because of the success of *Amadeus*. Critically, he told the magistrate that a director at the National did not procure anyone to do anything. A play has a written script, the director will discuss with the cast his ideas as to how the script should be best delivered to the audience, and during rehearsals the cast and director move to a consensus on the most satisfactory and faithful presentation. Here the author had written a violent scene where a man attempts to rape another man and fails in his attempt. The actors and director, following the stage directions, did their best to enact exactly that. Hall was candid in his evidence about that scene. He was aware that it would arouse controversy: 'I thought it would be found horrifying, as I think the gouging-out of Gloucester's eyes in *King Lear*, for instance, is horrifying, but the scene in question is in my view a precise and inevitable metaphor about the brutality of colonialism where the other side, the other race, becomes not a human being at all but simply plunder.'

It was eloquent and straightforward evidence. And it revealed a fascinating conundrum about the case. If a simulated rape performed on stage could, in the eyes of the law, be an act of gross indecency then would a simulated killing be an act of murder? The prosecution counsel, perhaps realizing that the more time he gave this lion of the stage to respond to the case against Bogdanov the clearer its underlying absurdity would become, shied away from any direct confrontation. Nonetheless, what emerged was that Mrs Whitehouse's case that Bogdanov had somehow 'procured' this act was feeble.

Reporters present during the hearing described the magistrate, Kenneth Harrington, looking increasingly agonized and ground down as the proceedings continued. Jeremy had insisted that he read the whole play overnight. The next day Harrington had a haggard, resigned look. Jeremy closed with a counterblast, inviting the magistrate to dismiss the summons as a blatant attempt to circumvent the Theatres Act. The preamble to that Act describes its purpose as an Act to abolish the censorship of theatrical productions. He taxed the magistrate with the absurdity of a situation where, had Mr Bogdanov been Ms Bogdanov then no offence would have been committed. Moreover the word 'procure' involved an element of persuasion, recruiting or inducement. This case, on the facts, was a mile away from that. If *Hamlet* was performed was one to say that the director had procured the death of Polonius? Nonetheless Harrington, taking the path of least resistance, and acknowledging the illogicalities surrounding the prosecution, ruled that the case should go to trial.

The competing camps now settled down to prepare for the battle to come. This time it would be before a jury in Court 1 of the Old Bailey, but not before a phony war of nine months had elapsed. One cannot overestimate the significance that the theatrical community attached to the prosecution which was now to be heard at a full trial. A Theatre Defence Fund was founded, raising over £10,000 for the defence costs. In support of the fund, Brenton embarked on a tour of regional theatres giving one-man readings of the play. There was a staged reading at the Old Vic, with proceeds going to the fund. The Oxford Playhouse planned to conduct late-night readings of the transcript after each day of the trial.

Again, just as had happened twenty years earlier in the defence of *Chatterley*, Jeremy had lined up several dozen witnesses for the defence, each to be called to speak to the integrity and seriousness of purpose of the play and playwright. Lord Olivier, Janet Suzman, Felicity Kendal, John Mortimer, Trevor Nunn, Peter Brook and Lord (Arnold) Goodman were all on the cast list. But there was a real question mark over whether these witnesses would be allowed to give evidence. This was a prosecution under the Sexual Offences Act and therefore, as we have seen, there was no provision for evidence of 'public good'.

During its run *The Romans in Britain* had provided marvellous copy for the cartoonists (in the *Evening Standard* a tremulous actor is shown waiting in the wings muttering, 'I'm buggered if I'm going on there'). Now it had achieved sufficient notoriety that it was being parodied on the London stage. The Collegiate Theatre was running *The Mad Show*, a 'riot of non-stop laughter featuring Mr Loonyverse' performing 'The Outrageous Romans in Britain Cha Cha'.

★

And so, on Monday, 15 March 1982, Jeremy found himself once again in Court 1 of the Old Bailey, preparing to defend an imagined act of buggery; or more precisely in this case attempted buggery. The trial had been billed as 'the most important case in the history of modern British theatre', and certainly the public interest was as great as in the run-up to the *Chatterley* trial in October 1960. In anticipation of the start of the trial, the press slavered over the prospect of a clash between the redoubtable Mary Whitehouse and the degenerate forces, as many commentators saw it, of the National Theatre. And for Jeremy the case had added piquancy. This was not just a straight fight between the forces of reaction and progress. Here the play had attracted hostility from all quarters. 'The protection of free speech is all the more difficult, but all the more necessary, where the speech in question cannot claim the protection of unequivocal artistic quality.'

The judge chosen to hear the case was Mr Justice Staughton, only forty-nine and appointed to the High Court bench just the year before after a career practising commercial and admiralty law. Educated at Eton, he had served in the 11th Hussars and listed his hobbies in *Who's Who* as bridge and growing dahlias. He was also a lay preacher. It was reported that an anonymous QC had described him as 'an extremely nice, decent, sensible man, of extremely limited experience in criminal law and, I think, fairly religious'. When Geoffrey Robertson had told Jeremy of the choice of judge he had exploded. 'Never heard of him, and I've been at the criminal Bar for forty years!' When Jeremy discovered that Staughton had written a book on shipping law, involving the law of bottomry,[13] he quipped: 'Ah, that's why he's been sent down to try this case.'[14]

John Smyth QC had been taken ill and his place as prosecutor was taken by Ian Kennedy QC. The case opened to a packed courtroom but with one notable absentee. Mrs Whitehouse was nowhere to be seen; it was said she had decided to remain at her home throughout the trial to pray for victory. As Mr Kennedy ran through the now familiar narrative of druids and soldiers he remarked that no doubt the defence would call a litany of 'experts' to justify the production and the scene in question. Jeremy rose to his full height to object to the prosecution's speculation about what evidence might or might not be called on behalf of the defence. 'My Lord, I have not come to any conclusions at all as to what evidence may be introduced by the defence.' The judge commented, 'Lord Hutchinson, I think Mr Kennedy was simply firing a shot across your bows.' It was the moment to make a joke: a joke not necessarily in good taste, but a joke that would start the process of establishing the absurdity of the allegations and of winning the sympathy of the jury. Jeremy retorted: 'In this case, My Lord, I might have expected a shot across my stern.' The judge's expression showed blank astonishment. It became known later that the judge was deeply shocked by his remark. 'So this is how advocates at the Old Bailey behave.' But Jeremy had obtained his first smile from the jury.

Just as at the magistrates court, Mrs Whitehouse called only one witness. Her case began and ended with the faithful Mr Ross-Cornes's testimony. Jeremy then got up to cross-examine. Geoffrey Levy, writing in the *Daily Express*, described him vividly: a tall, lean figure, with 'an air of languid tenacity', he put his questions to Ross-Cornes with 'the sonorous voice of an actor reading a Keats poem' and with the 'air of a man for whom the law no longer held any surprises'.

The cross-examination that followed is surely one of the most hilarious exchanges ever to take place in Court 1 of the Old Bailey. For a defendant, any allegation of a crime is no laughing matter. But, Jeremy comments, 'Sometimes to laugh a case out of court is the best way to help your client. It must always be, however, a very sensitive matter of judgement. The danger is that a jury will treat the case more seriously than the advocate.' He decided, after assessing Ross-Cornes's performance in the magistrates court, to take the risk. It was a move that turned out to be decisive. Jeremy started by asking Ross-Cornes whether he believed that there was any difference between indecency or foul language on stage, in the street, at a garden fête or at a 'vicar's tea party'. The answer, familiar from the committal proceedings, came back:

ROSS-CORNES: Something is either grossly indecent or it is not. The reason why people are doing it does not affect whether it is gross indecency in the eyes of people who are seeing it. [Gasps from the public gallery.]
JEREMY: Supposing a man and woman were making love on the

stage or on film. It is a very different situation from them doing it on the pavement, is that not right?

ROSS-CORNES: I think the degree of indecency would be the same, wherever it takes place.

As to the blinding scene in *King Lear*, Ross-Cornes explained that he had never seen the play (more gasps), but it was his view that it would be horrifying whether it was done on stage or at the vicar's tea party.

JEREMY: Would you also agree with me that homosexuality was not condemned historically in the time of the Roman Empire as an aberration?

ROSS-CORNES: I don't know about that.

JEREMY: This play, being about invasion, did it occur to you that this particular scene was symbolic?

ROSS-CORNES: It did not at the time.

The Olivier Theatre was and remains the largest theatre in England. It had been Ross-Cornes's evidence that he had distinctly seen a penis being held in an erect position by the third Roman soldier as he advanced towards Marben. This seemed somewhat far-fetched. Could it be true? Jeremy produced a plan of the theatre. It was solemnly handed to the witness. Where precisely had Ross-Cornes been sitting? The solicitor, slightly flustered, placed a cross on the plan and handed back the paper. 'I see,' Jeremy noted wryly. The cross showed that Ross-Cornes had been in the upper circle, the very furthest recess of the theatre and a full ninety yards from the stage. 'Mrs Whitehouse was only willing to pay for a ticket in the upper circle!' Appropriately enough, not far from the gods, as some-body later quipped. 'Did you bring a pair of binoculars with you?' (Laughter in court).

JEREMY: You sat in the back row! You go to this theatre, knowing your task is to collect evidence for a very serious prosecution of my client, a man who has never committed a single offence in his life, on a very nasty charge, and you sit in the back row.

ROSS-CORNES: Yes.

And then a change of tack:

JEREMY: Do you go to the theatre *much*, Mr Ross-Cornes? [The 'much' was accentuated, 'his Bloomsbury voice rising in mock-horror', as Geoffrey Robertson recalled.]

ROSS-CORNES: Not very much. I like to go to pantomimes and such like.

JEREMY: You know that theatre is the *art of illusion*?

ROSS-CORNES: If you say so, Lord Hutchinson.

JEREMY: And as part of that illusion actors use physical gestures to *convey impressions* to an audience?

ROSS-CORNES: Yes, I would accept that.

JEREMY: And from the *back row, 90 yards from the stage*, you can be certain that what you saw was the tip of the actor's penis?

ROSS-CORNES: Well, if you put it that way, I can't be absolutely certain. But what else could it have been?

Jeremy then did something that it can safely be said will never again be enacted in the Old Bailey. On the spur of the moment he placed his hand by his fly and stuck out his thumb. He veiled the hand with his gown. Bogdanov explains: 'Fist balled, thumb protruding, jammed into his crutch, Lord Hutchinson thrust away to the astonished and barely concealed amusement of the members of the jury, demonstrating exactly what Peter Sproule the actor had been doing: bunching his fist up and hitting Greg Hicks's thigh with his thumb.' 'Can you *see*, Mr Ross-Cornes?' asked Jeremy. The myopic solicitor blinked. Jeremy then swung round and let his gown loose. 'Are you sure you did not see the tip of the actor's thumb, Mr Ross-Cornes, as he held his fist over his groin – like *this*?' The witness gaped. He stuttered. He gasped for words. 'Well, I might have been mistaken.' Geoffrey Robertson himself later recalled that the 'jurors stared transfixedly at the QC's simulated erection'[15] while the rest of the court erupted in laughter. As for the judge, he remained stony-faced.

As the bedraggled solicitor limped from the witness box Jeremy made a submission of no case to answer. Having heard the barristers the judge then gave three rulings on the legal points argued by Jeremy. None of them augured well for the defence or indeed for the English theatre generally: first, said the judge, in a voice described by one journalist as like 'the sound of a wellington boot being extracted from deep mud', the Sexual Offences Act could indeed apply to events on stage;[16] second, he ruled that a simulated sexual act could still amount to gross indecency; third, he decided that the motive of sexual gratification was not an essential part of the offence.

Still, given the farce of Ross-Cornes's evidence, was it really likely that a jury would convict? Certainly it did not seem so to Mrs Whitehouse's counsel. And it was at this moment that the trial took yet another extraordinary turn. Ian Kennedy asked the judge for a short adjournment. He then asked to see Jeremy privately and told him that he had decided to withdraw the prosecution. He offered two explanations: first that Mrs Whitehouse's real purpose was to obtain the legal rulings from the judge confirming that just because a sexual act was simulated on stage did not mean that it was immune from the reach of the law; and second that Mrs Whitehouse had no wish to ruin the career of an obviously sincere man such as Michael Bogdanov.

Jeremy was used to hearing many different public explanations given by prosecutors for discontinuing prosecutions. In fact prosecuting counsel usually follow an admirable tradition at the Bar that if he or she at the close of the prosecution case takes the view that the evidence before the court at that stage is insufficient for a jury safely to convict, counsel is under a professional duty to seek leave to withdraw the case, a request that is invariably granted by the judge. In this case the evidence had been destroyed, and the judge's rulings were probably untenable on appeal. Jeremy's view is that Kennedy behaved in 'the best traditions of the Bar'.

The lawyers re-entered the court. Kennedy informed the judge that he was withdrawing the prosecution. What happened next was unprecedented. Staughton, having just given the green light to the continuation of the trial, took Kennedy's announcement badly. No, he would not allow the prosecution to be abandoned; he required it to continue and Kennedy's decision was 'misconceived and inappropriate'. Jeremy protested. 'With the greatest respect, it is not for Your Lordship to substitute your view for that of prosecution counsel.' He had already informed his client that the prosecution was no longer proceeding. It would be quite wrong to allow the case to continue in those circumstances. The judge was unmoved. 'That is my ruling.' Geoffrey Robertson and Jeremy went into a huddle to ponder their next move. How could they stop a prosecution that the judge required to be continued? The only possible solution was to attend the Attorney General's office in the Law Courts in the Strand and apply for a *nolle prosequi*,[17] a somewhat arcane procedure whereby the Attorney General is able to take over a prosecution and, if he sees fit, bring it to an end. So counsel repaired to the Strand. As Sir Michael Havers had already refused Mrs Whitehouse permission to prosecute under the Theatres Act, it was not surprising that he at once granted the application, and a case that should never have begun came to its sorry end.[18]

The prosecution had become a farce. It was ordered that the defence costs should come out of central funds. As for Mrs Whitehouse, she would have to bear her own costs, rumoured to be nearing £20,000. She attempted to put a brave face on the situation. She claimed, bafflingly, that it was 'a great day for the country and the theatre'. The judge's rulings had vindicated her stance. She had made her point. Now she could return to her garden in Colchester. 'All I wanted was a point of law. What the judge has said has established that an act of gross indecency can be committed on the stage. That was more important than whether we won or lost. It will stand as a backstop to help theatre managements, directors and writers understand what the law is . . . It is now for other people to act. It won't be Mrs Whitehouse on the back of theatre managements. It will be the law.' In fact the reality was that Mrs Whitehouse had become a laughing stock and this was all so much cant. The decision to stop the prosecution had been taken by Ian Kennedy alone.[19] In respect of her costs Whitehouse could only say that 'God would provide.' But presumably not the God worshipped by the chaplain to the National Theatre, Rev. Eric Mathieson, who, as the *Sunday Telegraph* reported, 'bursting to make a speech', denounced Mrs Whitehouse's 'spiritual fascism'. His rodomontade continued: 'Her claim to have the whole nation's moral conscience in her handbag must be resisted. There is a lot of support behind her, I know, but it is a vicious minority. Mrs Whitehouse has got a good deal of egg on her face today whatever she says – alleluia.'

The case and its chaotic collapse brought to an end Mary Whitehouse's career as a private prosecutor. The fact that there was no reference at all to the case in her next instalment of memoirs, published in 1985, speaks volumes. The case also sounded the death-knell to any further attempt to censor the theatre. Not one prosecution has ever been brought against a play since.[20] It is fortunate that Staughton's rulings on the compass of the Sexual Offences Act remain of interest only as footnotes to this extraordinary piece of legal history.

It is easy to look back on the case and treat it as a light-hearted 'Whitehouse farce'. But that is not how the protagonists saw it at the time. Geoffrey Robertson, himself a bruised veteran of the *Gay News* case, records that he was very nervous of the result. Many in the theatre world were fearful that in the event of a conviction a new era of self-censorship would prevail. And for Bogdanov, facing a two-year sentence if convicted, the prosecution was anything but a laughing matter. 'I was labelled a pimp. I found myself sitting in the dock of Court 1 of the Old Bailey, six months after it had been occupied by Peter Sutcliffe.' He had to endure sixteen months of anxiety between the launch of the prosecution against him and its final conclusion. His own reaction once the case was over veered from relief (there was a photograph of him having a celebratory drink on the balcony of the National Theatre) to unvarnished anger that, because of the withdrawal of the case, he had been deprived of his own day in court: the opportunity to explain himself to the jury and to the public at large. The outrage he must have felt was expressed by Jack Tinker, writing in the *Daily Mail*. In order to pursue her aim as censor of the theatres and the screen, Tinker wrote, Mrs Whitehouse had 'put a respectable married man through untold worry, misery and shame. While he sat in the well of the court, close to his counsel, the tall, urbane and patient Lord Hutchinson, Michael Bogdanov heard himself lumped together in the sight of the law with pimps, procurers and sleazy *madames*.'

As for *The Romans in Britain*, the play was finally revived in 2005, at the Sheffield Crucible, by Samuel West. A spokesman for Mrs Whitehouse's organization, now renamed Mediawatch-UK, was reported as saying: 'Any revival will have to take 1982 very seriously. The precedent set then still stands, so they'll have to consider if it's worth including this scene.' West duly ignored what Staughton had said twenty-three years earlier. There was no prosecution.

Postscript by Jeremy Hutchinson

WHEN THOMAS GRANT first approached me with the idea of writing this book my reaction was equivocal. I believe that the life of the criminal advocate is enjoyably ephemeral. No memorial is left behind and in the words of the greatest advocate of my time, Norman Birkett: 'The thing said can never be separated from the moment of its saying or from the person saying it and any attempt to recapture the fire and glow of past moments is foredoomed to failure.' Tom was persistent. 'Many of your cases throw light on a period of revolutionary change in society, and surely the record would be of lasting interest to your family.' Hard work has never been my idea of life in my nineties but nonetheless I agreed.

The writing, research and choice of case have been entirely Tom's. My part has been to dig out what documents and memories I still retain, to live up to the high standard of accuracy demanded, and to enjoy what has been a rejuvenating walk down memory lane.

No one becomes a criminal barrister to make large sums of money. A criminal practice has always been the least well paid and of the lowest status at the Bar. Yet in my opinion the rewards are of the greatest. You practise in circumstances that seriously affect your fellow human beings in their personal and everyday lives. Your clients are of every kind, privileged or deprived, bewildered and weak, or streetwise and strong. Each day you are coping with judges, magistrates, witnesses, police officers and your colleagues, and above all the jury, that great organ of the disestablishment and pillar of our democracy. You are confronted with their foibles, prejudices and demands. You are privileged in your work; privileged because, first, it falls to you to uphold at all times the principles of justice and the rule of law, and, second, unreservedly to uphold the interests of your client whose case becomes yours. You share for a short time the intimate life of a person in extremis and stripped bare whose reputation, livelihood or liberty have been placed in your hands.

Advocacy is the art of persuasive and attractive speech. Nowadays the student must attend many hours of 'advocacy training'. Indeed the main remaining role of the Inns of Court now appears to be just that. The upholding of integrity, duty to the court, the overwhelming importance of preparation, mastering the law and the facts, can all be taught. But, as Lord Birkett once pointed out, how can one teach that skill that could win from the diarist John Aubrey – when speaking of Lord Chancellor Bacon – the comment: 'It was the fear of all who heard him that he would make an end', or from Pitt the Younger, when replying to an expression of surprise at the huge reputation of Charles James Fox: 'Ah! But you have never been under the word of the magician.' There lies the Art of Advocacy.

How did I learn to practise this art? My father St John (Jack or Hutchie as he was known) was an outstanding criminal advocate. He died at the early age of fifty-eight in 1942 and I never heard him conduct a case. The first time I saw him in court was at the age of eleven when I was taken into Court 1 at the Old Bailey to hear his leader Norman Birkett QC plead in mitigation for their client Clarence Hatry in a famous case of fraud before Mr Justice Avory. Even then I was struck by the beauty of Birkett's voice in contrast to what seemed to me at that young age the cruel and ice-cold tone of the judge, as he passed a maximum sentence of fourteen years' penal servitude.

My father at no time encouraged me to follow in his footsteps and supported me in my original ambition to work with the League of Nations. It was only when I was at Oxford that I suddenly realized that my roots were too deep in my own country and that I would never be happy living abroad. As a result I changed course and decided to follow the same path as my father. Before qualifying in 1939 I managed to go as marshal to a High Court judge, on three occasions, sitting in the Assize Courts on three different circuits in England. This gave me the invaluable experience of observing the practice of advocacy in a great variety of cases from the judge's bench, and later hearing the judicial view on the qualities, or the lack of them, of the advocates appearing before him.

Sitting on the judge's left, I witnessed the dreadful ritual of the passing of the death sentence. 'You shall be taken to a place of execution and hung by the neck until you are dead,' followed by the comforting contribution of the judge's chaplain, sitting on the judge's right: 'Amen.' This experience later made me an active supporter of abolition.

I was called to the Bar in April 1939, but instead of donning my wig and gown I volunteered to join the Royal Navy, as war then seemed inevitable. So it was not until 1946 that I conducted my first case in an English court at the late age of thirty-one. However, I believe uniquely in the history of the Bar, the first case I conducted as a barrister was the prosecution of a murder. In 1944 I was serving as a signals officer on the staff of the C-in-C Mediterranean at Allied HQ in Caserta outside Naples in Italy when a naval rating went AWOL, joined three other servicemen from the US and Canadian armies, and while living rough in the Italian countryside had been present when another serviceman was killed by the gang. Each service was responsible for bringing its own servicemen to justice. When it was discovered that I was the only qualified lawyer on the staff, I was ordered to prepare and conduct the case. This I proceeded to do, acting as solicitor and barrister, discovering relevant witnesses, taking statements, employing interpreters, studying the law, and eventually appearing before a hastily convened naval court martial of five senior naval officers in full regalia in a converted and suitably grand room in the San Carlo Opera House in Naples. The defendant, in due course, was convicted and later dispatched by a naval firing squad: a different type of capital punishment.

Demobbed in 1946, I joined my father's old chambers in the Middle Temple, first as a pupil to James Burge, who later was to represent the unfortunate and persecuted Stephen Ward. Burge was a cultured man of spirit and humour, never the master of complex or 'heavy' cases, but in the great mass of less serious offences an outstandingly successful jury advocate. From him I learned the advantages of a light touch, good humour, a sense of fun, when appropriate, brevity and sincerity. Through Burge I came to see the wisdom of the old adage: 'Only ask the question to which you know the answer', to which I added later my own rule: 'When you get the wrong reply look as though it was precisely the one you were expecting.'

In the fourteen years before I took silk in 1961, I built up a practice in the criminal courts of London and to a lesser degree on the Western Circuit, where I was soon to be appointed counsel to the Post Office, prosecuting dishonest postmen on the one hand, and representing the National Union of Railwaymen defending allegedly dishonest railwaymen on the other. In this way I practised the Art of Advocacy. Unlike barristers today I received no training. I learned it from my pupil master and in the cauldron of the London magistrates courts. Ninety per cent of all criminal cases are tried in these courts, which in my time were tried by professional stipendiary magistrates, now called district judges. I made it my job to get to know these individuals and the legally qualified clerks who sat beneath them, and also the jailers who ruled the fascinating kingdom below the court where defendants who had been refused bail would assemble awaiting trial.

I always made a point of arriving early for my case, sitting quietly in counsel's seats, so that I could observe the manner in which the 'Beak' dealt with the stream of guilty pleas by prostitutes, street-traders, shoplifters and the like, a parade of the underprivileged and unfortunate in each area of the capital. I could assess the mood and character of the person who was to judge my client: their prejudices, qualities and deficiencies, even sometimes their interests, particularly in cricket. 'You may think, sir, that the reply of my client to the officer's question knocked back his middle stump.' Sometimes I would hear from the clerk that the Beak wanted to get away early to the Oval for the test match, in which case a quick plea of guilty to a lesser offence might be rewarded with a probation order or a small fine.

Trial by jury, of course, plays a central role in the life of a criminal advocate. When a person's liberty is at stake guilt or innocence is generally decided, not by a tribunal chosen by the state, but by twelve independent citizens chosen at random, who bring transparency and the involvement of the public into the criminal process. Applying the relevant law as explained by the judge, this lay jury has complete power to return the verdict that they consider proper in the particular case. Sometimes they return a verdict that is not strictly in accordance with the law: a 'perverse' verdict that accords with their own view of what is fair and just. They give no reasons and cannot be questioned by anyone afterwards – not even by the most respectable and conscientious academic researcher (a protection which I had a hand in when the Contempt of Court Bill was being debated in the House of Lords). It is this independence and immunity that is the ultimate guarantee of our freedoms and liberties and justifies Lord Devlin's description of trial by jury as being 'the lamp that shows that freedom lives'. Each juryman will be subject to his or her own prejudices, emotions, doubts and certainties, and to the same pressures and demands on the society in which we all live. The advocate who appears before a jury to plead his client's cause therefore should have an understanding of the Zeitgeist – the spirit of the age – and a deep interest in human nature. Juries are remarkably conscientious: they respond to pleas for fairness, for courage, for independence and the overcoming of prejudices, especially when there is a need to resist the pressures of an interfering judge.

Trials will often have moments of drama and, from the theatre, timing, projection and the use of the voice can be learned. But the fundamental difference between actor and advocate must never be forgotten: whereas the actor must lose himself and become somebody else, the advocate must always be him or herself. To copy or adopt the mannerisms or conduct of someone else in court is at once to lose all credibility. However unlikely or unattractive a defendant's case may be, the advocate's incentive throughout has to be the achievement of justice, the recognition by the jury that there is always another view to that put forward by the prosecution; for example, the old lag with many previous convictions set up by the police or the over-trusting solicitor employed by an overpowering and glamorous tycoon, who signs a fraudulent document without reading it through. Each illustrates the danger of presuming guilt. Brilliance in cross-examination is often emphasized in an advocate's performance; yet greater skill is often demanded in 'examination in chief', that is the process by which the defendant's evidence is initially presented to the jury before it is subject to hostile attack by the prosecutor. It is this process where the defendant is introduced to the jury, where the essential channels of his story are navigated, avoiding the shoals and rocks, yet never hiding them away only to be revealed in cross-examination. Time spent with the client before trial is never wasted. What lies behind the exterior? What needs to come out and what needs to be toned down? If there is a weakness that might lead to a disaster in cross-examination, better to bring it out and treat it with sensitivity in telling the story.

It is a trite thing to say but I found that it was preparation that so often wins or loses cases. The less the advocate looks at his papers during the trial the more attention he will be given. The facts must be absorbed. This will free up the advocate to think and act while on his feet during the trial. As the evidence unfolds, one comment, one aside, one negative when an affirmative was expected, may alter the whole complexion of a case. Suddenly an unexpected fact may emerge like the sun looming from behind a cloud. A long-prepared plan or argument may have to be jettisoned and something quite new substituted on the hoof.

Preparing a cross-examination of a witness who, if your client's case is true, must be giving false or inaccurate evidence may require long hours of thought and preparation. In my day there was much corruption in the Metropolitan Police. There was clearly close contact between many officers and the press. Defendants were repeatedly said to have made confessions or statements indicating guilt when in custody at the police station. Threats were made to 'nick' the wife or remove the children unless the defendant 'cooperated'. Much of such behaviour was privately justified by the perpetrators on the basis that the police knew from intelligence sources (informers, inadmissible evidence etc.) who the villains were and having to prove guilt beyond reasonable doubt was often an impossible task. Successfully to cross-examine an untruthful and experienced officer, well practised in giving seemingly credible evidence repeatedly before a case-hardened stipendiary magistrate, required a high degree of skill, in many cases very much more than when disputing an allegation of fraud or rape in a higher court.

Decisions have to be made how to run a case. Should it be given a high profile, requiring strong confrontation, an attitude of disbelief or even anger at the treatment of the accused; or would it be wiser and more effective to keep a low profile and an almost invisible presence, asking few questions and ultimately submit to the jury that there was no real evidence of guilt? In many cases it may be better to let the jury themselves draw favourable conclusions rather than spend time ramming home pleas for them to do so. Words are the ammunition of the advocate; simple but telling words placed in the right order. It is remarkable how powerful words can be. A love of literature and an appreciation of the written word, that which Norman Birkett refers to as the 'well-stocked mind', make a good background for an advocate. As an advocate I always wished that I had been better read.

There is a strong vocational element in our work: a desire to help people assert and protect their civil rights and defend them from the ever increasing power and intrusiveness of the executive; and, at the same time, when that power is properly exercised, to ensure that it is done with humanity and respect for the rule of law. When at long last in 1950 the Legal Aid Act was passed, the idea was that everyone should be able to obtain legal advice if unable to pay for it because, after health, the most important element in a civilized society is the ability of every citizen to assert and protect these rights: in other words 'a national legal service'. So there sprang up, across the country, the high street solicitor, often a single lawyer with staff. Anyone could enter the office and obtain a short preliminary legal opinion and advice. Such a practitioner would earn a modest income but provide an essential public service. Then came the Citizens Advice Bureau and the local law centre staffed by volunteer lawyers, and the legal aid advocate at the Bar. From the start the Bar was determined that the public should have the services of the best and not just the youngest or least successful (as in the USA) and, in my day, it was well understood that every criminal advocate would do a percentage of legally aided work throughout his or her career. In addition the advocate would observe the 'cab rank rule': you take the next brief offered however unpalatable it may be. The cost of this provision of course increases each year, not because of the grasping lawyers, but because of the increasing awareness of injustice in society, the continuing intrusion of the state into people's private lives, and the torrent of legislation creating new offences that continues to flow unabated. Yet compared to health and defence the cost is small.

This book was conceived as something of a celebration of the practice of advocacy in the second half of the twentieth century. Now, in 2015, it may appear more as a valediction to a process that has successfully been brought to an end: a goodbye to an era now seemingly long gone.

I read the headlines 'Is the Criminal Bar on the Brink of Extinction?'; 'Is the Criminal Barrister an Endangered Species?'; 'Is John Mortimer's Rumpole a Dying Breed?' From my own limited researches the answer seems to be 'Yes: indeed.'

When the chips are down, when executive power in the form of Lord Hailsham's elective dictatorship – the whipped and docile party majority in the House of Commons – becomes excessive, all that stands between the citizen and the all-powerful state is the judiciary, the jury and the wholly independent advocate. To undermine the ability of the advocate to practise, to remove the advocate's independence and access to the public, is the first act of the autocrat as we see across the world. As Thomas Erskine said when defending Tom Paine's book, *The Rights of Man*: 'From the moment that any advocate can be permitted to say that he will or will not stand between the crown and the subject arraigned in Court . . . from that moment the liberties of England are at an end.'

In 2003 Tony Blair, supporting his autocratic and oppressive Home Secretary David Blunkett, without consultation or advice, sacked his protesting Lord Chancellor, Lord Irvine, and abolished the office itself. Thus, on the whim of an arrogant and power-hungry politician the second greatest office of state was destroyed, after 800 years. The Lord Chancellor was the head of the judiciary: he sat in the Cabinet at the centre of power; he represented justice and the rule of law, and made sure that ministers respected that rule. He was a central pillar of our unwritten constitution.

Of course the presence of an unelected judge amid a group of democratically elected politicians was on the face of it an anachronism. But the modern 'acceptable' replacement turns out to be but a puny shadow of the past: enter Mr Grayling, whose job before entering Parliament is recorded as 'management consultant', a transient workaday politician on his way up the political ladder, Minister of Justice with the title of Lord Chancellor. With no experience of the law, no knowledge of how the criminal process works, no understanding of the delicate checks and balances we have put in place over the last fifty years to bring justice to all people, in the exercise of his 'management' skills he has deliberately destroyed the present system and in doing so in all probability the proper functioning of the criminal Bar. Provision of legal aid has been reduced to a ridiculously small number of franchised providers. Rates of pay have been cut by 42 per cent and are based on the type of offence involved. Providers will now have a strong commercial incentive to brief in-house advocates to keep the fee within their own firms. Already 50 per cent of prosecutions in the crown courts are conducted by civil servants, and nearly 50 per cent of all pleas of guilty by in-house solicitors belonging to a new and woeful species, the 'plea only' advocate. Now criminal barristers practise far less in the magistrates courts, where I learned my advocacy, and where so many unnoticed miscarriages of justice occur, and in parts of the country they only appear in the crown courts if privately funded. The Jeffrey Report,[1] from which my figures are taken, says that advocacy standards have fallen and the courts are finding it increasingly difficult to do their job.

Mr Grayling also seized on the embryonic Public Defence Service (the PDS), consisting of salaried and pensionable advocates, which was set up in 2001. Run by his department, he has expanded it as a safe haven for independent self-employed advocates who can no longer afford to practise and young practitioners seeking security: a state prosecutor (the CPS) to face a state defender (the PDS) in a safe and cosy relationship. Independence, choice, competition will have no place in this new subservient and managed brave new world. Types of offence can never measure the seriousness of an offence. A teacher falsely accused of assault by a child, a black student stopped and searched at night and having drugs planted in his car by a dishonest police officer, a civil servant falsely charged with indecency in a public lavatory may all be involved with a minor offence, yet each faces devastation in their life and requires the services of an advocate of the highest skill to bring justice and salvation. Such skill may be far higher than that required in a simple case of murder or fraud and cannot be measured by the number of documents involved or the hours of work required. Further, it should be said this calling is not a mere 'add on' to an in-house lawyer's demanding work within a firm. It is a highly responsible and whole-time profession in itself.

The final blow to independence is QASA, the 'Quality Assurance Scheme for Advocates' which will require a five-yearly assessment of every criminal advocate's competence, skills and suitability by the judiciary – the judges before whom the advocate performs in court. Not only will counsel now have to bow to the organization to which he or she may belong but also to the views of the presiding judge. The judge at a trial represents justice and for that reason, and not for his personal qualities, counsel defers to all the judge's rulings in court and shows the judge respect. In all other respects the advocate is the equal of the judge and it is counsel's professional duty to stand up to an interfering or overbearing judge in the interests of the client. In future it may well be in counsel's professional interest to toady to the judge to advance his career at the expense of the client. I cannot help but think that the response of F.E. Smith or Marshall Hall to such an unworthy proposal would have been to call for a QASA for the judges, managed by the advocates. I doubt I would ever have passed an assessment examination by the judges sitting at the Old Bailey.

Now we live in different times. As barristers' chambers amalgamate and are run as businesses, as self-employed barristers increasingly join firms of solicitors and are allowed to have direct access to the client without the need to be briefed by a solicitor, it would seem inevitable that for all those either committed or confined to doing publicly funded work, the two sides of the profession must start to fuse. We will finally move to the American-style system that has for so long seemed to be on its way, and which we have so stoutly resisted. For those with wealth a small and no doubt elite private criminal Bar will survive to serve them. Indeed that section of the Bar may thrive. For those of modest means or low income, their lot, as in the States, will be to be prosecuted by the state prosecutor (for which read 'district attorney') and defended by the local Public Defence Service advocate or his near cousin, the franchised in-house advocate (for which read 'public defender'). Do we really want a system in which the criminal advocate only serves the affluent?

No doubt the next target will be the jury, 'a luxury that we can no longer afford'. Its privacy, it will be said, is no longer sustainable and the historic ban on all research into its deliberations will be described as no longer in tune with the modern concept of transparency. A recent attack has been upon the other constitutional process whereby the judges, on behalf of the public, hold government and other public bodies to account as to the legality of their operations – Judicial Review. Here Mr Grayling describes the process as 'a promotional tool for countless left-wing campaigners' and is happily trying to legislate to reduce its availability in his own direct interest as a minister, causing Lord Woolf, one of the finest judges of my time and a former Lord Chief Justice, to describe his conduct as 'contrary to the rule of law', and adding the withering comment: 'If the government had understood judicial review they could not possibly have brought in the changes to legal aid . . . I fear it is due to ignorance and it underlines the need to understand what you are doing.'

Finally, because he stood in the way of the government's plan to repeal the Human Rights Act, the experienced and competent Attorney General Dominic Grieve QC was removed from his office as legal adviser to the government and was replaced by a junior barrister: an ex-government whip, promoted from his job as Under-Secretary of State in Mr Grayling's own Ministry of Justice. The new Attorney General was hastily made a QC, without having to undergo the lengthy and demanding qualifying process normally required by the Queen's Counsel Appointments Selection Panel. Upon resuming private practice he will of course bear the magic letters 'QC' after his name.

I eye my eight volumes of Campbell's *Lives of the Chancellors* and open Volume I to read: 'No office in the history of any nation has been filled with such a long succession of distinguished and interesting men as the Lord Chancellor and Lord Keeper of the Great Seal of England.' I reflect upon the irony that this process of destruction has been managed by a minister of justice whose official oath requires him 'to respect the rule of law' and 'defend the independence of the judiciary' and 'to ensure the provision of resources for the efficient and effective support of the courts.'[2] Not only that, but one who has a duty also to uphold article 6 of the Human Rights Convention: 'Everyone charged with a criminal offence has the following minimum rights: . . . to defend himself in person or through legal assistance of his own choosing, or if he has not sufficient means to pay for legal assistance, to be given it free when the interests of justice so require.'

All this in the name of saving money. To save many millions of pounds the Ministry of Justice has only to attend to another area of its responsibility: the crisis in our intolerably overcrowded prisons. The prison population has now grown to over 85,000 (it was 46,000 when I retired). Each of these prisoners costs the taxpayer around £40,000 a year to keep. The 'warehousing' and humiliation of offenders in grossly full and inhuman conditions make meaningful education, constructive work, rehabilitation and self-respect impossible. It produces inevitable recidivism and lowers the morale of the overworked and dedicated staff. Governors repeatedly point out that they have to cope with thousands of inmates who should not be there at all: the mentally ill, the drug takers, those serving indeterminate sentences under a law now long repealed, unconvicted defendants in custody awaiting trial for minor offences for which they clearly will not receive a custodial sentence. On top of all this costly new prisons are being built to absorb the relentless flow. Real prison reform calls for imagination, courage and determination; the dismantling of legal aid a mere stroke of the pen.

My profession has given me the most rewarding, enthralling and happy working life and I am sad to write this valediction. My words may be described by some people as those of a 'foolish, fond old man'; the silence of the senior judiciary and in particular of the Lord Chief Justices gives some credence to this view. Nevertheless I hope that this book will interest and amuse the reader – and be a warning too.

Jeremy Hutchinson
March 2015

Acknowledgements

Along the way Jeremy Hutchinson has become a great friend and an enormous inspiration to me.

The following have been very generous with their memories of Jeremy and the cases he was in, and I thank them all: Jonathan Aitken, Sir Geoffrey Bindman QC, Michael Bogdanov, Duncan Campbell, Margaret Drabble, John Ford, Christopher Kypreos, David Leigh, John Mathew QC, Geraldine Norman, David Posnett, Michael Randle, Geoffrey Robertson QC, Christopher Sallon QC, Brian Sewell, Robin Simpson QC, Stephen Solley QC, David Whitehouse QC.

Mark Holmes of Queen's College, Oxford, was very generous with his research into the *Sunday Telegraph* case.

Juliet Nicolson was godmother to the book and I owe her a huge debt of gratitude. My agent Caroline Dawnay and my publisher Roland Philipps of John Murray have been wonderfully supportive. I thank them for believing in this book.

I would also like to thank my friends Charles Anson, Edward Bindloss, Edmund Cullen, Mark Davies-Jones and Peter Zombory-Moldovan who read parts of the text with great care and made invaluable suggestions.

Greatest thanks must go to my wife Hester, without whom this project would never have been completed, as only she knows.

Illustration Credits

Notes

Jeremy Hutchinson: A Biographical Sketch

1. Now Prince Albert Road.
2. Michael Holroyd, *Lytton Strachey*, vol.2, pp.342–3. See also the description in Osbert Sitwell, *Laughter in the Next Room*, pp.16–23: 'All equally, soldiers, Bloomsbury beauties, and conscientious objectors – all except Diaghilew – danced. I remember the tall, flagging figure of my friend Lytton Strachey, with his rather narrow, angular beard, long inquisitive nose and air of someone pleasantly waking from a trance, jigging about with an amiable debility. He was, I think, unused to dancing.'
3. Hutchie is frequently mentioned in Cooper's letters to her son John Julius Norwich, published as *Darling Monster* (London, 2013).
4. In an unpublished letter to St John Hutchinson, D.H. Lawrence described Mary as 'one of the few women left on earth who actually listens to a man'.
5. *Letters of T.S. Eliot*, vol.1: *1898–1922*, ed. Valerie Eliot.
6. And see Chapter 11 below.
7. In the third volume of his autobiography *Downhill All the Way*, Leonard Woolf describes St John Hutchinson's heroic but futile submission when presenting the appeal of the self-styled Count Potocki de Montalk against his six-month prison sentence for publishing allegedly obscene poems – free translations of Verlaine and Rabelais.
8. Eliot, op. cit., p.473.
9. Sitwell, op. cit., p.22.
10. *Harold Nicolson's Diaries and Letters 1930–1939*, vol.1, ed. N. Nicolson, p.259.
11. Philip Toynbee, *Friends Apart*, p.50.
12. See generally Martin Green's *Children of the Sun*, p.327.
13. Isaiah Berlin, *Flourishing*, p.153.
14. *Harold Nicolson's Diaries and Memoirs 1930–1939*, vol.1, p.260.

15. She would go on to marry Jo Grimond in 1938.

16. He was killed in action on 11 August 1940.

17. In turn Maria Huxley would, in a letter, describe Jeremy in ecstatic terms: 'an adorable boy . . . very amusing and intelligent . . . I'd like to keep him here for ever' (see Sybille Bedford, *Aldous Huxley*, p.369).

18. Then the Dorset home of 'Bobbety' Gascoyne-Cecil, the 5th Marquess of Salisbury, a friend of Jeremy's father. Churchill was an occasional guest there in the 1930s.

19. Baron Rothschild was then head of the explosives and sabotage section of MI5.

20. On the McGilvary murder see generally Andrew Clark, *A Keen Soldier*.

21. See Tony Benn, *Years of Hope*, p.91.

22. Rebecca West writes about Rose's case in *The New Meaning of Treason*, pp.136–9.

23. For an account of the trial, which (understandably) horrified England at the time, see L. Fairfield and E.P. Fullbrook, *The Trial of John Thomas Straffen* (London, 1954).

24. Montagu writes about Jeremy's conduct in his autobiography, *Wheels Within Wheels*, p.108.

25. 10 April 1954, p.456.

26. In response Koestler wrote Jeremy a postcard bearing just three words – 'Gut gebrüllt, Löwe' ('Well roared, lion!').

27. Gerald Gardiner would become Lord Chancellor under the Wilson administrations of 1964 to 1970. His modesty is revealed in the letter he wrote to Jeremy when he was elevated to the House of Lords: 'I think that the thing is intended to be a job of work and not as an honour and I don't suppose that I shall be any good at it.'

28. A. Goodman, *Tell Them I'm on My Way*, p.257.

29. Clifford Luton, *Daily Express*, 16 July 1963.

30. The newspapers reported Jeremy's question to his client, Mr Roche: 'We know you were impartial politically because one canister landed on the Government side and one on the Opposition side.' There was sustained laughter in court when Roche replied, 'That's just what happened, sir.'

31. It is one of the anomalies of the Bar that barristers were, until very recently, unable to sue for their fees. Not getting paid for work done is one of the barrister's perennial anxieties.

32. The case was the subject of a book, *Smoke without Fire*, by Alfred Draper.

33. See Chapter 12 below.

34. See Chapter 12 below.
35. HL Deb, 12 March 2001, vol. 623 cc547–548.
36. See Chapter 12 below.
37. It is quoted in full in a NCCL monograph by Harriet Harman and John Griffiths, *Justice Deserted*.
38. It eventually became section 8 of the Contempt of Court Act 1981: 'Subject to subsection (2) below, it is a contempt of court to obtain, disclose or solicit any particulars of statements made, opinions expressed, arguments advanced or votes cast by members of a jury in the course of their deliberations in any legal proceedings.'
39. HL Deb, 20 January 1981, vol. 416 c372.
40. 10 July 1981.
41. Lord Hailsham had opposed Jeremy's proposed amendment.
42. See Chapter 7 below.
43. Stirling had to cater for Jeremy's demand that visitors to the new gallery must have contact during their visit with the world beyond the gallery and a view of the river: see Frances Spalding, *The Tate*, p.212.
44. It was Jeremy's decision to invite Cooper, perhaps the world's leading expert on Cubism, to curate the exhibition. He had been *persona non grata* at the Tate since an altercation with John Rothenstein, then the director of the Tate Gallery, in the 1950s, which led to physical violence between the two men.
45. Spalding, op. cit., p.209.
46. His retirement was delayed because of the controversy arising when the chairman–elect, Peter Palumbo, was quoted as having made certain critical remarks about the management of the Tate.
47. A younger member of his chambers wrote that Jeremy had been practically 'beatified' by his colleagues. David Whitehouse QC, whom Jeremy led on a number of occasions, commented to me on the great lengths to which Jeremy went to help and encourage junior members of his chambers.

Chapter 1: 'Lose his sanity or gain his freedom'

1. Sir Malcolm Hilbery, *Duty and Art in Advocacy* (London, 1946), p.8.
2. See Lord Hailsham's account in his memoirs, *A Sparrow's Flight* (London, 1990), p.367.
3. In fact these demands were wholly unjustified given that Carrington had only assumed this post in October 1959.

4. See generally John Bulloch and Henry Miller, *Spy Ring: The Full Story of the Naval Secrets Case* (London, 1961). No fewer than three accounts of the case had been published before the end of 1961.

5. Quoted in Rebecca West, *The New Meaning of Treason* (New York, 1964), p.290. Bruno Pontecorvo was an Italian physicist who became a British citizen and was working on the atomic bomb project before defecting to the Soviet Union in 1950.

6. Dominic Sandbrook, *Never Had it So Good: A History of Britain from Suez to The Beatles* (London, 2005), p.633.

7. For a detailed account see the excellent Roger Hermiston, *The Greatest Traitor* (London, 2013) and H. Montgomery Hyde, *George Blake Super-Spy* (London, 1987). Blake published his own autobiography in 1990, defiantly titled *No Other Choice*.

8. Blake, op. cit., p.86.

9. Philip Deane, *I was a Captive in Korea* (London, 1953). Jeremy later quoted these words in his speech in mitigation.

10. Blake, op. cit., p.142. An alternative theory is that the Russian secret service actively recruited Blake, to compensate for the gap in intelligence that followed the break-up of the Cambridge spy ring. Of the ring's three principal participants, two, Guy Burgess and Donald Maclean, had fled to the Soviet Union six months earlier. The third, Kim Philby, was under suspicion, and at that time of little use. Russian sources claim that a young Soviet agent, Nikolai Andreyevich Loenko, attached himself to the group of British and French diplomats being held by the North Koreans, for the purpose of discovering potential spies. According to this theory, Blake 'came over' after having been groomed by Loenko in meetings that took place over a period of several weeks.

11. Hermiston, op. cit., p.157.

12. Blake, op. cit., p.164.

13. Hermiston, op. cit., p.201.

14. The friendship is the subject of Ben Macintyre's recent book, *A Spy Among Friends: Kim Philby and the Great Betrayal* (London, 2014).

15. Hermiston, op. cit., p.222.

16. Blake, op. cit., p.192.

17. Ibid., p.197.

18. Ibid., p.198.

19. *The Macmillan Diaries*, vol.II, ed. Peter Caterall (London, 2011), p.380.

20. The D-Notice (now D-A Notice, or Defence Advisory Notice) was, and remains, a mechanism whereby an official request is made to news

organizations not to publish or broadcast items on specified subjects for reasons of national security. The notice carries no legal authority and compliance is voluntary.

21. Hermiston, op. cit., p.233.
22. At the time the leading criminal firm in London. It still maintains a very high reputation in the field.
23. The Rose case is considered by Rebecca West, *New Meaning of Treason*, pp.136–9.
24. Blake, op. cit., p.203.
25. See Chapter 4 below.
26. Blake, op. cit., p.203.
27. Patrick Devlin, *Easing the Passing* (London, 1985), p.39.
28. Parker's conduct during 'Lucky' Gordon's appeal in 1963 lends support to Jeremy's suspicion that he had discussed Blake's case with the Attorney General before the trial. The Stephen Ward case, and Parker's role in it, is described in Geoffrey Robertson's book, *Stephen Ward was Innocent OK!* (London, 2014), p.88ff. See further Chapter 3 below.
29. Though White would later express his 'shock' at the sentence: Tom Bower, *The Perfect English Spy: Sir Dick White and the Secret War 1935–1990* (London, 1995), p.269.
30. HC Deb, 4 May 1961, vol. 639, cc1609–18.
31. *Macmillan Diaries*, vol.II, p.380.
32. *The Times*, 20 June 1961. The decision was reported in the Law Reports at *R v Blake* [1962] 2 QB 377.
33. Chapman Pincher, *Dangerous to Know* (London, 2014), pp.67–8.
34. Bower, op. cit., p.268.
35. Ibid.
36. Hermiston, op. cit., Chapter 16 passim.
37. See the discussion about this at the end of the chapter.
38. See H. Montgomery Hyde, *Life of Birkett* (London, 1965), pp.587–9, 622. The relevant papers, including a memorandum from Jeremy, were found on his desk after he died, and returned to Jeremy by his widow.
39. Blake, op. cit., p.211.
40. See Chapter 10 below.
41. *A-G v Blake* [2000] AC. The case is one of the leading authorities on the assessment of damages for breach of contract.
42. See Chapter 10 below.
43. Blake, op. cit., p.207.
44. Hermiston, op. cit., p.181.
45. Ibid., p.182.

46. Ibid., p.184.
47. Ibid.

Chapter 2: 'Untough'

1. The words apparently used by the Director of Public Prosecutions (Sir Theobald Mathew) to the Solicitor General (Sir Peter Rawlinson) on the arrest of Vassall on 12 September 1962: see Rawlinson's obituary in the *Daily Telegraph*, 29 June 2006.
2. *Macmillan Diaries*, vol.II, p.501.
3. Alistair Horne, *Harold Macmillan 1957–1986*, vol.II (London, 1989), p.461.
4. John Vassall, *The Autobiography of a Spy* (London, 1975), p.14.
5. Ibid., p.21.
6. *The Times*, 23 April 1963, reporting the findings in the Report of the Tribunal appointed to Inquire into the Vassall Case and Related Matters (the Radcliffe Tribunal); see also paras 20ff. of the Report of the Radcliffe Tribunal itself.
7. Vassall, op. cit., p.90.
8. Ibid., pp.53–6.
9. Ibid., pp.62–8.
10. Peter Wright, *Spycatcher* (London, 1987), p.164.
11. Jeremy's junior was Robin McEwen, a personal friend of Vassall's whose knowledge of his character was invaluable and who helped Vassall considerably after he came out of prison.
12. Vassall, op. cit., p.147.
13. Ibid., p.144.
14. Ibid., p.148.
15. *The Times*, 23 October 1962.
16. Rebecca West, *The Vassall Affair* (London, 1963), p.9ff.
17. Vassall, op. cit., p.141.
18. In a speech Parker asserted that 'the judiciary is the handmaiden of the executive.' B. Abel Smith and R. Stevens, *Lawyers and the Courts* (London, 1967), p.308.
19. The former Commissioner of Prisons and a noted prison reformer.
20. John Lawton, *1963: Five Hundred Days* (London, 1992), p.12.
21. Horne, op. cit., p.462.
22. *Macmillan Diaries*, vol.II, p.519.
23. HC Deb, 5 November 1962, vol. 666, c714.
24. Horne, op. cit., p.462.

25. Richard Davenport-Hines, *An English Affair: Sex, Class and Power in the Age of Profumo* (London, 2013), p.236.
26. *DPP v Clough* [1963] 1 QB 773.
27. Bernard Levin, *The Pendulum Years* (London, 1970), p.60.
28. Ibid., p.62.
29. Vassall, op. cit., p.148.
30. *The Times*, 26 April 1963, reporting the findings of the Radcliffe Tribunal.
31. Wright, op. cit., p.164.
32. Chapman Pincher, *Too Secret Too Long: The Great Betrayal of Britain's Crucial Secrets and the Cover-up* (London, 1984), p.283.
33. C. Andrew and O. Gordievsky, *KGB: The Inside Story of its Foreign Operations, from Lenin to Gorbachev* (London, 1990).

Chapter 3: 'Society's pound of flesh'

1. See Chapters 1 and 2.
2. This is Christine's first account in her autobiography *Scandal!* (London, 1989), p.29. In her third account, *The Truth at Last* (London, 2001), the father was identified as a 'local boy', p.20.
3. Keeler, *Truth at Last*, p.110.
4. Philip Knightley and Caroline Kennedy, *An Affair of State* (London, 1987), pp.86–7.
5. Keeler, *Truth at Last*, p.95. Gordon disputed this.
6. Ibid., p.132.
7. Levin, op. cit., p.83.
8. Lord Denning's Report, para. 66.
9. It is one of the oddities of the affair that even so level-headed a commentator as Rebecca West should have been bamboozled into thinking that Stephen Ward was a Soviet spy: see *New Meaning of Treason*, p.337ff.
10. This is the conclusion reached by Richard Davenport-Hines in his excellent account, *An English Affair*, p.271. In Knightley and Kennedy, op. cit., it is suggested that Ward was behind the disappearance, p.149.
11. See generally Chapter 2.
12. HC Deb, 21 March 1963, vol. 674, c725.
13. Levin, op. cit., p.53.
14. Robertson, *Stephen Ward*, p.44ff., p.152ff.
15. Knightley and Kennedy, op. cit., p.165ff.

16. This is the theory of events put forward by Knightley and Kennedy, op. cit., p.170. Davenport-Hines supports this theory: op. cit., p.284.
17. See for instance Keeler, *Scandal!*, p.202.
18. Levin, op. cit., p.61.
19. *News of the World*, 16 June 1963.
20. *The Times*, 11 June 1963.
21. HC Deb, 17 June 1963, vol. 679, cc34.
22. Robertson, *Stephen Ward*.
23. See Ludovic Kennedy's brilliant account, *The Trial of Stephen Ward* (London, 1964).
24. West, op. cit., p.357.
25. See Jeremy's reminiscences about him in his Postscript.
26. See for instance the article that appeared in the *Criminal Law Review*, in September 1963, p.600. Even at the time the Court of Appeal's conduct of Gordon's appeal aroused criticism. Various Labour MPs as well as the Liberal leader, Jo Grimond, questioned why the court had not explained what the nature of the evidence was that had led to Gordon's sentence being quashed.
27. Kennedy, op. cit., p.294.
28. Davenport-Hines, op. cit., p.333.
29. Para. 106 of the Denning Report.
30. HC Deb, 17 June 1963, vol. 679, c151.
31. Levin, op. cit., p.63.

Chapter 4: 'Virtuous and puritanical'

1. Extraordinarily, between January 1950 and December 1953, magistrates issued orders for the destruction of more than 1,500 works of fiction, including *Madame Bovary*, *The Satyricon*, *The Decameron* and novels by Zola and Jean-Paul Sartre.
2. In the most notorious of those cases, brought against Lord Montagu, Jeremy had actually appeared as junior counsel for the prosecution.
3. See Jeremy Hutchinson: A Biographical Sketch, *supra*.
4. It is clear from the fascinating unpublished correspondence between Lawrence and St John, which Jeremy still has, that Dorothy Warren, the proprietor of the gallery, was keen to take a stand in relation to the paintings and force a prosecution. Lawrence would not countenance that: 'to burn my pictures just to get a sensational case seems to me a crime.' To sacrifice the pictures was to him 'false doctrine'. Lawrence

wrote about the incident in his pamphlet *Pornography and Obscenity* (1929).

5. Unsurprisingly, no attempt had been made in that case to suggest that publication was 'for the public good' for literary or other reasons.

6. Bernard Levin attended every day of the trial and, writing later in the *Spectator*, set out his reaction to this odd catalogue: 'Had the prosecution really employed an able-bodied man (it could hardly, in the light of some of the things Mr Griffith-Jones said later, have been a woman) to go through *Lady Chatterley's Lover* and count the appearances of words all of which you and I and Mr Griffith-Jones and Mr Justice Byrne and every member of the jury knew before reaching the age of twelve?'

7. The success of Jeremy's strategy was endorsed by Bernard Levin, writing in the *Spectator*: 'Looking round the court . . . one could see only rapt faces, utterly still hands, people being deeply moved by a great book. Almost all the great sexual episodes of the book came shining across in this way, demonstrating better than any witnesses the integrity of Lawrence's purpose, the beauty, purity and passion of his writing, the contemptible nature of the case against his book, the shame and hypocrisy of a country that can prosecute it at all.'

8. An observer at the trial noted that the transcript did not convey the way in which Griffith-Jones lingered over the word 'Leicester'. The innuendo was clear: 'the witness was not even an Oxbridge don.'

9. C.H. Rolph, *The Trial of Lady Chatterley* (Harmondsworth, 1961), p.114.

10. Later Bernardine Bishop, whose novel *Unexpected Lessons in Love* was shortlisted posthumously for the Costa Novel Award in 2013.

11. See David Kynaston, *Modernity Britain: A Shake of the Dice, 1959–1962* (London, 2014), p.111.

12. The only drawback to this idea was that Kipling was more than twenty years dead by 1960.

13. See the fascinating account in Alan Travis, *Bound and Gagged: A Secret History of Obscenity in Britain* (London, 2000), p.138ff.

14. Rolph, op. cit., p.221.

15. Geoffrey Robertson, Afterword to *Lady Chatterley's Lover*: 50th Anniversary Edition (London: Penguin, 2010), p.307.

16. Jeremy still has the original of this cartoon in his lavatory.

17. John Sutherland, *Offensive Literature: Decensorship in Britain 1960–1982* (London, 1982), p.28.

18. HL Deb, 14 December 1960, vol. 227 cc547

Chapter 5: 'Exciting, bawdy, extrovert'

1. See Chapter 3 above.
2. In an obituary of Cleland published shortly after his death it was said that he was granted a government annuity of £100 per year to *prevent* his writing further obscene books, though there is no documentary corroboration for this claim.
3. At the time a well-known novelist and a panellist on *What's My Line*.
4. *Guardian*, 17 November 1963.
5. *Guardian*, 20 November 1963.
6. At the end of 1963 in his 'Books of the Year' A.J.P. Taylor decided to play the curmudgeon and gave *Fanny Hill* a special award as 'the most over-rated book of the year'.
7. Mr Gold's nerve did not falter in the light of the events of 1963–4. He went on to found the Ann Summers sex-shop chain.
8. A statement that was false, and provocatively so.
9. Which provides: '(1) If a justice of the peace is satisfied by information on oath that there is reasonable ground for suspecting that, in any premises in the petty sessions area for which he acts, or on any stall or vehicle in that area, being premises or a stall or vehicle specified in the information, obscene articles are, or are from time to time, kept for publication for gain, the justice may issue a warrant under his hand empowering any constable to enter (if need be by force) and search the premises, or to search the stall or vehicle . . . and to seize and remove any articles found therein or thereon which the constable has reason to believe to be obscene articles and to be kept for publication for gain . . . (3) any articles seized under subsection (1) of this section shall be brought before a justice of the peace acting for the same petty sessions area as the justice who issued the warrant, and the justice before whom the articles are brought may thereupon issue a summons to the occupier of the premises or, as the case may be, the user of the stall or vehicle to appear on a day specified in the summons before a magistrates court for that petty sessions area to show cause why the articles or any of them should be forfeited; and if the court is satisfied, as respects any of the articles, that at the time when they were seized they were obscene articles kept for publication for gain, the court shall order those articles to be forfeited.'
10. At the time there were five copies of *Fanny Hill* in the House of Commons library.
11. 'Subject as hereinafter provided, any person who, whether for gain or

not, publishes an obscene article or who has an obscene article for publication for gain (whether gain to himself or gain to another) shall be liable—(a) on summary conviction to a fine not exceeding one hundred pounds or to imprisonment for a term not exceeding six months; (b) on conviction on indictment to a fine or to imprisonment for a term not exceeding three years or both.'

12. He would later be described by Roy Jenkins as 'that indefatigable scourge of the impure'.

13. It was a voice that had haunted Ludovic Kennedy during the Stephen Ward trial and is mentioned in his book *The Trial of Stephen Ward*.

14. Jeremy still remembers vividly Griffith-Jones's intervention. He remains baffled by it; as if somehow he had colluded with Quennell in the answer that was given.

15. Where Henry James had lived in the last twenty years of his life: it is now in the ownership of the National Trust.

16. Goaded by Sir Robert's moralizing, the police confiscated further copies of *Fanny Hill* in Manchester two weeks later. This time they also took copies of the *Kama Sutra* and *Tropic of Capricorn*. Again the summons was issued only in relation to the cheap edition of the book. The Manchester magistrate, Miss Eileen MacDonald, duly declared the book obscene. This time thousands of copies of the book were consigned to the flames.

17. Leo Abse, the Labour member for Pontypool, ascertained in questions to the Attorney General, Sir John Hobson, that the prosecution costs were over £296 3s. Money well spent, asserted the Conservative member for Twickenham.

18. Jeremy's solicitor.

19. The next day there was a counter-motion tabled by seven Conservative MPs applauding the learned magistrate for his decision and expressing the hope that the DPP would institute similar action in other areas throughout the country.

20. This was not a universal feeling. The *Daily Express* declared that there was 'universal relief at the ruling of the Chief Magistrate'. Peregrine Worsthorne, in the *Sunday Telegraph*, expressed concern about the threat posed by *Fanny Hill* to Christian marriage: 'It would surely be odd to allow any citizen with a few shillings in his pocket to buy *Fanny Hill*.'

21. See also Valerie Grove, *A Voyage Around John Mortimer* (London, 2007), p.215.

22. Also in that year a film was released: *Lady Chatterley versus Fanny Hill*,

starring Joanna Lumley. Its plot is described as follows: 'Two ladies of the evening are thrust into a bet between their "madams" as to who can seduce the un-seducable – a drag queen and a priest.'

Chapter 6: Decline and Fall

1. Robertson, *Obscenity* (London, 1979), pp.285–6.
2. Act II, Scene 1.
3. The 'cab-rank' rule is the professional obligation on barristers to accept instructions from a client regardless of any personal dislike of the client or the case provided that the fee offered is reasonable and the barrister has the professional capacity to undertake the case. The rule is designed to ensure that any client has access to representation of his or her choice.
4. Grove, op. cit., p.295.
5. See Chapters 13 and 14 below.

Chapter 7: The 'Theft' of the Duke of Wellington

1. The more familiar portrait, featured (in reverse) on Bank of England £5 notes from 1971, is by Sir Thomas Lawrence.
2. Curiously, this was exactly fifty years after the notorious theft of the *Mona Lisa* from the Louvre in 1911. On the theft generally see Sandy Nairne, 'How Goya's Duke of Wellington was Stolen', *Guardian*, 5 August 2011.
3. A reference to Sir Billy Butlin, the founder of Butlin's holiday camps, who had been knighted in 1964, and who had a contemporary reputation as a 'can-do' businessman.
4. Some sources say he was in fact an unemployed lorry driver.
5. His first appearance in court, in 1960, was even picked up by *The Times*, which reported that he had told the bench: 'This is a matter of principle with me. I believe that the air should be free. Why should millions of people be deprived of the pleasures of television . . . The standard of television may at times be ridiculed, but I still maintain that it is a grand time-killer and of a special benefit to our old folk.'
6. Jeremy remembers that Aarvold had earlier played rugby for England. He now wore his hair slicked back and gave the impression of a racehorse who had just run the Derby.
7. He would later become Director of the National Gallery.

8. In Jeremy's personal papers there is an intriguing telegram, addressed to him at the Old Bailey during the trial, and sent from Torremolinos, which reads as follows: 'Have identical portrait dated 1812 could be original contact Harwood 6 Knole Road Rottingdean Has examined Has photographs'. Unfortunately, this line of enquiry did not yield a lost original.

9. Which one might read as judicial code for saying that in fact the judge did not accept that verdict.

10. In his essay 'Temporary Appropriation should be Theft' [1981] Crim LR 129, Professor Glanville Williams claims that section 11 was inserted directly in response to Bunton's acquittal.

11. See Alan Travis, 'Revealed: 1961 Goya "Theft" from National Gallery was a Family Affair', *Guardian*, 30 November 2012.

Chapter 8: 'Like a Boeing 707'

1. For which she would be honoured by the British Press Awards as News Reporter of the Year in 1977.

2. Norman's investigations are set out at length in *The Fake's Progress* (London, 1977), p.208ff. It is impossible to do them justice here.

3. Published on 21 July 1976.

4. In a joint letter dated 3 August 1976 the artists Graham Sutherland OM and Paul Drury described their reaction to the drawings in question: 'It was as if an old friend – long dead – had been impersonated with the aid of liberally and clumsily applied make-up.' Geoffrey Grigson, the poet, and author of a major work on Palmer, called them 'cook-ups' (7 August 1976).

5. 20 August 1976.

6. The usual meaning in cockney rhyming slang of the phrase Sexton Blake is 'cake' but Keating had appropriated it to mean 'fake'.

7. In the event Geraldine Norman did produce *The Tom Keating Catalogue*, of the paintings she had actually managed to locate, which was a companion-piece to the biography.

8. No connection to Jeremy.

9. 29 September 1976.

10. Episodes can be seen on YouTube.

11. Quoted in Jonathon Keats, *Forged* (Oxford, 2013), p.135. Magnusson's essay, 'The Fake's Progress: Tom Keating', is in Magnus Magnusson, *Fakes, Forgers and Phonies: Famous Scams and Scamps* (Edinburgh, 2006).

12. *Guardian*, 4 March 1979.
13. Brian Sewell, *Outside II, Always Almost: Never Quite* (London, 2012), p.91.
14. 1 August 1981.

Chapter 9: Brotherhood of Love

1. The first being a BBC version of the trial of *Lady Chatterley's Lover* called *The Chatterley Affair*, first broadcast in 2006.
2. Howard Marks, *Mr Nice* (London, 1996), p.69.
3. It was actually known as the 'Brotherhood of Eternal Love'.
4. David Leigh, *High Times* (London, 1984).
5. 514 HL 1194 (25 January 1990).
6. Now Stephen Solley QC, later to become head of Charter Chambers.
7. Marks, op. cit., p.186.
8. 514 HL 1192 (25 January 1990), during a debate on the Courts and Legal Services Bill.
9. John Mortimer, *Rumpole and the Age of Miracles* (London, 1988), p.6. Quoted in David Pannick, *Advocates* (London, 1992), p.127.
10. For an account of the trial see Leigh, op. cit., p.270ff.
11. Quoted in ibid., pp.272–3.
12. Judy Marks, *Mr Nice and Mrs Marks* (London, 2006), p.175.
13. Quotations taken from Leigh, op. cit., p.273.
14. Judy Marks, op. cit., p.177.
15. It had been revealed in 1979 that Blunt had been granted immunity from prosecution in 1964 in return for his full confession of his spying activities.
16. Now Christopher Sallon QC.
17. See Chapter 14.

Chapter 10: 'Would you press the button?'

1. He would become Lord Chancellor later that year, as Lord Dilhorne.
2. Dominic Sandbrook, *Never Had it So Good* (London, 2005), p.241.
3. Ibid.
4. Michael Randle sees in the Direct Action Committee (DAC) the direct antecedent of the Committee of 100. He explains: 'It was the DAC which adopted what is now generally referred to as the CND symbol,

or "peace sign", designed by Gerald Holtom, and which, following the Aldermaston march, organized a six-week picket at the AWRE and then a week's sit-down at the entrance to the establishment. The following December it organized an occupation and sit-down at the Thor nuclear rocket base at North Pickenham near Swaffham in Norfolk, followed two weeks later by a sit-down blockade of the entrance when 45 people were arrested, among them Rev. Michael Scott, then a very well-known figure in the struggle against apartheid in South Africa and co-author with Bertrand Russell of *Act or Perish*, the founding document of the Committee of 100. Both demonstrations generated huge publicity and debate, and the DAC went on to organize, amongst other things, a campaign in Stevenage in 1959 against Blue Streak and Thunderbird missile construction, an international protest team against the French atomic test near Reggan in the Algerian Sahara, 1959–60, and a sit-down at the intermediate range rocket base at Harrington in Northamptonshire in January 1961 at which 82 people were arrested. One of the speakers at the first Aldermaston March, who also took part in the Sahara Protest Team, was Bayard Rustin, a close associate of Martin Luther King who went on to co-ordinate the famous civil rights march on Washington in 1963. The idea of Ralph Schoenman, Michael Scott and others was to create an organization that would employ on a mass basis the non-violent direct action methods pioneered by DAC. Most of us on the DAC enthusiastically supported the idea. There was, indeed, a big overlap in the membership of the two organizations which continued to exist side by side until the summer of 1961 when DAC dissolved itself on the grounds that the Committee of 100 was now taking the work forward on a more significant scale. Russell himself was a sponsor of the DAC, so when Ralph approached him he was, in a sense, knocking on an open door. Among DAC members who played an active role in the Committee of 100 Working Group were Pat Arrowsmith, Ian Dixon (one of the defendants in the Official Secrets Act trial), April Carter (Secretary of DAC), Ernest Rodker, Alan Lovell, Wendy Butlin and myself. (I was Chair of DAC from just after the Aldermaston March until the Committee folded, and Secretary of the Committee of 100 during the first year or so of its existence.) Michael Scott was on both committees though not on the Committee of 100 Working Group. Many of the other Committee of 100 members had been active at the grassroots of DAC and taken part in its demonstrations.'

5. Bertrand Russell, *Autobiography*, vol.3 (London, 1967), pp.104–10.

6. Schoenman's studies in the Italian Renaissance seem to have informed the naming of the new group, which recalls the Guelphs' 'Council of 100'.

7. Richard Taylor, *Against the Bomb: The British Peace Movement 1958–1965* (Oxford, 1988), p.195.

8. *Encounter*, February 1961, p.93.

9. Christopher Driver, *The Disarmers* (London, 1964), p.118.

10. Russell, op. cit., p.118.

11. Ibid., p.121.

12. Michael Randle and Pat Pottle, *The Blake Escape* (London, 1989), p.9.

13. Ibid.

14. Ibid., p.10.

15. Within Jeremy's archive is a note from a member of the Committee of 100 confirming that at a 'working Group meeting last night we agreed that distribution of leaflets within and around the Old Bailey shall stop immediately . . . Please accept our sincere apologies for the embarrassment caused to you. The lack of courtesy is now fully recognized and nothing further will be done during the remainder of the trial without first consulting the solicitors.'

16. Randle and Pottle, op. cit., p.13.

17. [1962] AC 788.

18. Taylor, op. cit., p.242. Nonetheless the Committee of 100 still managed to organize actions which had considerable impact, including the protests in 1963, organized in conjunction with the Save Greece Now Committee, against the visit to London of King Paul and Queen Frederica of Greece; the Spies for Peace revelations of 1963; and the occupation of the Greek Embassy in London in April 1967 following the Colonels' coup in Greece.

19. *Encounter*, February 1961, p.93.

20. *New Statesman*, 2 January 1960.

21. F.E. Myers, 'Civil Disobedience and Organizational Change: The British Committee of 100', *Political Science Quarterly*, 86.1, March 1971.

Chapter 11: 'Much ado about nothing'

1. What is now 3 Raymond Buildings, headed by Alexander Cameron QC.

2. Compton Mackenzie, *My Life and Times, Octave Seven: 1931–1938,* (London, 1968), p.89.

3. Jonathan Aitken, *Officially Secret* (London, 1971), p.56.

4. *Time* magazine, 1 September 1967.

5. Aitken, op. cit., p.86.

6. Ibid., pp.101–3.

7. Ibid., p.108.

8. The 'blurb', as it was called, was not available at trial, and there was some doubt as to its contents. Aitken suggests that, as well as being a summary of the report, the notes referred to the fact that pro-Biafran circles in London were aware of the report, and that it had been seen by MPs including Hugh Fraser. Johann Welser, who gave evidence for the prosecution, and who saw the report on 9 January 1969, recalled that the blurb made reference to the report being 'obtained from a secret highly guarded annexe of the defence adviser to the British High Commission in Lagos, flown to Lisbon, from where it eventually reached Biafran circles in London'.

9. For the purpose of a D–Notice see Chapter 1, note 20. The D–Notice Committee (now the Defence, Press and Broadcasting Advisory Committee) was a joint committee which contained government and press representatives, considering the content of D–Notices and giving advice to press organizations.

10. In his original statement to the police, Welser asserted that he had mentioned the Official Secrets Act in the course of his conversations with Brook-Shepherd. Welser did not repeat his evidence to this effect at trial.

11. Brook-Shepherd's evidence was that he did not recall Admiral Denning referring to the Official Secrets Act.

12. Declassified FCO diplomatic cables indicate that Colonel Scott was held in high esteem by General Gowon and his advisers, and that the key reason for his expulsion was not anger directed at Scott but in the nature of a face-saving exercise.

13. Aitken, op. cit., p.116.

14. See Chapter 2 above. The imprisoning of two journalists for contempt of court in the course of the Vassall enquiry had gravely damaged Harold Macmillan's standing with the press.

15. Aitken, op. cit., p.124.

16. Ibid., p.143.

17. *The Times*, 18 March 1970.

18. Although John Mathew recalls that there was simply no admissible evidence against Fraser, who had declined to comment when interviewed by the police.

19. *Sunday Telegraph*, 7 February 1971.

20. Mark Holmes, *The Official Secrets Act on Trial: The* Sunday Telegraph *Secrets Case, Public Opinion, and the Political Prosecution that Britain Forgot* (unpublished thesis, Queen's College, Oxford, March 2015).

21. Aitken, op. cit., p.139.

22. *R v Selvey* [1970] AC 304. This was one of the longest appeals in criminal history.

23. Peter Dunn, *Sunday Times,* 17 January 1971.

24. This is baffling given that, once it became apparent that the *Sunday Telegraph* was proposing to publish the Scott report, there were numerous telegrams emanating from the High Commission in Lagos to the Foreign Office in London urging that publication should be stopped.

25. Aitken, op. cit., p.169.

26. *Sunday Telegraph,* 7 February 1971.

27. *New Law Journal,* 3 April 1970.

28. See Chapter 3 above. John Mathew ascribes a somewhat different motive: 'I think Caulfield was terrified of getting a bad press if he showed any sympathy for the Crown's case.'

Chapter 12: 'This raddled and discredited prima donna'

1. Quoted in *The Times,* 6 September 1978.

2. See Chapter 11 above.

3. Aitken, op. cit., p.206.

4. Geoffrey Robertson, *The Justice Game* (London, 1999), p.105. His chapter 'Ferrets or Skunks? The ABC Trial' is an excellent and illuminating account of the case.

5. *A-G v Jonathan Cape* [1976] QB 752, 756.

6. John Campbell, *Roy Jenkins: A Well-rounded Life* (London, 2014), p.262.

7. Nigel West, *A Matter of Trust: MI5 1945–1972* (London, 1982), p.170.

8. It is suggested by David Hooper in *Official Secrets: The Use and Abuse of the Act* (London, 1987), p.134 that Philip Agee had provided information for 'The Eavesdroppers' article. Crispin Aubrey does not refer to this in his own excellent account of the trial, *Who's Watching You: Britain's Security Services and the Official Secrets Act* (London, 1981), to which this chapter is indebted.

9. Aubrey, op. cit., p.61.

10. Ibid.

11. Ibid., p.142.

12. Ibid., p.182.

13. Robertson, *Justice Game*, p.112.

14. Duncan Campbell, 'Official Secrecy and British Libertarianism', *The Socialist Register 1979*, pp.75 and 82.

15. Aubrey, op. cit., p.167.

16. The proceedings that were brought against the *Leveller* and *Peace News* and the *Journalist*, the magazine of the National Union of Journalists, for contempt of court were eventually dismissed by the House of Lords (see *A-G v Leveller Magazine Ltd* [1979] AC 440). No action was taken against the television networks and newspapers who published the colonel's name subsequently.

17. Robertson, *Justice Game*, p.120.

18. Ibid., p.121.

19. For a legal account of the trial see Andrew Nicol, 'Official Secrets and Jury Vetting', [1979] Crim LR 284.

20. See generally Harriet Harman and John Griffith, *Justice Deserted: The Subversion of the Jury* (London, 1979), p.23.

21. Aubrey, op. cit., p.170.

22. See generally *New Statesman*, 22 September 1978, where it was reported that a fellow juror later complained that the foreman was, from the start, the 'most vociferous' of the twelve, with 'firmly held opinions against the Defendants'. Of Campbell the foreman had remarked that, given that his information gathering was not done for money, he must have been intending to 'pass it on to somebody'.

23. Hooper, op. cit., p.143.

24. *Sunday Times*, 27 November 1978.

25. E.P. Thompson, *Writing by Candlelight* (London, 1980), p.106.

26. *New Society*, 19 October 1978.

27. Hooper, op. cit., p.145.

28. Ibid., p.149.

29. Aubrey, op. cit., p.180.

30. Ibid., p.184.

31. *Sunday Times*, 19 November 1978.

32. *Observer*, 19 November 1978.

Chapter 13: Last Tango

1. See Chapter 6 above.

2. As to whom, see Chapter 14 below.

3. Quoted in Sophie Taylor, obituary of Maria Schneider, *The Week*, 4 February 2011.

4. Claretta Micheletti Tonetti, *Bernardo Bertolucci: The Cinema of Ambiguity* (New York, 1995), p.127.

5. Ibid, p.126.

6. *New York Times*, 2 February 1973.

7. Quoted in Franco Arcalli and Bernardo Bertolucci, *Bernardo Bertolucci's Last Tango in Paris: The Screenplay* (New York, 1972), p.9.

8. Quoted in Charles Michener, 'Tango: The Hottest Movie', *Newsweek*, 12 February 1973.

9. See the BFFC 'Case Studies' website.

10. Quoted in Tom Dewe Matthews, *Censored: The Story of Film Censorship in Britain* (London, 1989), p.211.

11. BFFC 'Case Studies' website.

12. Quoted in *Sunday Times*, 1 December 1974.

13. *Blackburn v Attorney General* [1971] 1 WLR 1037. Lord Denning said this: 'In this case Mr Blackburn – as he has done before – has shown eternal vigilance in support of the law. This time he is concerned about the application of Her Majesty's Government to join the Common Market and to sign the Treaty of Rome. He brings two actions against the Attorney-General, in which he seeks declarations to the effect that, by signing the Treaty of Rome, Her Majesty's Government will surrender in part the sovereignty of the Crown in Parliament and will surrender it for ever. He says that in so doing the government will be acting in breach of the law.'

14. *R v De Montalk* (1932) 23 Cr App R 182.

Chapter 14: The Theatre of the Absurd

1. The play caused its own vast controversy. Eventually Sir Laurence Olivier was moved to write a lengthy letter to the *Observer*: '*Saved* is not for children but it is for grown-ups, and the grown-ups of this country should have the courage to look at it; and if we do not find precisely the mirror held up to nature in which we can see ourselves, then at least we can experience the sacramental catharsis of a very chastening look at the sort of ground we have prepared for the next lot.'

2. As John Sutherland put it in his book *Offensive Literature* (London, 1981), p.180.

3. One feels a certain amount of sympathy for an unnamed 'middle-aged woman' who was reported in the *Observer*, in one of the endless vox pop pieces that the play inspired in the press, as stating: 'I'm glad we're a long way from the stage . . . I shouldn't like to be too close to the action.' It was reported that at a later performance eggs, flour and fireworks were thrown in protest by the 'South London Action Group', which stood for 'moral standards'.

4. Mortimer had recently successfully defended *Inside Linda Lovelace* on obscenity charges.

5. It was reported that her bête noire, the director of the BBC Sir Hugh Greene, kept a satirical painting of her at his house showing a woman with five breasts, entitled *Sanctity*. Peter McKay, in the *Daily Mail*, wrote: 'This play on the French word for five . . . greatly amused Sir Hugh, if no one else.'

6. According to Ben Thompson, the editor of an anthology of Whitehouse-related letters: 'From Mumsnet to . . . feminist anti-pornography campaigns [and] the executive naming and shaming strategies of UK Uncut, her ideological and tactical influence has been discernible in all sorts of unexpected places in recent years.' Introduction to *Ban This Filth! Letters from the Mary Whitehouse Archive* (London, 2012).

7. *R v Lemon* [1979] AC 617.

8. For consideration of the Festival of Light, see generally Chapter 13 above.

9. See Chapter 13 above.

10. For a brilliantly funny account of the case see Chapter 7 of Geoffrey Robertson's *Justice Game*, to which this chapter is indebted.

11. This offence had originally been enacted as section 11 of the Criminal Law Amendment Act in 1885 at the instigation of the notorious Victorian moralist Henry Labouchere, who had inserted the clause in committee without discussion. It was this section, the so-called 'blackmailer's charter', that criminalized (for the first time) essentially all male homosexual activity. Under it Oscar Wilde was convicted in 1895 and Alan Turing in 1952.

12. In Caroline Blackwood's vivid phrase: *Observer*, 12 July 1981.

13. A legal mechanism for borrowing money on the security of a ship.

14. See also Robertson, *Justice Game*, p.174.

15. Geoffrey Robertson QC, 'Thumbs Up for a Great Act', *The Times*, 10 March 1998.

16. Staughton reasoned that he could not speculate whether Parliament, when passing the Theatres Act, had intended that all other statutory

offences should be exempted from the compass of the Act. But the promoter of the bill, George Strauss, had assured the House of Commons that 'no prosecution may take place without the consent of the Attorney General. We considered this necessary to prevent vexatious or frivolous prosecutions by outraged individuals or societies and to ensure uniformity of enforcement.'

17. Literally, 'I am unwilling to pursue the case'.

18. Havers later explained that he had agreed to the *nolle prosequi* because he thought it would be oppressive to Bogdanov to have to face a continuation of the trial when he had been told that it was to be stopped. But it is difficult to resist the conclusion that Havers had finally realized that he should have stopped the prosecution, as he had been invited to do, months earlier.

19. In a letter to *The Times* published on 30 March 1982 Mrs Whitehouse asserted that she knew nothing of the decision to withdraw until after it had been made.

20. The outcome did not commend itself to the *Daily Telegraph*. In the leader column of 19 March 1982 it was written: 'When the Lord Chamberlain's Office was abolished in 1968 an era of freedom, with some safeguard of law, was excitedly embraced, but it is now clear that the old system was in fact a better way of protecting the public from the more revolting ideas of directors and writers. A system of censorship, operated with judicious mildness, is what we have in the cinema. Its absence in the theatre produces complication, wrangling and offerings like *The Romans in Britain*, which disfigure the stage.'

Postscript by Jeremy Hutchinson

1. The Jeffrey Review, which published its final report on 7 May 2014, was an independent review, chaired by Sir Bill Jeffrey, looking into how criminal defendants are given independent legal representation in the courts of England and Wales.

2. Constitutional Reform Act 2005, section 17.

Select Bibliography

Ableman, P., *The Mouth and Oral Sex* (London: Running Man Books, 1969)

Aitken, J., *Officially Secret* (London: Weidenfeld & Nicolson, 1972)

Aubrey, C., *Who's Watching You: Britain's Security Services and the Official Secrets Act* (London: Pelican, 1981)

Bedford, S., *Aldous Huxley: A Life* (London: Collins, 1973)

——, *As It Was* (London: Sinclair-Stevenson, 1990)

Benn, T., *Years of Hope: Diaries, Papers and Letters 1940–1962* (London: Hutchinson, 1994)

Berlin, I., *Flourishing: Letters 1928–1946*, ed. Henry Hardy (London: Chatto & Windus, 2004)

Billington, M., *Peggy Ashcroft* (London: John Murray, 1988)

——, *State of the Nation: British Theatre Since 1945* (London: Faber & Faber, 2007)

Blake, G., *No Other Choice* (London: Jonathan Cape, 1990)

Bower, T., *The Perfect English Spy: Sir Dick White and the Secret War 1935–1990* (London: William Heinemann, 1995)

Catterall, P. (ed.), *The Macmillan Diaries*, vol. II: *Prime Minister and After: 1957–1963* (London: Macmillan, 2011)

Clark, A., *A Keen Soldier: The Execution of Second World War Private Harold Pringle* (Toronto: Knopf, 2002)

Cooper, D., *Darling Monster: The Letters of Lady Diana Cooper to Her Son John Julius Norwich 1939–1952* (London: Chatto & Windus, 2013)

Davenport-Hines, R., *An English Affair: Sex, Class and Power in the Age of Profumo* (London: Harper Press, 2013)

Denning, Lord, *Lord Denning's Report* (London: Her Majesty's Stationery Office, 1963)

Devlin, P., *Easing the Passing* (London: The Bodley Head, 1985)

Dewe Matthews, T., *Censored: The Story of Film Censorship in Britain* (London: Chatto & Windus, 1994)

Draper, A., *Smoke without Fire* (London: Arlington Books, 1974)

Driver, C., *The Disarmers* (London: Hodder and Stoughton, 1964)

Eliot, V. (ed.), *Letters of T.S. Eliot*, vol.1: *1898–1922* (New York: Harcourt Brace Jovanovich, 1988)

Goodman, A., *Tell Them I'm on My Way* (London: Chapmans, 1993)

Green, M., *Children of the Sun: A Narrative of Decadence in England After 1918* (London: Pimlico, 1992)

Grove, V., *A Voyage Around John Mortimer* (London: Viking, 2007)

Hailsham, Lord, *A Sparrow's Flight* (London: Collins, 1990)

Harman, H., and Griffiths, J., *Justice Deserted: The Subversion of the Jury* (London: Civil Liberties Trust, 1979)

Hermiston, R., *The Greatest Traitor: The Secret Lives of Agent George Blake* (London: Aurum Press, 2013)

Hilbery, Sir M., *Duty and Art in Advocacy* (London: Stevens & Sons, 1946)

Holroyd, M., *Lytton Strachey*, vol.2: *The Years of Achievement* (London: William Heinemann, 1968)

Hooper, D., *Official Secrets: The Use and Abuse of the Act* (London: Secker & Warburg, 1987)

Horne, A., *Harold Macmillan 1957–1986*, vol.2 (London: Macmillan, 1989)

Keats, J., *Forged: Why Fakes are the Great Art of Our Age* (Oxford: Oxford University Press, 2013)

Keeler, C., *Scandal!* (London: Xanadu Publications, 1989)

Keeler, C., and Thompson, D., *The Truth at Last: My Story* (London: Sidgwick & Jackson, 2001)

Kennedy, L., *The Trial of Stephen Ward* (London: Victor Gollancz, 1964)

King-Hamilton QC, His Hon. A., *And Nothing But the Truth* (London: Weidenfeld & Nicolson, 1982)

Knightley, P., and Kennedy, C., *An Affair of State: The Profumo Case and the Framing of Stephen Ward* (London: Jonathan Cape, 1987)

Kynaston, D., *Modernity Britain: Book Two, A Shake of the Dice, 1959–1962* (London: Bloomsbury, 2014)

Lawton, J., *1963: Five Hundred Days* (London: Hodder & Stoughton, 1992)

Leigh, D., *High Times* (London: William Heinemann, 1984)

Levin, B., *The Pendulum Years* (London: Jonathan Cape, 1970)

Macintyre, B., *A Spy Among Friends: Kim Philby and the Great Betrayal* (London: Bloomsbury, 2014)

Mackenzie, C., *My Life and Times, Octave Seven: 1931–1938* (London: Chatto & Windus, 1968)

Marks, H., *Mr Nice* (London: Secker & Warburg, 1996)

Marks, J., *Mr Nice and Mrs Marks* (London: Ebury Press, 2006)

Montagu of Beaulieu, Lord, *Wheels Within Wheels* (London: Weidenfeld & Nicolson, 2000)

Montgomery Hyde, H., *Norman Birkett: The Life of Lord Birkett* (London: Hamish Hamilton, 1965)

——, *George Blake: Super-Spy* (London: Constable, 1987)

Nicolson, N. (ed.), *Harold Nicolson's Diaries and Letters 1930–1939*, vol. 1 (London: Collins, 1966)

Norman, G., Norman, F., Keating, T., *The Fake's Progress* (London: Hutchinson, 1977)

Pannick, D., *Advocates* (Oxford: Oxford University Press, 1992)

Pincher, C., *Too Secret Too Long* (London: Sidgwick & Jackson, 1984)

——, *Dangerous to Know: A Life* (London: Biteback Publishing, 2014)

Radcliffe, Viscount, and others, *Report of the Tribunal appointed to Inquire into the Vassall Case and Related Matters* (London: Her Majesty's Stationery Office, 1963)

Randle, M., and Pottle, P., *The Blake Escape* (London: Harrap Books, 1989)

Rawlinson, P., *A Price Too High: An Autobiography* (London: Weidenfeld & Nicolson, 1989)

Robertson, G., *Obscenity* (London: Weidenfeld & Nicolson, 1979)

——, *The Justice Game* (London: Chatto & Windus, 1998)

——, *Stephen Ward was Innocent OK!* (London: Biteback Publishing, 2014)

Rolph, C.H., *The Trial of Lady Chatterley* (Harmondsworth: Penguin, 1961)

Russell, B., *Autobiography*, vol.3 (London: Allen & Unwin, 1969)

Sandbrook, D., *Never Had it so Good: A History of Britain from Suez to The Beatles* (London: Little, Brown, 2005)

Sitwell, O., *Laughter in the Next Room* (London: Macmillan, 1949)

Spalding, F., *The Tate: A History* (London: Tate Gallery Publications, 1998)

Sutherland, J., *Offensive Literature: Decensorship in Britain 1960–1982* (London: Junction Books, 1982)

Taylor, R., *Against the Bomb: The British Peace Movement 1958–1965* (Oxford: Oxford University Press, 1988)

Thompson, B., *Ban This Filth! Letters from the Mary Whitehouse Archive* (London: Faber & Faber, 2012)

Thompson, E.P., *Writing by Candlelight* (London: Merlin Press, 1980)

Toynbee, P., *Friends Apart: A Memoir of Esmond Romilly and Jasper Ridley in the Thirties* (London: MacGibbon & Kee, 1954)

Travis, A., *Bound and Gagged: A Secret History of Obscenity in Britain* (London: Profile Books, 2000)

Vassall, J., *Vassall: The Autobiography of a Spy* (London: Sidgwick & Jackson, 1975)

West, R., *The Vassall Affair* (London: Sunday Telegraph, 1963)

——, *The New Meaning of Treason* (New York: The Viking Press, 1964)

Woolf, L., *Downhill All the Way: An Autobiography of the Years 1919–1939* (London: The Hogarth Press, 1967)

Wright, P., *Spycatcher* (London: Viking, 1987)

Index

Note: Titles and ranks are generally the highest mentioned
in the text

International Times (newspaper), 180
Irvine, Derry, Baron, 368
Italy: JH's wartime posting to, 15
Ivanov, Yevgeny, 97–8, 100, 101, 103–4, 108

Jeffrey, Sir Bill: Report (on independent criminal advocacy), 369
Jenkins, Roy: friendship with JH, 31, 38; introduces Obscene Publications Bill, 122, 143, 340; as witness in *Lady Chatterley* case, 136, 142–3; on limited conviction of *Fanny Hill*, 156–7, 166; attempts to appoint JH as legal adviser, 301; and censorship in theatre, 343
John, Augustus, 242
Johnson, Stanley, 92
Johnstone, Colonel H.A. *see* 'Colonel B'
Jones, Sir Elwyn, 279, 299
Jones, Janie, 181
Jones, Kenneth (Mr Justice), 337, 339
journalists: and protection of sources, 91–2; and state, 299
juries and jurors: JH on, 364–5, 370
jury-vetting, 312, 319–21
Justice, Ministry of, 369, 371–2

Kael, Pauline, 330
Kalugin, Oleg, 74
Kauffer, Edward McKnight, 14
Keating, Tom: trial, 29, 204–9; background, 195, 197–8; letters to *The Times* confessing to fake paintings and pastiches, 198–201; motives, 201–2, 204; notoriety, 201, 203; eschews money, 202; charged, 203–4; JH defends, 203; case dropped, 210; health decline after injuring leg in road accident, 210; partial recovery and fame, 211; death, 212; *The Fake's Progress* (with Geraldine and Frank Norman), 201, 203–4
Keeler, Christine: depicted in Macmillan cartoon, 95; JH represents, 95–6, 113–17, 120; in Profumo affair, 95–6, 103; tried and sentenced, 95, 117; background and career, 96; and Ivanov, 97–8, 100; relations with Ward, 97, 101, 116; lifestyle and li-aisons, 98–100; sells story to *Sunday Pictorial*, 101; and Edgecombe trial, 102; supports Profumo's statement, 104; assaulted, 105–6, 108; interrogated by police, 105–6; sells story to *News of the World*, 107–8; testifies at Lucky Gordon's trial, 108, 111, 114; denounced by women, 109–10, 112; gives evidence against Ward, 109, 111–12; charged with perjury and tried, 112–13; receives money from Ward, 112; as passive victim, 113–14; voice, 113; later life, 117
Kelly, Sir Gerald, 189
Kelly, HMS, 13–14
Kelly, Jane, 195–7, 203–8
Kelvin, HMS, 13
Kendal, Felicity, 353
Kennedy, Ian, 354, 358–9
Kennedy, Ludovic, 38, 116
Kerouac, Jack: *On the Road*, 172
Kerpel, Tony, 331
KGB: and fate of agents revealed by Blake, 73–4; runs Vassall, 94
Khrushchev, Nikita S., 242
Kim Il-Sung, 45
King-Hamilton, Alan Barry, 175–6, 178–9, 181; *And Nothing But the Truth*, 181
Kipling, HMS, 13
Kipling, Rudyard, 146
Kirkup, James: 'The Love that Dares to Speak its Name' (poem), 181, 347
Kodak secrets case (1965), 301
Koestler, Arthur, 21
Komisarjevsky, Theodore, 11
Kondrashev, Sergei Aleksandrovich, 46–7
Korea: Blake in, 45–6, 59
Kubrick, Stanley, 331
Kypreos, Christopher: commissions *The Mouth and Oral Sex*, 172; premises raided, 172–3; prosecuted and tried, 173–4, 177–8; verdict and sentence, 178–9

Labour Party: JH joins, 9; JH leaves, 34; and nuclear disarmament, 240–1; supports Federalist Nigeria, 269–70;